MEDIA, STRUCTURES, AND POWER
The Robert E. Babe Collection

Media, Structures, and Power is a collection of the scholarly writing of Canada's leading communication and media studies scholar, Robert E. Babe. Spanning almost four decades of scholarship, the volume reflects the breadth of Babe's work, from media and economics to communications history and political economy.

Babe famously characterized Canadian scholars' distinctive contribution to knowledge as uniquely historical, holistic, and dialectical. The essays in *Media, Structures, and Power* reflect this strength. With a clarity of vision, Babe critiques mainstream economics, Canadian government policy, and postmodernist thought in social science. Containing introductions and contributions by other prominent scholars, this volume situates Babe's work within contemporary scholarship and underscores the extent to which he is one of Canada's most prescient thinkers. His interdisciplinary analyses will remain timely and influential well into the twenty-first century.

EDWARD COMOR is a professor in the Faculty of Information and Media Studies at the University of Western Ontario.

Robert E. Babe

EDITED BY EDWARD A. COMOR

Media, Structures, and Power
The Robert E. Babe Collection

UNIVERSITY OF TORONTO PRESS
Toronto Buffalo London

© University of Toronto Press 2011
Toronto Buffalo London
www.utppublishing.com
Printed in Canada

ISBN 978-0-8020-9860-3 (cloth)
ISBN 978-0-8020-9576-3 (paper)

Printed on acid-free, 100% post-consumer recycled paper with vegetable-based inks.

Library and Archives Canada Cataloguing in Publication

Media, structures, and power : the Robert E. Babe collection / edited by Edward Comor.

Includes bibliographical references.
ISBN 978-0-8020-9860-3 (bound)   ISBN 978-0-8020-9576-3 (pbk.)

1. Communication – Economic aspects.   2. Mass media – Economic aspects.   3. Telecommunication – Canada – History.   4. Telecommunication policy – Canada.   5. Communication – Canada – History.   6. Communication and culture.   7. Ecology – Economic aspects.   I. Babe, Robert E., 1943– II. Comor, Edward, 1962–

P96.E25M435 2011   302.2   C2011-903190-6

University of Toronto Press acknowledges the financial assistance to its publishing program of the Canada Council for the Arts and the Ontario Arts Council.

  Canada Council   Conseil des Arts   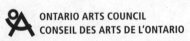 ONTARIO ARTS COUNCIL
for the Arts   du Canada   CONSEIL DES ARTS DE L'ONTARIO

University of Toronto Press acknowledges the financial support of the Government of Canada through the Canada Book Fund for its publishing activities.

Contents

PART THREE: CANADIAN COMMUNICATION THOUGHT

PART FOUR: CULTURAL ECOLOGY AND THE POLITICAL ECONOMY OF KNOWLEDGE

PART FIVE: CONCLUDING THOUGHTS

Preface

The idea for a book containing some of Robert Babe's most influential writings emerged in 2007. Given his status as one of Canada's outstanding social scientists, the far-reaching influence of his work, and the fact that he is now in the latter years of his career, it seemed to me that the time was right for such a collection.

After meeting with Bob about the project, I approached the University of Toronto Press, who immediately endorsed it. Soon thereafter, pre-eminent scholars were asked to write introductions for each of the book's four sections. Without reservation, the first four I asked – Sandra Braman, Robin Mansell, Paul Heyer, and Hanno Hardt – agreed to participate.

From the outset, the aim of the project was to go beyond publishing a relatively one-dimensional celebratory book. Instead, Bob and I agreed that the volume should represent his life's work; reflecting its interdisciplinary breadth. Furthermore, the readings were selected with an eye on their potential to stimulate debate. Likewise, its contributors – especially the four introduction writers – were invited to engage both Bob and prospective readers by contextualizing their assigned chapters through some amount of historical, intellectual, and critical rigour.[1]

The result, I hope, is a volume that demonstrates the precision and power of its author's years of thought-provoking work. Indeed, through what follows, I hope to stimulate the kind of grounded, critical, and, indeed, distinctly Canadian research that Robert Babe has been so well known for. In many ways, the importance of both the author's past writings and his passionate critiques on issues such as ecological sustainability, neoclassical economics, postmodernism, and Canadian culture, among many others, are models that younger academics may well choose to emulate.

Thank you to Sandra Braman, Hanno Hardt, Paul Heyer, Robin Mansell, Warren Samuels, and James Winter for your unwavering support for this project. Thanks also to University of Toronto Press editors Stephen Kotowych, Siobhan McMenemy, Ryan Van Huijstee, Frances Mundy, and copy editor Ian MacKenzie. In addition, thank you to Samantha Burton for her research assistance, and both Courtney Lundrigan and John Bosco Mayiga for their crucial preparatory work.

Support for this collection from the University of Western Ontario and its Faculty of Information and Media Studies is greatly appreciated. Likewise, without the kind permissions to republish the work of Robert Babe by many publishers and journals, this book would have been impossible (please see original references in 'Publications and Conference Papers by Robert E. Babe' at the end of this book). These, listed alphabetically, include:

- Greenwood Publishing Group, Inc., Westport, CT (for chapter 2, 'Communication: Blind Spot of Western Economics')
- Canadian Centre for Policy Alternatives (for chapter 15, 'Innis, Environment, and New Media')
- *Canadian Journal of Communication* (for chapter 6, 'Control of Telephones,' chapter 9, 'Foundations of Canadian Communication Thought,' and chapter 14, 'Economics and Information')
- Canadian Library Association and School of Library and Information Studies at Dalhousie University (for chapter 7, 'Convergence and Divergence')
- The Duke Center for Canadian Studies and Duke University Press (for chapter 5, 'Media Technology and the Great Transformation of Canadian Cultural Policy')
- *Fast Capitalism* (for chapter 16, 'The Political Economy of Knowledge')
- *Fifth-Estate-Online* and *Javnost* – The Public (for chapter 11 'Harold Innis and the Paradox of Press Freedom')
- Hampton Press (for chapter 18 'Political Economy of Economics')
- Innis Foundation (for chapter 3, 'Copyright and Culture')
- Lexington Books (for chapter 17, 'Cultural Studies, Poststructuralism, Political Economy')
- *Queen's Quarterly* (for chapter 4, 'Life Is Information')
- Springer Science and Business Media (for chapter 1, 'The Place of Information in Economics')
- *Topia, Canadian Journal of Cultural Studies* (for chapter 10, 'Innis, Saul, Suzuki')

- University of Toronto Press (for chapter 8, 'An Information Revolution?' and chapter 12, 'The Communication Thought of Herbert Marshall McLuhan')
- Wiley-Blackwell and *Journal of Communication* (for chapter 13, 'Red Toryism')

Finally and most obviously, this book would have been impossible without the ever-timely assistance of its tireless author, Robert Babe. Thanks, Bob, for this, your work and, of course, the generosity of your friendship. In all sincerity, it has been a great honour editing this book.

EAC

NOTE

1 Minimal changes have been made to these writings. Most simply minimize repetition. Full citations of the original versions are provided in the book's final section, 'Publications and Conference Papers by Robert E. Babe.'

Acknowledgments: Robert E. Babe

Without Edward Comor's initial idea, his formal book proposal, his diligence and generosity, there would be no place for these acknowledgments to appear. Thank you, Edward.

The support of the University of Toronto Press through three previous book projects over a twenty-year period, likewise, is pivotal. Many thanks to Virgil Duff, Stephen Kotowych, Siobhan McMenemy, Frances Mundy, and Ryan Van Huijstee, and as well to my former dean at Western, Catherine Ross, who secured subsidies in aid of publication. And of course, I express deep gratitude to the contributors in this volume – Sandra Braman, Edward Comor, Hanno Hardt, Paul Heyer, Robin Mansell, Warren J. Samuels, and James Winter.

Now, let me turn to the beginnings and trace chronologically some of my debts. Without the devotion, assistance, and insistence of my mother, Marjorie E. Babe (née Craig), I literally would not have finished high school. Nearly fifty years later, I am still in awe of the work she put into me. My older brother, Bill, set for me a high academic bar – even scoring 100 per cent on his province-wide Grade 13 history exam! He was a role model in my early years. I undoubtedly learned more from my big brother than I can even now appreciate.

Among my pre-university teachers I would single out just one: Don McIlveen, who was my high school basketball coach at Oshawa Central Collegiate Institute. At the time, I was an uncoordinated aspirant wishing to prove myself at something, and the coach stuck with me, always respecting my effort. The quote I received, second-hand, attributed to my coach, after he had watched me devote several lacklustre years trying to make the first string, was, 'I've never seen anyone do so much with so little talent.' I have always viewed that Churchilean-like statement most positively; like all great teachers, Don McIlveen managed to draw from his student the most this one, at least, was capable of. I am pleased to note I indeed made the first string in my final year, and that principle of extra effort has stayed with me ever since. Recently, in the fall of 2008, I had the privilege and joy of sending 'Mac' a draft of these acknowledgments, and subsequently sharing a dinner with him as arranged by my Oshawa friend, Ted Monchesky. In his response, the coach tactfully recalled that it had been football that he always envisaged for me! Thank you, Don McIlveen, for inspiring me, and for the life lesson learned thereby.

Of my professors during my undergraduate and MA years at the University of Western Ontario (1963–8) a number stood out. Louis Parai was my introductory economics teacher; at the time, I was in pre-meds. Parai, though, steered me into the dismal science, with helping hands from the late Stephen Peitchinis (a most august and respected professor) and from a certain Professor Walsh (whom I never had as an instructor but who summoned me to his office one day and, remarking on my relative grades, asked why in the world I was in sciences). Professor Walsh persuaded me to take a master's in economics. Another influential professor was Frank Roseman. In my qualifying year for MA studies, he stimulated my interest in the economics of industry (industrial organization), a speciality from which I did not waver during my formal higher education. Thank you Messrs Parai, Roseman, Peitchinis, and Walsh. (Incidentally, a decade or so later I testified before Frank Roseman, who was then a commissioner with the Restrictive Trade Practices Commission. For thirteen days I was an expert witness on behalf of the director of investigation and research, Combines Investigation Act, in a case opposing vertical integration in the telephone industry – a life-transforming experience! I was cross-examined in tag team by Bay Street's toughest lawyers; thereafter, I knew I could handle any question a student might throw at me. So, perhaps I should thank Bell Canada's lawyers – Warren Grover and the late Alex McIntosh – among other cross-examiners, although the thanks here still carry some bitterness).

It was Bruce W. Wilkinson, then at Western, who suggested I consider taking a PhD, and it was Carl Beigie who recommended that I apply to 'Michigan.' When I later told him I had been accepted by Michigan State, he responded, 'Why did you apply there? I meant University of Michigan.' So much in life is by chance, not planned, and one must be open to the unexpected. Soon thereafter Eric Maass, my landlord in

London, predicted I would be offered a fine job in the United States after I had graduated from MSU and that I would not return to Canada. I resolved immediately that I would return; without that prediction and resolution, I might easily still be in the United States.

The economics I learned at MSU was very different from what I had been trained in at Western. For the first time, I learned about economic power. All three of my thesis advisory committee members were institutional economists, and all three were highly influential. From Harry Trebing I learned not only public utility economics, but as well that an economist can make a career from the study of media and communication. From the late Walter Adams, my major professor, I learned that iconoclasm and non-conventionality are good, that above all one should be true to oneself rather than seek vain glory, that teaching really matters, that corporate malfeasances are rampant, and so much more. Walter suggested my thesis topic (economics of the cable television industry), and he secured for me both my first academic appointment (with the Department of Television and Radio at MSU) and my first book publication (with a press at MSU).

I need to tell a small anecdote about when and why Walter decided to take me under his wing and be my mentor. (In his long and distinguished career he was thesis supervisor to only a small handful of students – certainly fewer than ten.) We were standing together at the front of his undergraduate class as his 180 students were filing in (my job being to check off attendance on the seating chart) when he asked me convivially how the Leafs were doing. I responded, 'The Leafs! I could not care less about the Leafs. I'm a Montreal Canadiens fan.' Years later Walter explained that from that conversation he discerned in me an incipient non-conformity (my home town being, after all, virtually a suburb of Toronto, not to mention the English-French rivalry and divide) – thereby qualifying me to work under his supervision.

Finally, I cannot say enough about Warren J. Samuels. He blew me away in my first term as a PhD student with his erudition, breadth and depth of knowledge, his originality, and his detachment/fairness in presenting various schools of economic thought. (I was continually asking myself in his courses, 'Where does he stand? What does he think?' For Samuels, those questions were irrelevant for his understanding of education and scholarship; and he was uninterested in having disciples.) That I chose to switch from industry studies to intellectual history/critique in the second half of my career bears witness to the continuing, deep impact Professor Samuels had and continues to have. In a recent correspondence, I was very touched to read, 'I have been very proud of what you have made of yourself.' I had the joy of sending Professor Samuels, too, an early draft of these Acknowledgements, and I am so thrilled that he is a contributor to this volume.

I secured invaluable help in my dissertation research from several professionals in the broadcasting and cable television industries. In that regard, I would mention particularly Tom Williams and Alex Dworkin, who provided cost and revenue data on cable television. Tom even gave me an office at CHOH-TV in Ottawa. Thanks also to G. D. Zimmerman, to Norm MacDonald, and to John Hagborg of the CRTC who ran my computer analysis. Without the magnanimity of these individuals, my thesis would never have been accomplished.

I spent a year and a half teaching broadcasting economics in the Television and Radio Department at MSU (partially fulfilling Eric Maass's prophecy). Tom Baldwin, then an associate professor, sat in on my very first course, a graduate seminar, and helped greatly to increase my confidence. The graduate students, too, were fantastic. I still remember the names of several: not bad for a prof who today can barely recall names of students from one term to the next! It was here, in that first grad class, that I knew I would be a teacher.

When it came time to apply for landed immigrant status to remain in that post, however, I decided it was time to leave, or rather to return. After a summer consulting in Winnipeg, I moved to Ottawa and became a replacement professor in the Economics Department at Carleton University (1973–4). The year proved significant as I found that teaching economics paled before the enjoyment I had attained in the TV and Radio Department at MSU, and it was then I decided to seek a position in communication studies. I still reflect on an incident in my graduate seminar in microeconomic theory, the last course I taught at Carleton: a student at the back of the room finally spoke up at the conclusion of the very last session, having said nary a word all term; she remarked that she believed the conservationist position forwarded by the Club of Rome made a lot more sense than what I had been teaching. I was dumbfounded but soon became convinced she was right. I have forgotten her name, but I remain thankful to her. I can also remember the bemused look on the faces of a couple of my Carleton colleagues after they read a draft paper I had prepared challenging the revered Coase Theorem! The Coase Theorem, incidentally, has proven to be a recurring object of my inquiry, and antipathy.

My next year was in the service of Her Majesty in the now-defunct federal Department of Communications. That year was an eye-open-er. Previously, I had thought government was sincere in its idealistic broadcasting pronouncements, that it simply lacked the wisdom of how best to proceed, and that I, of course, could make a big difference in that regard. With all sorts of documentation on corporate malfea-sances and governmental complicities crossing my desk, I soon learned that policy pronouncements and speeches are crafted with an eye to public relations and too frequently have little or nothing to do with actual policy. The more I objected to what was going on, the fewer the number of memos I received, until finally there was but a trickle. Then I was told that if I altered one word of my original PhD thesis, which I was then revising for publication as a book (*Cable Television and Tel-ecommunications in Canada*, 1975), I should resign. So, I resigned. To the director-general who gave me that ultimatum, I owe a debt of grati-tude; otherwise, I might still be a frustrated public servant tilting at windmills or, more likely, a compromised one, jaded and dispirited, resigned to the 'inevitable.' My 1979 study for the Economic Council of Canada (*Canadian Television Broadcasting Structure, Performance, and Regulation*), as compared to my doctoral thesis (and book based ther-eon), displays the learning curve I experienced in that most valuable year of public service.

Another bright memory from the year in the DOC is of Fred Bigham, who graciously allowed me to review his incomplete PhD dissertation on the history of Bell Canada. It was not until an additional fifteen years had lapsed that my own research on the history of Canadian telecom-munications was finally published (*Telecommunications in Canada: Tech-nology, Industry, and Government*, 1990). I learned a lot about the vagaries of 'blind' peer review in the process of preparing that book for publi-cation. I am very grateful to Virgil Duff and the University of Toronto Press editorial team for the close attention they paid to my rebuttals to often ill-advised anonymous referees' reports. It is has long been a ques-tion in my mind as to why reviewers are presumed to be more candid in anonymity than if identified and thereby being made accountable for their assessments. In the end, that book made my career. Others deserv-ing thanks in this project include Thomas Grindlay, Kenneth Goldstein, Joe Schmidt, Antoine Zalatan, and Dennis Wardrop.

I did a lot of government and NGO consulting after leaving DOC (1975–8, and again 1979–83). In the first period, in addition to many small reports there were two major ones. First, I prepared *Canadian Television Broadcasting Structure Performance and Regulation* for the Economic Council of Canada; many thanks to H.E.L. 'Bert' Waslander for commissioning and supervising that work, and to Sylvia Ostry (then chair of the Council) for publishing it (and taking a lot of flak from industry and elected representatives both prior to and immediately following publication; one irate MP, for instance, suggested that Ms Ostry and I both be shipped to Cuba). The second project required well over a year of the most intense labour: preparing evidence for the director of combines investigation and testifying as an expert witness before the Restrictive Trade Practices Commission. I am very grateful to Don Braden, Gordon Kaiser, and the late Gordon Henderson for their support during this most challenging period. A summary of that evidence appears here as an appendix to Part Two.

In 1978–9, I taught at Simon Fraser University and was privileged to work alongside Bill Melody and Dallas Smythe. Bill's impact and support was immediate and strong (the final days of my RTPC testimony overlapped my early weeks at SFU). Dallas's influence was slower to take root, but as the present volume amply demonstrates, it was enduring.

Then back to Ottawa for four more years of consulting (1979–83). Two notable reports prepared at that time were *Competitive Procedures for Broadcasting: Renewals and Transfers* (with Philip Slayton, then dean of law at the University of Western Ontario), and *Broadcasting Policy and Copyright Law: An Analysis of a Cable Rediffusion Right* (with Conrad Winn, a political scientist at Carleton). Then, in the fall of 1983, I obtained a full-time position in the Department of Communication at the University of Ottawa, where I remained for eighteen years. Over that time I also gave some seven or eight times a graduate course in media economics at Concordia University in Montreal, and also (one time) a PhD course on media economics at McGill. Many thanks to William Gilsdorf, the late Gail Valiskakis, Jody Berland, and Gertrude Robinson for affording me those opportunities, particularly valuable as Ottawa U at the time had no graduate communication program. Jody Berland, incidentally, deserves extra thanks. Years later, in her capacity as editor of *Topia: Canadian Journal of Cultural Studies*, Jody invited me to prepare annual columns on the interface between cultural studies and political economy, five columns appearing between 2003 and 2006; they formed the base for my *Cultural Studies and Political Economy: Toward a New Integration* (2009).

It was assuredly at the University of Ottawa that I came into my own as a scholar. Four books were published during my tenure there, and almost a fifth: *Competitive Procedures for Broadcasting: Renewals and Transfers* (1983), *Telecommunications in Canada: Technology, Industry, and Government* (1990), *Information and Communication in Economics* (an edited volume, 1994), *Communication and the Transformation of Economics* (1995), and *Canadian Communication Thought: Ten Foundational Writers* (2000). The last, written while at Ottawa, was published after I moved to the University of Windsor. During those years Gary Hauch stimulated my interest in and concern for environmentalism, and the book on that topic (*Culture of Ecology: Reconciling Economics and Environment*), appeared in 2006 – several years after I had left Ottawa U. The most helpful among my colleagues were Gilles Paquet and David Staines. The communication students at University of Ottawa were very supportive and remarkable, and they regularly bestowed on me the honour of 'best professor.' Moreover, I jointly authored consulting reports with two students, Sheehan Carter and Angela Carter (no relation). Along with my esteemed colleague Kosta Gouliamos, I advised Kerry Pither and other students on staging an outstanding student-organized and student-funded multi-day conference on critical communication. Another former student, Danielle Cliche, edited a volume in which my work appears and invited me to England to deliver the paper at a conference held by the International Institute of Communications. During my final year at Ottawa U, my friend and colleague Hilary Horan successfully nominated me for an Ontario Colleges and Universities Faculty Association award for excellence in university teaching; Hilary laboriously gathered the necessary documentation, including student testimonials and petitions. Upon my leaving, Hilary also played a large role in the student-focused celebrations of my career at Ottawa U. Thank you, all.

I 'retired' from University of Ottawa in 2000, having the previous year taken up a position at the University of Windsor, where I was welcomed with open arms. Jim Winter has penned some kind words for this volume about my time at Windsor. My three years there were among the most congenial of my Canadian university career. Thank you, Jim, and colleagues at Windsor.

In 2002 I returned to the University of Western Ontario, now as a professor. I was appointed to the Jean Monty/BCE Chair in Media Studies – quite an honour. Being at Western completes a circle, which is very satisfying, and many thanks to my colleagues for making that available to me. At Western I seem always to be returning to the works of Harold Innis, and in that regard I have benefited much from the insights and expertise of my colleague, editor, co-author, and friend, Edward Comor. Even before we both arrived at Western, Edward was graciously reading and commenting on much of my writing. And he has certainly strengthened my resolve to expose the absurdities of post-structuralism. Thank you, Edward, indeed.

Every author benefits from writers he or she meets only through the printed page. I have prepared a Select Bibliography for publication in this volume, and those major influences are identified there.

Finally, to Jane, my wife of over thirty years, and to our fabulous children: Thanks! It's been a blast. I trust it will all continue for some time yet. I love you all.

REB

Abbreviations

AGT	Alberta Government Telephones
AT&T	American Telephone and Telegraph
BBG	Board of Broadcast Governors
BCE	Bell Canada Enterprises
BC Tel	British Columbia Telephone Company
CBC	Canadian Broadcasting Corporation
CBT	cognitive behavioural therapy
CCF	Cooperative Commonwealth Federation
CFDC	Canadian Film Development Corporation
CIA	Central Intelligence Agency
CPI	Committee on Public Information
CPR	Canadian Pacific Railway
CNCP	Canadian National / Canadian Pacific
CP	Canadian Pacific
CRBC	Canadian Radio Broadcasting Commission
CRTC	Canadian Radio-television and telecommunications Commission and Canadian Radio-Television Commission
CTC	Canadian Transport Commission
CTV	Canadian Television Network
DOC	Department of Communications
FCC	Federal Communications Commission
GATT	General Agreement on Tarrifs and Trade
GE	General Electric
LSR	League for Social Reconstruction
MPP	member of Provincial Parliament
MSU	Michigan State University
MTS	Manitoba Telephone System or Message Toll Service

NBC	National Broadcasting Company
NGO	non-governmental organization
OCUFA	Ontario Federation of University Faculty Associations
POTS	plain old telephone service
PR	public relations
PSP	Public Sector Pension
RF	radio frequency
RTPC	Restrictive Trade Practices Commission
SFU	Simon Fraser University
TCTS	Trans-Canada Telephone System
TNC	transnational corporations
UNESCO	United Nations Educational Scientific and Cultural Organization
U of O	University of Ottawa
UTP	University of Toronto Press
USIA	United States Information Agency
WATS	Wide Area Telephone Service

MEDIA, STRUCTURES, AND POWER
The Robert E. Babe Collection

Robert Babe, Canadian Scholar

EDWARD A. COMOR*

Over the course of a career, the collected works of most academics typically reveal the development of early insights into full-blown analyses. Central figures and schools of thought are fleshed out, gradually applied toward some sort of definitive conclusion. Indeed, for most, a career in the academy entails a journey in time through which concepts and political ideals run their course. Consciously or not, for most, the circle is squared.

Robert Babe, however, is not a typical scholar. Earning a PhD at one of America's elite economics departments – Michigan State University in 1972 – Babe left a predictably secure, prosperous career in the United States for a less certain future in his home country, Canada. After becoming an assistant professor in Carleton University's Economics Department, Babe turned to public service, becoming Canada's chief of telecommunications economic policy. Soon, however, Babe returned to the academy, in 1976 accepting a position at Simon Fraser University in the emerging field of communication studies. In the 1980s, he moved again, eventually becoming full professor in the University of Ottawa's Department of Communication.

Babe's move from economics to communication and media studies – from a prospective career as a professional economist to that of an interdisciplinary social scientist – had several antecedents. While his training in institutional economics impelled a holistic, historicist interest in structures shaping political economic relations, Babe's professional development reflected his quest to find an institutional home – one in which he could secure the time and space needed to explore, deduce,

---

* University of Western Ontario

and denounce. Whether questioning neoclassicists dominating the political right or, more recently, postmodernists in influential positions on the left, Babe's career has come to focus on empowering his readers through a scalpel-like disassembly of institutionalized thought.[1] Critiquing neoclassical economists, Babe writes, 'human relations are ... [for them] commodity exchange relations ... In fact, the focus of attention of mainstream economists is not on human relations at all, but on things (commodities).'[2] As for postmodernism, despite its progressive pretences, Babe dissects it in equally uncompromising terms. It has become, he writes, 'a paradigm [inadvertently] propping up established power, war, gross inequality and other forms of injustice.'[3]

As these and other uncomfortable truths were being articulated, yet another path of insight emerged from Babe's work, this one addressing his concern for ecological issues – both environmental and cultural. Just as information in his earlier work implies a shared symbolic environment, in Babe's later writings Earth constitutes the place upon which all creatures depend and in which all living things survive. Ecology – the understanding that everything depends on everything else – itself, he argues, requires a new economics involving a new theory of value. In a masterpiece of exposition – 'The Place of Information in Economics' (chapter 1) – he concludes that 'conceiving nature instrumentally as mere commodity emphasizes humanity's apartness or otherness vis-à-vis the environment, despite the reality that in ecological terms we are all a part of the earth and it of us.'[4]

Beyond critique, Robert Babe's work provides us with the nuance and precision needed to act strategically and efficaciously. From news media to educational systems, from corporate marketers to commercially structured digital technologies, Babe's training, policy background, and theoretical insights enable him to identify those key nodal points mediating contemporary power relations – in effect, defining them as important locales for reform and resistance. For example, today's corporate-dominated, time-annihilating Internet fosters, says Babe, 'a mindset that information is immaterial, and that information matters more than matter. In the spirit of Innis, we might say that digital information biases not only space over time, but also the immaterial over the material (and paradoxically so, given that Innis associated time-bias with religion, which addresses the unseen) – and that too has grave implications regarding how we care for the environment. Moreover, digital media help reinvigorate the doctrine of the infinite Earth, a posture toward nature that is anti-environmental in the extreme.'[5]

Predictably, not everyone has embraced such conclusions. Seen as a threat by some (especially those occupying the political right) and shunned by others (including some on the left), his writings have attracted few allies. In quoting Graham Spry, Babe could well be referring to himself: 'By nature I am compelled to be a reformer. I can always imagine improvements, always scent evils, and very easily hate some wrongly based institution.'[6]

The writings selected for this book reflect the depth and clarity of Robert Babe's developing thought. Not only is the range of subjects addressed remarkable, the quality and lucidity of his engagement is consistently superb. It is a corpus characterized by a continual expansion – pushing back boundaries, challenging realities.

In his first decade of scholarship, Babe published three books on telecommunications, broadcasting, and copyright regulations. His second decade saw the release of *Telecommunications in Canada* and his edited collection called *Information and Communication in Economics*. In the third decade, Babe completed *Communication and the Transformation of Economics* – a tour de force critique of neoclassicism and the conceptual and democratic possibilities of a communication approach – followed by his ambitious *Canadian Communication Thought: Ten Foundational Writers*. The last, published in 2000, was both a milestone and turning point: it defined a distinctive Canadian ontology while also bringing Babe's ecological concerns into focus. Six years later, Babe released *The Culture of Ecology*, a book that articulated humankind's environmental and cultural crisis while turning to past and non-Western sources for strategic insight on how to go forward. Now, as the fourth decade of his academic career unfolds, an ambitious new book has been published. In *Cultural Studies and Political Economy: Toward a New Integration*,[7] Babe reassesses the long-standing political economy versus cultural studies debate, tracing the lineage of poststructuralism and, in so doing, elucidating its destructive estrangement from cultural materialism (including political economy).

While his writings are consistently exploratory, ongoing themes and re-emerging analytical threads are discernable. Some are spelled out by Babe in his treatment of other scholars in *Canadian Communication*

Thought. As he puts it, the Canadian approach, particularly in contrast to the American, 'emphasizes the importance, and the power, of the human imagination, and it studies how our imaginations are moulded, or at least influenced, by prevailing institutions, by predominant media of communication.'[8] And in keeping with his typically Canadian emphasis on dialectics, Babe's analytical capacities surely involve a complex of biographical influences – choices Babe made in light of the structures in which he worked, as well as the historical dynamics influencing both the time and place of his studies.

Stemming from his formative years as both an 'insider' and 'outsider' in the American academy and as a Canadian public servant,[9] Babe's work resonates with a long tradition of similarly situated scholars. But rather than simplistically labelling Babe an 'eminent Canadian thinker' (which he is), the writings reproduced in this collection reveal an original academic, equally at home when assessing a spectrum of subjects – from the dialectics in Northrop Frye's writings to the sleight-of-hand complexities of the telecommunications industry to the global political economy's accelerating march towards ecological suicide.

As for Babe's nationalism, this is not the stuff of some kind of chauvinistic patriot. Rather, Babe's embrace of Canada, its people, and the institutions that mediate their culture more accurately involves a political strategy. For example, Babe recognizes that a commercial, commodified view of social relations in Canada constitutes a direct threat to freedom, justice, and social/ecological harmony. Instead of taking these cultural developments for granted, he understands that their political economic genesis and perpetuation involve a number of decisive mediators – the price system, mainstream economics, and postmodern ontologies among the most important. These, in structuring domestic relationships and, ultimately, norms of thought, constitute, for Babe, nodal points to be historicized, reformed, or resisted. Canadians generally and its scholars more particularly, as quite possibly the modern world's pre-eminent insiders/outsiders, possess (or potentially possess) both the insight and cultural capacities needed to redress what Innis termed an American-centred civilizational neglect of time and mechanization of knowledge.

For Babe, Canadian culture was (and, to some extent, remains) an important resource, not just for Canadians but also for the very survival of humankind. In reference to those addressed in *Canadian Communication Thought*, Babe writes that they are virtually univocal in their condemnation of the market as the chief means of organizing human activity, and, by implication, of subordinating communication systems to commercial concerns. In the view of these theorists, markets cause people to be unduly individualistic in their actions and present-minded in their thoughts, whereas human existence is contingent upon the actions of others and is, in some important regards, self-destructive when it divorces the past from the future. The price system and related concerns for economic power and efficiency, these theorists agree, tend to wipe out the ethic of community. Through commodification, objects, processes, and relationships are emptied, relegated to little more than containers of exchange value. With the price system, thresholds are eliminated. Death ensues.

To repeat, Babe's work consistently probes the underlying dynamics shaping thought. For him, those who control what information is available, as well as the kind of knowledge that emerges (itself the result of how it is understood and applied), are important subjects for cultures generally and political economists more particularly. Unlike the work of poststructuralists or postmodernists, a non-reductionist materialist analysis – as exemplified by holistic, dialectical Canadian thought – prospectively leads to knowledge that is genuinely empowering. A political economy approach, after all, uncovers power structures that status quo interests would rather not acknowledge. Amidst contemporary gaps between rich and poor, environmental degradation and accelerating species extinctions, and, for Babe, wars being waged under the cover of contrived simulacra, maintaining a material grounding to our discourses now is more important than ever.

The precise tools Babe developed to do this were forged from many sources. One was the Department of Economics at Michigan State University, where the members of his thesis advisory committee were particularly influential. From Harry Trebing, an expert in public utility economics, Babe learned that economists can, indeed, specialize in the economics of media and communication. From antitrust economist Walter Adams he was exposed to analyses of corporate power and corporate malfeasances and came to understand that mainstream economists' pretensions of 'objectivity' are hollow. From Warren J. Samuels, Babe was exposed to intellectual history and learned that neoclassical economics is just one among many approaches to the field.

Certainly another central figure influencing Babe's work is Harold Innis. For Innis, 'monopolies of knowledge' tend to emerge as a result of a status quo's use of 'biased' media that, over time, involve vested interests in a pernicious cycle of self-referential thoughts and policies. Civilizations, for Innis, rise and fall amidst mediated, structured ways of thinking and acting, ultimately generating contradictory outcomes. Innis also believed that developing the capacity to recognize and prospectively counter such dominant biases / ways of thinking is the essential task of the social scientist. Babe certainly would agree. Indeed, both Babe and Innis believe that a relatively favourable locale for this project lies at the margins of the imperial core (but not altogether in the hinterland, as this status and position entails more vulnerabilities than advantages). Canadians and, indeed, inside/outside intellectuals (such as Babe) are relatively well positioned to grasp the nettle of our civilization's biases.

Whether addressing how contemporary biases shape our neglect of ecological principles (as with neoclassicists), the contemporary left's rejection of structured human relationships (as with postmodernists), or, more generally, the probable escalation of violence and the collapse of our ecosystem (involving the core's reckless neglect of time), there is wisdom in Babe's writings – a wisdom that comes from an intellectual journey characterized by curiosity, insight, and political concern. As Babe understands Graham Spry's communication thought, so too we can recognize the depth of Babe's own work on media. As Babe writes, for Spry, 'media, and the individuals or groups controlling media, "condition" and "program" societies. Media as the "central nervous system" of the social organism transmit instructions on how members are to respond to environmental change and regulate in a general way society's relationships with its environment. Society's "genetic program" – its traditions, languages, laws, customs, institutions and so forth – are continuously conditioned and modified (mutated) as new information is diffused through its media of communication. The implication is that media can either contribute to the vitality and growth of a society, or can be entropic, inducing disintegration and death.'[10]

Resisting pessimism, Babe reaffirms that humanity does, indeed, share common interests, especially those concerning ecological conditions. For him, all living entities are interdependent. However, through the contemporary political economy's atomization of social relations, its neglect of continuity, and, indeed, its trivialization of life, too many in modern society (including most contemporary scholars) ignore this core reality. Having made this clear, Babe's writings – critiquing these norms through his use of history, philosophy, and theory – provide us with rays of light. Once the power of those who disproportionately influence our thoughts and activities is exposed, Babe has confidence that human beings will respond. This optimism repeatedly percolates to the surface, but it is an optimism that emerges only as a result of an often dark, critical engagement of the forces and complexities shaping thought itself. 'Denying or belittling human agency,' he writes, 'is tantamount to denigrating human dignity and is to understate the possibility of social reform.'[11]

The first part of this collection, focusing on Babe's communication-based critique of mainstream economics, consists of four chapters originally published between 1988 and 1995. By drawing on a broad range of theorists – particularly those illuminating the complex concept of information – he probes the relationship between economics and culture. As Sandra Braman, the author of this section's introduction explains, these initial chapters constitute some of Babe's most seminal and salient contributions, particularly when assessed in the context of contemporary policy issues. For Babe, understanding information itself – particularly its nature, characteristics, and dialectical status with materiality – is both fundamental and, today, remarkably under-assessed. In several ways this and related points, developed in Part One, lay the groundwork for Babe's subsequent assessment of knowledge–power relations.

Part Two, on telecommunications history and policy, represents the longest-running thread in Babe's career. These four chapters (plus an appendix), spanning the years 1981 to 1998, reflect Babe as an ever-developing thinker concerned with how power is forged, structured, and mediated. According to introduction writer Robin Mansell, here Babe demonstrates how and why the development of an autonomous public interest–oriented cultural industry in Canada has been undermined. Herein we also see his critical political economy being applied in ways that demystify taken-for-granted policy discourses, including today's ever-present technological determinism and rhetoric surrounding corporate globalization. What makes the critique presented in these chapters especially potent is Babe's own professional background in telecommunications policy. Throughout this part of the book, the author's intimate knowledge of what he is analysing resonates in ways rarely attained by 'policy outsiders.'

Part Three highlights Babe's groundbreaking research on Canadian communication thought, forging a distinctly Canadian ontology from which to assess both domestic and international developments. In addressing Innis, Frye, McLuhan, Macpherson, Grant, and Suzuki, among others, these five chapters make the case that the Canadian intellectual tradition is holistic, dialectical, and ecological (the last he conceptualizes in both environmental and cultural terms). Together, they span a decade of work that began in the mid- to late-1990s. Here we see Babe's adroit ability to synthesize and contextualize writers. Whatever their complexity or the era in which their work was carried out, Babe demonstrates that these intellectuals have commonality as Canadian communication scholars and, more importantly, they all have something important to communicate to contemporary readers. Among other things, the chapters in this section reaffirm the importance of history – particularly in Babe's vivid elaboration how social-economic developments and emerging mediations affected (and were affected by) Canada's unique intellectual community. Paul Heyer, in his introduction, concludes that in mapping Canadian communication thought, in Babe, we have 'a cartographer most worthy.'

Part Four – the last section of Babe's writings – is titled 'Cultural Ecology and the Political Economy of Knowledge.' Its five chapters show him at his most passionate, provocative, and, indeed, experimental. In these pages Babe's commitment to a holistic, non-reductive political economy is articulated as he confronts those organizations, structures, and, still more abstractly, media that continue to confound humanity's hopes for a peaceful, reflexive, and environmentally sustainable world. In writings published over a ten-year period dating from 1996, among other points, Babe argues that how we practise and think about our economic relationships and cultural lives explicate the inequalities that surround us. As Hanno Hardt (the author of this section's introduction) observes, Babe's approach reveals the complex power relationships structured into both human interaction (communication) and, more to the point, our cultural norms. Collectively, Hardt explains, these chapters elaborate a 'dynamic model of social communication that supports [Babe's] ... formulation of an ecological project'; they are, he continues, 'a rich example of a historically grounded effort to address the potential of a political economy of communication.'

The final section of this collection is made up of two rather different chapters. The first is by one of Babe's early mentors, Warren Samuels, while the second is by James Winter, a longtime friend and colleague. Samuels's contribution delves into the power of (and in) language, involving media and other institutions used in 'generating and marshalling ... information and ignorance.' Although Samuels shares these concerns with his former student, here he has chosen to explore them through his own lens – that of one of America's great intellectual historians. And although Samuels's focus is the writings of Adam Smith and T.D. Weldon rather than Babe's work directly, it constitutes a fitting addition to this collection. Robert Babe's work, after all, remains a going concern, complementing and extending the work of others (including his old mentor). As for Winter's brief, final chapter, the volume ends with some personal reflections on Robert Babe, the man.

Given the fact that Robert Babe's scholarship is ongoing, the reader might well ask the question, 'Why publish this collection now?' In response, let us place his work in three contexts: its influence on both policymaking and the academy; its timeliness in light of contemporary economic and cultural developments; and, finally, its place as a reflection and representation of Canada's uniquely historical, holistic, and dialectical approach to both social science and societal concerns.

For many years, Babe's contributions to political economy, telecommunications policy, ecological studies, and media theory have been widely recognized. The status and accomplishments of this volume's contributors itself underlines the extraordinary range and influence of his scholarship. Indeed, this collection's publication reflects Babe's standing in the academy and, more importantly, it presents, for the first time, his otherwise disparate writings as a coherent, developing body of work.

In historical terms, the timeliness of this collection is underlined by the contemporary collapse of neoliberalism and what, at this juncture, appears to be the beginning of an important shift in both economic thinking and public policy. As of 2011, decades of pro–free market regulations have intensified contradictions long recognized by Babe: unsustainable here-and-now cultural practices that have emerged alongside mass indebtedness and environmental decay. Thus, in the context of the contemporary crisis, this review of Babe's varied critical assessments coincides with efforts by political leaders, academics, and activists to construct new ways of organizing social-economic relations. Babe's work illuminates both past mistakes and future opportunities. In this regard, this collection is prescient.

Finally, when assessed in their entirety, the chapters in this volume constitute a model of the uniquely historical, holistic, and dialectical approach that Babe himself identified as Canada's distinctive contribution to knowledge. These writings, we suggest, reflect a uniquely Canadian perspective on social organization, economic life, and ecological survival.

As Robert Babe's intellectual journey continues, traversing further from both the mainstream academy and culture, we see his work probing deeper into contemporary mythologies and conceptual prejudices. His destination is nothing less than a humane and sustainable ontology. A just, sustainable future, for Babe, will require nothing less than substantive changes in how we, individually and collectively, choose to live our lives. But before any such sea change can take place, modern society's conceited, shortsighted norms must be confronted. Dialectically speaking, these mediated realities will have to be exposed and synthesized into new ways of conceptualizing life. As Babe's research propels him towards a more precise comprehension of the powers resisting this necessity, we find in him an audacious courage that, itself, continues to inspire. Citing Innis, Babe insists that 'we must continually strive through reflexivity to stand outside the biases of media and discourse sufficiently to at least glimpse truth, even if but as through a glass darkly, and that for him is precisely what the task and duty of scholarship is.'[12]

The writings in this volume are the fruit of thirty-five years of intellectual labour. For Babe, this work continues – steering us not towards safe intellectual harbours but, instead, forward in the direction of liberating insights. To paraphrase Innis, the intellectual history of Canada has been dominated by the discrepancy between the centre and the margin of Western civilization. For Babe, this discrepancy has generated a career characterized by tension – the tension generated by a man who both understands and disagrees with status quo ways of thinking and acting. Out of this tension and through his respect for both history and alternative cultures, Robert Babe has crafted a clear and creative critique – one from which tangible hope, in the end, thankfully emerges.

NOTES

1 Throughout Babe's writings, *postmodernism* and *poststructuralism* often are used interchangeably because he recognized that both perspectives generally reject modernist/structuralist notions of essences, natures, and other materialist postulates.

2 See p. 45.
3 See p. 337.
4 See p. 38.
5 See p. 332.
6 Spry quoted on p. 66.
7 Robert E. Babe, *Cultural Studies and Political Economy: Toward a New Integration* (Lanham, MD: Lexington Books, 2009).
8 See p. 197.
9 'Insider' in terms of the cultural milieux of his professional training (in the imperialist core) along with his work as a policy analyst; 'outsider' in terms of his critical political economic approach and Canadian sensibilities.
10 See p. 72.
11 See p. 364.
12 See p. 379.

PART ONE

Media, Information, and Critique of Economics

Introduction to Part One

SANDRA BRAMAN*

Robert Babe's work on economics is a hologram for his oeuvre as a whole. In it we find deep engagement with theory, whether orthodox or heterodox; theoretical pluralism; interdisciplinarity; and a deep concern for the real-world consequences of how we think and what we think about. Seeds of all of his other work can be found here, whether that is research on the history of communication theory, developing a framework for understanding relationships between cultural studies and political economy, or investigations into the epistemological underpinnings of environmental disaster. It may be ironic, but it is also valuable that Babe's critiques of the economic ideas that have dominated for over a century, and that continue to shape public and private sector decision-making, also yield insights of such value for communication theory.

Babe was ahead of the curve in examining the contributions of communication and cultural theories to understand economics. Those in cultural studies, for example, didn't begin to ask the questions about interactions between culture and the economy that Babe addressed in the edited volume *Information and Communication in Economics* (1994) and in his book *Communication and the Transformation of Economics* (1995) until more than a decade after these were published.

For those new to the study of the economics of information (micro-economics) and the information economy (macro-economics), Babe's work provides an excellent introduction. His synthesis of and additions to critiques of neoclassical economic thought make clear why those who use the associated set of analytical tools fail to cope with informa-

---

* University of Wisconsin at Milwaukee

tion, communication, and culture. Unlike some who insist that such questions have never been raised before – the ever-popular 'no one has ever' school of academic work – Babe reintroduces us to the contributions of such thinkers as Uri Porat on the heterogeneity of information from an economics perspective, and Beth Allen on information as a differentiated commodity. Babe mines the history of economic thought to find what is useful for thinking about information, including work by Frank Knight (1920s) on the importance of risk, uncertainty, and market imperfections to a sound evaluation of economic processes; Ronald Coase (1930s) on limits of neoclassical thought (recently borrowed substantially by Yochai Benkler); and Kenneth Arrow (1960s and 1970s) on prices and competition as information and decision structures. Babe also reintroduces 'renegade' economists such as John Kenneth Galbraith, Tibor Scitovsky, and Clarence Ayres, who have offered profound insights into interactions between culture and consumption.

Again and always, Babe also draws us back to the enduring contributions of Thorstein Veblen and Max Weber on relations between the symbolic and the material. Indeed, Babe draws on these thinkers to suggest an alternative history of communication theory, arguing that their ideas about communication were more profound and extensive than those of John Dewey, even if less recognized. Institutions, for example, can be seen as 'widespread social habits,' or 'habits of thought.' Looking at institutions allows us to see the gradual accumulation of small changes generated by social processes. By including Veblen and Weber among the intellectual sources of communication theory, Babe suggests, Chicago school ideas about communication as a constitutive force in society are complemented, extended, and enriched. Other elements of economic thought of use to communication theory include the emphasis on dynamic rather than static processes, and the linkage of the semiotic with the material.

Of course there are differences between how economists and communication scholars understand political economy, which Babe defines as the study of the nature, sources, uses, and consequences of Weberian power – the ability to impose one's will on others – whether that power is in an economic, political, communicative, or other form. While economists focus on legal systems (institutions) and class (the Marxist approach to social structure), communication scholars emphasize economic, institutional, and legal influences on message production and view media products as tools an established power system creates to preserve and extend itself.

The bulk of Babe's work on neoclassical economics is devoted to critique. The following selections from his work include these important, clear, and valuable analyses; here those critiques that offer insight into communication theory as well will be highlighted. Methodological individualism, for example, is problematic for both disciplines. In economics, theories of the firm and consumer behaviour are ahistorical and non-contextual. Collective, communal, and collaborative dimensions of organizational activities are ignored, and the consumer is depersonalized into an abstraction. Only transactional relationships among individuals are acknowledged. Even though such ideas can be described as 'quaint' and 'pernicious,' given contemporary economic (and environmental) problems, Babe notes that they remain the mainstay of mainstream quantitative approaches to the study of communication.

Similarly, economic analyses are flawed when they treat tastes as fixed, but the same problem is found in communication by those who take the position that the intentions of message producers have minimal effects relative to the power of users to make meaning. While many who take this position present themselves as more sensitive to political and cultural issues than those who continue to believe in and analyse media effects, Babe notes, in fact the minimal effects approach appeared not long after experience of Hitler's propaganda and Orson Welles's 'War of the Worlds' and has been useful for corporate content producers who seek to avoid accountability.

Babe also finds much of value in economic thought for those who study consumption as a set of communication and cultural processes. Nobelists George Stigler and Gary Becker, for example, both explored the difference between a market for products and consumer desire for commodities. By defining the latter as 'want-satisfying outputs produced by the consumer,' these economists join those in audience studies who emphasize the role of the viewer, user, or citizen in creating value from messages, information, and cultural experience. Inputs into meaning production include the consumer's time, skill, training, and other human capital in addition to other products purchased in the market. Here, however – as with many other moments in the history of economic thought – Babe argues that Stigler and Becker have trapped themselves by simultaneously treating content production (information) as a distinct economic sector with unique characteristics, even while they continue to argue that, like other sectors, it is only transactional in nature.

The application of neoclassical economic modes of analysis to all types of activities has been referred to as 'economic imperialism,' a notion generally attributed to later economists. Richard Posner, the leading proponent of the 'law and economics' approach to legal scholarship, has even gone so far as to produce economic analyses of such core communicative issues as First Amendment rights and privacy. Robert Babe gathers together his general critiques of neoclassical economic thought; his specific analyses of the failures of these theories when applied to information, communication, and culture; and his identification of relationships between economic and communication theories to argue that the directionality of intellectual colonialism should be reversed. The economy, he importantly tells us, is a communication system, and should be analysed as such.

In addition to theoretical implications of this perspective introduced above, taking this approach has methodological consequences. As discussed by Babe in the following selections, these include the need to link micro-economic (transactional and institutional issues) and macro-economic (sectoral issues) thought. Ideas such as 'efficiency,' 'equilibrium,' 'price,' and 'the market' need to be re-conceptualized and linked explicitly to policy analysis. While methodologically it is tempting to continue to view information as a commodity only – because doing so makes it so much easier to do quantitative analyses – Babe argues that the practice exacerbates policy problems such as the divide between the information-poor and the information-rich.

Babe has taken his own recommendations regarding how to use his ideas in policy analyses, providing immediate input into Canadian decision-making and building a research agenda for others. He looks at changes to copyright law in Canada, for example, and sees their impact on international flows of information and the global map of information production. He studies copyright law and cultural policy together, and finds ways in which developments in one area actively undercut the ability to achieve goals in the other. His detailed analysis of the Canada-U.S. Free Trade Agreement uncovers linkages between its economic and political consequences. And he poses challenges: What would happen, Babe asks, if we reviewed the history of policymaking in areas such as public broadcasting through the lenses of alternative ways of conceptualizing information? What attitudes towards the nature of information and what economic ideas implicitly underlie the work of influential communication policy scholars?

In his work on the economics of information, then, Robert Babe offers multiple and far-ranging contributions. In addition to his seminal work in this sub-discipline and his significant challenges to neoclassical economic thought, Babe's work enriches and sets new standards for work in the field of communication. These are tantalizing, not only theoretically and methodologically, but also as an insight.into the role of communication scholars in the world of policymaking. The numerous barriers to the effective use of the results of communication research in policymaking have been well documented,[1] while the privileged power position of economists in the world of policymaking is widely acknowledged. By inverting the directionality of intellectual colonialism between communication and economics, Babe's work suggests, communication researchers could offer work perhaps more evidently of use to policymakers. This could not only improve the relative position of communication scholars but, far more importantly, provide intellectual ground upon which we can stand in the effort to reverse what appears to be impending environmental disaster.

NOTE

1 Sandra Braman, ed., *Communication Researchers and Policy-making* (Cambridge, MA: MIT Press, 2003).

1 The Place of Information in Economics

> The very concept of a knowledge industry contains enough dynamite to blast traditional economics into orbit.
>   – Kenneth E. Boulding, 'The Knowledge Industry' (1963)

In recent decades, theorists such as George Stigler, Gary Becker, and Richard Posner have endeavoured to extend the applications of neoclassical theory into areas as diverse as family planning, racial discrimination, crime, marriage, divorce, drug addiction, politics, and suicide. Indeed, for such 'economic imperialists,'[1] *all* behaviour involving scarce resources can be illuminated by neoclassical price theory.

This chapter takes exception to that proposition. Focusing on information/communication, the chapter proposes instead that neoclassical economics be taken captive, contending that neoclassicists' notions of 'market,' 'price,' 'value,' 'commodity,' 'demand,' 'supply,' and 'exchange' are but specialized and reductionist renderings of broader communicatory phenomena. Acceptance of this proposition has far-reaching implications for such basic economic constructs as efficiency, comparative advantage, optimality, equilibrium, and as well for such standard neoclassical policy prescriptions as deregulation, privatization, free trade, and down-sizing the public sector. Information/communication poses severe challenges indeed for the neoclassical paradigm.

Four main parts follow this introduction. The first addresses treatments of information/communication by three principal approaches within the mainstream economics discipline: the macroeconomic or sectoral approach; the applied microeconomic or industry studies approach, known also as industrial organization; and the theoretical microeconomic approach, often called 'information economics.' While differences in treatment afforded information/communication among these approaches are readily evident, of far greater importance are the similarities. In particular, they are of one accord in treating, or in endeavouring to treat, information as commodity.

The main thrust of the argument of the ensuing section is as follows: mainstream economics, premised as it is on the ubiquity of commodity exchange, *needs* to treat information as a commodity in order to account for information within the mainstream or orthodox paradigm. Information, however, does not fulfil the definitional and conceptual requirements of commodities, thereby placing the discipline in a crisis concerning its own internal validity. Moreover, insisting that information is a commodity obscures not only many essential properties of information, but as well consequences of informational exchange, creating thereby also a crisis of external validity.

The penultimate section reverses the Becker/Stigler/Posner proposal and explores possibilities for 'economic colonization,' contending that economics' crises can be resolved only if the discipline is viewed more modestly, as but one way to investigate communicatory interactions. The concluding section touches on political economy aspects of the 'information commodity.'

Despite internal inconsistencies and incongruity with external phenomena caused by conceiving information as commodity, mainstream economics retains this analytical mode and itself remains remarkably influential. To understand the source of this unwarranted influence requires acknowledging the broader political economy that shapes mainstream analysis. There is wealth, status, and other emoluments to be had from 'proper' economics, and mainstream economics confers advantages to some. Put more positively, recognition of the limitations of mainstream economics, and positioning it within a broader communicatory context, offers the prospect of a more sustainable and equitable future.

Information and Communication in Mainstream Economics

Information Economy Treatment

Fritz Machlup's 1962 book, *The Production and Distribution of Knowledge in the United States*, was seminal in conceiving information and/or knowledge production, processing, and distribution as important economic activities. Prior to publication of Machlup's work, macroeconomic or aggregate analyses typically countenanced a three-fold division for the economy into agricultural, manufacturing, and service sectors. However, by calculating that nearly 29 per cent of U.S. output and 32 per cent of the U.S. employment in 1958 were accounted for by 'knowledge industries' whose annual growth averaged between 8 and nearly 11 per cent, Machlup justified constituting a fourth sector, one based on informational and communicatory activities and products.[2]

Subsequently Marc Porat took up and extended Machlup's work, pronouncing that the United States had become by 1967 an 'information economy.' Porat estimated that the information sector, in that year, accounted for about 46 per cent of U.S. GNP.[3]

In principle, macroeconomic or sectoral studies such as Machlup's and Porat's, by proposing a distinct informational sector, would seem to indicate that 'economic activities associated with processing information have unique attributes, and deserve to be studied separately from other activities in the national economy.'[4] To a limited extent some mainstream economists have pursued this line of thought, contending with Machlup, Porat, and Rubin, for instance, that information/communication will continue to outpace manufacturing and agricultural sectors in the most developed economies, a perception that led the United States in particular to adopt aggressive 'free trade' stances respecting informational products and services, both in GATT and in bilateral negotiations.[5]

Nonetheless, it also remains true, in a broader sense, that aggregate or sectoral analyses proposing a distinct, even predominant, informational sector imply that informational/communicatory activities are equivalent to other transactional activity, and can with equanimity be studied in money terms. This is to say that these analyses imply that informational/communicatory processes can and should be treated as subsets of broader processes of economic (commodity) exchange.

There are problems with this approach, however, as hinted at by Porat himself when he declared, 'Information is by nature, a heterogeneous commodity';[6] and 'there is no single definition of information that embraces all aspects of the primary sector';[7] and further, 'information cannot be collapsed into one sector – like mining – but rather the production, processing, and distribution of information goods and services should be thought of as an activity.'[8] Likewise, economist Beth Allen described information as a 'differentiated commodity.'[9]

The very notion of commodity requires, however, that units of the good in question be 'physically identical,' even though available 'in different places and at different times.'[10] Such standardization permits counting. Indeed *measurement*, according to Abraham Kaplan, 'in a word, is a device *for standardization*, by which we are assured equivalencies among objects of diverse origin ... When we count, we are always determining how many things there are of a certain *kind*' (emphasis in original).[11] This is precisely what Porat and Allen declared that informational commodities and activities lack – a standard with which to measure or count.

Porat tried to resolve, or rather avoid, the measurement problem respecting information by turning *from* 'heterogeneous' informational commodities *to* information *markets* and information *activities*, measuring such markets and activities in two ways: by employment, and by value added. Defining a 'primary information market'[12] as one that is established when 'a technology of information production and distribution is organized by firms, and an exchange price is established,' Porat combined such diverse 'markets' and 'activities' as education, banking, office furniture, mass media, telecommunications, advertising, insurance, finance, and the post office.

Labour content or labour intensity does not, of course, distinguish informational activities and commodities from other activities and commodities. Indeed there are huge disparities in 'labour-intensity' within Porat's information sector. While some informational activities may be highly labour-intensive (live theatre, ballet, and authorship, for instance), others are highly capital-intensive (data storage, information processing, and retrieval, for example).

Note also that Machlup/Porat-type sectoral analyses restrict communicatory activities to those 'organized by firms' and for which 'an exchange price is established.'[13] In other words, much if not most of our communication is excluded from the sectoral approach simply because it does not pass through markets and therefore does not command a price or 'value.'

Information Industry Studies Approach

The area within mainstream economics known as 'applied microeconomics' or 'industrial organization' investigates the structure and behaviour of industries in an economy. William Shepherd has remarked on characteristics of mainstream economic industry studies in general: (1) 'Each market is regarded as a distinct entity, in line with Marshallian partial analysis.' (2) 'The context of the market is considered to be extraneous.' (3) 'Behavior is normally perceived primarily as matters of pricing and interfirm strategies.' (4) 'Performance criteria are matters of minimizing costs and prices; there is usually little attention to content or equity.'[14]

Whatever the implications of these aspects of mainstream economic analyses may be for 'normal' industries, they are particularly disconcerting for economic studies of information industries, for the following reasons:

1. Information pervades economies, and among other things helps coordinate through prices activities of disparate economic agents (see the section on 'information economics' below). Therefore, it may well be unduly partial to apply 'Marshallian partial analysis,' i.e., supply and demand analysis, to information industries.
2. Since information is cumulative, or is at least dependent upon existing knowledge, and since symbols need to be comprehended in order for them to constitute information, it is a simplification to consider the context of an information market as being 'extraneous.' Information 'markets' both derive from the cultural/economic setting and, in turn, impinge upon it.
3. Behaviour in information industries entails more than mere pricing, since informational artefacts are unique creations that may, however, have many copies.
4. Content and equity, many would argue, are of the essence for informational activity. For purposes of analysis, however, economists tend to ignore content and depict output in terms of the medium, carrier, or substrate. Carriers include: paper, videotape, compact discs, celluloid, chalkboards, radio waves, and so on. Increasingly, firms charge per call, per view, per bit, and per screenful of information. In *this* sense there is indeed an increasing commodification of symbolic artefacts, but none of the quantitative measures used by economists touch directly upon the informational content; all relate rather to capacity for storing or transmitting symbols. Ignoring the informational content is a serious omission since it is the content that gives the substrate (medium) much of its value.

Information Economics Treatment

For years microeconomic theorists paid scant attention to information.

On the one hand, enraptured by the purely competitive model, which assumes perfect knowledge, and on the other, convinced that price theory provides abundant insight into real world phenomena, neoclassicists by and large rested content on the assumption that the price system automatically generates and processes information sufficient to ensure economic efficiency. Economies, neoclassicists assumed, are constrained by limited capacities for obtaining and processing materials, not by similar limitations concerning the information needed to organize and coordinate production and distribution.[15]

The great Marshall, for example, introduced his classic treatise extolling money as the means whereby even inward 'desires, aspirations and other affections of human nature' become measurable once expressed outwardly in market activity.[16] Marshall declared economics the most exact of the social sciences on account of the market's capacity to quantify.

Hayek, too, lauded the informational properties of the price system, viewing prices as 'quantitative indices (or "values").'[17] Each index or price, Hayek contended, should be understood as *concentrated information* reflecting the significance of any particular scarce resource relative to all others. The index or price borne by each commodity, Hayek enthused, permits autonomous economic agents to adjust their strategies 'without having to solve the whole puzzle [input-output matrix] *ab initio*.' Prices, then, for Hayek, as for modern information economists, *are* information.

Note also Arrow's more recent formulation of the idea: 'If the correct (equilibrium) prices are announced, then the individual agents can determine their purchases and sales so as to maximize profits or satisfactions. The prices are then, according to the pure theory, the only communication that needs to be made in addition to the information held initially by the agents. This makes the market system appear to be very efficient indeed.'[18]

One begins to see, in this context, the reasoning behind Kenneth Boulding's remarks quoted at the start of this chapter, for as extracts from Marshall, Hayek, and Arrow indicate, 'informational considerations [are] in fact, central to the analysis of a wide variety of phenomena,' constituting in Joseph Stiglitz's words, 'a central part of the Foundations of Economic Analysis.'[19] But with up to 50 per cent of the labour force engaged in informational activities, questions arise regarding the presumed capacity of markets spontaneously to generate information sufficient to ensure economic efficiency. Indeed, long before Machlup published his seminal work, intimations of doubt were being expressed in the mainstream economics literature.

One influential pioneer was Ronald Coase, who defined the firm as an organization purposefully bypassing or suppressing the price mechanism. Firms, according to Coase, consciously or deliberatively administer internal flows of resources, instead of relying on markets to accomplish this. Coase then questioned why firms, or 'islands of conscious power' as he called them, arise at all, given the purported efficacy of the price system. His response: 'There is cost of using the price mechanism,' namely the 'cost of ... discovering what the relevant prices are.' He continued, 'This cost may be reduced but it can never be eliminated by the emergence of specialists who *will sell* this information; the costs of negotiating and concluding a separate contract for each exchange transaction which takes place in a market must also be taken into account' (emphasis added).[20]

A second notable precursor was Frank Knight, who constructed a theory of risk, uncertainty, and profit.[21] True profit, Knight wrote, stems from uncertainty, since with perfect knowledge markets discount future shortages, obviating the possibility of economic profit. He defined profit as the reward over and above a 'normal' return. For him, profit was a measure of market imperfection attributable to imperfect knowledge (that is, to uncertainty). Profit is the entrepreneur's reward for engaging in activities whose outcomes are uncertain even in the probabilistic or actuarial sense, making them uninsurable.

Knight has had his critics. As Ben Seligman noted, his concept of profit, bereft of monopoly considerations, was a 'panegyric to the entrepreneurs.'[22] Nonetheless, as was true with Coase, Knight at least addressed relationships among imperfect knowledge, information, and money, anticipating thereby today's 'information economists' who define information precisely as reduction in uncertainty, and perceive it as commodity. According to Kenneth Arrow, for instance, 'The meaning of information is precisely a reduction in uncertainty.'[23]

Information economists undoubtedly adopt a much narrower conception of information than do either the macroeconomic analysts, or the information industries' analysts. By defining information as reduction in uncertainty, information economists endeavour to resolve the definitional problem besetting the other mainstream approaches. While their conception initially appears to be more precise (no talk here of information being a 'heterogeneous' or 'differentiated' commodity, for instance), information still remains ill-defined, as we shall see momentarily. Moreover, for information to be incorporated as a commodity into the neoclassical model, information must itself be quantified and treated on 'a par with ... a "regular" (noninformation) economic commodity, such as iron ore.'[24] This, however, has proved impossible.

We turn now to how neoclassicists have struggled with this conundrum. Proposing to begin rectifying the neglect of information within economics, George Stigler applied 'standard economic theory of utility-maximizing behavior'[25] to one important problem of information – the ascertainment of market price. Since prices are continually in flux, Stigler advised, there must exist at any given time and place ignorance as to what prices are. Buyers confronted with an array of prices for even homogeneous goods must 'search' in order to find the lowest price. A search will entail a cost, but also will produce a benefit. The 'value of information' in the face of this uncertainty, Stigler wrote, is 'the amount by which the information reduces the expected cost to the buyer of his purchases.'[26] Stigler concluded that the 'optimal amount of search' would be found 'if the cost of search is equated to its expected marginal return.'[27]

It is to be noted that Stigler's approach seems to preserve the purported automatism and effectiveness of the price mechanism, by turning prices ('information') into commodities. Ascertainment of knowledge respecting prices itself commands a price. The implication is that information required for markets to function effectively will be generated automatically in optimal quantities through the market mechanism.

But Stigler's 'solution' to the problem of uncertainty was more apparent than real, since he was unable to arrive at a general measure whereby information could be quantified, a requirement for supply and demand schedules to exist. Stigler assumed 'the cost of search for a consumer may be taken as approximately proportional to the number of (identified) sellers approached.'[28] Each 'approach' then yields one seller's price. But not all prices are equally informative: being apprised of one price is more informative if only one seller exists than if there are ten. Stigler himself remarked, 'The expected saving from a given search will be greater, the greater the dispersion of prices.'[29] What this statement essentially means is that the informational content of each ascertained price varies according to the dispersion in prices. There is no one-to-one correspondence between a price and its information content.

Stated more generally, information does not exist objectively in and of itself so as to be countable. It exists only in particular contexts; changing contexts changes (the 'quantity' of) the information conveyed by a given sign or combination of signs. These arguments and observations indicate, then, that there is no one-to-one relationship between the commodity acquired (here a price), and its information content.

Critique of Mainstream Treatments: Impossibility of the Information 'Commodity'

To be sure, information economists have noted that the 'information commodity' possesses some unique characteristics: Allen, for instance, remarked that 'satiation occurs at one unit of information *of any given type* [since] identical copies of the same information [the normal requirement for commodity] are worthless unless the duplicates can be sold [to other buyers].'[30]

Stiglitz pointed to another peculiarity of the information 'commodity.' 'How,' he asked, 'is an individual to resolve the infinite regress of whether it is worthwhile to obtain information concerning whether it is worthwhile to obtain information?'[31] Arrow posed a different formulation of the same dilemma: '[Information's] value for the purchaser is not known until he has the information, but then he has, in effect, acquired it without cost.'[32]

Other problems with information as commodity have been identified as well. For example, information is 'indivisible,' which means that partial information can be useless. Either one is informed of a price, or one is not informed.[33] Moreover, according to Arrow, since information can be reproduced at little or no cost while 'the cost of transmitting a given body of information is frequently very low,'[34] information can be difficult to appropriate; but capacity to be appropriated is a condition for commodification. Market exchange entails, after all, the transmittal of property rights.

Apart from the foregoing, however, the main problem as far as 'information economics' is concerned, is the absence of a measuring standard.

Mention should perhaps be made of the one means proposed to quantify 'information.' Ascribed to Claude Shannon and Warren Weaver, this 'mathematical theory of communication' has been immensely influential in fields as diverse as engineering, physics, biology, and cybernetics.[35] Shannon and Weaver defined information in the context of selecting choices from an array of predetermined and known possibilities, lending at first blush a correspondence to information economists' definition of information as uncertainty reduction.[36] According to Shannon and Weaver, the quantity of information in the simplest cases is the logarithm to base 2 of the number of available choices. If there are only two choices, a sender can inform a receiver of the selection of one of them with a single burst of signal (or 'bit') – an 'on' or a 'one,' instead of an 'off' or a 'zero,' presuming the receiver knows the options from which the selection is made and is cognizant of the code used to designate that choice. Likewise, if there exist sixteen alternatives, four 'bits' (or binary digits) are sufficient to signal any given selection ($16 = 2^4$; i.e., $\log_2 16 = 4$). For this latter instance, Shannon and Weaver denoted the 'quantity' of information as four units or four bits, since every one of the sixteen choices could be uniquely identified by a sequence of four binary digits. Unfortunately for 'information economics,' Shannon and Weaver's method quantifies something other than what is meant by 'information' in the economists' sense. As Weaver explained, 'information must not be confused with meaning.'[37]

Implications

Frustration is evident in the ranks of information economists. Upon reviewing the uncertainty literature, Spence sighed, 'There is no sweeping conclusion to be drawn from this survey.'[38] In like manner Stiglitz remarked, 'There seems to be a myriad of special cases and few general principles.'[39]

One reason for these lamentations is the fact that economists have not quantified and cannot quantify information. Each instance becomes then a special case, since 'information' means something different in each instance. 'Information' in information economics is akin to an error term or residual that restores tautologies: if uncertainty exists over prices, then a unique parcel of 'information' with 'value' may restore equilibrium, but its 'value' cannot be disassembled into price and quantity components (or alternatively, quantity is always equal to one for each unique informational 'packet,' information being, as Arrow suggested, 'indivisible'). The inability to devise a measure for information means, ultimately, that information stands outside of neoclassical modelling.

Since information on the one hand constitutes 'a central part of the foundations of economic analysis,' yet on the other stands outside neoclassical modelling, a fundamental inconsistency becomes apparent, giving rise to a crisis of internal validity. A more promising approach would be to stop 'force-fitting' information into the commodity mode and indeed to reverse the process, treating information no longer as commodity, but rather addressing 'commodities' as being informational and communicatory. Market exchange then would be viewed as an aspect of broader communicatory interaction.

Lack of internal validity is only one of neoclassicism's problems. Defining information as commodity, and indeed in the case of 'information economics' confining information to uncertainty reduction, renders invisible many important consequences of information interchange and transfer, thereby creating also a crisis of external validity. To illustrate with just one of an infinite number of possible examples, on 30 October 1938, Orson Welles's science fiction broadcast 'War of the Worlds' was heard by at least six million radio listeners. Of those, at least one million panicked or were seriously frightened, believing that Martians had indeed landed. According to Lowery and de Fleur, 'Terrified people all over America prayed and tried frantically in one way or another to escape death from the Martians ... Hundreds of people fled their homes. Bus terminals were crowded ... [In Pittsburgh] a man came home in the middle of the broadcast and found his wife in the bathroom with a bottle of poison in her hand and screaming, 'I'd rather die this way than that.'''[40]

Looking beyond the pale of information-as-commodity and information-as-reduction-in-uncertainty, new analytical possibilities open up concerning not only this particular broadcast, but communicatory activity broadly considered. Consider the following:

First, the capacity to communicate, to package and diffuse information, means power. It is not simply the case, as mainstream economists contend, that buyers survey an array of informational commodities and purchase the one or ones that seem most in tune with their needs, given prices and income constraints. Albeit unintentionally, Orson Welles drove hundreds, perhaps thousands, from their homes, none of whom had purchased the information he diffused. He affected, however briefly, the thoughts and emotions of six million or more people, many of whom took action based on these mental states. More generally, mass media give editors, writers, programmers, and other content providers, including advertisers, politicians, the military, public relations firms, news agencies, and entertainers, 'access to the thoughts and emotions of people in the audience.'[41] Communication *means* influence, and a capacity to exert influence over perhaps millions means power. Power, however, is not a primary concern for most mainstream economists, certainly not for neoclassicists; and commodity-alone / reduction-in-uncertainty treatments afforded information indeed enable mainstream analysts to skirt considerations of power.[42] Stated another way, less restrictive conceptions of information restore considerations of power to economic analysis and so entail the replacement or succession of mere economics by *political economy*.

Second, Welles's broadcast shows that information is not enveloped or contained in a single place, as are 'normal' commodities, but rather that information permeates both time and space.[43] Moreover, information generates or spawns more information, as press reports on Welles's broadcast, an ensuing study by the Office of Radio Research of Princeton University, policy statements from the Federal Communications Commission, Lowery and de Fleur's chapter, and indeed this very page, indicate. Societal evolution, as Veblen and more recently Boulding have understood, is in the first instance informational.

Third, information constitutes a shared 'space,' a symbolic environment, a communications ecology, in which people live.[44] Our physical environment is experienced or perceived in large part symbolically, and our symbolic constructs in turn influence action upon the material environment. I return to this at the close of the chapter.

Economics as Communication: Two Models

To infuse economics with internal and external validity, this section suggests that economic processes be viewed as special instances of more general communicatory processes.

At the outset it is to be noted that a superficial similarity exists between the economists' 'market' and the communication studies scholars' 'communication system.' Briefly, both models entail circular flows. In the former, a seller transmits property rights in, and perhaps physical possession of, a 'commodity' to a buyer and in return receives money, the amount being determined 'impersonally' through supply and demand. In the latter, a sender transmits a message by means of some medium of transmission (visible light, air, paper, radio, etc.), to a receiver, who decodes or interprets the transmission, and responds in some way ('feedback'). These similarities, however, mask profound differences. In the economics model, buyer and seller exert no influence on one another. They are assumed to be autonomous 'others,' rationally engaging in activities to maximize their individual welfare. By contrast, the communication system at a minimum posits influence by the sender on the receiver, and more often proposes that communicators engage in dialogic interactions, interpenetrating and transforming one another through 'mutual semiosis.'[45]

Which of these two models – the market or the communication system – is most apt for any given analysis hinges on whether it is a 'commodity' or 'information' that is at issue. If what is transmitted is 'inert,' exerting no effect or influence apart from satisfying pre-existing wants, and if monetary payment is made in compensation, then truly the economists' 'market' is operative. Communication scholars, however, question whether it is possible to participate in *any* exchange and remain unchanged.

What Then Is Information?

Physicist Carl Friedrich von Weizsäcker affirmed that *information* is rooted in form, or pattern, or structure. He wrote, 'This "form" can refer to the form of all kinds of objects or events perceptible to the senses and capable of being shaped by man: the form of the printer's ink or ink on paper, of chalk on the blackboard, of sound waves in air, of current flow in a wire, etc.'[46] Matter and form, von Weizsäcker continued, are conceptual complements: 'In the realm of the concrete, no form exists without matter; nor can there be matter without form.' He continued, 'A cupboard, a tree are made of wood. Wood is their "matter" ... But the cupboard isn't simply wood, it is a wooden cupboard. "Cupboard" is what it is intrinsically; cupboard is its *eidos*, its essence, its form. But a cupboard must be made of something; a cupboard without matter is a mere thought abstracted from reality.'[47]

Energy too, as with the telegraph, can be ordered or formed or organized so as to be capable of being understood.

Information, then, may be termed *dialectical*[48] in the sense that it entails both matter and form, both the material and the immaterial. This dialectical property of information is what makes it so difficult to appropriate. Different substances, and even human memories, can easily be shaped or formed to convey or hold the 'same' forms (but not necessarily the 'same' information, for reasons discussed now).

The mere existence of matter-in-form is not sufficient to constitute information; it is also required that meaning be conveyed. In addition to matter/energy and form, there must also be language, that is a code or codes assigning or imputing pre-arranged meanings to these 'forms.' As well, the receiver must be cognizant of the code that assigns meaning to the forms (or 'signs').[49] Hence, the dialectic of information goes well beyond matter/form to comprise also object/interpretation.

In this conception, information defies measurement, and for a number of reasons. First, as noted, information is more than just matter; information relates to the form matter takes.

Second, forms have no meaning unless and until a code or language exists that imputes or ascribes meaning to them. Not only that, but the code can change according to the context of the message, and indeed the context (life experience) of the reader or interpreter. In this view, meaning (information) exists not merely objectively as a physical sign so as to be countable, but also in subjectivity, that is in interpretation. For example, different languages or codes may ascribe different meanings to the 'same' form, and different message receivers or 'readers,' therefore, bringing different codes to the 'same' forms, may derive or impute markedly different meanings.

It is evident that we are bordering on the field of semiotics, which aspires to answer how forms (signs) take on meaning. Without dwelling there, an added point deserves emphasis. Languages, or codes, that enable us to decode or impute meanings relate to and are derived from cultures and subcultures. We learn languages and codes from our communities. To quote Lee Thayer, 'To be human is to be *in* communication in *some* human culture and to be *in* some human culture is to see and know the world – to communicate – in a way which daily recreates that particular culture.'[50] James Carey likewise defined communication as 'a symbolic process whereby reality is produced, maintained, repaired and transformed.'[51]

It follows, therefore, that information and communication should engage the analyst in a social or methodologically collectivist discourse (as opposed to the methodologically individualist discourse of the economist), for at least two reasons: First, messages frequently radiate into and permeate many minds, often simultaneously, producing, maintaining, and transforming societies, and the individuals comprising them. Second, any individual's interpretation of forms (signs, text, or information) comes not only from his or her unique life experiences, but also (and often more importantly) from the shared languages or codes of the culture(s) and subculture(s). As expressed by Mikhail Bakhtin, 'Language enters life through concrete utterances (which manifest language) and life enters language through concrete utterances as well.'[52]

The Political Economy of the Information Commodity

It may seem that we have strayed far from mainstream economics, but not as far as might at first appear. Following Carey, we can interpret mainstream economics as but a particular symbolic or 'informational' system *producing, maintaining, repairing,* and *transforming* economic reality. Even the physical sciences, as Boulding noted, do not merely investigate the world, but as well *create* the world they are investigating.[53] If that is true of the physical sciences (which, for example, have led to the creation of new basic elements), how much more must this be the case for social sciences such as economics?

It was indeed in full realization that the economics discipline acts upon and transforms the economic world, that the 'economics as discourse' and 'economics as rhetoric' literatures arose,[54] from whence it is (or should be) a short step to the political economy of mainstream economics, that is to the study of the power, money, and control lying behind and motivating mainstream economics analyses. Money is to be made from heightened commodity treatment of social interactions, and the mainstream economics paradigm is essentially *the* theoretical justification for extending the ambit of commodity exchange.

Heightened commodity treatment of social life processes carries with it, however, enormous costs. Three of these are now addressed briefly: injustice in international communication; breakdown of community; and ecosystem destruction. The implication of the analysis of this closing section is recognition of a pressing need for an alternative economics, a transformed economics, one that can help bring about a more sustainable and just future.

International Communication

By insisting within GATT (renamed and extended as the World Trade Organization) and in bilateral trade treaties that information be treated solely or primarily as a commodity instead of as gift or public resource, and that there be a dismantling of informational trade barriers and beefed-up copyright, the United States, which domiciles the world's largest information companies, positions itself to increase exports of informational products in exchange for energy, resources, foreign currencies, and labour-intensive manufactured goods. The United States and corporations headquartered principally in the United States, hold a competitive advantage in the mass production of informational 'commodities.'

Virtually all of the mainstream economics literature – from the sectoral analyses of Machlup/Porat, to the information industries studies, to the field of 'information economics' – is supportive of information's commodity status, despite critical problems concerning the discipline's internal and external validity that arise from this commodity-only treatment.

If information/communication, on the other hand, were defined as, say, the mutual engagement of dialogic partners, or as a basic human right, as was attempted in UNESCO's call for a New International Information and Communication Order,[55] then America's trading partners could rightly insist on a free and *balanced* flow of information: international 'communication' would no longer be a 'one-way street.'

But dialogic interaction interferes with the commodity status of information since receivers are no longer perceived and treated as mere 'consumers.' And communication as a basic human right is much less beneficial to the export trade of transnational 'communication industries.'

Commodity treatment of information perpetuates and exacerbates international inequalities and third world dependencies. Third world countries must concentrate on primary production (food production and resource extraction) for exports to pay for information and knowledge that the first world has commodified through intellectual property laws (copyright, trademarks, patents, and industrial designs). In the 'exchange,' however, the first world retains the knowledge it sells, an injustice that has been noted by many.[56]

Community

One of Kenneth Boulding's many remarkable achievements was to analyse the gift (or 'grants') economy and to compare that with the economy of commodity exchange. For Boulding, the information flowing through economies and other organizations can be of three basic types: threat information, exchange information, and love (or gift) information. For Boulding, 'all social organizations without exception are built by processes that can be classified into these three general types.'[57]

He further advised that a too heavy reliance upon exchange as the mode of communication can lead to social and economic breakdown. It is worth quoting him at length on this: 'The instability of capitalism may arise partly out of certain technical defects of an elaborate exchange system that results in unemployment and depression; it also results, however, from certain delegitimations of exchange, which may well arise because of strong preferences for integrative relationships, which are, after all, personally much more satisfying than exchange. To do things for love always seems to be more moral and progressive than to do things for money.'

So, he continued, 'capitalism undermines itself, as Schumpeter pointed out, despite its success, because of the failure of exchange institutions, such as finance, banking, corporations, and so on, to develop an integrative matrix that will legitimate them.'[58]

By contrast, the gift economy integrates rather than alienates. The integrative system, or gift economy, is based on status, on love and affection, and on one-way rather than two-way transfers. It comprises processes whereby 'culture is transmitted from one generation to another ... whereby persons and institutions acquire dignity, respect [and] legitimacy.'[59]

In the 1990s, North Americans are being increasingly enmeshed in processes that heighten the commodity treatment of social relations: continental and hemispheric 'free trade' agreements, higher education offered increasingly on the basis of user-pay and cost recovery; downsizing social programs such as unemployment insurance, medicare, old age security; introduction of technical devices and systems falling under the rubric of an 'information highway' that expand manifold pay-per transactional modes of human interaction. This movement toward heightened commodity treatment of human relations, in other words increased commodification of informational/communicatory processes, Boulding would say, reflects and contributes to a diminished sense of human community. Couple that with widening gaps between rich and poor (also an ineluctable concomitant of the market system) and societal breakdown through class warfare or massive individual alienation become real possibilities.

The Ecosystem

The transition to sustainable development, as recommended by the World Commission on Environment and Development,[60] entails rectifying a huge problem in symbolization. It means rejecting current practices of naming or symbolizing the ecosystem and portions thereof in money terms as commodity, and instead knowing it as gift. Conceiving nature instrumentally as mere commodity emphasizes humanity's apartness or otherness vis-à-vis the environment, despite the reality that in ecological terms we are all a part of the earth and it of us. Reconceiving the environment as gift, whether from God or from our ancestors, by contrast, would mean that we would again come to view ourselves as but temporary custodians or stewards of our environment, that we would again come to realize that we ought to act responsibly, with care, toward it in order that we can pass it along in love to future generations.

It is difficult to conceive how we might possibly reconceptualize nature as a gift if all our discourses about nature (and all else) remain commodified. Nature cannot truly become a shared resource and understood as a gift if our knowledge and conversation about nature remains commodified.

Treating nature as commodity, as our present economic system does, is, in the words of Herman Daly and John Cobb, 'an ideology of death,' and we can indeed see the working out of this deadly ideology all about us, from species' extinction, to water contamination, to ozone thinning, to desertification, to acid rain, to global warming. Treating the ecosystem as gift, by contrast, is an ideology of life, a mode of being, of perceiving, and of interacting with nature that humankind must retrieve if it is to have a future.

The challenge of renaming the ecosystem as gift rather than as commodity[61] is quite probably the most important communication/economic problem humankind faces. Indeed, 'It's a matter of survival.'[62]

NOTES

1 George J. Stigler, *Memoirs of an Unregulated Economist* (New York: Basic Books, 1988), 191–205.
2 Fritz Machlup, *The Production and Distribution of Knowledge in the United States* (Princeton, NJ: Princeton University Press, 1962).
3 Marc Uri Porat, 'Excerpt from *Definition and Measurement*,' in *The Information Economy, Information Economics and Policy in the United States*, ed. Michael Rogers Rubin (Littleton, CO: Libraries Unlimited, 1983), 1:16–24.
4 Michael Rogers Rubin, ed., *The Information Economy, Information Economics and Policy in the United States* (Littleton, CO: Libraries Unlimited, 1983), 1:1.
5 Sandra Braman, 'Trade and Information Policy,' *Media, Culture and Society* 12 (1990): 361–85.
6 Porat, 'Excerpt,' 16.
7 Ibid.
8 Ibid., 18.
9 Beth Allen, 'Information as an Economic Commodity,' *American Economic Review* 80, no. 2 (1980): 269.

10 Bruna Ingrao and Giorgio Israel, *The Invisible Hand: Economic Equilibrium in the History of Science* (Cambridge, MA: MIT Press, 1990), 5.

11 Abraham Kaplan, *The Conduct of Inquiry: Methodology for Behavioral Science* (San Francisco, CA: Chandler, 1964), 173, 182.

12 Beth Allen, 'Information as an Economic Commodity,' *American Economic Review* 80, no. 2 (1980): 269.

13 Porat, 'Excerpt,' 17.

14 William Shepherd, *The Treatment of Market Power: Antitrust, Regulation and Public Enterprise* (New York, NY: Columbia University Press, 1975), 11.

15 Charles Jonscher, 'Notes on Communication and Economic Theory,' in *Communication Economics and Development*, ed. Meheroo Jussawalla and D.M. Lamberton (Elmsford, NY: Pergamon, 1982), 62–3.

16 Alfred Marshall, *Principles of Economics: An Introductory Volume*, 8th ed. (1890; London, UK: Macmillan, 1938), 14–15.

17 F.A. Hayek, 'The Use of Knowledge in Society,' *American Economic Review* 35, no. 4 (1945): 519–30.

18 Kenneth J. Arrow, 'The Economics of Information,' in *The Computer Age: A Twenty-Year View*, ed. Michael L. Dertouzos and Joel Moses (Cambridge, MA: MIT Press, 1979), 313–14.

19 Joseph Stiglitz, 'Information and Economic Analysis: A Perspective,' *Economic Journal* 95 (1985): 21.

20 Ronald Coase, 'The Nature of the Firm,' *Economica* 4 (1937): 390–1.

21 Frank Knight, *Risk, Uncertainty and Profit* (1921; New York: Houghton Mifflin, 1957).

22 Ben Seligman, *Main Currents in Modern Economics: Economic Thought since 1870* (New York, NY: Free Press of Glencoe, 1962), 663–4.

23 Arrow, 'Economics of Information,' 307. Veblen, by way of contrast, remarked that information and knowledge *create* uncertainty, far from reducing it: 'It is something of a homiletical commonplace to say that the outcome of any serious research can only be to make two questions grow where one question grew before.' Thorstein Veblen, 'The Limitations of Marginal Utility,' *Journal of Political Economy* (1909); repr. in Veblen, *The Place of Science in Modern Civilization* (New Brunswick, NJ: Transaction, 1990), 33.

24 Jonscher, 'Notes,' 67.

25 George Stigler, 'Nobel Lecture: The Process and Progress of Economics,' *Journal of Political Economy* 91, no. 4 (1983): 539.

26 George Stigler, 'Information in the Labor Market,' *Journal of Political Economy* 70, no. 5 (1961); repr. in Stigler, *The Organization of Industry* (Homewood, IL: Irwin, 1968), 183–4.

27 Ibid., 175.

28 Ibid.

29 Ibid.

30 Beth Allen, 'Information as an Economic Commodity,' *American Economic Review* 80, no. 2 (1990): 269–70.

31 Stiglitz, 'Information and Economic Analysis,' 23.

32 Kenneth J. Arrow, 'Economic Welfare and the Allocation of Resources for Invention' (1962); repr. in *Economics of Information and Knowledge*, ed. D.M. Lamberton (Harmondsworth, UK: Penguin, 1971), 148.

33 Allen, 'Information as an Economic Commodity,' 270.

34 Arrow, 'Economic Welfare,' 147.

35 L. David Ritchie, *Information* (Newbury Park, CA: Sage, 1991), 7–8; Jeremy Rifkin, *Time Wars* (1987; New York, NY: Simon and Schuster, 1989), 208–18.

36 R.A. Jenner, 'An Information Version of Pure Competition' (1966); repr. in *Economics of Information and Knowledge*, ed. D.M. Lamberton (Harmondsworth, UK: Penguin, 1971), 83–108.

37 Claude E. Shannon and Warren Weaver, *The Mathematical Theory of Communication* (Urbana, IL: University of Illinois Press, 1949), 8.

38 A. Michael Spence, 'An Economist's View of Information, *Annual Review of Information Science and Technology* 9 (1974): 58.

39 Stiglitz, 'Information and Economic Analysis,' 21.

40 Shearon A. Lowery and Melvin L. DeFleur, *Milestones in Mass Communication Research: Media Effects* (New York, NY: Longman, 1988), 61–2.

41 Harold L. Vogel, *Entertainment Industry Economics: A Guide for Financial Analysis*, 2nd ed. (Cambridge, UK: Cambridge University Press, 1990), 155–6.

42 Walter Adams and James W. Brock, *The Bigness Complex: Industry, Labor, and Government in the American Economy* (New York, NY: Pantheon Books, 1986), chap. 2.

43 Harold Innis, *Empire and Communications* (1950; repr., Toronto, ON: University of Toronto Press, 1972).

44 Barrington Nevitt, *The Communication Ecology: Re-presentation versus Replica* (Toronto, ON: Butterworths, 1982).

45 R.S. Perinbanayagam, *Discursive Acts* (New York, NY: Aldine de Gruyter, 1991), 31.

46 Carl Friedrich von Weizsäcker, *The Unity of Nature* (New York, NY: Farrar, Straus and Giroux, 1980), 38–9.

47 Ibid., 274.

48 The original article characterized information as being 'epiphenomenal,' as opposed to being 'dialectical.' *Epiphenomenal* denotes that information is the form that matter takes without being itself matter; there is a sense that matter is prior to, or required for, form. However, severe analytical

problems arise from this conceptualization, as the discussion of entropy, for example, shows. It could equally well be argued, moreover, that matter is epiphenomenal to form since without form there can be no matter (a Platonic or idealist position). The author considers re-characterizing information as being dialectical to be a significant correction. Regarding information and entropy, see Robert E. Babe, *Culture of Ecology: Reconciling Economics and Environment* (Toronto, ON: University of Toronto Press, 2006), 141–52.

49 von Weizsäcker, *Unity of Nature*, 39.

50 Lee Thayer, *On Communication: Essays in Understanding* (Norwood, NJ: Ablex, 1987), 45; emphasis in original.

51 James W. Carey, *Communication as Culture: Essays on Media and Society* (Winchester, MA: Unwin Hyman, 1989), 23. See also **Peter L. Berger and Thomas Luckmann,** *The Social Construction of Reality: A Treatise in the Sociology of Knowledge* (Garden City, NY: Anchor Books, Doubleday, 1967).

52 Quoted in Perinbanayagam, *Discursive Acts*, front page.

53 Kenneth E. Boulding, 'Economics as a Moral Science' (1963); repr. in *Collected Papers* (Boulder, CO: Associated University Press, 1971), 2:451.

54 Warren J. Samuels, ed., *Economics as Discourse: An Analysis of the Language of Economists* (Boston, MA: Kluwer, 1990); Arjo **Klamer, Donald N. McCloskey, and Robert M. Solow,** *The Consequences of Economic Rhetoric* (Cambridge, UK: Cambridge University Press, 1988).

55 William Preston Jr, Edward S. Herman, and Herbert I. Schiller, *Hope & Folly: The United States and UNESCO 1945–1985* (Minneapolis, MN: University of Minnesota Press, 1989).

56 UNESCO, *Many Voices, One World* (Paris: UNESCO, 1980).

57 Boulding, 'Economics as a Moral Science,' 27.

58 Kenneth E. Boulding, *The Economy of Love and Fear* (Belmont, CA: Wadsworth, 1973), 110.

59 Boulding, 'Economics as a Moral Science,' 26.

60 United Nations, World Commission on Environment and Development (Brundtland Commission), *Our Common Future* (Oxford: Oxford University Press, 1987).

61 For an extended comparison of gift and commodity, see also Lewis Hyde, *The Gift: Imagination and the Erotic Life of Property* (New York, NY: Vintage Books, 1979); and E. F. Schumacher, *Small Is Beautiful* (London, UK: Sphere Books, 1974), chap. 13.

62 Anita Gordon and David Suzuki, *It's a Matter of Survival* (Cambridge, MA: Harvard University Press, 1990).

2 Communication: Blind Spot of Western Economics

There comes a time ... when the blind spots come from the edge of vision into the center.

          – Walter Lippmann, *Public Opinion* (1922)

This chapter compares the disciplines of economics and communication studies. In their mainstream versions, known respectively as neoclassical economics and as administrative communication research,[1] these scholarly areas appear at first glance to be quite similar. The economist's market, after all, comprising monetary and commodity flows between buyer and seller, has a seemingly close correlate in the communication system, comprising sender, receiver, medium, message, code, and feedback. Certainly it is interesting and important to compare and contrast these conceptual models that condition so much of what their mainstream practitioners have to say. Closer comparisons between these mainstream or dominant modes of analysis, however, reveal deep-rooted antinomies, as noted below.

In both the economics and communication studies disciplines, however, there is a subfield or specialty known as political economy, whose thrust is to analyse the nature, sources, uses, and consequences of power, whether economic, financial, legal, military, political, ideological, religious, customary, scientific, technological, communicatory, or otherwise – power defined as 'the possibility of imposing one's will upon the behaviour of other persons.'[2] It is a principal contention of this chapter that scholarly treatment of the 'economic' and of the symbolic (or 'communicatory') converge only with political economy, despite surface similarities between mainstream economics and orthodox communication research.

When scholars trained as economists practise political economy, they tend to emphasize the legal system in its apportioning of rights, or they look to the social (class) structure, depending on whether they are respectively institutionalists or Marxists. When communication scholars practise political economy, they tend to concentrate on economic/institutional/legal factors constraining and shaping message production, viewing media products as concoctions fabricated by the established power system to preserve and extend itself. Despite these differences in emphasis, political economy, whether undertaken by those grounded in economics or by those schooled in communication/media studies, melds the material and the symbolic, a most vital enterprise (as I argue in the closing section) in a world beset by injustice and facing environmental decay.

To explore the foregoing themes more completely, the chapter is organized as follows: The next section describes and analyses characteristics of mainstream economics, emphasizing particularly the unduly limited conception of communication countenanced by the orthodox version of the discipline. In the third section the chapter turns to administrative or mainline communication research, in order subsequently (in the fourth and fifth sections) to compare and contrast this field with neoclassical economics, particularly with regard to the treatment of communicatory processes. Neoclassical economics, it is argued, actually proffers a model of radical *non*-communication! Finally, the chapter finds reconciliation between these two academic 'solitudes' in political economy.

Mainstream Economics

Over the two centuries since the publication in 1776 of Adam Smith's *The Wealth of Nations*, mainstream economics has become theoretically refined, and has become increasingly formalistic, abstract, and mathematical. It has also become predominantly an economics of incremental change, based on the maximization principle (setting dollar costs and revenues equal at the margin). These characteristics help distinguish modern or neoclassical economics from its classical heritage.

In other respects, however, there is a historical continuity or sameness about the discipline. Three qualities in particular that characterized Adam Smith's formulation, and continue with the contemporary (neoclassical) are: methodological individualism, reification of the market, and the assumption of harmonious interaction. I treat each of these aspects in turn.

Methodological Individualism

For Adam Smith, the wealth of a nation was simply the summation of the wealth of its inhabitants. Whatever effectively promoted individual wealth necessarily promoted also wealth for the community. Smith argued that, since each individual knows best his or her own unique circumstances, national wealth is most effectively pursued by minimizing constraints on individual enterprise.

Methodological individualism in neoclassicism's reformulation of the economics of Adam Smith is apparent in its 'theory of the firm' and in its 'theory of consumer behaviour,' which, when combined, purport to explain, in the absence of historical context, relative prices and resource allocation. The firm in neoclassical price theory is an abstraction meant to represent any firm at any time and in any place. In the theory, the firm is seen not as a collective or communal undertaking, but rather as an individual enterprise for the sole benefit of the owner.[3] The consumer, too, is an abstraction meant to represent any consumer anywhere at any time. Buyers and sellers come together in markets where there results a circular flow, commodity travelling from seller to buyer and money flowing in the opposite direction. The economy is viewed as the aggregation of all such autonomous transactions.

For neoclassical economists, human relations are, then, commodity exchange relations mediated by commodities and by money. In fact, the focus of attention of mainstream economists is not on human relations at all, but on things (commodities). The central questions are how much of any given commodity will be produced, and what will be its exchange value vis-à-vis other commodities.

In the wake of today's ecological crises and the manifest heightening of environmental interdependence, methodological individualism (treating autonomous or quasi-autonomous individuals as the units of analysis), must appear quaint, even pernicious.[4] This methodological practice continues, however, as a mainstay of both contemporary mainstream economics and also (as we shall see) administrative communication research.

Reification of the Market

Adam Smith 'reified' the market. His 'obvious and simple system of natural liberty'[5] was said to arise spontaneously from the innate human 'propensity to truck, barter and exchange,'[6] not at all from human design and the conscious exercise of the human will. Once generated, Smith reckoned, the Market functioned automatically and was all-powerful; indeed, he likened it to an 'invisible hand,'[7] channelling economic activity to an end, namely promoting the common weal defined by Smith as the wealth of the nation, 'which was no part of [the participants'] intention.'[8]

While Smith understood that the Market could easily be subverted through monopoly power, particularly by the state bestowing exclusive privileges on its friends and supporters, modern day neoclassicists tend not to share this comprehension or conviction. According to George Stigler, for example, 'It is virtually impossible to eliminate competition from economic life. If a firm buys up all of its rivals, new rivals will appear. If a firm secures a lucrative patent on some desired good, large investments will be made by rivals to find alternative products or processes to share the profits of the firm.'[9]

While neoclassicists, deeming themselves to be neopositivists, substitute the model of pure competition for Adam Smith's 'invisible hand,' the change is superficial at best, and certainly no less idealist than the predecessor. Given consumer preferences, given the state of the industrial arts (technology), and given the initial distribution of wealth (endowments), all production and prices for neoclassicists are determined automatically by the Market and can be deduced logically by the principle of maximization. Provided that nothing 'interferes' with the free flow of inputs, output and hence welfare will be maximized automatically, given the (Pareto) criterion that no one can be made better off without someone else becoming worse off.

For this chapter, the 'givenness' in neoclassical theory of tastes and preferences is particularly important. 'For the vast array of problems,' neoclassicist George Stigler wrote, 'including most of those we shall encounter, it is customary to treat tastes as fixed.'[10] On those relatively rare occasions when tastes and preferences are presumed by neoclassical economists to vary, they are permitted to change only as a result of variations in 'exogenous variables,' that is, changes in factors residing outside the particular market being studied. Thus, for example, according to Stigler, 'in a study of the long-term demand for housing, one naturally investigates changes in family size [while] in a study of the trend in employment in the medical professions one considers the age and sex structure of the population and its organization.'[11] Seldom in the neoclassicists' world is it the case that promotional efforts of the producer (i.e., persuasion, propaganda) or past consumption of the commodity (i.e., habituation or addiction) affect consumers' tastes and preferences. As we shall see shortly, this practice of excluding shifts in tastes and preferences that could be attributed to the working of the market itself, radically distinguishes mainstream economics not only from heterodox economics, but from mainstream communication studies, too.

Harmony

Adam Smith hypothesized 'an obvious and simple system of natural liberty' premised on individual greed and the division of labour that he alleged promotes harmony among participants: 'It is not from the benevolence of the butcher, the brewer, or the baker that we expect our dinner,' admonished Smith, but rather from their 'self-love.' He continued, '[We] never talk to them of our own necessities but of their advantages ... and show them that it is for their advantage to do for [us] what [we] require of them.'[12]

Likewise, today's neoclassicists emphasize the harmonious nature of economic interactions – if and when mediated by unregulated, impersonal markets. In the model of pure competition upon which so much of neoclassical perception is based, no seller is large enough to control price; in fact each seller is so small that he or she can sell everything produced at the established market price, eliminating all possibility of cut-throat competition. Nor do buyers or sellers possess coercive power over one another. When incipient conflict is considered, as when production inflicts damage on third parties ('externalities'), the ingenuity and brilliance of neoclassicists has shown that under certain improbable conditions (namely, perfect competition, perfect knowledge, zero transactions costs), the Market will internalize the externality and resolve the conflict automatically, regardless of where legal liability resides.[13] The more closely one adheres to the neoclassical model of pure competition and the neoclassical mode of marginal analysis, however, the further removed one becomes from the everyday world of power plays, inequities, and injustices. It is to these latter dimensions of economic and communicatory life that political economy is addressed.

Mainstream (Administrative) Communication Research

Several scholars, for example Daniel Czitrom and James Carey, have claimed that the modern era of media/communication research was inaugurated at the turn of the twentieth century in the writings of John Dewey and associates.[14] Others, such as Wilbur Schramm and Everett Rogers, have argued that communication is a behavioural science, not part of the humanities, and hence did not really begin to take shape until the 1920s or 1930s.[15] Be this as it may, there has long been a consensus that 1948 was an important year for communication research, for even today it is still often purported that in that year Harold Lasswell formulated five questions as constituting the subject matter of the nascent discipline,[16] thereby serving to 'structure the thinking of a whole generation of communication scholars and students.'[17] The questions attributed to Lasswell were: 'Who, says what, in which channel, to whom, with what effect?'[18] Critics have noted that a sixth question – for them the most important – was omitted, namely, 'Why?' They also consider that too little attention is afforded the context within which the communication takes place.[19]

In any event, Lasswell (or rather, the consensus he represented) was highly influential, and in 1949 Claude Shannon and Warren Weaver synthesized and formalized his five questions by proposing a communication system wherein encoded messages travel a unidirectional path from source (or sender) to transmitter (encoder), via a carrier or medium to decoder and thence to ultimate destination. The model illustrated what, for Shannon and Weaver, was the quintessential communication problem: namely, reproducing at the destination a message from the source indicating a selection from an array of known possibilities.[20] Communication, for them, was successful if 'the meaning conveyed to the receiver leads to the desired conduct on his part.'[21] By merely incorporating feedback, or response from receiver to sender, Norbert Wiener, Ludwig von Bertalanffy, Kenneth Boulding, and others transformed Shannon and Weaver's linear model into a cybernetic system of mutual interdependence and mutual determinations.

While it is safe to say that pioneering communication researchers seldom considered complete communicating systems in their studies, nonetheless attention was afforded selective interpenetrations, even in the early years. As noted by Daniel Czitrom, during the 1940s and 1950s luminaries such as Frank Stanton (of CBS), Elmo Roper, George Gallop, Carl Hovland (working for the U.S. Army on the 'laws of persuasion'), Harold Lasswell, and Paul Felix Lazarsfeld set boundaries for the emerging field by concentrating on five closely related lines of research, namely propaganda studies, public opinion surveys and methods, market research, effects research, and interpersonal communication research.[22]

The research of this foundational period was positivist and empirical. Reality was conceived by researchers as being objectively given, with events being 'hard' and discrete; even psychic states, it was contended, could be detected, quantified, and aggregated through questionnaires, and norms thereby established.

Moreover, like neoclassical economics, this research was methodologically individualist. That is, researchers did not investigate how classes, groups, or institutions were formed, clashed, or interacted; at most they were concerned with how individuals functioned within groups or institutions, and how leadership could be exercised. Polls and surveys, principal methodologies of administrative research, also were (and are) methodologically individualist in the sense that individual respondents represent thousands or millions of autonomous others; society is deemed to comprise merely the summation of the individuals composing it: unions, coalitions, communities, and advocacy groups tended to be disregarded. Laboratory experiments too, another principal research method of administrative communication research, were and remain methodologically individualist, as it is the individual, not the class, group, or organization, that is the unit of analysis; the group, in other words, is represented by a small sample of autonomous individuals selected from the group.

A third characteristic of this research was its focus on behavioural or attitudinal change, a stance consistent with Shannon and Weaver's emphasis on how senders can influence receivers. Communication was presumed to result in overt effects that could be both measured and replicated. Sponsors of the research, intent on influencing more strongly the attitudes and behaviour of message recipients, were desirous to uncover 'the magic keys' of persuasion.[23]

Similarities of the Orthodoxies

One feature common to neoclassical economics and mainstream communication studies, then, is the existence at the very heart of both disciplines of circular flows upon which much else is constructed. Indeed, on the surface, the models seem almost identical. Both lend themselves readily to a methodologically individualist paradigm of single seller and single buyer, or sender and receiver, interacting – obscuring the importance of groups, coalitions, and other power concentrations, as well as the various contexts within which the interactions take place. Significantly, both models also abstract from asymmetries in power between seller and buyer or between sender and receiver.

Components of the two models bear striking surface similarities as well: the seller in the 'market' seemingly corresponds to the message source or sender; the buyer and the message recipient appear analogous; the commodity flowing from buyer to seller appears to link the parties in a manner not unlike the way in which messages or information link sender and receiver. On this basis one might well ask whether communication studies is not then 'really' but a special instance of the economist's market, or conversely whether the economics model depicts but a special instance of an information flow, in which case commodities and money could more generally be viewed as messages or as information. (See chapter 1.)

Orthodoxies Contrasted: Blind Spots Edge into Vision

The primordial model of a communication system suggests, at least implicitly, a number of profound questions concerning, for example: relationships between sender and message, between sender and medium, between codes and various other elements of the system, between medium and message, between medium and receiver, between message and receiver, between sender and receiver, and of course concerning how all these components interact in ongoing interdependence and mutual transformation. Mainstream communication researchers tend not to address all these questions at once, of course, but most at least recognize that an act of communication entails at least an attempt to exert influence, if not indeed control, by a sender over a recipient.[24]

But here we arrive at one of the great ironies and contradictions of mainline American media research. While much time, money, and energy have been devoted to discovering the 'laws of persuasion,' the sole media 'law' emerging from mainline researchers has been the law of minimal media effects, 'discovered' by Paul Felix Lazarsfeld in the early 1940s and elaborated by many others over subsequent decades.[25] According to Chaffee and Hochheimer, 'For four decades "limited effects" was a major defense of owners of new media technologies, including television, from government regulation in the United States.'[26] Significantly, the law of minimal effects is quite consistent with the Stigler/Becker postulate that consumers (here, message recipients) are 'sovereign' and unaffected by market transactions.[27]

Were economists to apply the questions media researchers routinely ask regarding the workings of the communication system to the circular flow of the market, that is, were economists to treat the market model as a communication system, they would undoubtedly become aware of issues heretofore neglected. They would come to see the market as being rife with influence or control. Prices, of course, embody information to which buyers and sellers respond (and neoclassical economists would give their assent to this). But, moreover, consumer goods may be viewed as messages. Apparel, for instance, has been analysed by media scholars as a language, with both 'vocabulary' and 'grammar.' Vocabulary includes hairstyles, accessories, jewellery, make-up, body decoration, and items of clothing. Like human speech, apparel actually comes in many languages, where 'dialects' and 'accents' coexist.[28]

More generally, consumer goods of all types 'carry and communicate meanings.'[29] Often commodities are purchased for the express purpose of communicating cultural meanings to third parties. In our economy, sellers through advertising frequently attempt to attach meanings onto products as a ploy to stimulate sales, and it is often precisely these meanings that consumers hope will be transmitted to third parties in their 'conspicuous consumption.' Not infrequently commodities are symbolically endowed by their manufacturers with 'magical' properties that will (it is implied but seldom stated directly) alleviate or resolve the most perplexing existential needs of users; through commercial imagery and incantations, manufacturers and advertisers communicate 'healing' to buyers, dispensing brand-name soaps, soft drinks, and automobiles as potions or placebos.[30]

Conceivably, economists could pose other questions, too, concerning, for instance, the two-way interactions of seller and commodity and of seller and buyer; the ramifications for workers of being treated as mere commodity; indeed the consequences of mediating so many human interactions by money; the change in meaning for commodities through their valuation in money terms; the range of impacts of different commodities on buyers, and so forth. While questions such as these are not avoided by political economists, neoclassicists either give perfunctory answers ('the value of a commodity is its money price'; 'the commodification of labour leads to efficiency in the flow of labour inputs') or avoid such questions altogether.

If, to take just two examples, either the producer of the commodity or the commodity itself were deemed to affect tastes and preferences of buyers, then the harmonious and 'simple system of natural liberty' proffered by Adam Smith would fall into disarray, and in its place would arise models comprising influence, power plays, and disharmony. Two renegade economists who have asserted that producers and/or commodities indeed affect consumer tastes are John Kenneth Galbraith and Tibor Scitovsky. Galbraith's emphasis was on the manipulation by producers through advertising of consumers' tastes and preferences, contending caustically that the free market 'protects not the individual's right to buy [but] the seller's right to manage the individual.'[31] Scitovsky, on the other hand, noted that the use of products tends to habituate users, meaning that increased consumption will not necessarily increase welfare, but simply appease temporarily the pangs of addiction.[32] Both possibilities pose formidable challenges to neoclassicism, decomposing its 'psychic balm.'[33]

While at first glance, then, similarities would seem to abound between the two models – namely, market and communication system – closer inspection reveals that they are interpreted much differently. Economists do not research 'communication' at all, or hardly at all. While prices are certainly regarded as indicators and signals to which buyers and sellers respond, the mainstream theory does not propose that buyers and sellers influence one another. Nor do commodities or money have impact upon the understandings, wants, needs, or psychic states of buyers and sellers. In important respects, then, the economist's ideal is one of perfect non-communication! Communication means influence; communication requires that someone or something affect someone else or many others. These requirements are precisely what neoclassical economists decry as 'imperfections' in the market – as instances of market power, and hence of 'market failure.' In perfect competition (the ideal against which the economic 'real world' is measured or interpreted), no seller exerts any influence on any buyer or other seller. Rather, each is pushed and pulled by the 'impersonal' forces that derive from aggregated, infinitesimally small influences of each participant. Likewise, products simply satisfy wants, certainly not influence or shape them.

It is not merely consumer products in general that are, for neoclassicists, devoid of message-carrying properties. So too (implicitly) are books, films, TV and radio programs, news stories, and so forth. Treating these cultural artefacts as commodities means precisely that buyers are understood as selecting messages in accordance with pre-existing tastes and preferences (subject to budgetary constraints and relative prices), and that buyers' tastes and preferences remain uninfluenced by 'consuming' the information. If these assumptions of minimal influence and control are not maintained, Smith's 'simple system of natural liberty' gives way to influence, power, and control – in brief, to critical political economy.

It is to be concluded that it indeed makes a difference whether one is an economist or a communication scholar, even in the mainstream. The former hypothesizes an impersonal, mechanistic world of individual autonomy and natural harmony; the latter envisages interdependence, influence, and control, even while providing analysis that furthers the capacity of those in power to maintain and extend the same. Many communication scholars (apart from poststructuralists and active audience theorists) would argue also that senders (sellers) necessarily alter psychic states of receivers inasmuch as messages are absorbed on account of novelty – otherwise no information has been imparted.

Political Economy

However, not all economists are neoclassicists. Critical political economists, unlike their neoclassical siblings, place the question of power front and centre. For them, as Frank Knight has written, 'the central issue of economic policy is the distribution of power.'[34] Or, in the words of Galbraith, 'Economics divorced from consideration of the exercise of power is without meaning and certainly without relevance.'[35] Rather than reify markets, political economists look to a host of factors, particularly law and social relations, to explain market outcomes. The market for them is an artefact, a human institution. Like other institutions, it too can be modified to achieve different results. There is no spontaneity or automatism to the market, and to think that there is is to be blinded to the underlying framework of power, including the legal system, which conditions market forces.[36]

Moreover, political economists writing in or from an economics tradition acknowledge the importance to economic affairs of the symbolic. Belief, knowledge, myth, 'common sense,' ideology – all contribute to the political economy framework within which goods are exchanged. Indeed, the very discipline of neoclassical economics can be interpreted and analysed as a symbolic or rhetorical system, serving to condition the economic system that it purports to describe.[37] Institutional economist Clarence Ayres went even further when he advised that 'all property rights derive from the culture which defines and honors them,' making the task of the economist, in his view, one of comprehending 'something of the nature and functioning of the ideology of our own society.'[38]

If not all economists are neoclassicists, neither are all communication scholars administrative researchers. Communication scholars with a political economy bent investigate the 'context' of cultural production – how the production of culture takes place; how it is organized, politically, economically, and institutionally; who produces it and why. These scholars routinely question the justice of the current distribution of communicatory power and analyse the consequences, broadly framed, of the deployment of the same.

It is with political economy, then, as stemming from both the economics and communication studies traditions, that the material and the symbolic, the economy and the culture, are conjoined. Political economy unites the economics and communications disciplines, which are misleadingly similar only in their mainstream forms.

In considering the origins of political economy as unifier of economics and communication studies, it is instructive to turn to the early institutionalists, and in particular to Thorstein Veblen (1857–1925), an acknowledged founder of institutional and evolutionary economics who pioneered the integration, or perhaps more properly reintegration, of the symbolic and the material. Veblen's contributions to communication studies, however, while certainly more profound and extensive than those of John Dewey, for example, have been scarcely acknowledged.[39] In summary, it may be noted that Veblen placed institutions at the very centre of his analysis, eschewing the methodological individualism of his economist colleagues. He defined institutions as 'widespread social habits' or as 'habits of thought.' For him 'the gradual accumulation of small changes in man's habits of thought are responsible for all achievements of the race.'[40] It is important to study institutions, Veblen contended, because they alone explain societal change or evolution. Whereas generations of individuals differ little in terms of intellectual capacities or in instinctive propensities, institutions (ways of seeing or 'habits of thought') undergo cumulative change, transforming culture, society, and economy.[41]

Through his definition of institution, then, Veblen emphasized the importance of the symbolic and the communicatory for the study of economic affairs. Furthermore, in *The Theory of the Leisure Class*, Veblen pioneered an embryonic analysis of the symbolic or informational properties of consumer goods. He declared that commodities are demanded not merely for their use value, but also, and often primarily, for their capacity to signal wealth and attract prestige. He argued, 'In order to gain and hold the esteem of men it is not sufficient merely to possess wealth and power. The wealth or power must be put in evidence, for esteem is awarded only on evidence ... Conspicuous consumption of valuable goods is a means of reputability to the gentlemen of leisure.'[42]

Furthermore, Veblen contravened the neoclassicists' contention regarding the neutrality of money. Prices, for Veblen, are messages that affect (not merely reflect) the value placed on goods: 'Precious stones ... are more esteemed than they would be if they were more plentiful and cheaper. A wealthy person meets with more consideration and enjoys a larger measure of good repute than would fall to the share of the same person with the same record of good and evil deeds if he were poorer.'[43]

Like Chicago school contemporaries – John Dewey, Robert Park, Charles Cooley – but unlike modern-day administrative communication researchers, Veblen conceived communication as being more than the mere imparting of information or the exertion of influence on receivers. Information for Veblen, as for Dewey, was 'the constitutive force in society'; communication was 'the entire process whereby a culture is brought into existence, maintained in time and sedimented into institutions.'[44]

NOTES

1 The term *administrative research* was coined in 1941 by a leading (administrative) communication scholar of the day, Paul Felix Lazarsfeld, to denote research 'carried through in the service of some kind of administrative agency of public or private character.' He added that such research usually is intended to 'solve little problems generally of a business character.' See Paul F. Lazarsfeld, 'Administrative and Critical Research' (1941); repr. in Lazarsfeld, *Qualitative Analysis: Historical and Critical Essays* (Boston: Allyn and Bacon, 1972), 158–60.

2 Max Weber, *Max Weber on Law in Economy and Society*, ed. and trans. Max Rheinstein, trans. Edward A. Shils (Cambridge, MA: Harvard University Press, 1954), 323.

3 Horace M. Gray, 'Reflections on Innis and Institutional Economics,' in *Culture, Communication, and Dependency: The Tradition of H.A. Innis*, ed. William H. Melody, Liora Salter, and Paul Heyer (Norwood, NJ: Ablex, 1981), 105.

4 Herman E. Daly and John Cobb, *For the Common Good: Redirecting the Economy toward Community, the Environment and a Sustainable Future* (Boston: Beacon, 1989), 85–96, 159–75.

5 Adam Smith, *An Inquiry into the Nature and Causes of the Wealth of Nations* (1776; repr., ed. Edwin Cannan, intro. Max Lerner, New York: Modern Library, 1937), 651.

6 Ibid., 13.

7 Ibid., 423.
8 Ibid.
9 George J. Stigler, *Memoirs of an Unregulated Economist* (New York: Basic Books, 1988), 164.
10 George J. Stigler, *Theory of Price*, 3rd ed. (New York: Macmillan, 1966), 39.
11 Ibid.
12 Smith, *Inquiry*, 14.
13 Ronald Coase, 'The Problem of Social Cost,' *Journal of Law and Economics* 3 (1960): 1–44.
14 James W. Carey, 'Culture, Geography, and Communications: The Work of Harold Innis in an American Context,' in *Culture, Communication, and Dependency: The Tradition of H.A. Innis*, ed. William H. Melody, Liora Salter, and Paul Heyer (Norwood, NJ: Ablex, 1981), 73–91; Daniel Czitrom, *Media and the American Mind* (Chapel Hill, NC: University of North Carolina Press, 1982); Jesse Delia, 'Communication Research: A History,' in *Handbook of Communication Science*, ed. Charles Berger and Steven Chaffee (Beverly Hills, CA: Sage, 1987), 20–98.
15 Wilbur Schramm, 'Human Communication as a Field of Behavioral Science: Jack Hilgard and His Committee,' in *Human Communication as a Field of Study: Selected Contemporary Views*, ed. Sara Sanderson King (Albany: State University of New York Press, 1989), 13–26.
16 Although Lasswell has routinely been credited with posing these questions, they were actually formulated jointly by several eminent media researchers (meeting in secret prior to the Second World War) who were intent to devise psychological warfare strategies for the US government. Since the questions needed a public author and the 'Communication Seminar' was secret, Lasswell was anointed. See Jefferson Pooley, 'The New History of Mass Communication Research,' in *The History of Media and Communication Research: Contested Memories*, ed. David W. Park and Jefferson Pooley (New York: Lang, 2008), 51–3.
17 Wilbur Schramm and D. Roberts, introduction to 'The Structure and Function of Communication in Society' by Harold D. Lasswell, in *The Process and Effects of Mass Communication*, ed. Wilbur Schramm and D. Roberts (Urbana: University of Illinois Press, 1971), 84.
18 Harold Lasswell, 'The Structure and Function of Communication in Society' (1948); repr. in *The Process and Effects of Mass Communication*, ed. Wilbur Schramm and D. Roberts (Urbana: University of Illinois Press, 1971), 84–99.
19 Scott R. Olson, 'Mass Media: A Bricolage of Paradigms,' *Human Communication as a Field of Study: Selected Contemporary Views*, ed. Sara Sanderson King (Albany: State University of New York Press, 1989), 73.

20 Claude E. Shannon and Warren Weaver, *The Mathematical Theory of Communication* (Urbana: University of Illinois Press, 1949), 7.

21 Ibid., 5.

22 Czitrom, *Media and the American Mind*, 123–7.

23 Shearon A. Lowery and Melvin L. DeFleur, *Milestones in Mass Communication Research: Media Effects* (New York: Longman, 1988), 137.

24 Shannon and Weaver, for example, defined *communication* as 'all of the procedures by which one mind can affect another.' Carl Hovland likewise stated that communication is 'the process by which an individual (the communicator) transmits stimuli (usually verbal) to modify the behavior of other individuals (the audience).' See L. Forsdale, *Perspectives on Communications* (Reading, MA: Addison Wesley, 1981), 9–11; also Schramm and Roberts, *Process and Effects*, 1–53.

25 'Limited media effects' was 'discovered' shortly after the rise of Hitler, who employed loudspeaker and radio to mesmerize Germany, and the radio broadcast of *War of the Worlds* (Halloween 1938), which sent millions into a panic. The limited effects model also deflected pressure from Hollywood and broadcasters by contending that media content is unimportant.

26 Steven H. Chaffee and John L. Hochheimer, 'The Beginnings of Political Communication Research in the United States: Origins of the "Limited Effects" Model,' in *Mass Communication Review Yearbook*, ed. Michael Gurevitch and Mark R. Levy (Beverly Hills, CA: Sage, 1985), 5:75.

27 In chapter 16 of this volume, the author suggests a resolution to the paradox of researchers on the one hand insisting that media have minimal effects, while on the other devoting much activity to strengthening the means of influencing audiences.

28 Alison Lurie, *The Language of Clothes* (New York: Vintage, 1985), 4.

29 Grant McCracken, *Culture and Consumption: New Approaches to the Symbolic Character of Consumer Goods and Activities* (Bloomington: Indiana University Press, 1988), 71, 83.

30 Raymond Williams, 'Advertising: The Magic System,' in *Problems in Materialism and Culture* (London: Verso, 1980), 177–91.

31 John Kenneth Galbraith, *The New Industrial State* (Boston: Houghton Mifflin, 1967), 217.

32 Tibor Scitovsky, *The Joyless Economy: An Inquiry into Human Satisfaction and Consumer Dissatisfaction* (New York: Oxford University Press, 1976), 136.

33 Warren J. Samuels, introduction to *The Place of Science in Modern Civilization* by Thorstein Veblen (New Brunswick, NJ: Transaction, 1990), xxvi. Note, in this regard, Stigler and Becker's seemingly desperate 'reformulation' of the theory of consumer demand. The two Nobel laureates proposed that

what consumers *really* demand are not 'products' but 'commodities.' They defined commodities as want-satisfying outputs *produced by the consumer,* using as inputs not only products purchased in the market, but also the consumer's time, skill, training, other human capital, and other inputs. By thus reconstructing the theory of consumer demand, the authors contended they had bypassed the dual problems of advertiser manipulation and product addiction. Changes in demand for products for Stigler and Becker are but a surface phenomenon, since underlying tastes and preferences (they hypothesized) are unchanging and everlasting: 'One does not argue over tastes for the same reason that one does not argue over the Rocky Mountains – both are there, will be there next year, too, and are the same to all men.'

That Stigler and Becker fail even on their own terms, can be seen by juxtaposing two sentences from contiguous paragraphs at the article's conclusion: 'We claim, however, that no significant behavior has been illuminated by assumptions of differences in tastes ... Needless to say, we would welcome explanations of why some people become addicted to alcohol and others to Mozart.' In the Stigler/Becker world, 'addiction' to Mozart vs. addiction to alcohol is of no 'significant' difference; nor are the foregoing addictions 'significantly different' from non-addiction. See George J. Stigler and Gary Becker, 'De Gustibus Non est Disputandum,' *American Economic Review* 67, no. 2 (1977): 75–90.

34 Frank Knight, *Risk, Uncertainty and Profit* (1921; Boston: Houghton Mifflin Company, 1957), 282.

35 John Kenneth Galbraith, *The Anatomy of Power* (Boston: Houghton Mifflin, 1983), xiii.

36 Warren J. Samuels, 'Interrelations between Legal and Economic Processes,' *Journal of Law and Economics* 14, no. 2 (1971): 435–50.

37 Arjo Klamer, Donald M. McCloskey, and Robert M. Solow, *The Consequences of Economic Rhetoric* (Cambridge: Cambridge University Press, 1988); Warren J. Samuels, *Economics as Discourse: An Analysis of the Language of Economists* (Boston: Kluwer, 1990).

38 Clarence E. Ayres, 'Ideological Responsibility,' in *The Methodology of Economic Thought,* 2nd ed., ed. Mark R. Tool and Warren J. Samuels (New Brunswick, NJ: Transaction, 1989), 29–30.

39 In American intellectual circles, Veblen was for years considered a bête noire, a 'mad prophet.' As noted by Horace Gray, 'reactionary capitalistic interests, to protect their economic power, launched a vicious propaganda attack against Veblen; they elevated him to the godhead of all devils ... Veblen was a wild man, a primitive, uncivilized creature, a libertine, an

anarchist, a communist, a revolutionary conspirator ... Some faculty men lost their posts for suspected Veblenism, others were denied appointments and promotions.' See Gray, 'Reflections on Innis,' 104–7.

40 Wesley C. Mitchell, *Types of Economic Theory: From Mercantilism to Institutionalism* (New York: Kelley, 1969), 2:605.

41 Thorstein Veblen, 'The Limitations of Marginal Utility' (1909; repr., *The Place of Science in Modern Civilization*, ed. Warren J. Samuels, New Brunswick, NJ: Transaction, 1990).

42 Thorstein Veblen, *Theory of the Leisure Class: An Economic Study of Institutions* (1899; New York: New American Library, 1953), 42, 64.

43 Veblen, 'Limitations of Marginal Utility,' 246.

44 James W. Carey, *Communications and Culture: Essays on Media and Society* (Winchester, MA: Unwin Hyman, 1989), 144.

3 Copyright and Culture

When Canada's federal government announced in October 1987 that it had negotiated a free-trade agreement with the United States it emphasized that Canadian culture had been safeguarded. While the pact covered resources, energy, manufactured goods, services, and capital, according to the government, culture had remained 'off the table' – except for commitments to abandon postal rates favouring Canadian magazines, to inaugurate a retransmission right for broadcasts rediffused by cable TV systems, and the ominous undertaking to hammer out an agreement over the next five to seven years on all remaining trade irritants.

Implicit in the government's assertions respecting the inviolability of Canadian culture were a number of key, but contentious, assumptions: that culture is able to be neatly segmented from all else included in the agreement; that culture, even when narrowly defined as excluding activities specifically enumerated in the agreement, would not be subject increasingly to international supply and demand; and that Canada then enjoyed significant autonomy in cultural matters. These implicit assumptions are worth exploring.

The claim that cultural sovereignty was being preserved in the face of Canada-U.S. free trade in goods, energy, services, and capital makes sense only if culture is indeed an activity or sphere that can be segregated from the others. There are a number of reasons for believing this is not so.

In November 1987, for example, the federal government published a discussion paper, 'Communications for the 21st Century,' wherein it stated, 'Using Organization for Economic Cooperation and Development (OECD) data and applying it to 1986 Canadian employment data, information workers account for 45 per cent of total employment. Even more significantly, information work is evident in the primary and manufacturing sectors as well as in services. As Statistics Canada has pointed out, the increasing importance of the service industries is related to the rise of the "information economy." For these industries, the processing, analysis and dissemination of information form the basis of the service they provide.'[1]

A free-trade deal mandating free flow and/or national treatment of services, capital, energy, resources, commodities, and manufactured goods must also be, in significant ways, a free-trade deal for information. Now the production, distribution, and exchange of information is not necessarily synonymous with cultural activity, but there is surely a wide overlap. Information comprises symbols and their manipulation, out of which meanings are constructed, emerge, or are at least represented. Culture, on the other hand, entails in part shared meanings, patterns of perceiving and thinking, having at its base shared pools of symbolic artefacts. It is in this sense that information workers may be termed 'cultural workers,' and as we have seen they constitute 45 per cent of the labour force. A further implication of the information economy literature is that international cultural flows embrace much more than movement of books, periodicals, movies, TV programs, and sound recordings across the international border, important as these may be. *All economic exchange involves culture.*

But this is hardly an insight originating with information economy literature. Harold Innis, for one, made the point long ago, emphasizing that economic activity of all kinds, particularly transportation and resource extraction, constitutes communication. He wrote, 'The history of the fur trade is the history of contact between two civilizations, the European and the North American ... [bringing about] a wholesale destruction of the peoples concerned by warfare and disease.'[2] Likewise, he wrote, 'The history of the Canadian Pacific Railway is primarily the history of the spread of Western civilization over the northern half of the North American continent.' He continued, 'The effects of the road were measured to some extent by the changes in the strength and character of that civilization in the period following construction.'[3]

Innis's insights on the conjuncture of economic activity and cultural activity were taken up and adapted by Marshall McLuhan, who maintained that media are defined by their effects. To McLuhan, housing, money, clothing, light bulbs, clocks, weapons, and so forth transmit messages and bring about changes, and hence are media.

Culture is then fully implicated with the economy, and the economy with culture. The sooner this is realized, the more realistically the consequences of free trade on Canadian culture can be projected.

In assurances regarding the continued integrity of Canadian culture in the face of economic free trade the government implicitly adopted a narrow definition of cultural activity, limiting its sphere of reference to the so-called cultural industries: book and periodical publishing, movies, broadcasting, recordings, art, dance, theatre, and so forth. However, accepting this narrow definition for discussion purposes, the concern then arises that heightened emphasis is being given to international supply and demand of cultural artefacts and activities at the expense of indigenously directed creations. On the one hand, cultural works are being given heightened status as commodity through copyright revisions, while on the other, shared-use or resource-like qualities of cultural productions are being downgraded as with·cutbacks in the funding of such institutions as the CBC. More intensely commodifying culture – particularly more stringent copyright and reduced importance of crown corporations – is part and parcel of the FTA.

The essence of copyright is to restrict the right to reproduce or perform individual creations to their originators or assignees. Through such restriction the originator (author, composer, arranger) attains a monetary reward bearing, in principle, some relation to the degree of acceptance that the work receives in the community. In the absence of copyright, it is claimed, others could attain monetary gain to the detriment of the originator without having undergone the trials and tribulations of creation.

Copyright has philosophical grounding in notions of private property, commodity, exchange, and markets, whereby works are distributed according to user-pay and ability to pay. Commodification of cultural works, then, exacerbates gaps between information-rich and information-poor, and all that spills out from that. But, from the perspective of Canadian cultural sovereignty, the most important implication of heightened commodity status for cultural works is the perverse incentive for domestic production and distribution that results. Since works once produced can often be shared by many with little added expense, the tendency will be for producers of commodified works to seek out wide markets and to gear their creative efforts to those markets. In the Canadian case, creators may have incentives to contemplate marketability south of the border when undertaking their creations. Likewise, distributors in Canada may be inclined to procure rights to American material where production costs are amortized over a much larger volume of users than is the case for indigenous productions.

It is in this context that we turn to *A Charter of Rights for Creators*,[4] the 1985 report of the Commons Subcommittee on the Revision of Copyright, upon which revisions to the Copyright Act were based. The document proposed creating new rights, strengthening penalties for misappropriation, and generally further commodifying information. Committee member Lynn McDonald explained at the time, 'There were great differences of opinion between the owners of copyright and those who wish to use the copyright. As a committee we addressed those and overwhelmingly came down on the side of the creators. Sometimes we limited the right, but overwhelmingly we made that decision in favour of creators.'

As consultant to the federal Department of Communications, I estimated the value for 1985 of these new rights at $171 million.[5] Interestingly, I was not requested to estimate how much of this would flow to foreign rights' holders. One may reasonably suspect most of it would so do, not only because the greatest proportion of copyrightable works in Canada is owned outside the country, but as well because of U.S. insistence that certain provisions (a retransmission right, for example) form a part of the Free Trade Agreement.

Few would begrudge creators receiving increased financial rewards for their creative endeavours, and copyright is one possible means of remunerating them. Its effectiveness, though, is another matter entirely. As an author, I have direct experience in assigning copyright to publishers, usually in return for royalties amounting to 5 per cent of the publishers' net sales, or about two cents on the dollar of retail sales. On a thirty-dollar book, author royalties at this rate amount to sixty cents. Best-selling authors undoubtedly strike better deals, but nonetheless it is virtually axiomatic that many creative talents get a mere pittance from copyright compared to the manufacturers, distributors, and retailers. Stringent copyright, primarily, is as boon to transnational media companies.

An additional problem, from the standpoint of Canadian culture, is when heightened copyright is accompanied by other measures that fail to recognize cultural artefacts and activities as shared resources – for instance, withdrawing funding from public broadcasting, libraries, and museums, and requiring user fees for primary, secondary, and post-secondary education. In combination such measures enhance the push and pull of international supply and demand on the production and distribution of cultural works and activities.

This brings us to the other side of information – information as resource. As Anthony Smith has written, 'It is possible to view information as a social resource of a special kind rather than as a produced commodity, a resource that enables other resources to function productively since it is the existence of salient information that determines the value and existence of other resources … Information, when treated as resource, automatically raises the wider question of social allocation and social control.'[6]

This type of reasoning has induced Edward Ploman and Clark Hamilton to add, 'The resource characteristics of information would lead to a different approach [other than that entailed in copyright] to the production and distribution of information. The emphasis would tend to be on a wide and unhampered dissemination and flow of information that is seen as essential for the economic, social and cultural activities of a society.'[7]

At first glance this emphasis on 'a wide and unhampered … flow of information' might appear consistent with international free flow that, as argued above, is part and parcel of the Free Trade Agreement. This notion breaks down, however, in the Canadian context if a consequence of enhanced free flow is to undermine indigenous productions. It was indeed in recognition of the dialectic inherent even in this resource characteristic of information – that the shared-use character of information can either maintain and strengthen indigenous culture, or weaken and subvert it if the information circulating is primarily of foreign origin – that public broadcasting was created in the first place. Reporting in 1932, the Special Parliamentary Committee on Broadcasting declared that only through public ownership could broadcasting help to strengthen cultural sovereignty rather than erode it.[8]

In the 1980s, however, these perceptions evidently have changed, in official circles at least. Even as the federal government enhances information's commodity status by beefing up copyright, it erodes information's resource-for-cultural-development character by downgrading the CBC. Cutbacks in federal funding of $85 million in 1985, of $50 million in 1986, and another $50 million in 1987 amply demonstrate this change.

In the early 1930s Graham Spry, lobbying for public broadcasting in Canada, coined his famous aphorism: 'The State or the United States.' Spry's reasoning, echoed by George Grant, was simple but correct: 'No small country can depend for its survival on the loyalty of its capitalists ... Only in dominant nations is the loyalty of capitalists assured. In such situations, their interests are tied to the strength and vigour of their empire.'[9]

The issues addressed so briefly in this article – economic free trade between two information economies, heightened commodification of information through revisions to the Copyright Act, downgrading resource aspects of information through cutbacks to the CBC, and the minority voice Canadians now have in culture within their own borders – are interrelated issues whose total thrust is not encouraging with respect to cultural sovereignty.

NOTES

1 Government of Canada, Department of Communications, *Communications for the Twenty-First Century: Media and Messages in the Information Age* (Ottawa: Supply and Services, 1987), 13–14.
2 Harold A. Innis, *The Fur Trade in Canada: An Introduction to Canadian Economic History* (1930), rev. ed. prepared by S.D. Clark and W.T. Easterbrook, foreword by Robin W. Winks. (Toronto: University of Toronto Press, 1962), 388.
3 Harold A. Innis, *A History of the Canadian Pacific Railway* (1923; Toronto: University of Toronto Press, 1971), 287.
4 Government of Canada, House of Commons, Standing Committee on Communications and Culture, *A Charter of Rights for Creators* (Ottawa: Supply and Services Canada, 1985).
5 Robert E. Babe, 'Size of Canada's Copyright Industries,' 3rd series, *Canadian Patent Reporter* 9, no. 4 (1986): 449–60.
6 Anthony Smith, *The Geopolitics of Information: How Western Culture Dominates the World* (London: Faber and Farber, 1980), 114.
7 Edward W. Ploman and Clark Hamilton, *Copyright: Intellectual Property in the Information Age* (London: Routledge and Kegan Paul, 1980), 220.
8 See chapters 4 and 5 herein.
9 George Grant, *Lament for a Nation: The Defeat of Canadian Nationalism* (1965; Ottawa: Carleton University Press, 1989), 69–70.

4 'Life Is Information': The Communication Thought of Graham Spry

> By nature I am compelled to be a reformer. I can always imagine improvements, always scent evils, and very easily hate some wrongly based institution.
> – *Passion and Conviction: The Letters of Graham Spry* (1992)

Graham Spry was exemplary in combining theory and praxis. On the one hand he was a historian, political analyst, and communication theorist; in addition to articles on Canadian communication policy, he wrote on ancient and Russian history, on 'India and Self-Government,' and on francophone-anglophone relations within the Canadian Confederation. This gentle, witty man was also, however, impassioned and tenacious in pursuing institutional reform through voluntarist politics, and his legacy continues to be felt in the fields of journalism, broadcasting, and health care.

In 1930, with Alan Plaunt (1904–41),[1] Spry formed, and until 1936 worked vigorously on behalf of, the Canadian Radio League, a volunteer association dedicated to establishing public broadcasting in accordance with recommendations of the 1929 Aird Royal Commission. Spry, Plaunt, and the League maintained that radio broadcasting, while important for certain limited commercial applications, should by no means be primarily a business. Rather, it should be treated as an instrument for cultivating an informed public opinion, for educating, and for entertaining; it should make the home 'not merely a billboard, but a theatre, a concert hall, a club, a public meeting, a school, a university.'[2] Spry admonished, 'Here is a majestic instrument of national unity and national culture. Its potentialities are too great, its influence and significance are too vast, to be left to the petty purposes of selling cakes of soap.'³

Nowhere, in Spry's view, was the dichotomy between unrestrained private, commercial interest and broader public and national interests more marked than in Canadian broadcasting. As he wrote in 1931, commercial pressure within an unregulated, advertiser-financed broadcasting system leads inexorably to 'stultified educational uses of broadcasting,' to programming 'designed for and serving principally companies desiring to advertise themselves or their products,' to concentration of control in the hands of a few powerful private interests, to malformed and uninformed public opinion, and to an association of Canadian stations 'with the American chains to broadcast American rather than Canadian programmes.'⁴ In the early 1930s Spry coined his famous and oft-repeated aphorism, 'It is a choice between the State and the United States,'⁵ to underline the fact that in broadcasting (as in so many other matters), Canada as a nation, as a community, as a social organism, cannot survive without government actively coordinating and in some measure directing activities.

Much has been written about the volunteer efforts of the Canadian Radio League and of Graham Spry in bringing about public broadcasting in Canada.⁶ To this day, its campaign is considered a 'classic study on the art of lobbying.'⁷ The League articulated clear and simple goals, most particularly 'the operation of Canadian broadcasting as a national public service.'⁸ It recruited members from all walks of life. It studied the prejudices and idiosyncrasies of members of Parliament and of other influential citizens and took into account such information in forming its arguments and making its representations. In the case of Conservative Prime Minister R.B. Bennett, for instance, Spry 'stalked' his prey, learning his daily movements. According to filmmaker Bruce Steele, 'Spry "accidentally" meets Bennett outside the steam bath of the Chateau Laurier Hotel: the Prime Minister naked beneath a towel; Spry in full formal dress, comfortable in suit and tie. Spry respectfully puts the case of public broadcasting before the startled leader and wins him over.'⁹ And that, despite Bennett's zeal in the depths of the Great Depression to cut back public expenditures in an effort to balance the federal budget!

According to broadcast historian Margaret Prang, 'All the evidence suggests that the League's role was a major one, that it did much to prevent the radio issue from becoming a partisan question, and that it forestalled a postponement of the formation of a policy during the exigencies of the depression, a postponement which might have been fatal to the cause of public control.'[10]

In addition to his radio activism, between 1932 and 1934 Spry was also publisher of the *Farmers' Sun*, always a money-losing venture, renaming it *New Commonwealth* to reflect its new alignment with the newly founded social democratic party, the Cooperative Commonwealth Federation (CCF). In 1935 Spry also purchased, for one dollar, the *Canadian Forum* (founded in 1920), thereby rescuing from bankruptcy that venerable but now defunct journal of arts and commentary. The early and mid-thirties also saw him join and become active in the League for Social Reconstruction (LSR), organized in 1931 by Frank Underhill and Frank Scott as a 'Canadian Fabian Society,' and in this connection he became a contributing editor of *Social Planning for Canada*, published in 1935. As well, Spry joined the CCF, was a signatory of the Regina Manifesto (1933), and served as vice-chairman of the CCF's Ontario Council.

Lacking an income, however, Spry was forced to relinquish some of his volunteer connections. Branded a radical, by 1936 he was simply unemployable in Canada.[11] Eventually he secured an executive position in England with a U.S. oil company, and thereupon wrote his fiancée, Irene Biss, 'Here I am, the nationalist, working for Americans and in England. And here am I the socialist serving the biggest of big business. All contrary to my wishes, contrary to my hopes, and accepted by an act of will.'[12]

During the Second World War, still in England, Spry served as personal assistant to Sir Stanford Cripps of the British War Cabinet. He also became a member of the Home Guard, complete with tin hat, gas mask, and rifle. In 1942 he accompanied Cripps on his mission to negotiate independence for India.

In 1948, endeavouring to re-establish formal ties with his native country, Spry became, at Saskatchewan Premier Tommy Douglas's behest, agent general for Saskatchewan in Britain. Among other accomplishments Spry recruited medical personnel to help neutralize the 1962 doctors' strike against the introduction of provincial medicare.

Whether at home or abroad Spry maintained a keen interest in Canadian public affairs – particularly broadcasting and francophone-anglophone relations. He secured leaves of absence as needed to return home to help influence policy. 'Retiring' in Canada in 1968, Graham Spry continued to lend his energy, engaging personality, and substantial intellect, both individually and through a revitalized Canadian Broadcasting League, to support his beloved CBC, until 24 November 1983, when he died peacefully while asleep at his home in Rockcliffe Park near Ottawa. He had spent the previous evening discussing broadcasting policy with his friend and collaborator Kealy Wilkinson.

Over his lifetime Graham Spry made many close friends, and of these many were extraordinarily influential individuals – Lester B. Pearson, Tommy Douglas, Frank Scott, King Gordon, Eugene Forsey, Walter Gordon, Brooke Claxton, and of course Irene Biss, whom he met in 1933 at a LSR skating party and who was his wife for forty-five years: 'We had such fun,' she exclaimed in an interview I conducted with her in the summer of 1993. Although moving easily in circles of power and wealth, Graham Spry retained an ability to empathize with the less privileged; perhaps his experience of penury and unemployment in the 1930s contributed to that capacity. In his eulogy, Tommy Douglas suggested that, although renowned for contributions to Canadian broadcasting, Graham Spry had achieved even more for the Saskatchewan farmer.

In this chapter I now recount Spry's communication thought as it concerns two related areas: anglophone-francophone relations, and the notion of community.

Anglophone–Francophone Relations

As a child Spry lived for a time in Montreal. As an adult he learned French by listening to recordings. Throughout his adult life he retained a keen interest in the concerns of francophone Canadians, and in writings and speeches he addressed relations between French- and English-speaking peoples within the Canadian confederation. Some of his thoughts appear in notes prepared for two addresses given in England in 1966 and circulated privately to interested parties as a typescript bearing the title, 'French Canada and Canadian Federation.' Where not otherwise noted, this is the source document for this section.

According to Graham Spry, the Quebec separatist movement had origins in a traditional theory of nationalism as propagated in former years by the church in Quebec. The theory maintained that 'as the family is a natural human unit, confirmed by the institution of marriage, so the nation is a natural unit, defined by a language group with a common history in occupation of a particular territory. A nation does not realize itself, thus the thesis runs, and is not a nation until it has been expressed through the institution of an independent State, encompassing within a single government the "collectivity" of the language group and the territory the language group occupies.'[13]

But race and language, Spry continued, are dangerous foundations upon which to build political life: race, he declared in 1929, is 'like a car left with its engine running; the slightest touch will put it in gear and set it speeding towards some bitter accident.'[14] Indeed, he continued, an 'unqualified emphasis upon racial or linguistic factors ... [was] the right-wing and disastrous theory of nationalism which wracked Europe for at least the last 150 years.'

The opposite of racial and linguistic nationalism, according to Spry, is 'political nationality,' as advanced, for instance, by Lord Acton in 1862. A *political nation*, Spry explained, is 'a "moral and political being," wherein different races [are] embraced within a single state.'[15] Such was the philosophy that formed the Canadian Confederation of 1867 and was understood as such by both French and English leaders of the time. Their goal then had been to create a community of two peoples, strong enough on the one hand 'to resist continentalist pressures from the south,' and on the other sufficiently flexible 'to ensure the identity of each of the French and English societies.'

According to Spry, the essence of the Canadian *political nationality* ever since has been the ideal of 'two peoples living not separately but both differently and above all together.' Canada, for Spry, has been 'a test case,' albeit on a modest scale, 'for the concept of a world-wide, multi-racial Commonwealth.'

However, it is precisely this concept that Quebec separatists oppose. Spry declared, 'Thus primitive, European theory [i.e., racially or linguistically based nationhood] threatens the more difficult but richer Canadian theory of "political nationality,"' primarily as a result of primitive theory's deep, visceral, and simplistic appeal to emotions.

Quebec nationalism today differs in an important respect from the nationalism of former years. No longer is nationality expressed primarily through a church intent on maintaining a pastoral way of life, but rather through a political party intent on economic growth, trade, and development. Nonetheless, the present spirit of independence at a deeper level, Spry insisted, resonates with the past: the separatist party retains the longings for and attachment to ethnicity and language.

Spry, then, contrasted the racial and linguistic nationalism of Quebec to the political nationalism of Canada. For him, however, the very existence of Canada as a political nation was and remains attributable to the French fact in North America. Without French colonization of the St Lawrence valley during the fur trade, the region would have been swept into the American Revolution of 1776.[16] Likewise today: if Quebec were to secede, the 'larger vision of a Canadian nation of two languages and cultures peacefully mastering without bloodshed or hatred a territory as great as the whole of Europe' would be split into three geographic areas. He continued, 'The vision would dissolve, and the federal "political nation" disappear. In the course of time and of increasing economic and communications pressures, the several parts would almost certainly fall, whatever the political terminology, into total subordination to the United States.'[17]

Spry's Thought on Information and Community

Graham Spry often remarked that 'life is information.' In a 1972 paper, 'Culture and Entropy: A Lay View of Broadcasting,' prepared for the Royal Society of Canada, he went some distance toward unpacking these three words. *Culture* and *entropy*, he wrote, are opposing terms, the former being an expression for social organization or integration, the latter for disorganization or disintegration. These terms, he continued, although opposed, are joined through the concepts of information and communication.

Culture, according to Spry, *is* information, or at least is the product of information. 'Information is the prime integrating factor creating, nourishing, adjusting and sustaining society.'[18] Spry appears to have used the terms *culture, community*, and *society* almost interchangeably, for he defined *society* as 'a people in communication,' and citing cyberneticist Norbert Wiener declared, 'Properly speaking the community extends only so far as there extends an effectual transmission of information.'[19]

The dual concepts of information and communication for Spry point to important parallels between the individual organism and society (the social organism). He wrote, 'A society, a community, a nation, like any other organism, is a function of a network; society is organized, integrated and made responsive by information. In the human being, the central nervous system including the brain is that most powerful, most complex and highest of all networks of life – a network of 12,000 to 20,000 million neurons. [In a marginal note of 1981, Spry revised this estimate upward to 100 billion neurons.] Each of these cells is, so to speak, a two-way electric and chemical re-broadcasting station, creating by means of its axons, dendrites and synapses, an incalculable total of channels or inter-relationships.'[20]

For individual organisms, Spry continued, life depends upon and may be defined in terms of the existence and continued use of the neural communication network; death, conversely, entails the disintegration or non-use of this neural network. Likewise, in society, communal vitality requires reciprocal transmission and reception of messages; social disintegration, the analogue of individual death, results from too much noise, from insufficient feedback (necessary for homeostasis), or from silence (breakdown or non-use of the communication system).

While significant parallels between individual and social organisms can be drawn, Spry averred, there is also an important difference. He explained, 'The wisdom of the community or society, balanced against the wisdom of the body, is elementary, rudimentary, inexperienced and very, very recent ... Whereas the human body, as inherited through the genetic code generation after generation, has millennia of experience as a single, unified system, sensitive and responsive to changes in the internal and external environment, human societies have only very recently developed rudimentary processes of social adjustment and social response.'[21]

What, then, Spry asked, permits societies, comprising separate individuals, to attain and maintain organization (social homeostasis) in the face of entropic pressures inclining them toward social breakdown or social death? His reply: the means of communication – that is, the media. Media, and the individuals or groups controlling media, 'condition' and 'program' societies. Media as the 'central nervous system' of the social organism transmit instructions on how members are to respond to environmental change and regulate in a general way society's relationships with its environment. Society's 'genetic program' – its traditions, languages, laws, customs, institutions, and so forth – are continuously conditioned and modified (mutated) as new information is diffused through its media of communication. The implication is that media can either contribute to the vitality and growth of a society, or can be entropic, inducing disintegration and death.

Spry's Vision and Canadian Media Today

When Graham Spry set about forming the Canadian Radio League in the early 1930s, the challenge was clear: make room in a crowded and finite radio frequency spectrum, dominated largely by American commercial stations and networks, for a substantial, non-commercial, Canadian presence. To this day the ideal has persisted, but the challenge has grown more severe. Technological trends, commercial pressures, and philosophical/political currents combine to undermine the predominance within Canada of Canadian and of public broadcasting.

In terms of evolving technology, three trends can be highlighted. First is the exponential expansion in transmission capacity: cable systems each year diffuse new packages of specialty (non-broadcast) television services; thousands of movie titles are now available on demand through video stores for playback on VCRs and digital video disc players; direct-to-home satellite broadcasting systems have been licensed whereby viewers can receive by means of small and relatively inexpensive dishes, hundreds of television channels; and then too, of course, there is the 'information highway.' The spectrum of constraint of the 1930s, in other words, is increasingly a spectrum of abundance.

Second, through satellites particularly, but increasingly also through transoceanic and landline fibre optics, the world shrinks into the proverbial 'global village.' Information increasingly can be gleaned instantaneously from geographically dispersed locations, while conversely programming/instructions are sent worldwide at lightning speed.

These foregoing technological trends combine with a third, and also with commercial considerations. In the 1930s the medium of communication of most concern to Spry was relatively inexpensive radio broadcasting that diffused programming indiscriminately to all within the coverage area of a transmitter. Today radio has been largely superseded by much more expensive video, whose cost characteristics bestow tremendous financial advantage to programmers reaching large, often international audiences. Through cable and through scrambling/descrambling technologies (the third technological trend highlighted here), people are required increasingly to pay directly to access the bulk of the expanded programming fare.

For both technological and financial reasons, therefore, electronically distributed information inclusive of all citizens, including particularly the financially underprivileged, is becoming marginalized, raising the prospect of yet further and more pronounced cleavages, domestically and internationally, between the information rich and the poor. Also, technological innovations permit people increasingly to receive and send messages in real time according to communities of interest distinct from and independent of location; *people-in-communication* (Spry's definition of community), therefore, is increasingly less likely to be defined by geographical or political boundaries. Moreover, due in part at least to information's inexhaustible economies of scale, the pronounced tendency is toward heightened concentration of control internationally through the formation of transnational informational conglomerates, exacerbating unidirectional flows from central, primarily American, production centres. This became particularly evident, and ominous, during the Persian Gulf War as citizens, political leaders, and news agencies alike relied on essentially a single news source.[22]

Technological and commercial trends in broadcasting and communication correspond to, help reinforce, and are in important respects dependent upon neoconservative movements in North America and elsewhere. Theoretical neoclassicism, particularly as it emerged from long gestation in the Economics Department at the University of Chicago, has provided intellectual ground for neoconservative policy – particularly privatization, deregulation, heightened commodification, reduction in social programs, user fees, reduced governmental activism, and globalization through deregulated international markets for commodities, capital, and information. At the very heart of neoclassical philosophy and of neoconservative policy is a conception of information/communication that is diametrically opposed to the perspective Spry articulated. One way to appraise the relevance of his thought for the present and the future is to compare his depiction of information/communication with its opposite.

Neoclassicists have viewed information as mere commodity (akin to toasters, according to a former chairman of the U.S. Federal Communications Commission), while communication for them is but a variant of commodity exchange. Neoclassical economists George Stigler, Ronald Coase, and Gary Becker won Nobel prizes in large part for expounding on this theme. Human relations, they have contended, are utilitarian and fleeting: autonomous economic agents come together briefly to trade and then go their separate ways, untouched and untouchable. Society is merely the summation of individuals, not an entity distinct in itself. For Gary Becker, social phenomena seemingly as diverse as marriage, family planning, racial discrimination, crime, divorce, drug addiction, politics, and suicide can be understood adequately through the principles and concepts of neoclassical economics (price, cost, individual utility maximization, supply, demand) – in brief, in terms of what Harold Innis described and warned of in his classic 1938 essay, 'The Penetrative Powers of the Price System.'

But refusal to acknowledge, let alone highlight, society as a social organism and as an entity comprising groups and individuals in dynamic interaction, transforming one another and the social whole through informational exchange, Spry would say, will inevitably result in entropy or social breakdown. Applying Spry's analysis we could say that American cities have long been experiencing entropy on account of the price system's penetrative powers. Those lacking money, that is the means to communicate, in a society premised on the ubiquity of commodity exchange are precluded from meaningful participation in social affairs, leaving available only other, destructive modes for articulating their plight – riots, blockades, theft, vandalism, or as the alternative, silence. For the affluent, too, although not likewise deprived of material comforts and delights, the price system can be erosive of hitherto permanent and deep-felt connections, commodifying one's sense of nation, of community, and of self.

For Spry, however, human relations are not, and should never be allowed to become, mere commodity exchange relations. For him, rather, people influence and transform one another in unpredictable ways, and they also are components of, and participants in, an evolving social whole. Furthermore, Graham Spry feared that in Canada the commercial, commodified view of information/communication was achieving such ascendancy that his country could wither and be swallowed up in what today we may call the transnationalized, commercialized, New World Order.

'What is the information upon which the Canadian society takes its decisions; who controls its selection and its distribution; and for whose purposes?' Spry asked. For advocates of information-as-commodity-alone, questions such as these cannot even be raised; they lie quite beyond the pale of thought. And hence, the immense utility of neoclassicism for the agencies of global commercialization and transnationalization.

In 1972, Spry declared, 'What we have today is a large measure of concentrated control over more and more of this great national instrument of stations and cable systems – a one-way node for distributing information and influencing public opinion by business and commercial interests. They are a part of the Canadian community but a conflict of interest is inevitable between using revenues for Canadian programming and using them to increase profits and push up quotations on the stock market … In terms of Canadian purposes, strategy and Canadian reception of Canadian entertainment, education and information in the home, the trend seems to be irresistibly towards running down, disorganization, randomness, that is towards entropy.'[23]

Given such ample cause for despair, note that it was also Graham Spry who admonished, '"Nothing is here for tears, nothing to moan." What the situation now commands is an urgent and renewed sense of the prime and essential purposes … a fresh and wise use of imagination and, above all will, will, will, the determination to achieve these purposes.'[24]

NOTES

1 See Michael Nolan, *Foundations: Alan Plaunt and the Early Days of CBC Radio* (Montreal: CBC Enterprises, 1986).
2 From news release announcing the founding of the Canadian Radio League, quoted in Rose Potvin, *Passion and Conviction: The Letters of Graham Spry* (Regina: Canadian Plains Research Center, University of Regina, 1992), 72.
3 Graham Spry, 'A Case for Nationalized Broadcasting,' *Queen's Quarterly* (Winter 1931): 169.
4 Ibid., 151–69.
5 Presentation by the Canadian Radio League before Parliamentary Committee on Radio Broadcasting (18 April 1932), quoted in Potvin, *Passion and Conviction*, 81.
6 For instance, Frank Peers, *The Politics of Canadian Broadcasting 1920–1951* (Toronto: University of Toronto Press, 1969); E. Austin Weir, *The Struggle for National Broadcasting in Canada* (Toronto: McClelland and Stewart, 1965).
7 Potvin, *Passion and Conviction*, 2.
8 Alan Plaunt, *The Canadian Radio League: Objects, Information, National Support* (Ottawa, 1931); also Nolan, *Foundations*.
9 Bruce Steele, 'Radical Dreamer: The Passionate Journey of Graham Spry; Treatment for a Documentary Film,' privately circulated, n.d., 23.
10 Margaret Prang, 'The Origins of Public Broadcasting,' *Canadian Historical Review* 46, no. 1 (March 1965): 30.
11 Potvin, *Passion and Conviction*, 111.
12 Ibid., 118.
13 Graham Spry, 'One Nation, Two Cultures,' in *The Canadian Nation* (Ottawa: Association of Canadian Clubs, 1929), 14.
14 Ibid.
15 Graham Spry, 'Canada: Notes on Two Ideas of Nation in Confrontation,' *Journal of Contemporary History* (July 1971): 173.
16 Spry, 'One Nation, Two Cultures,' 18.
17 Spry, 'Canada: Notes,' 196.
18 Graham Spry, 'Culture and Entropy: A Lay View of Broadcasting,' in *Studies in Canadian Communications*, ed. Gertrude Joch Robinson and Donald F.

Theall (Montreal: McGill University Graduate Programme in Communications, 1974), 91.
19 Spry, 'Culture and Entropy,' 91.
20 Ibid.
21 Ibid., 91–2.
22 See Bruce Cummings, *War and Television* (London: Verso, 1992); also, Hamid Mowlana, George Gerbner, and Herbert I. Schiller, *The Triumph of the Image: The Media's War in the Persian Gulf* (Boulder, CO: Westview, 1992).
23 Spry, 'Culture and Entropy,' 96, 98.
24 Ibid., 90.

PART TWO

Communications History and Policy

Introduction to Part Two

ROBIN MANSELL*

The chapters in this section illustrate Robert Babe's insightful critiques of Canadian policymaking in the fields of media and telecommunication. Through his historical analyses, Babe's work demonstrates how the vested interests of industrialists and governments have been advantaged structurally, undermining the development of an autonomous and broadly public interest–oriented cultural industry in Canada.

Babe's work exemplifies what Dallas W. Smythe advocated as the proper subject of inquiry into the political economy of communication. Smythe suggested that research should reveal the strategies of those whose power is antithetical to human welfare – 'It seems to me from the standpoint of understanding where we are, we'd better find out how we got this way, and we'd then be better able to deal with where we are.'[1] Babe's insights into major changes in the communication industry in Canada and into the justifications for policy regimes and interventions go a long way towards achieving this aim.

It was at Simon Fraser University in the late 1970s that I met Robert Babe, who was on the faculty. As a PhD student I was very interested in his work, but it was not until much later that I understood how far he was willing to venture beyond the mainstream of the economics discipline. Before my arrival at Simon Fraser I had been trained as a social psychologist, and one of my central interests was in how power relations influence the way people communicate with each other. Initially, I pursued that interest at Simon Fraser under the supervision of a social psychologist, but I kept encountering economists in the department who were not like the neoclassicists whom I had encountered in the past.

* London School of Economics and Political Science

Bob Babe arrived at Simon Fraser at a time when William H. Melody, then head of department, and Smythe, the former head, were building up the strength of the department in the field of the political economy of communication. They were doing so from different vantage points: Smythe aiming to stem capitalist accumulation as far as possible and Melody seeking the reform of existing institutions in line with the public interest. Melody was concerned with the institutional structures of the telecommunications sector, and more generally the information and communication industry in Canada. It was as a result of discussions with Babe, Melody, and Smythe during the early years of my PhD that I came to realize that the same power relations that had interested me at the individual and social group levels were also very much at work at the level of institutions including firms, government policymaking bodies, and regulatory organizations.

Just as my own research was shifting into this rich area of study, I encountered Bob Babe. Here was another unusual economist – someone who challenged the idea that all aspects of technological innovation are profoundly new, such that history no longer matters, someone who argued against the inevitability of economic and social change in the interests of capital and was willing to take issue with policies informed by technological determinism, seeking empirical evidence of the specific and historically situated ways in which both the continuities and discontinuities of developments in the Canadian information and communication industry were influencing existing power relationships. I became an avid reader of Bob Babe's work. I have been invited to review several of his books over the years. In fact, I have actively sought out his published work to inform my own.

In 2002 to mark William H. Melody's retirement, I co-edited a volume entitled *Networking Knowledge for Information Societies: Institutions and Intervention*, to which Bob was a valued contributor. In his chapter he stated that 'efforts should be made to extricate as far a possible human activities and nature from commodity exchanges and the price system. This would be in explicit recognition that humans and all other species share a common future.'[2] This view prefigured much that has since been argued about the need for a shift to a commons-based sharing culture and economy, to an economy based on respect for all citizens and the environment, and to one that aligns the strategic interests of the most powerful actors in the interests of a sustainable future.

My thinking has been much influenced by Bob Babe's work over the years, especially as it is these values that I have sought to encourage through my own analyses of the institutionalized power relations that govern the strategic interests of the firms, governments, and other actors that are shaping the information and communication landscape today, albeit now on a global basis. The rest of this introduction sets out some of the key ideas that are recurring themes in Babe's work specifically in the telecommunication and information economy fields. It is a privilege to write this introduction to a selection of his works on the history of the communication industry in Canada because his work in this area is representative of political economy at its best.

My first encounter with Babe's work was with the appendix in this section, 'Vertical Integration and Productivity: Canadian Telecommunications,' published in 1981 in the *Journal of Economic Issues*. This is the journal of the U.S. Association for Evolutionary Economics, home to institutional economists working in the 'old' institutional tradition informed by Thorstein Veblen, John R. Commons, Wesley Mitchell, and many others. Here Babe provides a comparative analysis of the relative productivity gains between vertically integrated telecommunication carriers (Bell Canada and Northern Telecom) and carriers that were not integrated. Babe was working in a way that did not have the hallmarks of the neoclassical tradition – instead, he was offering a direct challenge to received wisdom. He found that the policy choice of letting Northern Telecom and a small number of other equipment manufacturers serve as Bell Canada's preferred suppliers had led to smaller gains in productivity than might otherwise have been achieved if procurement had taken place on the open market. He argued that institutional arrangements can 'entail significant social costs in terms of forgone productivity gains.'

It is well known that productivity measures can be interpreted in different ways. For instance, other factors such as the fact that the two classes of carriers might have been operating at different economies of scale or that they might have had different age structures of equipment might have explained the differences in productivity gains. In this case, the Restrictive Trade Practices Commission report on this issue found that 'the evidence of this inquiry does not establish that, on balance, the separation of Bell and Northern would improve performance in the telecommunication equipment industry or in the delivery of telecommunication services by Bell and other carriers.'[3] The Commission's overriding concern, however, was to ensure that Northern Telecom would not fail, as it was argued that this would create high risks for employees, investors, customers, and the country. Canada's 'high-tech' industrial strategy was in full swing. What distinguished Babe's work was not only his particular reading of the data, but his willingness to broach the subject of power relations at work in the economic structures that were being fostered and to show who was being disadvantaged.

In the four other works in this section, Babe addresses themes that he illustrates through his historical analysis of the institutional features of the Canadian 'consciousness industry.'[4] He calls for a demythologizing of technology to understand the implications of this industry for society and for reassessments of policy rhetoric through critiques of terms like *convergence* and *information society*. He argues that these need to be understood as embodying power relations. He offers us detailed analyses of the dynamics through which policymakers have often sought to protect the interests of the private sector and to defend the interests of incumbents.

The works included here were written before the full force of 'globalization' began to permeate policy circles. Castells suggests that informational strategies are 'the new, and most effective, frontier for the exercise of power on the world stage.'[5] The great value of Babe's historical analysis is to call into question just how 'new' many of today's strategies really are.

In his paper 'Control of Telephones: The Canadian Experience,' Babe refers to Serafini and Andrieu's 1981 report, *The Information Revolution and Its Implications for Canada*. This was used to galvanize shifts in Canadian industrial policy aimed at championing Canadian innovative prowess across a range of information and communication technologies as a means of stimulating international competitiveness. Babe recounts the knock-on impact of the celebration of technological innovation on the Canadian domestic telecommunication industry. The privileging of industrial policy coincided with the liberalization of this industry. This occurred in a context in which the OECD member states were debating how their former monopolists should adjust to the introduction of competition. Historically, with their monopoly status preserved, carriers such as Bell Canada, like its U.S. counterpart AT&T, had been able to charge high rates (or tariffs) for long distance communication to 'subsidize' local calls that were billed on a flat rate. The former monopolists also resisted competitive entry by refusing to interconnect with new entrant carriers on an equitable basis. Smelling competition in the air, the incumbent carriers 'rebalanced' their rates – raising prices for local calls and reducing them for long distance. This gave rise to public policy concerns about access for the poor and those in rural areas who would see substantial rises in the costs of their calls. Although this rebalancing of rates took some time and was the subject of numerous regulatory hearings, ultimately it was accomplished. In a period in which liberalization was gaining popularity (as witnessed by the inclusion of telecommunications within the remit of the General Agreement on Trade in Services in 1997), the relative autonomy of the Canadian telecommunication industry was diminished.[6] Babe shows how, in fact, from the 1880s onwards, corporate and regulatory practice combined to disadvantage smaller independent telecommunication operators in Canada as well as new entrants, and this continued through the liberalization era of the 1980s and 1990s. He documents the reluctance of large incumbents to share their long distance revenues fairly with carriers with whom they interconnected and how they persisted in regarding new technology as a threat, whether the new technology was coaxial cable or a domestic satellite.

It is frequently asserted that 'the way we got this way' is attributable to rapid technological change – digitalization – which in turn is said to lead inevitably to technological convergence (disrupting market structures and leaving little if any space for governments to manoeuvre when it comes to retaining domestic control over the communication industry, including its content or entertainment output). This myth is dispelled by Babe's chapter on the 'Information Revolution' (1990) and in his 1996 paper on 'Convergence and Divergence: Technologies, Old and New.' In the former, we are invited to consider a wide-ranging critique of essentialist and technology deterministic arguments. Babe reveals the rationales for some of the myths about the information society, showing that policy discussions take place far too frequently in an idealized world without regard to 'the real world of power struggle and powerplay.' Here, Babe may have again been influenced by Smythe, who argued that technology should be understood in the following way: 'One part is bureaucracy (in both the private and public sector) ... The second part is science which is being taken over increasingly by the third part, capital. The fourth part is tools and machines created by engineers. The fifth part is ideology which provides the raw materials with which the sixth part, propaganda, seeks to mould public opinion to accept the myth.'[7]

Resisting the myth of technological solutions to social and economic problems, Babe challenged the views of Alvin Toffler, Daniel Bell, and others who had suggested that the trajectory of innovation in information and communication technologies ultimately might produce a powerful and beneficial synthesis of 'man and machine.' This might occur in a marketplace where human beings would no longer be able to exercise control over these developments. Instead, market liberalization, light touch regulation, and often 'no touch' regulation would become an increasingly familiar refrain for the communication industry in Canada as elsewhere.[8] Following Jacques Ellul, rather than being 'out of control,' Babe highlights how neatly the rhetoric of technological inevitability supported the consciousness industry's interest in bolstering its profits through the commodity sale of information and entertainment products. This is the kind of analysis that succeeds in demythologizing technology.

Similarly in 'Convergence and Divergence' (1998) Babe considers why we should not understand technological convergence as inevitable. He interrogates this view about inevitability through a discussion of the technical, functional, corporate, and legislative/regulatory implications of the 'information highway' metaphor. Through his historical account, Babe shows that industry structure has not been preordained; instead, different structures were the negotiated outcomes of political and economic interests, whether in telecommunications, publishing, or broadcasting. Driven by interests in profits, there have been arguments about whether various sub-markets of the consciousness industry have been overly concentrated through the decades. The tale told here is not one of technological inevitability. It is one that acknowledges that there were possibilities to choose other policies that might have provided the kinds of cultural screens that Smythe envisaged; that is, those 'aspects of a national culture or ideological system which serve to protect its cultural realism against disruptive intrusion [from the U.S. neighbour to the south].'[9]

The 1981 Serafini and Andrieu report on the information revolution, referred to above, gave rise to a report by the Science Council of Canada, titled *Planning Now for an Information Society: Tomorrow Is Too Late*.[10] It concluded that 'we live in what has come to be known as an "information economy,"' and referred to a crisis created by technical change in the form of convergent technologies. It called on government and the private sector to invest in order to ensure Canadian leadership in semiconductors and software, without which Northern Telecom's then-president, Walter Light, claimed Canada would have a peripheral existence. Linked to this technology-driven strategy was an equally forceful message for the content side of the consciousness industry. It would flourish best if a 'free marketplace of ideas' could be fostered.

This meant freeing markets from regulatory restraint as much as possible – except where an incumbent's status needed to be protected.

William Melody, Babe's contemporary at Simon Fraser University, had clearly demonstrated the bankruptcy of the idea of a 'free market' in ideas. Babe shows in his work how regulatory interventions kept the cable and telecommunication industries separate, despite all the talk of convergence. By the mid-1990s technology was said to be driving the market and the Canadian government was championing the new 'electronic marketplaces and virtual communities.' As Babe wrote, 'In fact, "convergence" is by and large a code word for the deregulation of capital flows in media industries.' Of course policymakers did not reveal that it was mainly the transnational corporations that were driving the extension of the reach of commodified information, albeit not for sale in 'free markets.'

Babe's work witnesses what in hindsight we can see as a continuous corrosion of the space for broad public interest considerations by policymakers. That corrosion promoted the interests of incumbent private sector actors in Canada, and later, a more extensive set of increasingly global economic interests in all aspects of the information and communication technology and content sectors.

Could it have been otherwise? Undoubtedly, at various historical junctures different pathways could have been followed. The paper on 'Media Technology and the Great Transformation of Canadian Cultural Policy' (1998) is Babe at his best in terms of the range of intellectual resources he brings to bear on the problem of Canadian cultural autonomy. Here he explains 'how we came to be as we are' in terms of the overtaking of a public commitment to a distinctively Canadian pursuit of cultural developments by an attraction to 'the universal beneficence of profits' (drawing on Karl Polanyi's account of economic transformation). Babe argues there was a shift from a policy commitment to the intrinsic value of cultural outputs, to an increasingly strong support for their commodity value. He seems to imply that there was a halcyon time of a commitment to culture when Canadian cultural production resided beyond capitalist forces. It is perhaps more appropriate to suggest, following Garnham (1990),[11] that while all cultural production is 'determined' under capitalism, determinations should be understood to refer to a set of limits that make some outcomes more likely than others. These outcomes are, however, not uncontested or unchanging. This suggests that we need to ask not only whether it could have been otherwise, but also what scope there is today for creating incentives through policy intervention for new outcomes that value citizens and their interests rather than, predominantly, those of the large corporate players.

As Babe highlights in his work, the Canadian government drafted the private sector into the project of developing Canada's cultural industries by licensing private radio stations and, later, by seeking competition for CBC television. He demonstrates how by the 1950s it was being acknowledged that there was an economic cost involved in efforts to shift the cultural 'terms of trade' from their 'natural' north-south axis, towards a 'north of the 49th parallel' east-west axis. However, although this policy was couched in public service, nationalist and cultural policy language, it also can be argued that this was merely tinkering with economic incentives. In 1968, when a new regulator, the Canadian Radio-television and Telecommunications Commission, was set up, it exhibited signs of understanding that market intervention was needed to promote the east-west axis of cultural production, but this policy gave way by the 1980s, as Babe shows, to a policy of 'technological nationalism.' Melody challenged the Canadian government's policy in this area over its domestic satellite initiative, calling them the 'tinker toys' of an industry agenda that was, in the main, dedicated to profit making rather than to finding ways to foster Canadian content production.[12]

As Babe recounts, the then–Department of Communications view was that technological prowess was essential, whether satellites, teletext systems, or other digital technologies were the subjects of its consideration. The emphasis then shifted from a concern about symbolic content to a much stronger focus on access to the infrastructure of communication. Whether it was described as a 'technological imperative' or as an 'information revolution,' Canada joined the bandwagon of the great transformation towards the digital and in so doing created a basis for a new rhetoric that was partly couched in terms of technological neutrality and partly in terms of promoting the diversity of content distribution outlets. Now competition was expected to stimulate the strong gales of innovation.

In Canada, historically, there has been neither a strong political will to implement policy in line with a public interest that favoured the citizen, nor a propensity towards public investment that might have preserved the institutions of cultural production in a way that could have mitigated counter-flows encouraging the north-south axis of the cultural industry. However, towards the end of the first decade of the twenty-first century, there is an anti-globalization counter-flow that is appearing in some of the newer spaces for cultural production enabled by the Internet. Although it is difficult to discern how the new social movements can be associated with a distinctively Canadian project of resistance to the rhetoric and the material reality of the dominant structural incentives for Canadian content production, there are perhaps grounds for renewed attention to 'dealing with where we are' today.

In this respect, Babe's insights from the 1980s and 1990s are applicable today. The rhetoric has moved on, but cultural policy in Canada and elsewhere is being driven by the juggernaut of technological inevitability that his work calls so clearly to account. If today we are informed that Canada's and other nations' economic prosperity hinges on its leadership within a global knowledge-based economy, issues of incumbency, economic interest, regulatory intervention, and the potential for domestic cultural developments that respect values beyond those of the market remain in play. Historical analysis of market, institutional, and cultural dynamics remains essential to understanding the limits of capitalist determinations and the opportunities for creative, distinctive outcomes in the consciousness industry in Canada.

NOTES

1 Quoted in J.A. Lent, ed., *A Different Road Taken* (Boulder, CO: Westview, 1995), 42.

2 Quoted in R. Babe, 'The "Information Economy," Economics and Ecology,' in *Networking Knowledge for Information Societies: Institutions & Intervention*, ed. R. Mansell, R. Samarajiva, and A. Mahan (Delft: DUP Science, Delft University Press, 2002), 259.

3 Restrictive Trade Practices Commission, *Telecommunications in Canada: Part III: The Impact of Vertical Integration on the Equipment Industry* (Ottawa: Department of Consumer and Corporate Affairs, Supply and Services, 1983).

4 Or the 'cultural industry.' Babe uses Smythe's (1981) terminology in some of his work. Earlier use of the term *consciousness industry* was by H.M. Enzensberger in an article in 1970, and in his *The Consciousness Industry* (New York: Seabury, 1974); and Stuart Ewen in his *Captains of Consciousness* (New York: McGraw Hill, 1976).

5 M. Castells, *The Internet Galaxy: Reflections on Internet, Business and Society* (Oxford: Oxford University Press, 2001), 161.

6 For further historical context, both critical and mainstream, see R. Mansell,

Telecommunication Network-Based Services: Policy Implications, OECD/ICCP report no. 18 (Paris: OECD, 1987); N. Garnham and R. Mansell, *Universal Service and Rate Restructuring in Telecommunications*, OECD/ICCP report no. 23 (Paris: OECD, 1991); W.H. Melody (with H.M. Trebing), 'An Evaluation of Pricing Practices and Policies in Domestic Communications,' *President's Task Force on Communications Policy* (Springfield, VA: Federal Clearing House, 1969); W.H. Melody, R. Mansell, and A. Oliver, 'Telecommunications in Nova Scotia: A Cost of Service Study for Maritime Telegraph and Telephone Co., Final Report,' prepared for the Nova Scotia Board of Public Utilities, July 1983.

7 D.W. Smythe, 'New Directions for Critical Communications Research,' *Media, Culture and Society* 6 (1984): 2.

8 During this period, Babe was not alone in contesting these arguments. See W.H. Melody, 'Technological, Economic and Institutional Aspects of Computer/Telecommunications Systems,' in *Applications of Computer/Telecommunications Systems*, ed. OECD (Paris: OECD 1975).

9 D.W. Smythe, *Dependency Road: Communications, Capitalism, Consciousness and Canada* (Norwood, NJ: Ablex, 1981), 232.

10 Science Council of Canada, *Planning Now for an Information Society: Tomorrow Is Too Late* (Ottawa: Ministry of Supply and Services, 1982), 11.

11 Nicholas Garnham, *Capitalism and Communication* (London: Sage, 1990).

12 See also R. Mansell, 'Is Policy Research an Irrelevant Exercise? The Case of Canadian DBS Planning,' *Journal of Communication* 35 no. 2 (1985): 154–66.

5 Media Technology and the Great Transformation of Canadian Cultural Policy

At work in the Canadian mind is, in fact, a great and dynamic polarity between technology and culture, between economy and landscape.
– Arthur Kroker, *Technology and the Canadian Mind* (1984)

In a deservedly famous work, economic historian Karl Polanyi depicted the passing of feudalism and the rise of capitalism as comprising three basic transformations: Nature, in becoming commodified, was transformed into 'land,' a mere factor of production; human beings in being commodified were transformed into 'labour,' also merely a factor of production; and finally social inheritance became the commodity 'capital.'[1] The price system, in other words, penetrated not only allocations of final outputs, but as well social processes of production.

For Polanyi these transformations, while fundamental, were not unmitigated blessings. Indeed, he lamented, in coming to rely almost exclusively on prices and profits as indicators of social conditions, the trading classes lost thereby all means of sensing 'the dangers involved in the exploitation of the physical strength of the worker, the destruction of family life, the devastation of neighborhoods, the denudation of forests, the pollution of rivers, the deterioration of craft standards, the disruption of folkways, and the general degradation of existence including housing and arts, as well as the innumerable forms of private and public life that do not affect profits.' Nonetheless, Polanyi observed, 'the middle classes fulfilled their function by developing an all but sacramental belief in the universal beneficence of profits.'[2]

And there, of course, we stand today. In our economic/political system, markets have indeed become *the* 'organizing principle of society,' and many aspects of social, cultural, and economic life now conform to market logic and to market values.[3] Jerome Davis is one who has set forth aspects of pecuniary cultures conforming to the logic and values of markets. Some of the central cultural values promoted in and required by the market system, according to Davis, are:

- *Acquisitiveness.* In market-centred economies it is deemed desirable that individuals are able to acquire and hold as much property as they can. Restrictions on acquisitive behaviour, therefore, are to be as slight as possible. Selfishness and greed are virtues; altruism and empathy, while not necessarily vices, are at best second-order virtues, ones not to be promoted extensively.
- *Individualism.* For Adam Smith, the wealth of a nation was simply the aggregation of the wealth of the individual inhabitants. Whatever effectively promoted individual wealth, Smith believed, promoted also wealth for all. And, Smith continued, since each individual knows best his or her own unique circumstances, including personal wants, needs, and skills, national wealth is most effectively pursued by minimizing constraints on individual enterprise. Collectivities, associations, and cooperative action therefore, according to the logic and values of the marketplace, are evils, and consequently are afforded epithets such as *monopoly, monopsony,* and *collusion,* names whose negative connotations may indeed, unfortunately, be apt on account of the ethics of acquisitiveness and greed characterizing our economic and cultural order. In a non-capitalist gift economy, words such as *cooperation* and *joint effort* might be more suitable.
- *Competition and laissez-faire.* Competition, according to marketplace ideology, is the agent transforming acquisitive behaviour and the greed 'instinct' of individuals into the broader social good. Competition, when effective, means that no producer or buyer has significant market power, that no one is able therefore to exploit customers or suppliers (including 'labour'), and that each producer will be responsive to market demand. Davis quotes *Nation's Business,* official organ for the United States Chamber of Commerce, as follows: 'Our rulers will best promote the improvement of the nation ... by leaving capital to find its most lucrative course, commodities their fair price, industry and intelligence their natural reward, idleness and folly their natural punishment.'[4] How current this statement does seem!

- *Profit.* Profit motivation, according to Davis, 'is undoubtedly the most important of all the norms of capitalism.' Indeed, 'the fundamental assumption upon which [the] capitalist system has been established, and which alone can justify its existence, is the belief that every man, being free to seek his personal gain in competition with his fellow men, will profit only inasmuch as he is able to serve others efficiently and effectively.'[5] Profit in pecuniary economies is the single most important signifier of what is good, what is true, and what is beautiful. Large profit rates signal not only a job well done, but point also to areas deserving expansion in the future.
- *Materialism.* As Davis notes, 'no system could be more materialist than capitalism itself … *Social* ends and values are not important or are given mere lip service … Possession and consumption of things are the real goods. Liberty, freedom, equality, and other non tangible values [such as justice, equality, a healthy environment, community, and, in the case of Canada, Canadian nationhood] are thought [at best] to be by-products in that struggle.'[6]

The Great Transformation of Canadian Cultural Policy

Upon inception in 1867, Canada was already essentially a capitalist or market-oriented state, albeit one concentrating on resource extraction – principally fish, fur, timber, agriculture – and on commercial transactions. Therefore its manufacturing sector was underdeveloped and its infrastructure of transportation and communication was built primarily to support the export of 'staples.' As Innis put it, 'The economic history of Canada has been dominated by the discrepancy between the centre and the margin of western civilization.'[7]

Canada, then, did not experience the dramatic transformations in factors of production set forth by Polanyi as typifying the emergence of capitalist economies from feudalism. Nonetheless, it is argued here, Canada underwent, and continues to undergo, an analogous transformation in the field of *cultural policy.* Cultural activities and artefacts, previously deemed to have either an *intrinsic* worth (that is, an inherent beauty, goodness, or truth) or a value deriving from contributions made in pursuing communal, collective, non-market/anti-market goals, are increasingly judged, financed, and undertaken on the basis of market criteria, like those set out by Davis. This great *transformation in Canadian cultural policy* is the overarching theme of the present chapter.

Given the writings of Karl Polanyi, Jerome Davis, Harold Innis, and others, one would expect a priori that nations like Canada with market economies would as a matter of course pursue cultural policies conforming to the logic, functioning, values, and norms of the Market. In market economies, commodified cultural artefacts, after all, command prices and so contribute to GNP – that is, to the 'wealth of the nation' – at least according to Market ideology. Public policy in the cultural sphere, therefore, one would expect, would most likely be designed to eliminate all or most obstacles to the commodification of culture and be supportive of 'cultural industries.' Indeed, current manifestations of this expectation include bilateral and multilateral trade treaties that entail the 'free flow' and heightened commodity status of information.[8] Furthermore, one would expect that non-market or anti-market cultural artefacts (which in Canada often comprise the truly indigenous cultural artefacts) would increasingly be viewed, in a sea of commercial culture, as anomalies, if not indeed as being alien and subversive – that pressures (monetary, political, moral) would arise to remove or reduce them, if not entirely, then at least from the mainstream media. As this filtering proceeds, public 'taste' will in turn tend to become even more attuned to the form and content of cultural artefacts in the commodity mode, and people will accordingly tend increasingly to reject even more strongly cultural items and activities not conforming to market norms.

Historically, however, the expectations regarding cultural policy for capitalist economies have not been entirely fulfilled in Canada. From 1928, the year the Aird Royal Commission was appointed to report on broadcasting, until even the present, there has in fact been an explicit stream of cultural policy, possessing a substantial measure of public support, that has been designed to *oppose* market forces and the concomitant drift toward continental cultural integration.

Recent decades, however, have seen a withering of public resolve in this regard, and hence there has been a continuing and accelerating transformation of Canadian cultural policy – from one designed to preserve and foster nationhood, into one congruent with and supportive of the commodity mode. Cultural policy, in other words, increasingly is being set to be in conformity with the logic and the cultural values of markets, including the principle of continental or indeed worldwide cultural/economic/political integration.

This 'great transformation' of cultural policy has necessarily carried with it changes in attitudes, rhetoric, and policy stances toward media (or more generally, toward 'technology' as the means of culture).

In what follows, primary attention is accorded broadcasting, although parallels with film policy are noted briefly.

The First Stage: Cultural Policy as Anti-Market

Initial Non-intervention

Prior to 1928 the Canadian government was essentially passive with respect to radio broadcasting. While provisions for issuing radio telegraph licences to private commercial stations were in place as early as 1922, the federal government remained otherwise largely aloof.[9] Its passivity is illustrated particularly by its non-intervention in fundamental industry restructurings taking place in 1923.[10] The non-intervention years 1920 to 1928 were characterized also by the dominance of unregulated market forces in broadcasting. Canadian station owners displayed little originality, concentrated on recorded music and popular American programs, some even affiliating with U.S. networks, the noteworthy exception being a radio service provided by Canadian National Railways, a Crown corporation, which provided an original, albeit limited service as a competitive ploy to lure rail passengers from its arch rival Canadian Pacific. Other features of this essentially unregulated era included interference from stations broadcasting from the United States and Mexico, and a dearth of facilities serving less populated regions.[11]

'The State or the United States'

It was against this background that the government in 1928 appointed the first royal commission, headed by Bank of Commerce President Sir John Aird, to examine 'the broadcasting situation in the Dominion of Canada and to make recommendations to the Government as to the future administration, management, control and financing thereof.'[12] The Aird Commission, reporting in September 1929, declared, 'We have heard the present radio situation discussed from many angles with considerable diversity of opinion. There has, however, been unanimity on one fundamental question – Canadian radio listeners want Canadian broadcasting' – a service, however, unlikely to be provided in abundance, the Commission adduced, under private enterprise with advertiser funding. Consequently, Aird adjudged that the interests of Canadian listeners and the Canadian nation alike would be better served by introducing 'some form of public ownership, operation and control behind which is the national power and prestige of the whole public of the Dominion of Canada.'[13] 'In short,' as Frank Peers concluded, 'the commission recommended a publicly owned system with no private stations, and programs which should have only a limited commercial content in the form of "indirect advertising."'[14]

Stated otherwise, the Aird Commission recommended that attempts should be made to deploy the technology of radio broadcasting in the manner of a 'time-binding' (or culture-preserving) medium of communication;[15] radio should be used purposefully to contravene market ('space-binding') forces that were then threatening Canadian political and cultural sovereignty. Aird's position was expressed not only in the report's concrete policy recommendations, but as well by various phrases sprinkled throughout, such as: 'education in the broad sense,' 'public service,' 'fostering a national spirit and interpreting national citizenship,' 'promoting national unity,' 'mould the minds of the young people to ideals and opinions that are ... Canadian.'[16]

Significantly, the Aird Commission recognized that pursuing time-binding or culture-conserving goals by means of essentially space-binding media would require consciously modifying market forces, particularly with regard to the proliferation of facilities. Indeed, Aird recommended closing down transmitters not needed by the public broadcaster.

The Aird Commission's anti-market, pro-culture position was adopted subsequently by the influential Canadian Radio League, a volunteer organization formed to lobby for general implementation of Aird's recommendations. Appearing before the 1932 parliamentary committee charged with studying the Aird report and making recommendations, Graham Spry delivered his famous dictum, 'The State or the United States,' to highlight the fact that in broadcasting free markets lead inexorably to continental cultural homogenization. Spry asked,

Why are the American interests so interested in the Canadian situation? The reason is clear. In the first place, the American chains have regarded Canada as part of their field and consider Canada as in a state of radio tutelage, without talent, resources or capacity to establish a third chain on this continent ... In the second place, if such a Canadian non-commercial chain were constructed, it would seriously weaken the whole advertising basis of American broadcasting. The question before this Committee is whether Canada is to establish a chain that is owned and operated and controlled by Canadians, or whether it is to be owned and operated by commercial organizations, associated or controlled by American interests. *The question is, the State or the United States.*[17]

The Public Service Era

Promoting a bill in Parliament in May 1932, the very depths of the Depression, to establish a public broadcasting agency, Prime Minister R.B. Bennett declared,

> First of all, this country must be assured of complete control of broadcasting from Canadian sources, free from foreign interference or influence. Without such control radio broadcasting can never become a great agency for the communication of matters of national concern and for the diffusion of national thought and ideas, and without such control it can never be the agency by which national consciousness may be featured and sustained and national unity still further strengthened ...
>
> Secondly, no other scheme than that of public ownership can ensure to the people of this country, without regard to class or place, equal enjoyment of the benefits and pleasures of radio broadcasting. Private ownership must necessarily discriminate between densely and sparsely populated areas. This is not a correctable fault in private ownership, it is an inescapable and inherent demerit of that system. It does not seem right that in Canada the towns should be preferred to the countryside or the prosperous communities to those less fortunate.[18]

As noted subsequently by the 1957 Royal Commission on Broadcasting, these remarks of the prime minister 'were endorsed by the Opposition and the leader of the third party represented on the Parliamentary Committee. Parliament, with only one dissenting voice, accepted the recommendations of the Committee and the Canadian Radio Broadcasting Commission [CRBC] ... was created by Act of Parliament.'[19]

One significant way in which the legislation departed from the recommendations of the Aird Commission, however, was in the preservation of private stations, albeit subject to the understanding that they could be taken over at some later date. In the interim, they were to be regulated by the CRBC.[20]

In 1936 the CRBC was replaced by the Canadian Broadcasting Corporation (CBC), a Crown corporation intended to be more independent of government. Despite overt and covert politicking by private sector interests, however, the CBC remained pre-eminent in Canadian broadcasting for over twenty years, a status reaffirmed by successive parliamentary committees and as well by the 1951 Massey Royal Commission on National Development in the Arts, Letters, and Sciences.[21] Note, for instance, the following ringing endorsement by the 1942 House of Commons Special Committee on Radio Broadcasting: 'The principle laid down by previous parliamentary committees that the Corporation should extend its services so as to give a complete national coverage, if necessary by taking over privately-owned stations, should be followed and the Corporation should take over any privately-owned broadcasting stations considered essential for national coverage. The private broadcasting stations have no vested interest in the sound waves they are allowed to use. The Government should not hesitate to terminate any licence when it is in the public interest to do so.'[22]

Turning Point

A turning point of immense importance occurred in 1957 with publication of the report of a second Royal Commission on Broadcasting (Fowler Commission). On the one hand, the Commission reiterated the nationalist, cultural, public service, anti-market goals that had been associated with Canadian broadcasting since the Aird Commission. It stated, for instance, 'The *natural*[23] flow of trade, travel and ideas runs North and South. We have tried to make some part, not all, of the flow run East and West. We have only done so at an added cost, borne nationally. There is no doubt that we could have had cheaper railway transportation, cheaper air service and cheaper consumer goods if we had simply tied ourselves into the American transportation and economic system. It is equally clear that we could have cheaper radio and television service if Canadian stations became outlets of American networks. However, if the less costly method is always chosen, is it possible to have a Canadian nation at all?'[24]

One could hardly ask for a clearer, more concise statement of the inherent opposition between indigenous control and market economics, between non-market goals and economic efficiency, between government intervention and laissez-faire. Clearly in this extract the Fowler Royal Commission expounded the anti-market philosophy articulated by the Aird Commission, the Canadian Radio League, R.B. Bennett, and other nationalist, pro-culture forces. In stating that countries should not always choose the cheapest option, Fowler stood firmly against economic orthodoxy's doctrine of 'comparative advantage,' which maintains that all countries benefit by forbearing to produce items that can be produced relatively more cheaply elsewhere, instead concentrating on producing items for international trade that can be produced relatively more cheaply at home, a doctrine that over the years has proven to be of immense value to the stronger of the trading partners.[25]

On the other hand, and this of course is the main point, the Fowler Commission departed markedly from the philosophy enunciated by Aird and from its own just-quoted endorsement of Aird's philosophy by declaring that 'private broadcasters are integral parts of a single system' of broadcasting, and in recommending that 'the presence of private elements in Canadian radio and television should be continued and accepted as a permanent part of the Canadian pattern.'[26]

Parallels with Movies

Parallel to broadcasting is the history of motion pictures in Canada. From 1896 to 1939 market forces totally dominated,[27] until creation by the federal government of the National Film Board as an instrument of cultural policy to help oppose market forces.[28] Moreover, attempts were made, beginning particularly in 1968 with creation of the Canadian Film Development Corporation,[29] to enlist private enterprise to pursue cultural and nationalist goals, goals that are fundamentally antithetical to the logic of markets.[30]

The Second Stage: A Faustian Bargain

Enlisting Private Enterprise

The federal government acted quickly upon receiving the 1957 *Report of the Royal Commission*. First, it authorized creation of a second television service (CTV) to be made up entirely of private stations to compete with the CBC. Next, it created a Board of Broadcast Governors (BBG), independent of the CBC, to regulate activities of both public and private sector stations and networks. In this way private elements of Canadian broadcasting were apportioned a status commensurate with that hitherto reserved for the public sector.

Perhaps believing that pursuit of anti-market, pro-cultural goals depended less on ownership patterns (public versus private) than upon free versus constrained market forces, the government charged the BBG with regulating both public and private broadcasting in a manner that would ensure that both sectors contributed to Canadian cultural, anti-market goals. Pursuant to that mandate, the BBG soon promulgated the first Canadian content quotas for television: 55 per cent of the air time, the Board decreed, was to be filled with programs 'basically Canadian in content and character.' Programs deemed by the Board to be in compliance with that rule, however, included broadcasts of events occurring outside the country in which Canadians participated, and events that were 'of general interest to Canadians.'[31]

Enshrouding the private sector with the mantle of public purpose meant that private stations, no longer deemed an alien force, now and henceforth needed to be protected by government from the strains of the marketplace in order for them to be better positioned to pursue the noble anti-market goals with which they had been entrusted. The BBG, as noted by John Beke, was not negligent in affording such protection.[32]

Reporting in 1965, however, the Committee on Broadcasting, headed by Robert Fowler (who had chaired also the 1957 Royal Commission on Broadcasting), was quite critical of the performance of both private television broadcasters and the BBG. The Committee noted, for example, that the advent of private television stations in areas served previously only by the CBC, had caused a *decrease* in the audience to Canadian programming: private stations had concentrated on diffusing U.S. programs in their prime time hours. According to Fowler, about two-thirds of the programming on private stations in prime time was American, compared to 39 per cent on the CBC. Nor did private stations, according to Fowler, widen the scope of programs available to Canadian viewers; rather, they 'merely increased the broadcasting of popular entertainment, mainly American in origin.' Fowler added that 'although the volume of available programs increased, there was little if any increase in more serious programs directed towards limited audiences.'[33]

Fowler, however, assigned blame for inadequacies in performance not so much to private sector stations that were, after all, only pursuing profits within constraints established by the regulator, the BBG. Fowler viewed the BBG as being quite inadequate as a regulator, and this for a number of reasons. One was that it had not vigorously enforced its own Canadian content regulations. According to the Committee, 'Only recently has the BBG taken enforcement action; four stations were prosecuted and each was fined the ridiculous amount of twenty-five dollars.' Fowler continued, 'No licence has been suspended for non-compliance with the Canadian content regulations.'[34] Indeed, the content quotas had been continuously suspended by the Board. In addition, according to the Commission, the BBG's content regulations were full of loopholes: the Committee commented wryly that 'compliance with the Canadian content regulations should clearly not depend, for example, on the number of foreign state funerals or major sporting events that happen to fall within a particular period.'[35]

More generally, the Fowler Committee concluded that time-based content quotas were quite impractical: 'A half-hour program of excellent quality may cost far more than several hours of quiz-shows and the like, and will undoubtedly be worth more in this context, but will still only be chalked up as half an hour of Canadian content. We believe that, taking all these factors into account, enforcement of Canadian content by universally applicable regulations is impractical.'[36]

The federal government evidently accepted Fowler's declaration that deficiencies in the conduct and performance of the Canadian broadcasting system were attributable ultimately to inadequacies of the BBG as a regulator, rather than to entrusting private enterprise to accomplish non-market, indeed anti-market ends. The BBG, therefore, was to be sacrificed on the altar of Canadian nationalism, and replaced by a more powerful agency, the Canadian Radio-Television Commission (CRTC). Furthermore, the government concluded, it was advisable that the new regulator receive more explicit and detailed guidance as to its purposes, namely supervising Canadian broadcasting to achieve cultural, anti-market goals.

Broadcasting, then, immensely lucrative at least in potential, already having been penetrated, particularly beginning in 1958, by profit-oriented, private enterprises, meant that the government, a decade later, was loath to try to ease private stations out of a field still cloaked with cultural, anti-market purposes and rhetoric. As the government's 1966 *White Paper on Broadcasting* confirmed, 'Any statement of policy related to broadcasting in Canada therefore starkly poses this question. How can the people of Canada retain a degree of collective control over the new techniques of electronic communication that will be sufficient to preserve and strengthen the political, social, and economic fabric of Canada, which remains the most important objective of public policy? ... Broadcasting may well be regarded as the central nervous system of Canadian nationhood.'[37]

Legislation creating the Canadian Radio-Television Commission was enacted in 1968.

The Canadian Radio-Television Commission

The Broadcasting Act of 1968 went much further than had the predecessor act in entrenching private broadcasting. According to the new legislation, 'Broadcasting undertakings in Canada make use of radio frequencies that are public property and such undertakings constitute a *single system*, herein referred to as the Canadian broadcasting system, *comprising public and private elements.*'

While the new act still proclaimed a special role and importance for the CBC, nonetheless henceforth broadcasting (echoing a recommendation of the 1957 Royal Commission) was to be viewed as *'a single system comprising public and private elements.'* Furthermore, *both* elements of the system were to contribute to pro-cultural, anti-market goals.

To cajole, persuade, require, force, or otherwise induce private stations to adhere to the spirit of the new act, the CRTC was empowered to license new stations, to renew, suspend, or revoke licences, to attach conditions to licences, to enact and enforce regulations, and to hold public hearings.[38] By the act, private broadcasters were again affirmed in their status as chosen instruments. Hence the CRTC, like the BBG before it, concluded that private stations needed protection from the strains and tensions of competition, whether domestic or foreign, in order that they might better pursue the anti-market charge that had been set for them.

Chosen instrument status for private broadcasting, it is now to be emphasized, foreshadowed the present-day ideology of *technological nationalism*[39] insofar as there ensued a conscious government policy of encouraging the extension of private broadcasting facilities throughout the country. After all, chosen instruments, at least in theory, should not be confined to the major 'markets'!

However, the time was not yet ripe (which is to say that pro-market ideology had not yet totally supplanted pro-cultural, anti-market sentiments) to allow a full-blown ideology of technological nationalism (discussed below) to replace the rhetoric of cultural nationalism, cable television being a particularly poignant case in point.

The Blight of Cable

For the period 1968–76 particularly, and continuing until about 1980, the CRTC assumed a jaundiced view of cable TV. For the Commission in these early years, cable was at best a blight upon broadcasting. In a major 1969 policy statement, the Commission fretted that unencumbered cable growth and the concomitant increase in penetration into Canada by American signals 'posed the most serious threat to Canadian broadcasting since 1932 before Parliament decided to vote the first *Broadcasting Act*.' In the Commission's opinion, cable growth 'could disrupt the Canadian broadcasting system within a few years.'[40] Consequently the CRTC tried to promulgate a set of highly restrictive policies toward cable television.[41] Whatever else the Commission's declarations, policy proposals, and initiatives may have meant, they certainly did not presage that cable television had been enfolded by the CRTC within the doctrine of *technological nationalism*. That fundamental shift in ideology or rhetoric, as far as the CRTC was concerned, awaited publication of the Therrien Report, discussed below, in 1980.

Nonetheless, right from the beginning, the CRTC seemed to recognize that something was amiss. In the 1969 policy statement in which it set forth some of its most restrictive cable policies, the Commission mentioned certain misgivings it had with regard to the fairness and logical consistency of its policies. It is worth quoting the CRTC on this: 'The Commission feels strongly that no part of the Canadian population should be penalized in order to preserve or to protect vested interests: either financial interests of investors in private broadcasting or privileges accumulated by particular groups in public broadcasting. The Canadian broadcasting system is worth safeguarding only if it provides the Canadian population with essential services which could not be provided otherwise. It would not make sense to protect a Canadian system based essentially on the retailing of programs "using predominantly non-Canadian creative and other resources."'[42]

Performance of the Private Sector as Chosen Instrument

Television broadcasting profits during the 1970s soared, but culturally the performance of the private sector was weak. The CRTC, however, like the BBG before it, frequently cast a blind eye toward non-compliance with its Canadian content quotas and showed itself also to be quite 'understanding' when stations failed to keep their 'Promises of Performance' attached as conditions to their licences.[43] On the other hand, the Commission on occasion did express frustration with the performance of its chosen instruments, as the following extract illustrates:

The Commission on other occasions expressed its concern about the disproportionate influence of mass-marketing strategies on North American broadcasting and particularly, of course, on Canadian broadcasting ... Techno-economic considerations place constraints on the striving for cultural originality and artistic excellence in broadcast production. Unique, carefully crafted programs involving concentration of resources and orchestration of talent become merely the exception. Instead, everything which can move or speak is subject matter for the industrial image manufacturers, who exploit live resources on a scale without precedent in the history of communications ... Broadcast programs often seem intended to titillate rather than to touch, to entertain rather than to initiate, to shock rather than to reassure, or keep in perspective, to simplify rather than to refine, to satisfy an anonymous audience rather than to facilitate individual opportunities for expression, and they impose on their audiences a limited number of expeditious and lucrative formulas instead of enlarging the possibilities of viewer choice.[44]

Given such patent deficiencies, one could well question the wisdom or sincerity of continuing to treat private sector television broadcasting as a chosen instrument to pursue goals of Canadian culture and Canadian nationalism. It was, in other words, becoming all too apparent that Canadian private broadcasters were not merely making extraordinary profits, but that these profits stemmed from the deftness with which they selected American television programs for rediffusion in Canada – a sharp antithesis to the goals set for broadcasting and to the ostensible reason for the existence of private stations and networks. The fiction that had been inaugurated by the Fowler Royal Commission in 1957, that private enterprise could be regulated or cajoled into serving anti-market goals, had about run its course.[45]

Fortunately for the private sector stations, however, a modified ideology or rhetoric, again justifying their existence, promotion, and support, was readily at hand to substitute for the doctrine of cultural nationalism. The new doctrine, of course, was that of *technological nationalism.*

Phase Three: Technological Nationalism

Two Doctrines of Technological Nationalism

Maurice Charland defined *technological nationalism* as ascribing to technology 'the capacity to create a nation by enhancing communication.'[46] An additional – and today more current – meaning, however, is the notion that countries cannot really achieve economic status in the world without being at the cutting edge of technological advance; that evolving technology, particularly in the communication field, is the key to national economic success and respect in the global marketplace. These two meanings of technological nationalism, while inconsistent in certain respects, are however of one accord in the implication that technological development is *inherently* desirable, and therefore should be given full sway.

Foreshadowing Doctrines of Technological Nationalism

As Charland remarks, Canada particularly has been prone to the first of these doctrines of technological nationalism. Our creation mythology, after all, centres on the CPR, ascribing Canadian nationhood to the space-binding railway, making it but an easy extension to apply purported nation-building properties to communication media as well. Indeed Charland points out that the rhetoric of nation building through communication technology was applied to broadcasting as early as 1927 by Prime Minister Mackenzie King, whose voice had been broadcast for the first time across the country earlier that year.

Publication of the 1957 *Report of the Royal Commission on Broadcasting*, as we have seen, gave further credibility to the notion of nation building through communication technology, what I will henceforth refer to as the '*primitive* doctrine of technological nationalism.' The Royal Commission advised in effect that radio and television transmitters, regardless of modes of ownership, and even when funded by advertising, could serve anti-market, pro-cultural, and nation-building goals. The Commission, however, qualified that conclusion in advising that a regulatory board be established to mould the conduct of the private sector so as to achieve anti-market, social purposes. In other words, the Royal Commission did not deem communication technology in and of itself to be sufficient to achieve nation-building purposes, and in that sense had not totally appropriated the primitive myth of technological nationalism.

Likewise, the Board of Broadcast Governors, in being reluctant to further expand the private sector subsequent to licensing a private television service in the larger communities, was not acting fully in accordance with the primitive myth of technological nationalism. Nor was the CRTC in its early years when it regarded cable television as a serious threat to the very survival of the Canadian broadcasting system.

On the other hand, however, private television broadcasting facilities certainly did proliferate under the aegis of the CRTC, evidently as the result of an understanding that such facilities and services were good things in and of themselves, despite occasional protestations by the Commission. In thus expanding the private sector, despite obvious and deep deficiencies, the CRTC was acting in accordance with a doctrine that ascribes ultimate goodness to technology per se.

Implementation of the Doctrine: Technology as Nation Builder

The federal government's 1968 *White Paper on a Domestic Satellite System for Canada* endeavoured to forge strong links between communication technology and nation building, contending that satellites would be a means of 'integrating remote communities into the Canadian mainstream,' and of 'protecting and strengthening Canada's cultural heritage,' adding that 'a domestic satellite system is of vital importance for the growth, prosperity, and unity of Canada.'[47]

The year 1968 also saw creation by the federal government not only of the CRTC (which, as we have seen, initially adopted a stance of *cultural nationalism* as opposed to a full-blown *technological nationalism*), but as well of the Department of Communications (DOC), staffed largely by engineers, lawyers, and economists. As noted by Caplan-Sauvageau in their report to the federal government, from the outset the DOC 'was particularly anxious to link culture, which it sometimes described as a form of software, to the potential of new communications technologies.'[48] Initially, however, the DOC had little direct role in implementing broadcasting and cultural policy, the Secretary of State's Department retaining most responsibility for the federal government's cultural initiatives. Rather, the DOC was confined primarily to spectrum management, to fostering technological initiatives such as communication satellites and videotex ('Telidon'), to negotiating jurisdictional matters with the provinces in the fields of culture and communication, and to conducting/ sponsoring research studies. In that last regard, the DOC organized the Telecommission, chaired by Allan Gotlieb, as a joint government-private sector inquiry into the role of telecommunications in Canada. Reporting in 1971, the elite panel called the Telecommission went a great distance in promulgating a doctrine of nation building through communication technology. The report opened by quoting Francis Bacon, often held to be the patriarch of scientism and technology, establishing thereby the tone for the entire document.[49] In the view of the writers of the report,

'The technologies of telecommunications and computers, effectively used in combination, could make a striking contribution to economic prosperity and the general quality of life in Canada; to the development of remote and sparsely populated regions of the country; to the extension of French and English broadcasting services from coast to coast; to the ability of individuals and groups in Canada to express themselves and communicate their views in the language of their choice; and to Canadian acceptance of responsibility for participation in the achievement of international objectives, especially social and economic development of less fortunate countries in many parts of the world.'[50]

In articulating this primitive doctrine of technological nationalism, the Department of Communications in these early years revised history in attempts to incorporate communication technology into the Canadian creation myth, and also mythologized the future by positing nation-building prospects as being contingent upon communication technology.

Likewise, in proposing a new framework for communication policy in 1973, then–communications minister Gérard Pelletier stated that 'the existence of Canada as a political and social entity has always been heavily dependent upon effective systems of east/west communication … [counterbalancing] the strong north/south pull of continentalism.'[51] Even by the late 1980s the mythic discourse of Canadian nationhood through communication technology had not entirely disappeared, as the following extract from the DOC's 1987 policy document, *Communications for the Twenty-First Century*, illustrates: 'Communications have always played a central role in Canada's history. From the fur trade of the seventeenth and eighteenth centuries, to the canals and railways of the nineteenth, from the broadcasting networks, airlines and highways to the telephone and satellite systems of the twentieth, communications technologies have helped Canadians reach new frontiers, settle and develop the wilderness, and build both a society and culture that are unique in the world for the degree to which they depend on good communications systems.'[52]

The Mature Myth: Technological Imperative

But nation building through communication technology is a hard myth to sustain in an age of globalization and burgeoning transnational communication. Put simply, communication technologies weaken nation states.

This fact has been acknowledged by none other than the Canadian government. In its review of Canada's foreign policy, for example, the 1994 Special Joint Committee of the Senate and House of Commons opined, 'Globalization is erasing time and space, making borders porous, and encouraging continental integration.' The Joint Committee continued, 'National sovereignty is being reshaped and the power of national governments to control events, reduced.'[53] Inducing globalization, according to the Special Joint Committee, has been an 'explosion of technology ... a revolution in transportation, communications and information processing.' And behind these technologies, the Joint Committee affirmed, stand transnational enterprises: 'Non-governmental actors have become major international players. The primary agents of globalization are in fact the transnational corporations (TNCs).'[54]

It is not difficult to see why the Special Joint Committee reached these conclusions. Improvements in telecommunications permit transnationals to administer in real time the activities of foreign divisions from central locales, gleaning information and electronically monitoring activities, dispensing orders, and exploiting international divisions of labour. Satellite and other advanced forms of telecommunications enable transnational managers hastily to relocate production sites to non-unionized locales, to zones offering more favourable tax treatments, to jurisdictions with lax but 'business-friendly' environmental regulations, and to zones proffering 'pro-business' health and safety legislation.[55] This, too, the Special Joint Committee acknowledged: 'The transnational mobility of capital generates pressures for deeper harmonization of national policies. In the competition for competitive advantages governments must deal with pressures to cut back on social programs and environmental programs that may raise the cost of producing goods and services, and to lower corporate taxes.'[56]

Against this backdrop, the myth of nation building through telecommunications begins to ring quite hollow. Hence, the need once more to revise a myth if private, corporate interests in broadcasting and telecommunications are to be accommodated.

In recent years, therefore, the federal government's nationalist rhetoric has once more shifted ground, largely forsaking the doctrine of nation building through communication technology to promote instead the *mature* doctrine of technological nationalism – the technological imperative – the notion that Canada has *no choice* but to be at the forefront in introducing communication technology.

Rhetorically, a definite turning point occurred with publication in 1981 by the Department of Communications of *The Information Revolution and Its Implications for Canada*. Written by two senior DOC bureaucrats, Shirley Serafini and Michel Andrieu, the booklet argued that irrespective of any misgivings Canadians might have concerning national sovereignty or other matters, an information revolution was indeed underway, necessitating the deployment of new communication technologies. According to the authors, 'The information revolution is a worldwide phenomenon causing significant structural changes in the economies of all countries, regardless of national differences in institutional arrangements or public policies. This strongly suggests that, like the industrial revolution, the information revolution is unavoidable. Consequently, the objectives of public policy should be not to prevent the revolution from occurring, but rather to turn it to our advantage.'[57]

And further,

Canada has no choice but to promote vigorously the introduction of the new technology in order to maintain and increase its international competitiveness ... The information revolution is international in nature and reflects a fundamental structural change through which all developed economies are passing ... The only strategy with a chance of success is one which attempts to take advantage of the benefits of the technology with respect to devising new products and improving productivity. Any attempt to slow down the revolution out of concern for possible employment effects will backfire. Such an approach would inevitably lead to an erosion of Canadian industry's competitiveness, resulting in declining exports, falling output and collapsing employment.[58]

Serafini and Andrieu acknowledged, perhaps for the first time in a document published by the government of Canada, that communication technology erodes national sovereignty, and in so doing they implicitly repudiated the primitive myth of technological nationalism that their department had been promoting since its inception. Nonetheless, they went on to insist that this 'information revolution' was simply unavoidable in the context of global developments, and in so doing they thereby became harbingers for the revised mythology that is so current today.

Two short years later, the DOC was enfolding even program content, not just the hardware, into the new rhetoric. In a position paper published in 1983, TV programming was seen as a means for stimulating demand for new technologies: 'Canadian high technology industries should benefit directly as cable operators retool their plants to carry these new programming and non-programming services. Cable companies will require significant amounts of new capital equipment – such as earth stations, scrambling and descrambling equipment and a variety of other types of cable hardware. Canadian high technology industries manufacture much of this equipment, and jobs should be created as a result.'[59]

In 1987 the DOC charged that Canadians had not yet become sufficiently imbued with the revised mythology. Claiming that a 'persistent lag in information technology diffusion [posed] a serious problem of national proportions,' the DOC lamented, 'We do not have a culture that promotes the use of new technology.'[60]

At about the same time, the CRTC, too, began being imbued with the technological imperative doctrine. A factor that slowly came to influence the Commission in this regard was transference in 1976 to the CRTC, renamed the Canadian Radio-television and Telecommunications Commission, of regulatory responsibilities for federally regulated telecommunications common carriers such as Bell Canada. Historically telecom carriers had been regulated under provisions of the Railway Act, which provided that rates should be 'just and reasonable' and free of 'undue preference' and of 'unjust discrimination' – provisions far removed from its broadcasting mandate of safeguarding, enriching, and strengthening the cultural, political, social, and economic fabric of Canada!

A landmark in the shift of the CRTC's stance toward technology was the Therrien Committee's 1980 report on extending broadcasting services to northern and remote communities. That Committee had been formed by the minister of communications, who wanted broadcasting services by satellite, including pay television, to be extended throughout Canada, particularly to remote areas, in both official languages. Therrien, a CRTC commissioner, responded with a ringing endorsement: 'For the past ten years or more, advisory or consultative committees have been urging governments to start planning so as to ensure that Canada will be able to maintain its rightful place in a totally new telecommunications universe, but for the most part their urgings have been in vain. This new technological universe is already taking shape at a pace that is inexorable. An astonishing variety of broadcasting services are now available thanks to satellite carriage, and this is only the tip of the iceberg.'[61]

Given this presupposition, Therrien recommended that the government 'regard new technology and innovative approaches to services as a welcome opportunity to provide better broadcasting for everyone in Canada.' It continued, 'The Committee believes that there is no longer room for retrospective tunnel-vision about television. We are already living in a new communications universe. The total nature of that universe cannot be precisely identified, but many of its features and its outlines are already clearly visible ... With regard to what can be done now to get the whole machine moving, the Committee [recommends] ... that immediate action be taken to provide alternative [i.e., private, commercial] Canadian programming for reception in remote and underserved areas. The next steps must be to initiate action, without any delay, aimed at achieving the objective of providing as wide a range of services as possible to be carried on Canadian satellites.'[62]

The CRTC acted quickly, and thereafter continuously, on Therrien's advice. Between 1982 and early 1995 it licensed over thirty new Canadian pay, pay-per-view, and specialty channels, and as well authorized numerous U.S. satellite services for distribution by cable.[63] As the 1986 Task Force on Broadcasting (Caplan-Sauvageau) put it, 'Over the years the CRTC has significantly diluted the notion of a "predominantly Canadian" broadcasting system, always in the name of the *Broadcasting Act*.'[64]

In 1991 Parliament enacted a revised Broadcasting Act. Among the provisions of the new Act were the following: 'The Canadian broadcasting system should be regulated and supervised in a flexible manner that ... is readily adaptable to scientific and technological change; [and that] does not inhibit the development of information technologies and their application or the delivery of resultant services to Canadians.'[65]

The CRTC accepted enthusiastically the implied technological imperative of this provision. In 1994, for example, evidently awe-struck by an ostensible 'political, economic and cultural revolution' that is outpacing 'the ability of regulators to recognize and define, let alone control,'[66] the Commission proposed revamping its entire regulatory framework, 'converging' telecommunications and broadcasting.

Several decades ago, in *Lament for a Nation*, George Grant informed us of what is at stake for Canada in embracing the technological imperative. He wrote, 'North American liberalism expresses the belief in open-ended progress more accurately than Marxism. It understands more fully the implications of man's essence being his freedom. As liberals become more and more aware of the implications of their own doctrine, they recognize that no appeal to human good, now or in the future, must be allowed to limit their freedom to make the world as they choose ... Nationalism [in a technologized, liberal state] can only be asserted successfully by an identification with technological advance; but technological advance entails the disappearance of those indigenous differences that give substance to nationalism.'[67]

Today, of course, information highway initiatives are routinely framed within the rhetoric of technological imperative and technological nationalism. According to Industry Canada, a relatively new department that absorbed portions of the now defunct Department of Communications, 'If Canada is to succeed in a global economy based on the creation, movement, storage, retrieval and application of information, our communications networks must be knitted into a seamless and powerful information infrastructure serving all Canadians ... Canada's information highway must be linked and integrated with the networks of our trading partners as part of a seamless, global information infrastructure. This global reach will allow businesses and individuals to access information markets, clients and partners around the world.'[68]

The Myth of Technology

For Dallas W. Smythe, 'modern technology is a mystifying term which describes the ongoing capitalist system, nothing more.' While appearing to be 'nonpolitical,' Smythe continued, 'in reality, [technology] is one of capitalism's most potent propaganda weapons.'[69]

Historical analysis of Canadian broadcasting/communication policy and rhetoric lends credence to and amplifies Smythe's position. Upon inception in 1921, radio broadcasting was controlled by private sector interests, and therefore broadcasting technology meant advertising, 'entertainment' (i.e., diversion or distraction of audiences), American programs, profit seeking, and propagation of a consumerist ethic; as remarked by Daniel Czitrom, radio became the 'latch key' whereby advertisers invaded nearly every home, or at least homes located within the more lucrative and populous zones where broadcasting facilities were concentrated.[70] The congruence of radio 'technology' and capitalism in this early period is, then, apparent.

The 1929 Aird Commission, however, endeavoured to change fundamentally the meaning of radio. Aird wanted to transform radio broadcasting into a communication medium that would be set in opposition to continentalist cultural pressures. Radio, Aird believed, should be non-commercial, used to enlighten and educate. Aird envisaged a radio medium predominantly Canadian in content and character, serving rural and remote regions as well as populous centres, a medium owned and controlled as a public enterprise by Canadians to help build community and nationhood. Aird, then, denied the 'technological imperative' by contending that the consequences of radio, merely a human invention, depend upon *choices* regarding the deployment of media technologies and concerning patterns of ownership and control. If retained by advertisers and private sector broadcasters, Aird adduced, radio would certainly continue to serve continentalist economic interests, concomitantly eroding Canadian community, while on the other hand if consciously deployed in the public sector to achieve non-pecuniary ends, radio could prove useful as a counterpoint to continental, market-induced integration. As we have seen, the Conservative government of the day, by and large, acted in accordance with Aird's recommendations, and for over twenty years Aird's alternative – anti-market, pro-cultural meaning, first for radio and then for television – held sway.

Commercial forces, however, even with the advent of the CRBC in 1932, persisted, grew stronger, and finally came to dominate, with the result that the meaning of broadcasting shifted back once more to what commercial enterprisers, in their profit seeking, wished to make of it. No longer, evidently, is the distinction between public and private, non-commercial and commercial, seen by policymakers as being essential, or even as important. Today, rather, the spectre of privatization hovers over even educational broadcasters (e.g., TV Ontario), and one questions how many years the CBC has left as a public sector institution.

Technology, convergence, and *information revolution* in our day are code words, rhetorically standing for 'global capitalism,' 'transnational enterprise,' 'international market forces,' 'dominant economic interests,' and so forth. In a 1983 policy document, for instance, the Department of Communications declared, 'The new broadcasting environment is simply one facet of that sweeping, international movement. Based on the proliferation of new technologies and computer-communication services for the creation of knowledge and transmission of information, this 'information revolution' is now taking Canada into a new, cultural, economic and social world where there are few existing rules.'[71] Substitute the phrase *global capitalism* or *transnational enterprise*, or *a compliant Canadian government* or *capitalist ideology* into the above quote for the term *information revolution* and the code is broken; with that substitution, political/economic powerplays come to the fore once more, new insights become possible, and resistance once more seems feasible.

Smythe asked, 'Is the *idea* that technology is autonomous, i.e., politically neutral and universal, itself a political concept?' 'Yes,' he answered, 'it is a political concept and reactionary as well.' For, he continued, 'the reification of technology as a universal tendency (an autonomous factor) inevitably leads people to regard technology as something that is happening *to them* without their consent, awareness, or the possibility of their controlling it ... In every sense of the word, "technology" is a reactionary political fact in the present state of the peoples of the world.'[72]

Power, in the absence of responsibility is, of course, the essence of totalitarianism. The mythic doctrine of technological imperative, now being promoted so fervently by the Canadian government and by Corporate Canada, by denying the *possibility* of human choice, and hence denying also human responsibility, is most assuredly a totalitarian ideology, advantageous of course to those who would relieve themselves of the burden of responsibility for outcomes.

To de-mythologize technology, by showing once again that artefacts are innovated and deployed by human agents is, as Jacques Ellul affirmed, equivalent to resuming the fight for freedom.[73] With Canadians being propagandized by their governments and business leaders into believing that convergence, information highways, privatization, and deregulation of communication are necessary and inevitable, voices such as those of Smythe, Ellul, Grant, Polanyi, Davis, and Spry are well worth harkening to once more.

NOTES

1 Karl Polanyi, *The Great Transformation: The Political and Economic Origins of Our Time* (1944; Boston: Beacon, 1957), 68–76.
2 Ibid., 133.
3 Ibid., 75.
4 Jerome Davis, *Capitalism and Its Culture* (New York: Farrar and Rinehart, 1935), 33.
5 Ibid., 37.
6 Ibid., 30–1; emphasis added.
7 Harold A. Innis, *The Fur Trade in Canada: An Introduction to Canadian Economic History* (1930), rev. ed. prepared by S.D. Clark and W.T. Easterbrook (Toronto: University of Toronto Press, 1967), 385.

8 Sandra Braman, 'Trade and Information Policy,' *Media Culture and Society* 12 (1990): 361–85.
9 Canada, Royal Commission on Broadcasting (Fowler Commission), *Report* (Ottawa: Queen's Printer, 1957), 297.
10 At that time Bell and radio equipment manufacturers (e.g., General Electric), hitherto deadlocked on radio patents, agreed to split broadcasting (one-way, point-to-mass communication) from telecommunications (two-way, point-to-point), and to preserve these divisions as exclusive domains.
11 Royal Commission, *Report*, 298.
12 Quoted in ibid., 299.
13 Ibid., 300.
14 Frank Peers, *The Politics of Canadian Broadcasting 1920–1951* (Toronto: University of Toronto Press, 1969), 47.
15 Harold A. Innis, *The Bias of Communication* (1951; Toronto: University of Toronto Press, 1971).
16 Cited in Peers, *Politics of Canadian Broadcasting*, 47–8.
17 Spry, excerpted in ibid., 89. Emphasis added.
18 Quoted in Royal Commission, *Report*, 303.
19 Ibid.
20 In the legislation the CRBC was given powers to purchase existing stations, to construct new ones, and to 'take over all broadcasting in Canada,' subject to parliamentary approval. Funding for the CRBC was to be entirely through parliamentary appropriation in amounts no greater than the revenues accruing from annual licence fees paid for broadcasting receivers and transmitters.
21 For example, Massey recommended that no private television stations be licensed until the CBC had firmly established itself in the field, and thereafter any and all private stations should be required to affiliate with CBC and be regulated by it.
22 Canada, House of Commons, Special Committee on Radio Broadcasting, *Minutes of Proceedings and Evidence* (Ottawa: King's Printer, 1942), 1095.
23 In deeming market forces to be 'natural,' of course, the Commission is tipping its hand as to what will follow.
24 Royal Commission, *Report*, 9. Emphasis added.
25 For a general (i.e., not culture-specific) critique of comparative advantage, see H. Daly and J. Cobb, *For the Common Good: Redirecting the Economy toward Community, the Environment, and a Sustainable Future* (Boston: Beacon, 1989), 213–18.
26 Royal Commission, *Report*, 94.
27 Peter Morris, *Embattled Shadows: A History of Canadian Cinema 1985–1939* (Montreal and Kingston: McGill-Queen's University Press, 1978).

28 Gary Evans, *John Grierson and the National Film Board: The Politics of Wartime Propaganda* (Toronto: University of Toronto Press, 1984).

29 The CFDC now is Telefilm Canada.

30 S.M. Crean, *Who's Afraid of Canadian Culture?* (Don Mills, ON: General, 1976), 71.

31 See A. John Beke, 'Government Regulation of Broadcasting in Canada,' *Saskatchewan Law Review* 36 (1971): 104–44; and Robert E. Babe, *Canadian Television Broadcasting Structure, Performance and Regulation* (Ottawa: Supply and Services for the Economic Council of Canada, 1979), 20–2.

32 According to Beke, once additional broadcasters were licensed, the Board pursued protectionist policies, limiting further expansion. Indeed, the BBG's institutional function was the economic well-being of private broadcasters. Beke, 'Government Regulation,' 116.

33 Canada, Committee on Broadcasting. *Report* (Ottawa: Queen's Printer, 1965), 35.

34 Ibid., 46.

35 Ibid., 49.

36 Ibid.

37 Canada, Department of the Secretary of State. *White Paper on Broadcasting* (Ottawa: Queen's Printer, 1966), 4.

38 Babe, *Canadian Television Broadcasting*, 29–48; also C. Christopher Johnston, *The Canadian Radio-television and Telecommunications Commission: A Study of Administrative Procedures in the CRTC*, prepared for the Law Reform Commission of Canada (Ottawa: Supply and Services, 1980).

39 *Technological nationalism* is explained later in this chapter.

40 CRTC, 'Public Announcement: The Improvement of Canadian Broadcasting and the Extension of U.S. Television Coverage in Canada by CATV,' 3 December 1969.

41 Robert E. Babe, *Cable Television and Telecommunications in Canada* (East Lansing: Bureau of Business and Economic Research, Michigan State University Press, 1975), 228–42. For example, it announced that it would authorize neither distant head-ends nor microwave for cable systems, thereby preventing systems far from the border from re-diffusing U.S. signals, a policy that would have precluded the development of cable in much of Manitoba, the Atlantic provinces, and in all northern regions of the country. Furthermore the Commission announced that cable re-diffusion of foreign signals would be limited to one commercial and one non-commercial signal. As well the Commission twice refused to license pay-TV, and it prohibited cable program originations deemed to be 'competitive' with over-the-air broadcasting.

42 CRTC, 'Public Announcement.'
43 Babe, *Canadian Television Broadcasting*, 64–99, 141–56.
44 CRTC, 'Radio Frequencies Are Public Property,' 31 March 1974, 10, 16.
45 See the retrospectives provided by Herschel Hardin, *Closed Circuits: The Sellout of Canadian Television* (Vancouver: Douglas & McIntyre, 1985); and Babe, *Canadian Television Broadcasting*.
46 M. Charland, 'Technological Nationalism,' *Canadian Journal of Political and Social Theory* 10, nos. 1 and 2 (1986): 197.
47 Canada, Department of Industry, *White Paper on a Domestic Satellite System for Canada* (Ottawa: Queen's Printer, 1968), 36, 8.
48 Canada, Task Force on Broadcasting Policy (Caplan-Sauvageau), *Report* (Ottawa: Supply and Services, 1986), 18.
49 'Telecommunications policy may have to be re-shaped if full advantage is to be taken of the opportunities that technology affords and if socially undesirable effects are to be avoided. For, in the words of Francis Bacon, "he that will not apply new remedies must expect new evils; for time is the greatest innovator."' Canada, Telecommission, *Instant World: A Report on Telecommunications in Canada* (Ottawa: Information Canada, 1971), i.
50 Canada, *Instant World*, 7–8.
51 Canada, Minister of Communications G. Pelletier, *Proposals for a Communications Policy for Canada* (Ottawa: Information Canada, 1973), 3.
52 Canada, Department of Communications, *Communications for the Twenty-First Century* (Ottawa: Supply and Services, 1987), 5.
53 Canada, Special Joint Committee of the Senate and the House of Commons Reviewing Canadian Foreign Policy, *Canada's Foreign Policy: Principles and Priorities for the Future* (Ottawa: Publications Service, Parliamentary Publications Directorate, 1994), 1.
54 Ibid., 4.
55 David Suzuki, *Time to Change* (Toronto: Stoddart, 1994); William Melody, 'The Information Society: The Transnational Economic Context and Its Implications,' in *Transnational Communications: Wiring the Third World,'* ed. Gerald Sussman and John A. Lent (Newbury Park, CA: Sage, 1991), 27–41.
56 Canada, *Canada's Foreign Policy*, 4.
57 Shirley Serafini and Michel Andrieu, *The Information Revolution and Its Implications for Canada* (Ottawa: Supply and Services, 1981), 13.
58 Ibid., 96, 94. Subsequently Francis Fox, minister of communications, took up these thoughts virtually verbatim in *Culture and Communications: Key Elements of Canada's Economic Future*, brief to the Royal Commission on the Economic Union and Development Prospects for Canada (1983).

59 Canada, Department of Communications, *Towards a New Broadcasting Policy* (Ottawa: Supply and Services, 1983), 7.
60 Canada, *Communications for the Twenty-First Century*. A useful critique of this document is provided by James R. Taylor, 'The Twenty-First Century in the Rear Mirror,' *Canadian Journal of Communication* 13, nos. 3 and 4 (1988): 63–85.
61 CRTC, Committee on Extension of Service to Northern and Remote Communities, *The 1980's: A Decade of Diversity – Broadcasting, Satellites and Pay-TV* (Ottawa: Supply and Services, 1980), 2.
62 Ibid., 36–7.
63 CRTC, *Competition and Culture on Canada's Information Highway* (Ottawa: Public Works and Government Services Canada, 1995), 6.
64 Canada, Task Force on Broadcasting, *Report*, 14.
65 Broadcasting Act 1991, s. 5.2.
66 CRTC, 'Review of Regulatory Framework,' Telecom Decision CRTC 94-19 (16 September 1994), 49, 51.
67 George Grant, *Lament for a Nation: The Defeat of Canadian Nationalism* (1965; Ottawa: Carleton University Press, 1995), 56–7, 76.
68 Canada, Industry Canada, *The Canadian Information Highway: Building Canada's Information and Communications Infrastructure* (Ottawa: Supply and Services, 1994), 5, 25.
69 Dallas W. Smythe, *Dependency Road* (Norwood, NJ: Ablex, 1981), 20.
70 Daniel Czitrom, *Media and the American Mind* (Chapel Hill: University of North Carolina Press, 1982), 77.
71 Canada, *Towards a New Broadcasting Policy*, 4.
72 Dallas Smythe, 'After Bicycles, What?' (1973); repr. in *Counterclockwise: Perspectives on Communication*, ed. Thomas Guback (Boulder, CO: Westview, 1995), 236, 237. Emphasis added.
73 Jacques Ellul, 'The Power of Technique and the Ethics of Non-power,' in *The Myths of Information: Technology in Post-Industrial Society*, ed. Kathleen Woodward (Madison, WI: Coda, 1980), 246.

6 Control of Telephones: The Canadian Experience

In popular literature on new media,[1] in academic literature on the information revolution,[2] and most significantly in policy documents from the government of Canada (see chapter 5), a recurring theme is evident: *technological imperative*, the doctrine maintaining that technology's march is largely inevitable, autonomous, foreordained. Indeed, a range of governmental soothsayers have endorsed the doctrine of technological inevitability: Arthur J. Cordell, writing for the Science Council of Canada,[3] Francis Fox, minister of communications,[4] and the panel known as the Telecommission,[5] are notable examples, among many others. This technological imperative, it is to be noted, provides a veneer of inevitability, naturalness, and hence goodness to technological developments and deployments that otherwise might raise questions concerning the distribution of economic power, cultural change, environmental impact, investment priorities, the democratic balance, and so on. Such questions become academic, however, as soon as one subscribes to a doctrine of technological inevitability.

As well, the technological imperative neatly absolves the wielders of technology of responsibility for outcomes. In this context it is most instructive to recall remarks of Roland Barthes, who wrote, 'Myth deprives the object of which it speaks of all History. In it, history evaporates ... Nothing is produced, nothing is chosen: all one has to do is possess these new objects from which all soiling trace of origin or choice has been removed. This miraculous evaporation of all history is another form of a concept common to most bourgeois myths: the irresponsibility of man.'[6]

The present paper endeavours to reintroduce this same 'soiling trace of origin or choice.' By drawing upon a range of evidence from Canadian telecommunications history, including local and inter-exchange telephone service, cable television, and communication satellites, one of the most pernicious myths of our day, namely the technological imperative, is dispelled. The paper demonstrates that governmental policymakers, and more particularly corporate power-players, have been instrumental in shaping Canadian telecommunications infrastructure; mere technology has been largely passive. Human responsibility for outcomes is hence reasserted.

Telephony: Prior to Regulation

The history of Canadian telecommunication has been dominated by one company, Bell Canada. Federally regulated, it was formerly parent of the Bell Canada Group but in 1983, through a controversial corporate reorganization, became a wholly owned subsidiary of Bell Canada Enterprises Inc. In 1985 BCE amassed revenues of $13.3 billion from a diverse array of activities ranging from pipelines to publishing. But at the core of this corporate complex squarely stood one company, Bell Canada, and it is to the emergence of that corporate entity that we now turn.

Bell Canada (or the Bell Telephone Company of Canada, as it was then known) was incorporated in 1880 by federal charter on behalf of agents of the National Bell Telephone Company of Boston. Earlier that year National Bell secured Canadian rights to Alexander Graham Bell's remarkable invention and so its dominance in Canada seemed assured.[7] Although the patent was declared void in 1885, for the next 100 years the charter endured, permitting the company inter alia to string lines along all public rights of way – an important, albeit imperfect, instrument for monopolization.

Beginning in 1893 when telephone patents expired in the United States, helping inaugurate an American independent telephone industry,[8] Canadian independents started springing up too. Between 1892 and 1905 in Ontario alone some eighty-three independent companies came into existence.[9] They generally depended on U.S. manufacturers for equipment, since Bell and its manufacturing subsidiary, the Northern Electric and Manufacturing Company, were less than enthusiastic purveyors of telephone equipment to these interlopers. Indeed, entry by independents gave rise to a flurry of anti-competitive activity on the part of Bell, carefully designed to stall and, if possible, reverse growth of the insurgents. In the case of companies offering multiparty rural lines, for example, Bell often granted urban interconnections but only on condition that Bell be afforded control over all further connections. Sometimes Bell interconnected with one company to eliminate connections for others.[10] Predatory pricing was well honed as an anticompetitive tactic also. In communities like Sherbrooke, Peterborough, Port Arthur, and Fort William free service served admirably to unnerve competitors;[11] in Montreal, too, prices were shaved to rock bottom as a competitive response.

Beginning in 1891 and continuing until 1909 when finally outlawed by the Board of Railway Commissioners for Canada, Bell also secured agreement from major railroads to exclude independents from their railroad stations and railroad rights of way.[12] Furthermore, Bell procured exclusive franchises from municipalities (thirty of them by 1905) by promising not to increase telephone rates for the life of the agreements.[13] Exclusionary tactics such as these, coupled with perceived excessively high rates in monopolized areas and lack of rural service, eventually resulted in the inauguration of federal regulation, beginning in 1906.[14]

Years of Regulation

Among the powers granted the Board of Railway Commissioners in 1906 was oversight of connections between Bell and other companies. Interconnection proved to be a thorny regulatory issue for about a century thereafter. From 1906 to the 1950s, the main interconnection issue concerned Bell's relations with predominantly local telephone companies. Since the 1950s, however, interconnection controversies embraced cable television and rival long distance carriers. This section addresses all these instances, and also terminal interconnection, the attachment of customer-owned ('foreign') terminal devices.

Interconnections with Local Telephone Companies

Between 1906 and 1915, some 676 independent telephone companies were established in Ontario. Growth was so dramatic that by 1915 independents accounted for nearly one-third of Ontario's telephones, a level never since equalled.[15] Bell succeeded in halting, then reversing, the growth of independents, first through its long distance interconnection and pricing policies, and subsequently through local exchange pricing policies, ultimately absorbing most of them. Indeed Bell bought up 160

Ontario independents between 1950 and 1959 and an additional 218 between 1960 and 1975.[16] These takeovers are explained by noting pricing tactics employed by the carrier and the sequence of rulings handed down by Bell's federal regulator.

From the onset of competition to the 1920s, Bell claimed that long distance (toll) service was unprofitable and was being cross-subsidized by local exchange service. This contention is supported by noting that pressures for entry at the time were primarily into local service, not long distance. As long as Bell retained discretion over long distance connections, this pricing strategy made sense. It allowed the company to retain high local rates despite direct competition. Rivals, after all, were handicapped by having few, if any, long distance lines. The pricing strategy also dissuaded competitive entry into long distance.

However, once Bell was required by its regulator to afford even competing companies connections to long distance, this form of non-compensatory pricing became less expedient. Indeed, Bell found itself in the undesirable position of *subsidizing* its competition! Consequently, by the turn of the decade, Bell had implemented its first phase of 'rate rebalancing,' reversing the loss–profit relationship between long distance and local whereupon independents began to subsidize Bell for their use of long distance. 'Rebalancing' reached such immense proportions by 1979 that Bell declared its costs to be $1.32 to produce $1.00 in local exchange revenues but only $0.31 to produce $1.00 in toll.[17]

Phase one 'rebalancing,' then, had two consequences as regards the structuring of the telephone industry. First, it created a severe financial strain on independent companies thereafter pressured into charging non-compensatory local rates and unable to share (adequately) in toll revenues.[18] Second, it created incentives for entry into long distance by other carriers.

Independent telephone companies most definitely suffered under the first round of 'rate rebalancing.' However, since all agreements between Bell and the independents were subject to regulatory scrutiny, the commissioners of the day also played an important role in the demise of independent companies. The record clearly reveals a lack of concern on the regulator's part. In a 1951 decision approving a toll-sharing agreement[19] between Bell and 'line haul companies' (companies owning some long distance lines), for example, the Board of Transport Commissioners emphasized that it had 'no responsibility for the revenue plight of companies not subject to our jurisdiction.'[20] Likewise in 1954 the Board reiterated that it was 'not responsible for the financial welfare of such companies.'[21] Here, Union Telephone Company, which lacked toll lines of its own, had applied to share more adequately in long distance revenues generated by calls originated by it. Union argued it should at least be compensated for expenses incurred in billing its subscribers and for use of equipment provided by Union that was used jointly for local and toll traffic. The Board, however, in dismissing the application, adopted the so-called board-to-board method of cost allocations, whereby it is assumed that local switching, local distribution, and telephone instruments are not used in long distance calls and hence warrant no compensation.

Only after 1976, the date when federal jurisdiction over telecommunications was transferred to the Canadian Radio-television and Telecommunications Commission, were such outrageous rulings reversed. Unfortunately, the new sympathetic treatment by the regulator toward independent telephone companies came many years too late, as most had long since passed into oblivion. Nonetheless, in Ontario today [1985], some thirty independent companies survive, providing 179,000 of the province's telephones – a small but persuasive reminder that a substantially different industry structure could now be in place.[22]

Cable Television Interconnection

Analogous to Bell's harsh treatment of independent telephone companies was its interaction with another locally based telecommunications industry, the cable television industry. Although at the time precluded by its charter, as amended, from operating cable television systems, Bell exerted effective control over the industry through contractual restrictions, beginning with the inception of the cable industry in the early 1950s and continuing until 1977. Bell's interest in restricting cable is obvious. The message-carrying capacity of the coaxial cable used in cable systems was over 300 times greater than the copper pair wire (or local loops) used by Bell to connect the telephone instrument to the local exchange. Unrestricted, cable systems could have proven to be formidable competition for Bell (and so it has turned out).

The cable industry since its inception was dependent on telephone companies for access to poles, ducts, and rights of way. In order to minimize competitive incursions, Bell Telephone (and some, but not all other Canadian telephone companies) offered access to poles and ducts only under highly restrictive conditions. Under Bell's 'partial system agreement' cable companies were required to contract with Bell to construct their systems, were required to pay for the labour and materials used in construction, and then were required to lease the facilities back from Bell. Bell, in other words, refused to allow cables *owned* by cable companies on its poles and over its rights of way.[23] Since Bell owned the cables in cable systems, it was also in a position to restrict the types of messages that could be transported. Typical prohibitions included:

1. preclusion of material not part of, or ancillary to, broadcasts or cablecasts;
2. messages for distribution point-to-point or to only a portion of the network, thereby pay television and certain educational and industrial programming were forbidden;
3. bidirectional messages and conversations; and
4. facilities used in conjunction with, or interconnected to, the telephone switching centre.[24]

On appeal in 1975, the Canadian Transport Commission (CTC) ruled that one company, namely Transvision (Magog) Inc., should be allowed to attach its own cables to Bell's poles.[25] Then in 1977, having assumed telecommunications jurisdiction from the CTC, the CRTC passed a general ruling whereby licensed cable companies could attach their own cables to Bell's poles.[26] Rates for pole attachments since that time have been set by the Commission to prevent monopoly pricing. As a result, the cable industry in recent years has been offering pay television, alarm service, meter reading, and other services that had been banned under the 'partial system agreement' (such as local and long distance phone services). It is to be noted that the status of cable vis-à-vis the telephone industry has depended more on regulatory policy and contractual arrangements than upon the technologies in question.

Terminal Interconnection

A century-old claim undergirding 'natural monopoly' in Canadian telecommunications had been the notion of systemic integrity, the belief that network performance could be maintained only through centralized administration of end-to-end operations. By analogy to the weak link in the chain, telephone companies contended that subscriber-owned equipment would pollute the system. In 1968, however, Parliament reduced Bell's authority to ban subscriber-owned equipment by revising the Bell Charter, empowering the CTC to become final arbiter regarding the 'reasonableness' of Bell's 'requirements' for the attachment of customer-owned equipment.

In 1975, Morton Shulman, millionaire stock speculator, author, former coroner, and maverick MPP in Ontario's Parliament, complained to the CTC that Bell had disconnected his phone in the provincial legislature. Bell countered that Dr. Shulman had illegally attached his own terminal to Bell's line, and that Bell had drawn up no 'requirements' for such attachment. With impeccable logic the CTC agreed with Bell, ruling that since Bell had published no 'requirement,' there was 'no such requirement before the Commission which the Commission could judge to be reasonable or not.' Thereupon, the case was dismissed, the CTC maintaining 'we have no jurisdiction to grant the relief sought in the case.'[27]

Challenge Communications Ltd fared better once telecommunications jurisdiction had been transferred to the CRTC in 1976. Challenge Communications was a mobile telephone carrier competing with Bell, but it required access to Bell's network to complete its service. In 1977 Bell unilaterally announced that mobile telephone customers leasing dial telephones from companies other than Bell would not be connected to Bell's switched network. Bell justified this exclusion on the grounds of systemic integrity. In oral proceedings, however, a less sublime reason came to light, proffered by none other than Bell's normally crafty counsel, Ernie Saunders: 'Having gone to the trouble to take the steps to make this service available to the public, Bell Canada quite understandably desires to reap the benefits of this new offering.'[28]

The Commission, while perhaps marvelling at Sanders's candour, ruled the tariff to be illegal, conferring as it did undue preference in Bell's favour and unduly discriminating against Challenge. The decision was subsequently ratified, on appeal, by the Federal Court of Appeal.[29] Rebuffed by the courts and regulator alike, Bell Canada filed an application in November 1979 requesting the CRTC to make a general ruling on the extent to which attachment of customer-owned equipment was in the public interest. During the ensuing hearings neither Bell nor BC Tel invoked the now-outworn shibboleth of 'systemic integrity.' Instead both companies agreed that provisioning of all terminals should henceforth be on a competitive basis.[30]

Long Distance Interconnection

As noted above, the first era of 'rate rebalancing' created incentives for entry into long distance markets by independent carriers. This section describes Bell's relations with three rival long distance carriers: Northern Telephone Company, CNCP Telecommunications, and Telesat Canada.

Northern Telephone Company

In 1964 the town of Kenora, Ontario, which operated a municipal telephone system, and Northern Telephone Limited, servicing 150 communities or settlements in Northern Ontario and adjacent regions of Quebec, jointly applied for an Order of the Board of Transport Commissioners to require Bell Canada to provide the applicants with toll interconnection at Fort William to enable Northern to transmit long distance telephone calls between Kenora and Fort William in place of (or in competition with) Bell. While the local exchanges and distribution facilities in Fort William were owned by the municipality, Bell controlled the city's long distance toll-switching centre and hence its toll connections. In support of its application, Northern stated that Bell Telephone had always neglected northern regions, noting that even at that time Bell still owned no long distance transmission facilities between the two communities, merely leasing circuits from Canadian Pacific Telegraph. Northern also stated that toll revenues generated by approval of the application would enable it to lower local rates and upgrade service throughout its sparsely settled territory. The Board, however, saw things differently, ruling that approval of the application would cause a revenue fall for Bell of between $150,000 and $300,000 per year, an undesirable occurrence in the Board's view. The Board thereupon denied the application, stating, 'The fact that a competing carrier is prepared to offer more is not a ground for substituting it for the existing carrier.'[31] Bell acquired Northern Telephone in 1966.

CNCP Telecommunications

On 14 June 1976, Canadian Pacific Ltd applied to the CRTC to order Bell Canada to interconnect CP's telecommunication system to Bell's switched network. For many years CNCP Telecommunications had been offering services competitive to some services of Bell Canada and the consortium of telephone companies known as the TransCanada Telephone System (TCTS). However TCTS members possessed the important advantage of owning and controlling the local switched distribution facilities, agreed by CNCP to be properly monopolized. CNCP therefore faced a significant competitive disadvantage in being excluded from such facilities. While CNCP was permitted to lease local distribution facilities (local loops) on a 'dedicated' (unswitched, or point-to-point) basis from TCTS members, enabling CNCP to connect business customers with its own offices and to its own long distance network, it was prohibited from interconnecting with telephone switching centres and with those customer-owned terminals that were in turn connected to TCTS switching offices. The result was that CNCP was limited to providing private line services and the limited amount of switched services that its own switching and distribution facilities could handle. Thousands of small businesses were thereby foreclosed from CNCP's offerings since the leasing of dedicated local loops could be justified only by institutions with high volumes of telecommunications traffic.

In weighing arguments on both sides the CRTC departed significantly from positions established previously by the CTC and its predecessors. Whereas the Board of Transport Commissioners had asserted that the Board was 'not responsible for the financial welfare' of companies not under its jurisdiction, the CRTC stated that it was required to take a wide view of its obligations to protect the public interest and that, in particular, it would consider the indirect effects of granting the application upon subscribers to other telephone systems, such as those in the Maritime and Prairie provinces.[32] Furthermore, the Commission ruled, again in contrast to the precedent established in the *Northern Telephone* case, that CNCP was required to make a prima facie case only, namely that access to Bell's facilities would be useful to CNCP, that duplication of such facilities would not be in the public interest, and that 'no unreasonable technical harm would result from the interconnection.'[33]

Reviewing the evidence, the CRTC concluded that Bell had grossly overstated the revenue erosion effect of interconnection. The Commission estimated 'as an upper limit' the revenue loss to Bell in 1982 from interconnection to be no more than $45.7 million, as opposed to the $253.3 million Bell had estimated.[34] Furthermore, the CRTC stated that 'Bell failed to provide adequate empirical evidence to support its contentions regarding the nature and extent of any economies of scale enjoyed by it.'[35] On the other hand the Commission foresaw substantial benefits from interconnection. 'The evidence in this case indicates that competition would be greatly enhanced with interconnection and that interconnection would provide significant benefits to users in terms of improved responsiveness, particularly on the part of the telephone company, in satisfying their telecommunications requirements.'[36] Thereupon Bell was ordered to interconnect CNCP for certain private line voice and data transmission services, and a more competitive era was foreseen.

CNCP, however, was unsuccessful in a subsequent application filed in 1983 to extend the range of authorized, interconnected services to include long distance voice, principally Message Toll Service (MTS) and Wide Area Telephone Service (WATS). Even while applying the criteria used in its previous interconnection decision, the CRTC concluded in this instance that 'the granting of CNCP's application would *not* be in the public interest.'[37] On the one hand, the CRTC stated if CNCP were required to make contributions to help Bell maintain low (non-compensatory) local telephone rates, it was unlikely that CNCP would ever be profitable. On the other hand, if such contributions were not made, the toll subsidy to local service provided by Bell would inevitably decline as a result of the competitive pricing of toll services, resulting in an undue escalation in local rates. Low local rates had, in the years subsequent to being introduced to eliminate independent telephone companies, become a matter of social policy to foster universal telephone service. This desirable goal notwithstanding, it may be noted that Bell used this second CNCP proceeding to advance its proposal to once more 'rebalance rates,' this time by sharply reducing long distance prices to erase incentives for long distance entry, and by doubling local rates. Bell estimated the effect of phase two 'rebalancing' could be to deprive 400,000 of its customers of local telephone service.[38]

Telesat Canada

Turning finally to Telesat Canada, it becomes again apparent that technology per se has dictated no particular market structure. Telesat Canada was created by Act of Parliament in 1969, an outcome of recommendations contained in the *White Paper on Domestic Satellite Communications System for Canada* (1968). In rejecting proposals by TCTS to themselves own, control, and finance satellites as part of an integrated, terrestrial/space telecommunications system, the *White Paper* took the position that satellites should be able 'to compete effectively in those areas where competition is appropriate.' The government also rejected proposals by TCTS that the member companies own all ground stations, a proposal designed to afford the telcos effective control.[39] A further suggestion, that Telesat sell services only to designated common carriers, that is that Telesat become a 'carriers' carrier,' was also rejected.

Nonetheless, the government needed the cooperation of TCTS, anticipating that the telephone companies would be Telesat's largest customers. Therefore the government agreed to TCTS's demands that Telesat be allowed to lease only full radio frequency channels, each with a capacity of 960 telephone circuits (equivalent to one TV channel), that all leases be for continuous use, that five-year leases would be required, and that resale and/or sharing of channels by and among customers be prohibited.[40] These restrictions effectively confined Telesat's potential customer base to the carriers themselves and the CBC; the latter, a Crown corporation, was envisaged by the government as helping to keep Telesat afloat during the initial years.

Upon incorporation of Telesat the government and the carriers each subscribed to 50 per cent of the shares, with the possibility of allowing the general public to participate to the extent of one-third ownership at a future date. Between 1972 and 1976 three Anik A satellites were launched in the 4–6 GHz range; a fourth Anik B satellite, leased full-time to the federal Department of Communications, was also sent aloft; it operated in the 12–14 GHz range. The three Anik A satellites had twelve transponders each, and by 1976 Telesat found itself able to lease only one-third of its capacity.[41] Even the few channels that *were* leased were underutilized. Telesat was financially troubled, despite the public funding through CBC and Department of Communications. Moreover, by 1975, there was some question whether TCTS would renew leases unless members could get full control of Telesat.

In these circumstances, Telesat and the government reached an agreement whereby Telesat would become a member of the telephone consortium and in so doing would receive a guaranteed rate of return. In exchange, Telesat agreed that its earth stations would henceforth be operated by TCTS members, and that Telesat would become a carriers' carrier, selling channels only to designated carriers. The agreement was approved hastily by the Department of Communications and was submitted for approval to the CRTC in early 1977. The CRTC, however, rejected the agreement! In doing this, the CRTC made the following observations, among others: (1) the guaranteed rate of return provision would make assessment of Telesat's rates difficult and would erode incentives for efficiency; (2) the agreement minimized advantages of satellite compared to terrestrial microwave, since all facilities would be bundled together in setting distance-based prices; (3) there was likelihood of undue preference in favour of the telephone companies and to the disadvantage of other carriers such as CNCP; and (4) there was a substantial lessening of competition.

On appeal, predictably, Cabinet overturned the CRTC's decision. The main reason cited for this re-reversal was that without the agreement the carriers were not expected to utilize Telesat to any great extent, throwing into question the future financial viability of satellites in Canada. Nonetheless, the government did announce that the matter of earth station ownership and Telesat's policies of leasing only complete channels would be reviewed. The government's statement concluded that 'Telesat is a complement to, not a competitor with, existing tele-communications carriers and ... a closer association with these carriers must develop if efficient, effective integration of satellite and terrestrial facilities is to be ensured, thereby making new services available to Canadians at the lowest possible cost.'[42]

Indeed, some of the more restrictive provisions of the original agreement were relaxed after 1977. In 1979, for example, the federal Department of Communications announced that cable systems would be permitted to own ground stations. In 1981 the CRTC ruled that Telesat's customer base could no longer be restricted to authorized common carriers and that Telesat's policy of providing only full period RF channels to its customers was unduly prejudicial, disadvantaging smaller users.[43] (Full implementation of this decision was waylaid for a time, however, by another Cabinet reversal.) Then, in 1984, the Commission required Telesat to permit licensed broadcasting undertakings to resell excess capacity to other such undertakings for broadcast programming purposes.[44] In May 1986 a revised connecting agreement between Telesat and TCTS was approved by the Commission whereby Telesat's customer base was no longer to be restricted to broadcasting undertakings and specified common carriers; TCTS's subsidies to Telesat were to cease as well, effective 1 January 1988.[45]

Conclusions

By closely investigating pricing and interconnection arrangements in the Canadian telecommunications industry since 1880, one is struck by the wide range of conceivable industry structures that the various technologies permitted. This is important to remember in an era in which the shrill cry of the technological imperative and technological determinism is heard so often.

NOTES

1 John Naisbitt, *Megatrends* (New York: Warner, 1982); Alvin Toffler, *The Third Wave* (New York: Bantam, 1981).
2 Daniel Bell, 'The Social Framework of the Information Society,' in *The Computer Age: A Twenty-Year View*, ed. M. Dertouzos and J. Moses, 163–211 (Cambridge, MA: MIT Press, 1979); Marc Uri Porat, 'Communications Policy in an Information Society,' in *Communications for Tomorrow*, ed. Glenn Robinson (New York: Praeger, 1978), 3–60.
3 Arthur J. Cordell, *The Uneasy Eighties: Transition to an Information Society* (Ottawa: Supply and Services, 1985); also, Science Council of Canada, *Planning Now for an Information Revolution: Tomorrow Is Too Late* (Ottawa: Supply and Services, 1982).
4 Francis Fox, *Culture and Communications: Key Elements of Canada's Economic Future* (Ottawa: Supply and Services, 1983).
5 Canada, Department of Communications, Telecommission, *Instant World* (Ottawa: Information Canada, 1971).
6 Roland Barthes, *Mythologies* (New York: Hill and Wang, 1972), 151.
7 William Patten, *Pioneering the Telephone in Canada* (Montreal: Patten, 1926).
8 Richard Gabel, 'The Early Competitive Era in Telephone Communications, 1893–1920,' *Law and Contemporary Problems* 34, no. 2 (Spring 1969): 340–59.
9 Thomas Grindlay, *A History of the Independent Telephone Industry in Ontario* (Toronto, ON: Ontario Telephone Service Commission, 1975), 254–305.
10 Canada, House of Commons, Select Committee on Telephone Systems, *Proceedings* (Ottawa: King's Printer, 1905), 238–41.
11 Ibid., 77–98.
12 Ibid., 179–209, 680.
13 Ibid., 660.
14 Canada, *Railway Act*, 1906.
15 Rural Telephone Committee, *Report to the Hydro-Electric Commission of Ontario concerning Rural Telephone Service in Ontario* (Toronto: Hydro-Electric Power Commission, 1953), exhibit 2.
16 Ontario Telephone Service Commission, Transcripts of Hearings (3 August 1977), 186.
17 Canadian Radio-television and Telecommunications Commission (CRTC), 'CNCP Telecommunications: Interconnection with Bell Canada,' Telecom Decision CRTC 79-11 (17 May 1979), 216.
18 CRTC, 'City of Prince Rupert, Connecting Agreement with B.C. Telephone Company' (9 November 1978), 31.
19 Toll-line is equivalent to long-distance telecommunication line, which at

the time in Canada was charged on a metered basis while local calls were charged on a flat rate basis.

20 Board of Transport Commissioners for Canada, *Judgements, Orders, Regulations and Rulings* 41, no. 15 (1 November 1951).

21 Board of Transport Commissioners for Canada, *Judgements, Orders, Regulations and Rulings* 44, no. 9 (1 August 1954).

22 Ontario Telephone Service Commission, *Annual Report* (Toronto: OTSC, 1986), 13.

23 Robert E. Babe, 'Public and Private Regulation of Cable Television: A Case Study of Technological Change and Relative Power,' *Canadian Public Administration* 17, no. 2 (1974): 187–225.

24 Ibid., 209.

25 Canadian Transport Commission, Order No. T-726 (15 October 1975).

26 CRTC, 'Bell Canada Tariff for the Use of Support Structures by Cable Television Licensees,' Telecom Decision CRTC 77-6 (27 May 1977).

27 Canadian Transport Commission, Decision File No. 49645-26 (14 April 1975).

28 CRTC, 'Telesat Canada Proposed Agreement with Trans-Canada Telephone System,' Telecom Decision CRTC 77-10 (24 August 1977), 15.

29 Gordon Kaiser, 'Competition in Telecommunications,' *Ottawa Law Review* 13, no. 1 (1981): 95–122.

30 CRTC, 'Attachment of Subscriber-Provided Terminal Equipment,' Telecom Decision CRTC 82-14 (23 November 1982), 32.

31 Board of Transport Commissioners for Canada, Decision, file no. 3839-1054 (3 June 1964).

32 CRTC, 'CNCP Telecommunications,' 102–5.

33 Ibid., 127.

34 Ibid., 186, 140.

35 Ibid., 241–2.

36 Ibid.

37 CRTC, 'Interexchange Competition and Related Issues,' Telecom Decision CRTC 85-19 (29 August 1985), 43.

38 Canadian Press, 'Doubling of Local Rates Could Leave 400,000 without Telephone,' *Montreal Gazette* 18 October 1984.

    Author's note: Through a series of name changes and takeovers, the former CNCP Telecommunications is now part of Rogers Communications; Rogers, along with a few other companies, today (2011) offers long distance, local, and mobile telephone services in competition with the older telephone companies.

39 Charles Dalfen, 'The Telesat Canada Domestic Communication Satellite System,' *Canadian Communications Law Review* 1 (1969): 182–211.

40 David A. Golden, 'Anik,' unpublished speech, Washington DC, 29 January 1974.

41 CRTC, 'Telesat Canada Proposed Agreement with Trans-Canada Telephone System,' Telecom Decision CRTC 77-10 (24 August 1977).

42 Department of Communications, 'Statement by Minister of Communications, Jeanne Sauvé, in Respect of an Order-in-Council to Vary CRTC Decision 77-10,' news release, 3 November 1977.

43 CRTC, 'Bell Canada, British Columbia Telephone Company and Telesat Canada: Increases and Decreases in Rates for Services and Facilities Furnished on a Canada-wide Basis by Members of the TransCanada Telephone System, and Related Matters,' Telecom Decision CRTC 81-13 (7 July 1981).

44 CRTC, 'Telesat Canada – Final Rates for 14/12 GHz Satellite Service and General Review of Revenue Requirements,' Telecom Decision CRTC 84-9 (20 February 1984).

45 CRTC, 'Telesat Canada and Bell Canada,' Telecom Decision CRTC 86-9 (8 May 1986).

Author's note: In 1991, consistent with neoliberal policies of privatization and deregulation, by Act of Parliament the federal government divested its shares in Telesat. In 1998, BCE acquired all outstanding shares in Telesat, thereby increasing its ownership from 58 per cent to 100 per cent. In December 2006, however, BCE announced the sale of its satellite services subsidiary, Telesat Canada, for $3.42 billion to a new acquisition company formed by Canada's Public Sector Pension Investment Board (PSP Investments) and Loral Space & Communications Inc. This sale was consistent with BCE's more recent refocusing on its core telephone markets and its sale of several other non-essential subsidiaries, including Nortel Systems.

7 Convergence and Divergence: Telecommunications, Old and New

Until recently the term *telecommunications* (literally 'communicating from a distance') was reserved for point-to-point, as opposed to point-to-mass and point-to-multipoint, electronic communication. As media converge, however, old distinctions give way. Increasingly, telecommunications is an omnibus term denoting all modes of electronic communication.

Indeed, analysts now refer to the 'new' telecommunications.[1] Major features distinguish the new from the old: (1) the rapidity of technological change, particularly the shift from analogue to digital transmission; (2) convergence among hitherto distinct sectors of the industry; (3) increased competition, even in sectors previously deemed 'natural monopolies'; (4) heightened commodity status accorded information and communication; and (5) a much altered legal/regulatory/policy framework. Moreover, these changes are aspects of, and contribute to, broader geopolitical trends and issues, often referred to as *globalization*.

Three main sections follow this introduction. The first compares the new and the old telecommunications with regard to the first four of the dimensions highlighted above. The next section addresses the evolving legal/regulatory/policy framework in the context of convergence. The last section focuses on broader geopolitical trends and issues.

Comparison of the Old and New Telecommunications

Technological Change

Over the past several decades telecommunications have been characterized by rapid technological change. Whereas until the 1950s large portions of the telephone plant and equipment had a useful life of thirty to fifty years or more, this is seldom the case for modern telecommunications. Switching and some transmission equipment now become obsolete long before they are physically worn out. Since the 1960s, technological innovation has resulted in annual declines in transmission costs of at least 11 per cent. Moreover, coaxial cable and more recently fibre-optic cable are multiplying the capacity of the telephone network's original transmission medium (copper pair wire) by several hundreds of thousands. Advances in compression techniques and the development of new wireless technologies, in conjunction with digitalization, have also expanded transmission capacity and evidently are lowering entry barriers – to such an extent that competition is now encouraged even in local telephone service. Furthermore satellite communications have extended the geographic reach of interconnected telecommunications systems to encompass, in principle, the entire globe.

It is tempting to ascribe convergence and the emergence of policies promoting competition to technological change. In this view, digitalization not only erodes monopoly but also facilitates interconnection among rival telecommunications companies. Arguments to the effect that digitalization is the force driving competition and convergence in the new telecommunications should not, however, be accepted uncritically. As noted below, competition in some countries arose long before the modern era, and communication sectors were highly converged at the outset.

Convergence

A second aspect of the new telecommunications is convergence, that is, the blurring of industry or sector boundaries. In former years, facilities and companies offering point-to-point communication services were distinct from both broadcasting and publishing in terms of ownership, products, services, and characteristic technologies. Recently there has been a lessening in these demarcations. Convergence has technical, functional, corporate, and legal/regulatory aspects.

Technical convergence means that, increasingly, a single mode of transmission (for example, a coaxial or fibre-optic cable, or a satellite transponder) simultaneously transmits voice, text, data, sound, and image. Digitalization is often proclaimed to be a key factor in permitting this intermingling.

Functional convergence, sometimes referred to as 'multimedia,' points to new, hybrid services combining voice, data, text, and/or image. Electronic encyclopedias, for example, combine text, video, and sound. While functional convergence is closely linked to technical convergence, it is nonetheless distinct. Functional convergence emphasizes services and products, as opposed to modes of carrying or transmitting signals.

Corporate convergence refers to mergers, amalgamations, and diversifications whereby media organizations come to operate across previously distinct industry boundaries. Until recently, telephone companies such as Bell Canada were precluded from holding broadcasting licences, for instance, but this restriction has now been removed. Likewise, 'cross ownership' of media, such as common ownership of broadcasting and newspapers in the same community, was deemed to be a policy concern. Here too, restrictions have been relaxed, with the result that media conglomerates have emerged. In the United States, Time Warner, for example, operates in such previously distinct communication sectors as book and periodical publishing, recorded music, movie production, Internet services, and cable TV. In Canada, Rogers operates radio, television, cable television, specialty television, cellular telephone, home telephones, and video rental companies, and it has become a major periodicals publisher.

Legislative/regulatory convergence refers to governmental initiatives that are erasing the distinctions that characterized the legal/regulatory/policy frameworks set for telephony, broadcasting, and publishing. In the United States, for example, the Telecommunications Act of 1996 opened virtually all communication services to competition and in so doing created added impetus for corporate and functional convergence. In Canada, the Canadian Radio-television and Telecommunications Commission (CRTC) has likewise introduced a continuing series of measures supporting convergence.

From a historical perspective, however, convergence is not new to telecommunications. In the United States and Canada alike, the telegraph and the daily press at the turn of the century constituted a closely integrated operation, even to the extent that telegraph operators were the principal news reporters; moreover, telegraph companies either owned or had firm and exclusive contractual arrangements with the major news agencies. This 'vertical integration' between content and carriage was terminated not on account of technological innovation, but rather through public policy decisions designed to reduce the monopoly in news gathering and distribution.[2]

Likewise, telegraph and telephone companies in the late 1870s and early 1880s, at least in some jurisdictions, made use of common facilities; the two services were sometimes even provided by the same entity. In North America, divergence took place around 1880 when the telegraph interests centring on the Western Union Telegraph Company turned telephone patents over to the Bell interests and exited the telephone field; in return, Bell promised not to enter telegraphy. Again, technology provides little explanation for the divergence between sectors.

Finally, radio and telephony were highly integrated from the 1890s until the 1920s. It was an agreement to pool patents and segment markets among such entities as AT&T, RCA, General Electric, Westinghouse, Western Electric, the Bell Telephone Company of Canada, and Northern Electric that caused radio and telephony to diverge.[3] Technology imposed neither convergence nor divergence upon these sectors.

Since technology does not explain past divergence among communications sectors, one might conclude that technology likewise provides at best a superficial explanation for convergence (or reconvergence) in the present. Eschewing technological determinist explanations, however, places one firmly in the political economy tradition, which asks by whom and for whom technological innovations are introduced, who benefits and who suffers from such innovations, why some innovations are suppressed, and how the legal/regulatory structure is used to facilitate or obstruct industry restructurings. Reconvergence, from a political economy perspective, then, issues from and contributes to changing distributions of political/economic/cultural power: between telecommunications suppliers and their various user groups; among user groups themselves; between domestic and international businesses; between governments and business; and between business and labour.

Competition versus 'Natural Monopoly'

By at least the 1920s, the old telecommunications had been widely designated a 'natural monopoly,' whereas publishing and the emerging broadcasting industries, in much of North America, at least, were designated competitive. Two major arguments were invoked in support of the 'old' telecommunications as a natural monopoly. The first was the claim that large portions of telecommunications plant and equipment are characterized by large if not inexhaustible economies of scale that make it inefficient to have more than one supplier. The second was the claim that the laudable goal of universal service could best be achieved by the monopoly corporation averaging its costs across all service classifications in order to effect cross-subsidies among customer groups.

The new telecommunications, on the other hand, denote an era in which much less credence is paid to the concept of *natural* monopoly. One reason for this is increased awareness of the historical record regarding the manner in which monopoly was attained. That record reveals that monopoly was not 'thrust upon' telecommunications firms; rather, the telecommunications firms aggressively sought and achieved monopoly in a highly predatory manner.[4]

As well, however, the notion of inexhaustible economies of scale for all portions of the telecommunications system became suspect; indeed, some studies showed that smaller, non-vertically integrated telephone companies, albeit publicly owned, were far more efficient.[5] Furthermore, the fact that rural territories in the United States and Canada had first been served by independently owned or publicly owned telephone companies, not by a dominant carrier, was finally recognized as being somewhat inconsistent with this 'old' doctrine.

During the 'natural monopoly' era, the main thrust, or at least the ostensible purpose, of regulation (or of public ownership, as the case might be) was to protect the public against unduly high prices and to ensure universal service. By contrast, with the emergence of competition and the transition to the 'new' telecommunications, a primary regulatory goal has been to proscribe predatory business practices by dominant companies. More recently, a definite goal of public policy also has been to advance the interests internationally of domestically based telecommunications firms.

Information and Communication as Commodities

A fourth and highly significant distinction between the new and the old telecommunications is the increasing status of information and communication as commodities. Although information has been bought and sold in markets for centuries, it is also the case, as noted by Herbert Schiller, that social movements throughout history have resisted the total commodification of information. They have, in other words, struggled to reserve 'for common use' portions of the community's production and supply of information.[6]

Schiller writes that the public library system and, in the United States the land-grant universities, are among the 'signal achievements' of these social movements. Laws guaranteeing access to information, the creation and support of public radio and public television, state sponsorship of the arts, the regulatory/policy goal of universal service for telecommunications and broadcasting systems, programs to increase literacy and to facilitate access to basic education, and constitutional guarantees of freedom of speech, freedom of the press, and freedom of assembly are other examples of policies premised on shared information as serving the common good.

Since at least the 1980s, however, institutions and practices treating information and communication as a shared good, or as a public resource, or indeed as a basic human right, have been in decline. Emblematic of this shift were the withdrawals in the 1980s by the United States and the United Kingdom from UNESCO over the issues of whether a free and balanced flow of information should characterize world communication (that is, whether the Third World should have a right to create and distribute information), and whether communication should be considered a basic human right.[7]

The dominant trend toward more thorough commodification of information has numerous manifestations, including:

- information highway initiatives;
- the development of online work and other computer-based modes of workplace surveillance;
- erosion in many countries of publicly funded education;
- the unbundling of telecommunications services, that is, the setting of separate prices for each service;
- a transition in telecommunications from 'value of service' to cost-based pricing;
- a heightening tendency to charge user fees for access to information;
- privatization of hitherto publicly owned telecommunications and broadcasting systems;
- enactment of stiffer copyright laws and the incorporation of copyright and other intellectual property into bilateral and multilateral trade negotiations and treaties;
- the scrambling and descrambling of television signals for pay-per-view;
- the privatization of government databanks, publications, data collection services, and publishing operations; and

- the creation of the transactional commodity, such as lists of customers and users.

Computerization/digitalization of telecommunications has been a precondition for many of these developments. Computers have the capacity to record and quickly process vast amounts of information, to monitor electronic messaging, to measure 'bits' of information, to direct these bits to specified addresses, and to facilitate the billing process. Another, albeit related, factor spurring the heightened commodity treatment of information and communication has been a developing perception that the wealthier economies are now information based, in other words, the emergence of the notion of the information economy.

It is a major paradox of the present era that, whereas the economy is increasingly premised on the ubiquity of information as a commodity, information itself is ill-suited to being treated that way. (See Part One of this book.) To review, information is dialectical with regard to matter-energy and the form or structure that matter-energy assumes. Information is not just matter that can be counted; it is also shape or pattern or form that must be 'read.' A second dialectical tension, therefore, concerns the objective existence of matter-in-form on the one hand, and the subjective, interpretive, or culturally specific import of these matter-in-forms on the other. The dialectic of information presents multitudinous problems for treating information as a commodity – a basic premise and goal of the new telecommunications. Third, these 'forms' can often be replicated at almost zero cost, and in any event people can 'share' these forms without lessening their use or enjoyment.

Legislative/Regulatory/Policy Issues

The old and new telecommunications differ fundamentally with regard both to their underlying philosophies and to the goals that policymakers have set and are setting. This section looks at the differences between the old and the new telecommunications regarding their respective legal/regulatory/policy frameworks.

Legal/Policy Framework for the Old Telecommunications

To appreciate fully the dimensions of the revised legal/regulatory/policy framework, we need to review the old, pre-convergence frameworks as they applied to telephones, broadcasting, and publishing. A

Table 1
Characteristics of the three-sector communication field

	Publishing	Broadcasting	Telephones
Characteristic technology	Printing press; hard copy	Transmitters	Wires, cables, switching centres
Competition and entry conditions	Unlicensed entry; market forces	Limited entry through restricted licensing of radio frequencies	Monopolistic; licences, franchises, and charters; high entry barriers
Vertical integration	Complete between carriage and content	Complete between carriage and content	Absent, common carrier only, not a content originator
Regulatory focus and special legislation	Market forces; copyright laws; anti-monopoly laws	Cultural regulation, licensing; publicly owned broadcasting systems	Public utility regulation of prices and profits; public ownership
Services	Information distributed from central point to customers who pay directly, frequently financed also by advertising	Information radiated spatially; financed by advertisers and/or taxation	Transport of messages originated by customers who pay directly
Nature of the communication	Point-to-mass, largely one-way	Point-to-mass, one-way	Point-to-point, two-way
Declared aims of public policy	Marketplace of ideas; protection of authors' rights; often support for indigenous cultural productions	Nation building, social and cultural improvement, marketplace of ideas; universal service; indigenous cultural productions	'Just and reasonable' access; no undue preference or unjust discrimination; low-cost, efficient, universal service; common carriage; profit regulation

Source: Adapted from Robert E. Babe, *Telecommunications in Canada* (Toronto: University of Toronto Press, 1990), 17.

summary of these frameworks is presented in Table 1. With convergence and competition, of course, the sector divisions set out in this table are eroded and the legal/regulatory/policy distinctions lessened. Increasingly the presumption is that competitive markets will ensure a (redefined) public interest for all sectors. The framework for publishing, in other words, is increasingly being applied to telephones and broadcasting.

During the era of the telecommunications monopoly, certain measures of public control were invoked, either directly through government ownership (as in much of Europe and the Prairie provinces of Canada), or indirectly through regulation by an independent, quasi-judicial tribunal such as the Federal Communications Commission (FCC) in the United States and the Canadian Radio-television and Telecommunications Commission and its predecessors in Canada. In the case of regulation, the three principal concerns were the prevention of undue monopolistic profit taking, the setting of 'just and reasonable' rates for individual services, and prevention of undue or unjust discrimination among customer groups.

Once the 'revenue requirements,' or total permissible revenues, were set by the regulator to guard against monopoly profiteering – no easy task, it may be added – attention in regulatory proceedings turned to the rate structure, that is, to the system of relative prices and to the rate level that would generate the authorized revenues. For much of the period of 'natural' monopoly, prices for individual services were set according to what was frequently called the value-of-service principle, although this generally was a misnomer. Local service was more 'valuable' in the sense that one needed access to the local exchange in order to place or receive long distance calls. But, according to the practice, local exchange service recovered relatively little of the common costs it shared with long distance. What the term *value of service* did accurately connote, however, was that there was little or no attempt to set prices according to estimates of cost.

Value-of-service pricing, despite its seeming arbitrariness, actually made some sense in the old telecommunications, for at least two reasons. First, various telecommunications services, such as local and long distance, use common plant and equipment. Determining just how such equipment-related costs should be apportioned among the various joint services is very problematic, if indeed not altogether arbitrary. By fixing prices according to the value-of-service principle, the regulator made no pretence at apportioning costs. Second, the goal of universal service was more attainable under a value-of-service pricing system than it is with a cost-of-service pricing system. Through the dual principles of cost averaging among service categories and cross-subsidization among user groups, service to rural or remote areas and to low-income groups could be provided at a price nearly everyone could afford.

Value-of-service pricing grew problematic, however, as competition began to be permitted – first at the boundaries of the regulated utility's service area (terminal equipment, private lines, etc.), and soon even at its core. Under rate base / rate of return regulation, it came to be realized, a firm with a core monopoly could have financial incentive to invest unduly heavily in competitive services and to price these services below cost. In recognition of these tendencies and incentives, regulators embarked on complex but ultimately arbitrary programs of separating and allocating costs among service categories with the intent, if not of implementing a cost-of-service pricing system, then at least of ensuring that prices for competitive services were compensatory.

In one early but influential study, the U.S. Federal Communications Commission concluded that AT&T had indeed engaged in non-compensatory pricing in competitive markets, subsidizing below-normal returns in competitive markets with excessive returns from monopolized services.[8] As a result of this 1965 'Seven-Way Cost Study,' the FCC instigated Docket 16258, said to be its first overall investigation of AT&T since 1935. This investigation ultimately culminated in the break-up of AT&T through antitrust on 1 January 1984. The antitrust action was intended, in part, to separate, through ownership, plant and equipment dedicated to the then-competitive interstate long distance services market from what was still at the time deemed to be the naturally monopolized local exchange services market. This separation was undertaken so that a competitive long distance market could be sustained with reduced likelihood of anti-competitive cross-subsidy, this despite the long-standing claim of telephone companies that long distance cross-subsidized local service.

Official Policy Concerns in the 'New' Telecommunications

Official policy concerns in the era of the new, converged telecommunications are substantially different from the 'consumer protection' concerns of the natural monopoly era. Countries worldwide are increasingly apprehensive lest they be left behind in the global race to innovate new communication technologies, a precondition (or so it is believed) for success in the global marketplace. In this context, the extraordinary profits that can be made domestically by telecom companies are no longer viewed by policymakers as the bane they once were. High profitability at home, it is argued, boosts the ability of domestically based companies to compete internationally.

Thus we arrive at one factor that has induced regulators to substitute 'price caps' for rate-of-return and other modes of profit regulation. Under price caps, services for purposes of regulatory supervision are bundled together and a price index for the bundle is monitored; the index is not to exceed a set relation over time to the movement in the retail price index. With price caps, a firm's profits can increase in accordance with greater productivity, and these profits can then in turn be used to help finance foreign ventures, as opposed to lowering prices for domestic customers.[9]

Second, it is often argued, national economies have become units of an increasingly integrated world economic system.[10] Hence national governments see as one of their primary tasks lowering or eliminating barriers to the transnational flow of goods, services, information, and capital. For this reason, national governments are relaxing their foreign ownership restrictions on domestic telecommunications companies and are also deregulating operations of domestic telecommunications carriers in other ways.

A third goal of policymakers in the era of the new telecommunications, as we have seen, is to increase competition. Thus the CRTC, for example, encourages the entry of cable television companies into the local telephone services market and permits telephone companies to offer broadcasting-type services.

Finally, in the new telecommunications, the venerable goal of providing a universally accessible and affordable telecommunications service, while still affirmed, is being redefined and reduced. Rather than being applied to the full range of telecommunications services, as was the case in the old telecommunications, the goals of universal and affordable access increasingly pertain only to 'basic' services, also known as POTS – plain old telephone service. Enhanced or value-added services, such as e-mail and other Internet services, voice mail, electronic database services, video-on-demand, and so forth, are now to be governed predominantly by market forces rather than by direct public policy.[11] Indeed, distinctions between basic and enhanced telecom services have been set out in bilateral and multilateral trade treaties such as the North American Free Trade Agreement and the General Agreement on Tariffs and Trade. These agreements severely constrain the freedom of signatory governments to enact domestic policies in the area of enhanced services.

From the foregoing, it becomes apparent that the new, converged telecommunications are part and parcel of a process often called globalization. It is in that context that the real policy issues, often unarticulated in official circles, are to be understood.

The Real Issues

Any number of geopolitical trends and issues are raised by the new, converged telecommunications. This is because the new telecommunications entail the unleashing of global market forces, not only in the provision of transmission services (carriage) but also in the flow of international information (content). Even as the capacity of telecom systems continues to expand exponentially, hitherto separate systems of broadcasting, the press, and even postal services and banking are being interlinked to form a seamless, digitalized, global infrastructure. These events, moreover, are taking place within a context of a diminished public sphere. While many significant issues are raised by these developments, in this section there is space to note only a few.

Global Divisions of Labour

Today there continues to be an ever-increasing predominance in world commerce of transnational corporations (TNCs). Mulgan argues that information technologies have fundamentally transformed TNCs. Early TNCs were *multinational firms*, which owned relatively autonomous branch plants in various countries.[12] Multinationals were succeeded, first, by *international corporations*, which used standardized procedures and managerial practices, and more recently by *global corporations*, which exploit global economies of scale through international divisions of labour.

Global enterprises, obviously, are dependent upon instantaneous communication links to coordinate and control geographically dispersed activities. The new telecommunications make cross-national coordination and control much easier. Indeed, in global networking, where the preponderant flow of data is within organizations (albeit among internationally dispersed sites), the economic significance of information shifts from mere commodity to a vital means of coordination and control.

The overriding consequences for labour of these developments, however, are subject to some disagreement. According to Carnoy et al., the corporate search for global profit as facilitated by the new telecommunications creates a new, four-fold division in the world. First, they argue, there are the clear winners (the United States, parts of Europe and Japan, for example), which are succeeding in producing information-related goods and services. Second are potential winners, such as

Mexico and Brazil, which may succeed in producing the knowledge- and information-based goods and services that are required by the evolving new world order. Third are the large continental economies of India and China, which are integrating with the world economy on account of their huge markets and large stock of skilled labour. Finally, there is the 'fourth world,' what Carnoy et al. call the 'clear loser' – the marginal rural economies and sprawling urban peripheries.[13] The authors caution that with transnationals' quest for absolute advantage, 'a significant part of the world population is shifting from a structural position of exploitation to a structural position of irrelevance.'[14]

Unfortunately, in positing a four-fold division of the world based on the degree to which countries adopt new telecommunications infrastructure and the speed at which they do so, Carnoy et al. may well be helping to perpetuate and extend global economic, cultural, political, and technological dependence and to deepen global inequalities along geographic lines. Their analysis, which is all too typical, implies that the only way developing nations can extricate themselves from poverty is by becoming ever more dependent on first world countries and on transnational enterprises by adopting yet more quickly the new telecommunications.

Another view maintains that the new telecommunication is part of a massive technological restructuring in developed and developing countries alike, whose concomitants include 'jobless growth,' automation, virtual workplaces, massive layoffs, deskilling, the demeaning of work, and computer monitoring of the workplace.[15] According to this view, when jobs in industrialized countries do emerge, they are often for part-time, term, temporary, or contract workers. White collar and blue collar workers alike face greater anxiety, less job security, less power, and often lower wages. According to Heather Menzies, the coming into place of the new infrastructure, variously known as the new telecommunications and as the information highway, 'represents a staggering social transformation, equivalent to that of the Industrial Revolution.'[16]

These trends and concerns are explained in large measure by the simultaneous appearance of free trade areas and the new telecommunications. In the new global economy, transnational companies apportion production activity among internationally scattered sites to secure their greatest absolute advantage. They withdraw capital from locations where profit margins are low and invest where they are high. Regions and countries heretofore bypassed by transnational capital are encouraged to attract new investment by lowering wages and other costs of doing business within their borders. As noted by Daly and Cobb, therefore, 'those who advocate free trade and free capital mobility are simultaneously advocating [global] equalization of wages.'[17]

Decline in National Sovereignty

In 1974, almost two decades before the break-up of the Soviet Union and the ending of the Cold War, Richard J. Barnet and Ronald E. Muller remarked that national governments would continue to be pre-eminent in a world dominated by military might, but that in a world governed by economic power, corporations would become the controlling force.[18] In retrospect, Barnet and Muller seem prophetic. In 1994, for instance, a special joint committee of the Canadian Senate and House of Commons charged with reviewing Canadian foreign policy remarked in a rather unconcerned if not indeed commendatory fashion that national governments were ceding measures of control over social and environmental programs, over tax policy, even over foreign policy, to transnational corporations. This trend was the result of the heightened ability of transnationals in the era of the new telecommunications and freer commodity and capital flows to divest quickly in any one nation or region and relocate elsewhere.[19]

Because the new telecommunications permit rapid processing and transfer of information, both short- and long-term decision making by distant managers located at the head offices of transnational businesses are proving to be increasingly the norm. According to William Melody, TNC managers are increasingly empowered through global telecommunications and computer networks to play government against government, country against country, local labour against foreign labour, and local suppliers against foreign suppliers. By threatening to shift production to other sites, TNCs gain concessions and shift risks. In this light, urging developing countries to modernize by investing heavily in the new telecommunications becomes highly problematic. Doing so may actually deepen their dependence and prolong their poverty.[20]

Today, in developed and developing countries alike, transnational business is having greater sway. In developing areas, policies consisting of privatization, deregulation, wholesale production of staples for export, lifting of constraints on foreign ownership and investment – all termed 'structural adjustments' – are being imposed by agencies such as the International Monetary Fund and the World Bank.[21] In developed countries, the same genre of 'free market' policies is being implemented, often under the guise of deficit reduction and free trade agreements.

But the effects are the same. In either instance, transnational business is empowered; local business, labour, and national governments are enfeebled.

Disparities between Rich and Poor

Finally, heightened commodity status for information, one of four main elements of the new telecommunications, has significant implications for global wealth distribution. Information as commodity means, for instance, that information-rich First World countries can and do trade information in world markets to attain foreign exchange. They use this foreign exchange to purchase energy, natural resources, and products of cheap labour. Information-poor countries, on the other hand, need to attain information/knowledge to emerge from destitution. 'Education is the ultimate resource,' according to E.F. Schumacher.[22] But to get essential elements of this ultimate resource, dependent nations must trade their endowments of resources, often non-renewable, to core countries. The First World, of course, benefits inordinately from these arrangements. In proffering 'mere' information, the First World gains access to other countries' scarce and not renewable resources at virtually zero real incremental cost to itself. This is because the 'form' component of information is infinitely reproducible; the First World even retains the information/knowledge it sells! No wonder the United States, as world leader in producing information, insisted that the General Agreement on Tariffs and Trade incorporate intellectual property in its treaties. Copyright provisions have figured prominently in bilateral and trilateral trade agreements to which the United States has been a signatory as well.

Even in First World countries, however, heightened commodification of information expands cleavages between rich and poor. We currently see a diminution (at least relatively and often in absolute terms) in the funding of public education, of public health care, of public libraries, and of public broadcasting, and a concomitant heightening of user fees for many genres of information supply – tuition fees, pay-per-view and specialty television channels, online databanks, stiffer drug patent laws, access to government data, and so forth. More complete commodification of information may well have deleterious implications for community, as money comes to mediate an ever-increasing array of human interactions, leaving 'silent' those lacking in financial resources.

Conclusion

Telecommunications have always been closely related to power – economic, political, and cultural. Changes in telecommunications, therefore, reflect and foretell changes in the possession and/or exercise of power.

Today much of the world is experiencing a shift from an old to a new, converged telecommunications. The old regime was characterized by the regulated monopoly firm, by segregation among communication services, technologies, and modes of regulation, by universal service through cost averaging and cross-subsidization, and by national (or even state or provincial) regulation. The new telecommunications, in contrast, are characterized by increased competition, convergence, and deregulation, and by harmonization among states of their telecommunications policies.

These changes foretell a shift in communicatory, and hence also in economic, political, and cultural power. This shift is away from national governments to private businesses, particularly transnational corporations; away from labour to capital; away from providers and users of public communication services to providers and users of commodified information and communicatory products and services. Countries that are net exporters of information as commodity and of advanced means of communicating will benefit at the expense of net importers of information products and services.

These developments are taking place despite, not because of, properties inherent to information. Nonetheless, there is a waning in the concept and practice of public communication and conversely a steadily increasing reliance on market forces to allocate informational and communicatory resources.

Given ecological and environmental crises, whether the world can withstand ever-increasing relations of commodity exchange is a moot point. What is clear, however, is that those seeking greater equality, justice, and community should contemplate critically the new telecommunications and the accompanying practice of further commodifying communicatory interactions. Increased commodification of information is a most significant force transforming our world.

NOTES

1 Robin Mansell, *The New Telecommunications: A Political Economy of Network*

Evolution (Thousand Oaks, CA: Sage, 1993); Robin Mansell and Roger Silverstone, *Communication by Design: The Politics of Information and Communication Technologies* (Oxford: Oxford University Press, 1996).

2 Robert E. Babe, *Telecommunications in Canada: Technology, Industry and Government* (Toronto: University of Toronto Press, 1990).

3 Ibid.

4 United States, Federal Communications Commission, *Investigation of the Telephone Industry in the United States* (1939; repr., New York: Arno, 1974); N.R. Danielian, *A.T.&T.: The Story of Industrial Conquest* (New York: Vanguard, 1939). See also chapter 6 in this volume.

5 Robert E. Babe, 'Vertical Integration and Productivity: Canadian Telecommunications,' *Journal of Economic Issues* 15, no. 1 (1981): 1–31; excerpted in this book as Appendix to Part Two.

6 Herbert I. Schiller, *Information Inequality: The Deepening Social Crisis in America* (New York: Routledge, 1996), 35.

7 Colleen Roach, 'Dallas Smythe and the New World Information and Communication Order,' *Illuminating the Blindspots: Essays Honoring Dallas W. Smythe*, ed. J. Wasko, V. Mosco, and M. Pendakur (Norwood, NJ: Ablex, 1993), 278.

8 Dallas Smythe, *The Relevance of United States Legislative-Regulatory Experience to the Canadian Telecommunications Situation. A Study for the Telecommission* (Ottawa: Information Canada, 1971), 124.

9 H.M. Trebing, 'Common Carrier Regulation: The Silent Crisis,' *Law and Contemporary Problems* 34 (Spring 1969): 299–329.

10 M. Carnoy, M. Castells, S. Cohen, and F.H. Cardoso, *The New Global Economy in the Information Age: Reflections on Our Changing World* (University Park: Pennsylvania State University Press, 1993), 6.

11 Mansell and Silverstone, *Communication by Design*, 223–5.

12 G.J. Mulgan, *Communication and Control: Networks and the New Economies of Communication* (New York: Guilford, 1991), 29–30.

13 Carnoy et al., *New Global Economy*, 7.

14 Ibid., 37.

15 H. Menzies, *Whose Brave New World? The Information Highway and the New Economy* (Toronto: Between the Lines, 1996), 29–37.

16 Ibid., 7.

17 H.E. Daly and J. Cobb, *For the Common Good: Redirecting the Economy toward Community, the Environment and a Sustainable Future* (Boston: Beacon, 1989), 219.

18 R.J. Barnet and R.E. Muller, *Global Reach: The Power of the Multinational Corporations* (New York: Simon and Schuster, 1974), 96.

19 Canada, Special Joint Committee of the Senate and House of Commons Reviewing Canadian Foreign Policy, *Canada's Foreign Policy Principles and Priorities for the Future* (Ottawa: Publications Service, Parliamentary Publications Directorate, 1994).

20 W.H. Melody, 'The Information Society: The Transnational Economic Context and Its Implications,' *Transnational Communications: Wiring the Third World*, ed. G. Sussman and J. Lent (Newbury Park, CA: Sage, 1991), 35–7.

21 See J. Cavanaugh, D. Wysham, and M. Arruda, eds., *Beyond Bretton Woods: Alternatives to the Global Economic Order* (London: Pluto, 1994).

22 E.F. Schumacher, *Small Is Beautiful: Economics as if People Mattered* (London: Sphere Books, 1974), 64–83.

8 An Information Revolution?

If the information revolution may be said to have had a father, surely it would be Fritz Machlup, formerly economics professor at Princeton. Machlup's 1962 book, *The Production and Distribution of Knowledge in the United States*, was the inaugural attempt to identify and explore the pervasive importance for the U.S. economy of information and knowledge production. That seminal work inspired two burgeoning literatures: most directly, one on the information economy, but also another on the information society. The latter incorporates social, cultural, and political analyses and forecasts deemed attributable to the perceived exponential growth in information-related activity. Together these two literatures, one on economy and one on society, make up the conceptual underpinning of the information revolution.

It was Machlup's contention that in the United States since 1900 there has been a gradual but distinct shift in the occupational composition of the labour force, entailing 'a continuous increase in "knowledge producing" workers and a relative decline in what used to be called "productive labor."'[1] Cumulatively these gradual shifts have been dramatic. By 1958, according to Machlup, the 'knowledge industry' accounted for roughly 29 per cent of U.S. gross national product.

Fifteen years later a monumental study encompassing nine volumes was completed under the auspices of the U.S. Department of Commerce. Again attempting to quantify the economic importance of information-related activity, *The Information Economy* declared that the information sector in 1967 accounted for more than 46 per cent of U.S. GNP. Marc Porat, one of the principal authors, estimated information workers to have increased from 13 per cent of the U.S. labour force in 1900 to 25 per cent in 1940 and 46 per cent in 1974.[2] Hence, he summarized, 'we are now an information economy.'[3] Shortly thereafter,

Serafini and Andrieu of Canada's federal Department of Communications applied Porat's methodology to Canadian data, reporting that information workers had increased from 29 to 40 per cent of the Canadian labour force between 1951 and 1972, a trend generally replicated, according to the authors, in all other developed economies. Later that department reported that information workers comprised 45 per cent of Canadian employment in 1986.[4]

While Machlup and Porat, at least initially, concentrated on economic aspects of the information revolution, it is to sociology professor Daniel Bell of Harvard that credit or responsibility must be given for extending the revolution to culture and society. For Bell, history comprises threes: three distinct infrastructures (transportation; electrification; and now, computer communications), three principal epochs (pre-industrial, based on agriculture and mining; industrial, or manufacturing; and now, post-industrial, that is, information-based), and three transforming resources (first, natural power; next, created energy; and now, information).[5] In other words, like other post-industrial prophets, Bell hypothesized a new centrality for information-related activities; and this centrality, he believed, represents a fundamental break with the industrial past.

Techniques

Although electronic techniques and devices for communicating are over 150 years old, the literature of the information revolution emphasizes engineering developments since the Second World War, especially calling attention to dramatic increases in capacity, speed, and ubiquity and to equally dramatic reductions in cost and size. In this regard analogies and metaphors are both copious and imaginative. Alexander King, for example, remarked that in three decades a whole roomful of vacuum tubes and other components had been reduced to the size of a cornflake.[6] Likewise, Christopher Evans compared developments in computing to a make-believe world of automobiles: 'Suppose for a moment that the automobile industry had developed at the same rate as computers and over the same period [about thirty years]: how much cheaper and more efficient would the current models be? If you have not already heard the analogy, the answer is shattering. Today you would be able to buy a Rolls Royce for £1.35; it would do three million miles to the gallon, and it would deliver enough power to drive the *Queen Elizabeth II.* And if you were interested in miniaturization, you could place half a dozen of them on a pinhead.'[7]

Developments in computing have been paralleled by advances in transmission. Coaxial cable and now fibre-optic cable have multiplied transmission capacity of the telephone network's original transmission medium (copper pair wire) by several hundreds of thousands, while satellites provide yet a further illustration: in 1965 the annual cost per telephone circuit on satellites was $22,000; in 1980, $800; and in 1985, $30.[8] During the past several decades, telecommunications costs, conceived broadly for all transmission media, have declined by 11 per cent per annum.[9]

Considered separately, innovations in both computing and transmission have been impressive enough. Of still greater significance, however, has been the integration of these two industrial arts into computer networking. On the one hand, dramatic reductions in cost and size have allowed computing power to be distributed throughout telecommunications networks (distributed processing). On the other, telecommunications networks are being digitalized – made capable of transmitting information in the same machine-readable form used in computing. Now all human-readable information (pictures, text, voice, data) can be coded into on/off bursts of energy, permitting texts to be instantaneously acted upon by computers (delayed or stored, edited, corrected, processed, combined in new ways) – even while in transit – prior to being retranslated at their destination into human-readable language (if in fact such retranslation takes place at all).

Power

Such developments bring us much closer to the essence of the information revolution. In describing the integration of computers and telecommunications, then–communications minister Francis Fox noted sagely,

> The important thing about information technology is not so much that it uses and processes information – which it does in abundance – but that it is fundamentally a *control* technology. This has led to a confusion about the nature of its impact, with much effort focused on the emergence of 'information economies,' 'information societies,' and such like. But in fact information stands in relation to *the real agent of technological change* in much the same way as smoke to fire or dust to a sandstorm: it is an index, or superficial manifestation, of a deeper phenomenon. If we are to understand the nature of the new information technologies, it is necessary to focus less on their content and more on their function (i.e. regulation – in the cybernetic sense of the term – of systems, or in other words control).[10]

The revolution, then, in the view of Francis Fox, concerns the rapid development and application of new and increasingly powerful techniques of control, and is to be contrasted with the Machlup-Bell-Porat paradigm that merely emphasizes an exponential growth in information-related activity in an idealized or depoliticized world. Mr Fox's statement invites us to reconsider communication devices in the real world of power struggle and powerplay.

Unfortunately, much of the literature on the information revolution addresses what is happening and projects what will happen in an idealized world, far removed from the nitty-gritty of actual institutions, rivalries, corporate and governmental power plays, greed, propaganda, and public relations. In the idealized world of the policymaker and futurologist, engineered devices are mythologized as 'technology,' and human agents become transformed into mere spectators, moulded by an ineluctably evolving technical environment.

The Myth of the Machine[11]

New Technologies, Old Idolatries

As may be readily apparent, the literature on the information revolution often encourages readers to stand in awe of 'new technologies.' Humanity in awe of its artefacts is nothing new to the information revolution. Isaiah berated his countrymen for worshipping the 'works of their hands, [bowing down] to what their own fingers have made.' He continued, 'So man is humbled and men are brought low.'[12] And so it is in our day. Much of the literature on the information revolution attributes to information-related artefacts both inevitability and omnipotence in effects. In particular, two interrelated doctrines (or myths) are frequently propagated: *technological determinism* and *the technological imperative*. The former posits all important human phenomena to be attributable to or explainable by 'technology.' The latter postulates 'technology' to be autonomous, having a life, growth, and development of its own; it is dependent perhaps on human agents for support but, in a more profound sense, is inevitable.[13]

Ubiquity

Mythologizing 'technology' is not limited to science fiction. Rather, the proclivity to mythologize can be detected in both non-fiction/academic literatures on the information revolution and government policy pronouncements. This section samples the former literatures to help establish ubiquity; extracts from Canadian policy documents have been presented in a previous chapter.

One of the most widely read exponents of an information revolution has been Alvin Toffler, who developed the metaphor of the wave to describe (not explain) rapid innovation in the areas of electronics and computers, the space industry, oceanics, and biotechnology. Toffler's metaphor was intended not only to imply simultaneity of innovation across seemingly diverse fields, but also to connote the all-inclusive and unavoidable nature of the consequences. He wrote,

A powerful tide is surging across much of the world today, creating a new, often bizarre, environment in which to work, play, marry, raise children, or retire. In this bewildering context, businessmen swim against highly erratic economic currents; politicians see their ratings bob wildly up and down; universities, hospitals, and other institutions battle desperately against inflation. Value systems splinter and crash, while lifeboats of family, church and state are hurled madly about ... [However] many of today's changes are not independent of one another. Nor are they random ... They are, in fact, parts of a much larger phenomenon: the death of industrialism and the rise of a new civilization ... The grand metaphor of this work, as should already be apparent, is that of colliding waves of change.[14]

Throughout Toffler's writings there are allusions to the inexorability of this third wave, which transforms everything in sight. Nothing remains untouched, nor can anything stand in its wake. This change, while systematic and all-inclusive, itself remains unexplained, is evidently uncaused, and is therefore unexplainable.

In like fashion, Daniel Bell pronounced, 'With the revolution in communications, all ... will change.'[15] Why? Because information-related 'technologies' are pictured as proliferating (exponentially). Information is seen as growing in volume (again, exponentially). These occurrences are deemed to be quite natural, evidently part of the order of things – despite Bell's conviction that traumatic cultural social and psychological consequences may result from our 'transition' to post-industrial society.

Marc Porat, too, after completing his quantitative studies on the information economy, succumbed to mythic explanations for an information revolution, maintaining technology to be 'the big wheel that drives all the little wheels.' 'Little wheels' to Porat include economy, ideology, society, culture, and polity.[16] Even more unfortunately, from our perspective, Porat's conjecturing has been embraced uncritically by some Canadian policy analysts and academics addressing policy issues.[17]

An imaginative and possibly powerful twist to themes of technological omnipotence and inexorability was invented by Arthur C. Clarke, who merged the myth of 'technology' with evolution. *Technological evolution*, Clarke announced, is transforming, if not utterly obliterating, humanity. He asked, 'Can the synthesis of men and machine ever be stable, or will the purely organic component become such a hindrance that it has to be discarded? If this eventually happens – and I have ... good reasons for thinking that it must – we have nothing to regret and certainly nothing to fear ... The Tool we have invented is our successor. Biological evolution has given way to a far more rapid process – technological evolution. No individual exists forever: why should we expect our species to be immortal? Man, said Nietzsche, is a rope stretched between the animal and the superhuman – a rope across the abyss. That will be a noble purpose to have served.'[18]

Clarke's theme was taken up a decade and a half later, albeit in moderation, by Christopher Evans. Reminiscent of Isaiah's countrymen, Evans evidently deemed human artefacts to be superior to their creators:

> During the 1990s computers will increasingly serve as intellectual and emotional partners. We are about to embark on a massive programme to develop highly intelligent machines, a process by which we will lead computers by the hand until they reach our own intellectual level, after which they will proceed to surpass us ... When they *do* overtake us, computers will, in my opinion become extremely interesting entities to have around. Their role as teachers and mentors, for example, will be unequalled. It will be like having as private tutors the wisest, most knowledgeable and most patient humans on earth: an Albert Einstein to teach physics ... a Sigmund Freud to discuss the principles of psycho-analysis, and all available where and when they are wanted.[19]

Nor should the writings of Marshall McLuhan be ignored when considering influential myth-makers. That great guru of the electronic era interpreted media as prosthetic extensions, re-orchestrating the senses, and creating a new humanity: 'To behold, use, or perceive any extension of ourselves in technological form is necessarily to embrace it. To listen to radio or to read the printed page is to accept these extensions of ourselves into our own personal system and to undergo "closure" or displacement that follows automatically ... By continually embracing technologies, we relate ourselves to them as servo-mechanisms. That is why we must, to use them at all, serve these objects, these extensions of ourselves, as gods or minor religions.'[20]

Because humans are remade by their manufactured extensions, and because humans serve them as well as use them, McLuhan believed that media transform virtually all aspects of culture and society; by comparison, uses made of media (the 'content') are 'ineffectual.'[21] Significantly, McLuhan refrained from addressing the topics of how, why, and by whom new media are introduced and diffused. In brief, to quote Roland Barthes on the property of myth, all 'soiling trace of origin or choice'[22] is absent from McLuhan's writings, or at least from those written during his period of celebrity.

Demythologizing Technology

One requirement for freedom, Jacques Ellul stated, is to demythologize technology, because 'technique has come to represent both necessity and fate for modern man, and thus, the effort to recover our ethical identity is the equivalent of resuming the fight for freedom.'[23] Technology as necessity and as fate, Ellul continued, has inculcated our hearts with an 'insidious ethics of adaptation,' resting on the notion that 'since technique is a fact, we should adapt ourselves to it'; 'anything that hinders technique ought to be eliminated, and thus adaptation itself becomes a moral criterion.'[24]

We cannot be free, Ellul insisted, if technique is or becomes an end in itself, thereby reorienting the very values and criteria that should be used to make decisions concerning the development and implementation of our artefacts. To be free, Ellul concluded, we must view our machines as mere tools, helping us to accomplish explicitly articulated goals. Simply because something is possible to accomplish does not in itself make it desirable to do so.

Why Mythology?

Three related suggestions are now offered to help explain the mythological allure of fabricated devices: the human condition; Western culture; and purposeful propagation (the consciousness industry).

The Human Condition

Innately, movement and change attract attention; constancy tends to be hidden. Alluding to McLuhan, Hugh Kenner once wrote that fish, always submerged, know nothing of water; while it is futile to explain water to them, they do understand swimming and will take particular note of how well one uses one's flippers. On the one hand, organisms must be sensitive to sudden environmental changes to survive. On the other, essentially unchanging or slow-to-change features of the environment tend not to be perceived – a defence against sensory overload. Gregory Bateson has wisely remarked that 'the unchanging is imperceptible unless we are willing to move relative to it.'[25] No wonder then that so much attention is today riveted on new technologies, with underlying and enduring human traits and proclivities, such as the quest for dominance and power, being obscured in the process.

It is not merely attentiveness to change that is at work here, however; innate human frailty is surely a factor too. We are all born naked into the world, without power and vulnerable. And inventions provide an illusion at least of power and protection, seemingly equipping us to withstand better the vagaries of circumstance. To illustrate: with the onset of electric telegraphy in the nineteenth century, commentators not infrequently cited the following rhetorical question from the biblical Book of Job to underscore heightened confidence in humanity's ability to control its destiny:[26] 'Canst thou send lightnings, that they may go and say unto thee, "Here we are?"' The supreme irony, of course, is not that we can now do what God implied Job could not; rather, it is to be found in our increased vulnerability as we develop and deploy increasingly powerful techniques. Theodor Adorno once commented, 'No universal history leads from savagery to humanity, but one indeed from the slingshot to the H-bomb; it culminates in the total threat of organized humanity against organized human beings, in the epitome of discontinuity.'[27]

In this light, the human propensity to mythologize 'technology' becomes more comprehensible. We don godlike powers as we 'put equipment on,' but we find ourselves yet more vulnerable as a result.

Western Culture

Apart from the human condition, we can also look briefly to historical development in Western thought and culture. It is instructive to begin with Francis Bacon (1561–1626), author of *New Atlantis*, a utopian vision of a society ordered on scientific principles. Bacon is sometimes held to be father of technologism and scientism.[28] With him arose the idea that there is a kind of knowledge that grows incrementally and systematically, not as a result of hit-and-miss discovery, but as the product of a deliberate activity of the mind. Bacon proposed that the inductive method (inference of general principles consistent with many particular observations) replace the a priorism of medieval scholasticism. Consequently, Bacon's new *will to know* left behind 'all philosophy and theology which end in passive meditation on a cosmic order held to be fixed and unalterable.'[29] For Bacon the only true knowledge was practical knowledge, since 'truth and utility are here the very same things.'[30] Therefore knowledge for Bacon 'is that which yields a steady increase of human control over the environment ... and which is forthcoming upon deliberate exercise of "the will to know"'[31]

While Bacon promulgated a will to know to attain instrumental knowledge, Friedrich Nietzsche (1844–1900) promoted its perhaps inevitable successor, the *will to power*. For Nietzsche, all values, limitations, and beliefs are relative and man-made, and are exposed as such through environmental, institutional, and cultural changes wrought by applications of Bacon's instrumental knowledge.

But this belief creates an existential dilemma: more and more powerful means but less and less confidence in the ends or purposes for which the means are deployed. At the limit, George Grant has argued, our innovating and application of instrumental knowledge could become quite unencumbered of any intimations of what is good to will. Nietzsche's nihilists, Grant tells us, are those who know nothing of what is good to will but nonetheless would 'rather will nothing than have nothing to will.'[32] The proclivity to mythologize becomes easily comprehensible in light of Nietzsche's insight. Technology provides ever-more-powerful means for accomplishing deeds, even while eroding criteria whereby the deeds, and hence the means, can be judged.

Consciousness Industry[33]

Finally, not to be neglected, is *the consciousness industry*, through which concerted effort is made to propagate technologism as inevitable, and hence as goodness and truth. Firms and industries producing hardware and software, nations and transnational corporations seeking to extend international influence and dominance, telecommunications carriers, and the scientific elite – all have vested interests in mythologizing 'technology.'[34]

How much easier it is, for example, for the government of Canada to proclaim that Canadians face an ineluctable information revolution producing its own dramatic, unforeseen, but inevitable effects, than to admit that information devices and their consequences are *variables* that get worked out only within a legal/policy framework of which the government is chief architect and for which the government bears ultimate responsibility!

How much more profitable is it for transnational high-tech firms to foster an aura of awe and inevitability respecting engineered artefacts than to acknowledge that emerging communication techniques are powerful devices wielded in a continuing battle for international influence and dominance!

Mythologizing 'technology' serves well the interests of both government and industry. Mythologizing 'technology' transforms conscious acts (frequently entailing billions of investment dollars, tax write-offs, and subsidies) into the mythically inevitable and 'natural' order of things. Moreover, mythologizing 'technology' obscures the locus of responsibility, no small advantage for those who deploy advanced techniques; after all, how can anyone be held responsible for the inevitable? Finally, mythologizing 'technology' sweeps aside debate concerning the distribution of power domestically and internationally, and the utilization of communication media towards those ends.

Myths of communication 'technology' thus inform us that nothing is selected, nothing chosen. Rather, all one has to do is to possess these new devices from which all soiling trace of origin and choice has been effaced.

Hence, we find a third reason for the current pervasiveness of these myths; they are simply useful for some to propagate.

NOTES

1 Fritz Machlup, *The Production and Distribution of Knowledge in the United States* (Princeton, NJ: Princeton University Press, 1962).
2 Marc Uri Porat, *The Information Economy: Definition and Measurement, Special Publication*, 77-12 (Washington DC: Office of Telecommunication, U.S. Department of Commerce, 1977), 1; also, Michael R. Rubin, ed., *Information*

Economics and Policy in the United States (Littleton, CO: Libraries Unlimited, 1983), 20–4.

3 Porat, *Information Economy*, 1.

4 Canada, Department of Communications, *Communications for the Twenty-First Century* (Ottawa: Supply and Services, 1987), 13.

5 See, particularly, Daniel Bell, 'The Social Framework of the Information Society,' in *The Computer Age: A Twenty-Year View*, ed. M. Dertouzos and J. Moses, 163–211 (Cambridge, MA: MIT Press, 1979); and Daniel Bell, 'Teletext and Technology,' in *The Winding Passage* (New York: Basic Books, 1980), 34–65.

6 Alexander King, 'A New Industrial Revolution or Just Another Technology?' in *Micro-electronics and Society*, ed. G. Friedrichs and A. Schaff (New York: Mentor, 1982), 4.

7 Christopher Evans, *The Mighty Micro: The Impact of the Computer Revolution* (London: Gollancz, 1979), 76.

8 Thomas Ronald Ide, 'The Technology,' in Friedrichs and Schaff, *Micro-electronics*, 52–9.

9 Manley Irwin, *Telecommunications America* (Westport, CT: Quorum Books, 1984), 48.

10 Francis Fox, *Culture and Communications: Key Elements of Canada's Economic Future* (Ottawa: Supply and Services, 1983), 4. Emphasis added.

11 It was from conversations with Dallas W. Smythe that I first became aware of our proclivity to mythologize 'technology.' Smythe generally would write the word only when surrounded by quotation marks, a practice I sometimes adopt here.

12 Isaiah 2:8–9.

13 See, generally, Langdon Winner, *Autonomous Technology* (Cambridge, MA: MIT Press, 1977).

14 Alvin Toffler, *The Third Wave* (New York: Bantam, 1981), 1–5.

15 Bell, 'The Social Framework,' 188.

16 Marc Uri Porat, 'Communications Policy in an Information Society,' in *Communications for Tomorrow*, ed. Glenn O. Robinson (New York: Praeger, 1978), 19–25.

17 R. Brian Woodrow and Kenneth B. Woodside, 'Players, Stakes and Politics in the Future of Telecommunications Policy and Regulation in Canada,' in *Telecommunications Policy and Regulation*, ed. W.T. Stanbury (Montreal: Institute for Research on Public Policy, 1986), 105–22.

18 Arthur C. Clarke, *Profiles of the Future* (New York: Bantam Books, 1964), 212–27. Clarke, of course, was author of *2001: A Space Odyssey*.

19 Evans, *The Mighty Micro*, 229.

20 Marshall McLuhan, *Understanding Media: The Extensions of Man* (New York: Mentor, 1964), 55.

21 Ibid., 24.

22 Roland Barthes, *Mythologies* (New York: Hill and Wang, 1957), 151. Emphasis added.

23 Jacques Ellul, 'The Power of Technique and the Ethics of Non-Power,' in *The Myths of Information: Technology in Post-Industrial Society*, ed. Kathleen Woodward (Madison, WI: Coda, 1980), 246.

24 Ibid., 243.

25 Gregory Bateson, *Mind and Nature: A Necessary Unity* (New York: Dutton, 1979), 97.

26 See Daniel Czitrom, *Media and the American Mind* (Chapel Hill: University of North Carolina Press, 1982), 8–10.

27 Theodor Adorno, *Negative Dialectics*, trans. Dennis Redmond (1966), http://www.efn.org/~dredmond/ndtrans.html.

28 For example, Theodore Roszak, *Where the Wasteland Ends* (Garden City, NY: Anchor Books, 1973), 29.

29 Ibid., 138.

30 Quoted in ibid.

31 Ibid.

32 George Grant, *Time as History* (Toronto: CBC Learning Systems, 1969), 34.

33 See Dallas Smythe, *Dependency Road: Communications, Capitalism, Consciousness, and Canada* (Norwood, NJ: Ablex, 1971), to whom I am indebted for use of this term.

34 Or, in Ellul's terms, means or methods or *la technique*, because of their enormity, take precedence over ends; goals are lost sight of in the face of ever more powerful means. (See his *Perspectives on Our Age*, ed. William Vanderburgh [Toronto: CBC, 1981]).

Appendix. Vertical Integration and Productivity: Canadian Telecommunications[1]

Vertical integration between telephone operating companies and equipment manufacturing companies has been highly controversial in both the United States and Canada. On the one hand, it has been argued that vertical integration results in lower costs to telephone operations than would be the case were telephone companies to procure equipment from unaffiliated suppliers on the basis of competitive bids. Cost savings are said to result from reduced contracting costs, reduced selling costs, reduced equipment compatibility problems, system-wide planning of technology, and so forth.[2] On the other hand, it is argued that vertical integration induces inefficiency on the part of telephone companies due to incentives to pay high prices or purchase too much equipment from unregulated affiliates and due to the possibility that desirable technology available only from unaffiliated suppliers will be foreclosed.[3] Indeed, it is suggested that vertical integration between a regulated public utility and an unregulated equipment supplier may constitute a principal means whereby the regulated entity escapes regulation.

While case studies have been developed that indicate that abuses on occasion do occur from heavy reliance upon a single integrated equipment supplier,[4] it has remained to be demonstrated whether the net overall effect of vertical integration is to aid or harm efficiency. One reason such studies have not been carried out in the United States is the structure of the U.S. telephone industry, making comparisons of integrated and non-integrated companies difficult.[5]

In contrast, the Canadian telephone industry [of the 1970s] is more ideally structured for an investigation of the net effect of vertical integration upon telephone company efficiency. Distinct regions of Canada are served by different companies, each with responsibility for local exchange and toll service. The companies are distinguished by their equipment procurement practices; the non-integrated firms employ competitive bidding procedures, whereas the vertically integrated companies tend to eschew competitive bids.

In 1966, the director of Investigation and Research Combines Investigation Act, Canadian Department of Consumer and Corporate Affairs, launched a ten-year study of the effects of vertical integration in the Canadian telecommunications industry. In December 1976, he submitted his report to the Restrictive Trade Practices Commission (RTPC). Beginning in June 1977, the RTPC conducted a public inquiry into the effects of vertical integration. The major portion of this article summarizes and revises a study commissioned by the director and entered as evidence before the RTPC.

This study makes productivity comparisons of integrated and non-integrated telephone companies in Canada to gain insight into the net effect of vertical integration upon the efficiency of telephone operations.

The following section provides a brief description of the structure of the Canadian telephone industry in the 1970s and early 1980s ...[6] The next section justifies productivity analysis as a means of assessing the impact of vertical integration, and the productivity analysis is then developed. The final section offers some policy implications of the preceding analysis.

The Canadian Telephone Industry and Equipment Policies

Telephone service in Canada, as elsewhere [in 1981], is provided on a monopoly basis. Although certain markets may be termed competitive (or at least characterized by rivalry), for example the provision of private lines, over 90 per cent of the revenues of telephone companies are attributable to monopolized services.

In 1978, Bell Canada accounted directly for 60 per cent of all telephones in Canada and for 95 per cent of all telephones in its territory. Bell is a shareholder owned publicly regulated company that is the dominant shareholder of three other major Canadian telephone companies: New Brunswick Telephone, Maritime Telegraph and Telephone, and Newfoundland Telephone. As of 31 December 1976, Bell Canada also owned 69.2 per cent of the shares of Northern Telecom Limited, Canada's largest telecommunications equipment manufacturer.[7] In a normal year, Bell Canada purchases 80 per cent to 90 per cent of its telecommunications equipment from Northern Telecom.[8]

In 1976, Northern Telecom had sales of $1.1 billion, of which 54 per cent were to Bell Canada and affiliates; an additional 30 per cent were to other Canadian telephone companies. Northern has in excess of 70 per cent of the Canadian operating company equipment market.[9] Bell Canada and Northern Telecom have an agreement whereby Northern's 'prices and terms [to Bell] are to be as low as those offered to its most favored customers for like materials and services under comparable condition.'[10] Since Bell Canada is regulated by the CRTC as to a permissible rate of return on a non-consolidated liabilities rate base, Bell Canada's share of Northern Telecom's earnings escapes regulatory supervision except insofar as Northern pays dividends to Bell Canada; in 1976, Northern declared dividends equal to approximately 20 per cent of net earnings.

The second-largest telephone company in Canada is British Columbia Telephone Company (BC Tel), which is essentially the sole provider of telephone service in its province. BC Tel and two equipment manufacturing firms, Automatic Electric (Canada) and Lenkurt Electric (Canada), fall under the common control of General Telephone and Electronics Corporation (United States). Since BC Tel, prior to 1979, did not itself own Lenkurt and Automatic Electric, none of the earnings of BC Tel's manufacturing affiliates were considered by the regulatory authority in setting BC Tel's revenue requirements. In 1975, BC Tel purchased 8 per cent of its telecommunications equipment from Northern Telecom and 70 per cent from its affiliates.[11] BC Tel is about one-fourth or one-fifth the size of Bell Canada.[12]

The major telephone companies in Canada have formed an association known as the Trans-Canada Telephone System (TCTS) for purposes of national telephone interconnection, long distance revenue sharing, and capacity planning. Interprovincial toll rates in Canada have been essentially non-regulated over the period covered in this study.

Telecommunications Efficiency, Productivity, and Vertical Integration

Efficiency at the firm level may be defined as the degree of correspondence between the actual costs experienced by the firm and the lowest attainable costs were the firm to use the lowest cost techniques available to it, given the level of output. The greater the deviation of actual costs from lowest attainable costs, the more inefficient the firm; the closer is the correspondence, the more efficient the firm.

Direct assessments or comparisons of efficiency in the telephone industry are at best difficult, if not totally impractical, however, for the reason that each firm operates in an exclusive territory. Differences in population density and distribution, climate, terrain, and so forth may well cause the lowest attainable level of costs to differ substantially across companies (for each output level); in any event, such lowest attainable costs will not be observed.

As one example of the problems inherent in direct efficiency comparisons, note the difficulties posed by differences in population density. Research supports the presumption that total unit distribution costs are less in more densely settled areas.[13] Moreover, population density in the Bell Canada operating territory is two to three times greater than in the territories of the other companies. On this basis, one would expect the lowest attainable level of costs (for each output level) for Bell Canada to be significantly below those of the other companies, but the extent to which such attainable costs are lower is unknown.

Productivity gain comparisons are an indirect method of assessing the relative efficiencies of the various companies. They possess the distinct advantage of using only actual observed costs; estimates of lowest attainable levels of costs are not required. Gains in productivity describe the success that various companies have in conserving inputs through improved techniques as embedded in capital items as well as in other factors of production (including management and labour). As noted previously, vertical integration may bias the choice of technology (capital equipment), distort the quantity of capital employed, and influence the prices paid for equipment, all to the detriment of the company's efficiency. *Ceteris paribus*, gains experienced by vertically integrated companies in such circumstances would be lower than those achieved by non-integrated companies that do not operate under such conflicts of interest. However, if vertical integration is indeed synergistic with telephone operations, *ceteris paribus*, the integrated companies will display higher productivity gains.

Before discussing comparisons of gains in productivity it is necessary to enlarge upon the *ceteris paribus* assumption. Productivity gains have been attributed primarily to economies of scale and technological advance (the latter being intimately related to equipment procurement policies).[14] In the telephone industry, the practices of rate averaging and cross-subsidization among services may mean that productivity gains are also attributable to a substitution of non-compensatory services (perhaps local exchange service) by lucrative services (long distance service). In addition, Northern Telecom has alleged that Bell Canada's relatively low gains in productivity are attributable to Bell's having implemented major switching advances embedded in Northern's equipment ahead of other companies.

To be assured that discrepancies in productivity observed between integrated and non-integrated companies are substantially attributable to the existence or absence of vertical integration, it is necessary to establish that three conditions exist. First, economies of scale are relatively unimportant at the firm level. Second, differential gains in productivity are not attributable to low *levels* of productivity (efficiency) in the base year. Third, shifts to 'profitable' services are not more important for companies demonstrating high gains in productivity.

Evidence on Economies of Scale

Two types of studies on economies of scale in telecommunications have been undertaken. One attempts to measure economies for portions of the system only, such as intercity communications links. The other seeks to depict the behaviour of costs as the consolidated enterprise expands, and this is the type of study most relevant here. Of course, cost characteristics of the consolidated enterprise depend upon characteristics of components, and if economies are negligible at the component level, they will not be observed, in all likelihood, at the consolidated level.

Among all the aspects of a telecommunications system, it is commonly believed that intercity transmission is the most likely to display scale economies. Even for this single component, however, the evidence on the existence of economies is at best mixed and ambiguous. For example, a consulting firm commissioned by the U.S. Federal Communications Commission to critique responses to Docket 20003 (an inquiry into the effect of selective competition in telecommunications) concluded that the available evidence lends 'no support for claims of substantial economies of scale in long distance transmission.'[15] Similarly, Leroy Mantell concluded 'that what appears to have been important and increasing returns to scale in the Bell System over the period 1946–70, were largely the result of technological improvement; when technological change is accounted for, in fact, the substantial returns to scale for long lines convert to rather large diseconomies.'[16] In addition, Leonard Waverman concluded that 'there are economies of scale for total costs when ultimate capacity of a microwave system ranges up to 996 circuits' (a very small capacity).[17]

In contrast, Ephraim Sudit found 'impressive economies of scale' but concluded, 'Which part of these impressive scale economies was due solely to technological advance [is] impossible to tell.'[18] This latter admission points up an important failing if advanced techniques of production are available to large and small firms alike.

Of more relevance to the present discussion, however, are findings regarding economies of scale in Canadian telecommunications for the consolidated enterprise. Two studies have concentrated on the firms that are discussed in this article.[19] The Institute of Applied Economic Research (Concordia University) concluded that both Bell Canada and BC Tel experience constant returns to scale, while the three non-integrated companies as a group experience diseconomies of scale. Rodney Dobell and his colleagues estimated that Bell Canada experiences 'modest returns to scale,' and that 'a doubling of all inputs would raise output by 110 percent rather than 100 percent as would be the case with a constant return to scale function.' Non-Bell members of TCTS, however, were found to experience constant returns to scale, although the authors admitted data problems. They concluded, 'It is possible that slight increasing returns to scale typify the growth of the large telephone companies.'

In summary, while it is possible that a portion of the differential gains in productivity experienced by the various companies is attributable to economies of scale, the supporting evidence is certainly not extensive.

Indeed, in reviewing material presented by Bell Canada purporting to demonstrate widespread economies of scale, the CRTC concluded, 'On the basis of all the material submitted on this issue, the Commission considers that Bell failed to provide adequate empirical evidence to support its contentions regarding the nature and extent of any economies of scale enjoyed by it.'[20]

It also is to be noted that economies of scale become much less important when the rate of technological advance is rapid. Equipment designed for large capacity may become obsolete long before it is filled,[21] and the telephone companies have argued that technological obsolescence is continually decreasing service lives of equipment in the industry.

Base Levels of Efficiency

It is conceivable that an inefficient company may experience greater gains in productivity over time than an efficient company simply because the former may be introducing cost-saving measures already introduced by the latter. The base year for this study is 1967.[22] Consequently, as a test of this 'catching up' hypothesis, Table 2 gives percentage rate increases implemented by the various companies over the periods 1950–67 and 1950–77.

Table 2
Percentage rate increases introduced by five Canadian telephone companies, 1950–67 and 1950–77

| | 1950–67 | | 1950–77 | |
Company	Local rates	Intra-territory toll rates	Local rates	Intra-territory toll rates
Bell Canada	49.0	22.0	101.0	65.0
BC Tel	87.0	47.0	197.0	112.0
Manitoba Telephone	17.6	18.0	45.0	46.0
Saskatchewan Telecommunications	29.0	9.0	67.0	37.0
Alberta Government Telephones	20.0	n.k.	62.0	n.k.

n.k. = not known
Source: Restrictive Trade Practices Commission, 'Exhibit T-487F,' table A-3, *Telecommunications Equipment Inquiry* (1978), table compiled by author.

Telephone companies practise a form of cost-plus pricing. Although prices for individual services need not be based on the cost of providing that particular service, the overall rate structure and level are designed to cover all costs and provide a reasonable return on capital. Therefore, rate increases reflect rising costs that are not compensated for by rising output; a company experiencing no inflationary pressure and no gain in productivity would not be required to implement any rate increases over time, even though the level of output were to change.

The fact that Bell Canada and BC Tel introduced rate increases over the period 1950–67 that were orders of magnitude greater than those implemented by the three non-integrated companies is prima facie evidence that the latter experienced greater gains in productivity over the seventeen-year period *prior* to the base year of this study.[23] This is strong inferential evidence that in the base year (1967) the non-integrated companies were at least as efficient as the integrated companies.[24]

Productivity Comparisons

Telephone Company Studies

Both Bell Canada and Alberta Government Telephones (AGT) have

Table 3
Total factor productivity gain comparisons, Bell Canada and Alberta Government
Telephones, 1967–76

Year	Bell Canada	Alberta Government Telephones
1967	100.0	100.0
1968	104.6	106.9
1969	108.2	114.3
1970	112.4	120.6
1971	111.4	126.3
1972	117.3	140.8
1973	123.5	153.4
1974	132.0	175.1
1975	143.3	189.8
1976	146.0	190.0

Sources: Bell Canada, 'Memorandum on Bell Canada's Productivity,' updated as RTPC
Exhibit T-832; Alberta Government Telephones, 'AGT Productivity Relationships,' printed
as Appendix 4 in 'Evidence in Chief of Alberta Government Telephones, Saskatchewan
Telecommunications and Manitoba Telephone System, the Canadian Radio-television
and Telecommunications Commission between Canadian Pacific Limited and Canadian
National Railway Company, Applicants, and the Bell Telephone Company of Canada,
Respondent,' April 1978; and RTPC Exhibit No. T-833.

conducted studies estimating their own productivity gains over the
period 1967–76. Table 3 sets forth the results of these studies.

The methodology used in the Bell and AGT studies was similar to
that developed by John Kendrick.[25] Indices of real value added (revenues after deduction of purchased inputs, and deflated for price
increases) are divided by indices of capital and labour input weight-
ed by their relative contribution to the production process in the base
year. Capital service input is derived from an age-adjusted estimate of
capital stock.

It is to be noted from Table 3 that AGT's gain in productivity over the
decade 1967–76 was twice that experienced by Bell Canada. AGT states
that the methodology employed by Bell Canada for Bell's measurement
of productivity was 'applied to data from the AGT system.'[26] These two
studies are the only publicly available total factor productivity analyses
in Canadian telecommunications to have been carried out prior to the
study discussed here. To date, the required database for traditional productivity studies (in particular, time series data pertaining to physical
capital inputs) has not been generated for MTS (Manitoba Telephone
System), BC Tel, or Sask Tel (Saskatchewan Telecommunications).

Five-Company Productivity Comparison

Comparison of Methodologies

The most common method of estimating productivity is to compare changes in the ratio of estimates of physical output and estimates of physical input over time; an increase in the ratio is declared to be an increase in productivity. Such is the approach followed by Bell Canada and AGT in measuring productivity gains.[27] At present it is impossible to carry out similar productivity analyses for the three remaining companies for lack of data, especially with regard to capital service input.

The methodology employed here circumvents data problems; in the process, it also avoids certain conceptual difficulties (chiefly pertaining to the assumption of pure competition) inherent in the traditional approach. This article employs an alternative measure of productivity that is in keeping with regulatory methodology in rate setting. This implied productivity measure (termed Relative 'e') is defined as the difference between the value of rate increases and the inflationary element of factor costs. If a telephone company experiences no inflationary pressures (for example, average factor payments, defined as wage rate and percentage return to capital, are unchanged), and if the company experiences no change in productivity (that is, the number of units of input required to produce a unit of output is constant, given increasing or decreasing output), no rate increases will be required. If, however, a telephone company experiences inflationary pressures over time (for example, wages are rising, the reward to capital increases), rate 'relief' will be required to the extent that productivity increases (decline in number of units of input required to produce a unit of output) are unable to compensate for inflationary costs. It is conceivable that productivity increases could more than compensate for inflationary rewards to factors of production, in which case we would observe a reduction in rates. The index of productivity isolates productivity increases from the truism that increased revenues due to rate increases must equal the sum of cost increases attributable to the increased rate of compensation accruing to each factor of production, less increased (or decreased) productivity.

It is to be noted at the outset that this measure of productivity gain can be applied to unregulated as well as to regulated firms. In other words, the measure does not depend upon the fact that regulatory bodies attempt to set the permissible rate of return on capital approximately equal to the opportunity cost of capital. Productivity increases can be shared among the various factors of production through higher rewards as well as through lower prices to consumers; an increased return to capital with no increase in prices or reduction in reward to other factors is indicative of a productivity increase of which capital is the sole beneficiary.

The second preliminary point is that, in the accounting sense, revenues equal costs plus profits. In this article, for ease of exposition, the reward to capital (comprising interest and earnings), is termed a cost, not in the economic sense of opportunity cost, but in the accounting sense of a reward to a productive factor. It may or may not include the economists' concept of 'rent,' which is a return over and above the payment needed to attract the resource. Therefore, each year, total costs equal total revenues, in the sense that total revenues accrue to factors of production.

With these conceptual statements in mind, it is now appropriate to construct the index mathematically.

Change in total revenue from year 0 to year 1 comprises two components: increased revenues attributable to increased real output and to increased prices for telephone service. The growth in real output is symbolized as

$$\Sigma P_0 Q_1 - \Sigma P_0 Q_0$$

with P and Q representing price and quantity, and the numerical subscripts the years, and the Greek sigma indicating summation of revenues from all service categories.

The growth in revenues attributable to rate increases is symbolized as

$$\Sigma P_1 Q_1 - \Sigma P_0 Q_1$$

Henceforth, for simplicity, the sigma will be dropped.

Growth in revenues attributable to rate increases is explicable by two underlying factors: i, inflationary reward to factor inputs, and e, change in productivity. While factor i is generally 'positive' for all companies (that is, factor costs [rewards] are generally rising for all companies), item e may be 'negative' or 'positive.'

In analysing factor i, that is, inflationary costs, assume two general factors of production: L (labour) and K (capital). Total increased wage payments from year 0 to year 1, $w_1 L_1 - w_0 L_0$, comprise (1) increased growth of labour employed at constant wages, $w_0 L_1 - w_0 L_0$, and (2) the remainder attributable to higher wage rates, $(w_1 - w_0) L_1$. Similarly, increased capital payments (costs) attributable to increased returns to capital can be represented by $(k_1 - k_0) K_1$.

In addition to increased returns to labour and capital, telephone companies face inflationary pressures stemming from purchased services, materials and supplies, and so forth. The inflationary impact of these other costs is depicted as $(c_1 - c_0) C_1$, where c_1 represents average price of these components in year 1.

The inflationary factor, i, then, is given as

$$i = (w_1 - w_0) L_1 + (k_1 - k_0) K_1 + (c_1 - c_0) C_1.$$

Since the remainder of revenue increases attributable to rate increases (as opposed to real growth) is attributed to productivity, e, then

$$- e = P_1 Q_1 - P_0 Q_1 - i$$
$$= P_1 Q_1 - P_0 Q_1 [(w_1 - w_0) L_1 + (k_1 - k_0) K_1 + (c_1 - c_0) C_1].$$

To make e comparable among firms, divide it by a scale factor, namely, $P_0 Q_1$ (real output). When divided by real output, the resulting term is known as Relative 'e.'

$$- \text{Relative } 'e' =$$

$$\frac{(P_1 Q_1 - P_0 Q_1) - (w_1 - w_0) L_1 - (k_1 - k_0) K_1 - (c_1 - c_0) C_1}{- (P_0 Q_1)}$$

At first glance, this index may appear to measure increased profitability, rather than productivity; the index shows differences in revenues and costs. Such is not the case, however, as increased profits are treated as a cost of production ($k_1 - k_0$ is defined as the change in the *realized* return to total capital).

It can be shown that Relative 'e' as developed above actually depicts the change in the gap between the growth in real output and the growth in real costs. For simplicity, let's develop the argument with e, rather than Relative 'e.'

$$e = [P_1 Q_1 - w_1 L_1 - k_1 K_1 - c_1 C_1 - (P_0 Q_1 - w_0 L_1 - k_0 K_1 - c_0 C_1)].$$

But $P_1 Q_1 - w_1 L_1 - k_1 K_1 - c_1 C_1 = 0$, by definition. Therefore,

$$e = - (P_0 Q_1 - w_0 L_1 - k_0 K_1 - c_0 C_1).$$

Since $P_0 Q_1$ is real output in year 1, measured in year 0 prices, and since $w_0 L_1 + k_0 K_1 + c_0 C_1$ represents real costs in year 1 measured in year 0 prices, the productivity index depicts real output minus real input, and when divided by real output the result reduces to

$$\frac{1 - \text{real input}}{\text{real output}}$$

The traditional productivity index is defined as

$$\frac{\text{real output}}{\text{real input}}$$

It will be noted that the present index can assume values between -1 and $+1$.

[In the original text, Babe next provides an extended section entitled 'Calculating the Terms in the Index.']

Computation of the Index

Relative 'e' is calculated here on the basis of $k_1 - k_0$ being defined as the change in the percentage gross return to capital (that is, changes in the ratio of depreciation to capitalization are assumed to be wholly 'inflationary'). The index for Bell Canada as of 1977 is 0.094; for MTS, 0.345; for Sask Tel, 0.155; for AGT, 0.302; for BC Tel, 0.062.

Interpretation

The indices of productivity show, as a proportion of real output in each year (base 1967), the real resource savings achieved since 1967 by the companies in question. It will be noted that the three non-integrated companies achieved significantly greater productivity increases over the period than did the two integrated companies.

It can be shown that Bell Canada's productivity increases for the period 1968–77 are valued at $151.4 million for the single year 1977 (constant 1967 prices), but that had Bell achieved the same relative productivity improvements as achieved by MTS, the savings would have been $555.7 million. Had Bell Canada been able to implement productivity increases equal to those of MTS, it would have saved subscribers an additional $404.3 million in 1977, or approximately 25 per cent of real output in 1977. Similarly, considering the year-by-year cumulative discrepancies in productivity between Bell Canada and the non-integrated group as a whole, it can be shown that the average productivity gains achieved by the non-integrated companies are valued at about $1.6 billion (constant 1967 dollars) over and above the productivity improvements achieved by Bell Canada, for the period 1968–77. This is about 14 per cent of Bell's real output for the period and about 95 per cent of the value of rate increases through the period.

Compared to BC Tel, the non-integrated companies achieved productivity gains valued at $315 million over and above that achieved by BC Tel for the full period (constant 1967 prices); the excess productivity on the part of the non-integrated companies equals approximately 13 per cent of BC Tel's real output for the period and 91 per cent of the value of rate increases since 1967.

Evaluation of the Methodology

The methodology for measuring productivity gains developed above is based on the generally accepted notion that productivity increases offset inflationary pressures, thereby lessening price increases for final output. In using this identity, one is not required to estimate the age distribution of plant and equipment, which entails substantial measurement problems; nor is one required to allocate capital usage by year under restrictive assumptions such as those of pure competition. This is not to say that the database discussed above cannot (and should not) be refined further; the use of the economy-wide GNP deflator for an important grouping of costs is not fully satisfactory.

The index described here has been tested for bias. Because the non-integrated telephone companies are owned by provincial governments, they are not required to pay corporate income tax; however, the integrated companies, being shareholder owned, are required to do so. In principle, it should not matter whether tax is included in the return to equity (the procedure followed above) or is removed from the relevant terms (revenues, return to capital). In the case of Bell Canada, however, removal of tax raises the index for 1977 from 0.094 to 0.119. The difference in the index calculated under these two procedures is due to changes in the capital-output ratio through time. The discrepancy in the index when calculated in these alternative ways is insignificant when compared to the discrepancies in productivity gains among the companies and does not disturb the conclusion that the productivity gains achieved by the non-integrated companies over the decade have been significantly greater than those achieved by the integrated companies.

Policy Implications

The preceding analysis leads to the conclusion that non-integrated telephone companies can achieve and do achieve productivity gains substantially in excess of those attained by integrated companies; this conclusion is supported by studies carried out by the telephone companies themselves.

In attributing cause to the above findings, one must consider the possibility of economies of scale, differences in growth rates of profitable as compared to non-compensatory services among the various companies, and initial levels of efficiency, as well as the existence and absence of vertical integration. The evidence suggests, however, that among these factors, vertical integration is the most important.

Technological advance in the telephone industry was extensive and rapid in the decade after 1967, making possible impressive gains in productivity.

In 1967, the first electronic exchange in Canada was put in service; by the end of the decade, digital switching systems threatened to make them obsolete. The decade prior to 1977 also witnessed the introduction of digital data transmission networks based on packet switching, pulse code modulation coaxial cable, communications satellites, and, of course, microelectronic circuitry, among other innovations.[28] These new techniques are available to large and small companies alike.

While it is conceivable that economies of scale were of significance in the industry prior to the mid-1960s, thus disadvantaging smaller companies, it is likely that such economies have now [1981] been overwhelmed by the much faster pace of technical advance and equipment obsolescence. Smaller companies are no longer disadvantaged, and productivity gains will be greatest for those firms that are most astute in the selection and introduction of the new techniques.

Institutional arrangements that distort management's choice of new equipment, therefore, can entail significant social costs in terms of forgone productivity gains.

In this decade it is highly unlikely that any single equipment manufacturing company can attain or will maintain a position of 'technological self-sufficiency' across the broad spectrum of telecommunications equipment. Irrespective of how progressive Northern Telecom, Automatic Electric, and Lenkurt Electric may be in certain lines of equipment, the vertically integrated telephone companies appear to be sacrificing their own efficiency of operations by not giving thorough consideration to equipment available from rival manufacturers.

There may be, of course, benefits attributable to the existence of vertical integration that have not been considered here. Northern Telecom possesses Canada's largest private research and development capability, and it has been argued that a large captive market is required for significant expenditures in that area. There may also be associated issues of employment and balance of trade entailed in vertical integration. In making public policy decisions, the full range of benefits and costs attributable to vertical integration should be considered. Nevertheless, the finding that vertical integration appears to induce considerable inefficiencies in telephone operations is an important one.

Addendum (June 2008)

The government of Canada did not require Bell Canada to divest Northern Telecom. Nor did the Restrictive Trade Practices Commission recommend divestiture. In its final report the RTPC stated, 'While Dr Babe's evidence on growth in productivity raises a question regarding B.C. Tel and Bell's performance, there are too many uncertainties regarding the causes of the measured differences to ascribe them to vertical integration.'[29]

In 2000, Bell Canada Enterprises (the holding company formed to own shares in Bell Canada, Northern Telecom, and other companies) voluntarily divested its ownership in Northern Telecom, by then renamed Nortel Networks. In the period immediately following the divestiture, Nortel accounted for about one-third of all Toronto Stock Exchange valuations. From a high of $398 billion in market capitalization in September 2000, however, Nortel's value plunged to less than $5 billion by August 2002; its stock price sunk to $0.47 from a high of $124.00![30] Arguably, BCE divested itself of Nortel so it would be better positioned to compete in the new, competitive telecommunications environment mandated by the regulator, and Nortel, no longer enjoying status as Bell's captive supplier, displayed, through its fall in market valuations, costs it had imposed over the years on Bell's subscribers through unrealized gains in productivity.

NOTES

1 Reprinted from the *Journal of Economic Issues* by special permission of the copyright holder, the Association for Evolutionary Economics.

2 See, for example, H.W. Bode, *Synergy: Technical Integration and Technological Innovation in the Bell System* (Murray Hill, NJ: Bell Laboratories, 1971).

3 See, for example, Director of Investigation and Research Combines Investigation Act, *The Effects of Vertical Integration on the Telecommunications Market in Canada* (Ottawa: Department of Consumer and Corporate Affairs, 1976).

4 Canada, Department of Communications, *Review of the Procurement Practices and Policies and the Intercorporate Financial Relationships of the British Columbia Telephone Company* (Ottawa: Minister of Communications, 1975).

5 In the late 1970s the American Telephone and Telegraph Company (AT&T) accounted for 90 per cent of all long distance (toll) revenues and over 80 per cent of local exchange revenues in the United States; AT&T controlled Western Electric, America's largest telephone equipment manufacturer. The remaining telephone companies, some of which were vertically integrated, were principally local exchange companies using the long distance lines of AT&T. In addition, the operations of the largest independent telephone companies were fragmented geographically. Therefore, direct comparisons of efficiency and/or productivity were of limited validity because of discrepancies in operating characteristics.

6 Editor's note: Deleted from this version is a section in which Babe summarizes 'some evidence that led observers to be concerned with the existence of vertical integration in Canada.' Also omitted is a subsection titled 'Noncompensatory and Lucrative Services.'

7 Bell Canada, *Statistical Report 1976* (Montreal: Bell Canada, 1977), 5–7.

8 Restrictive Trade Practices Commission (RTPC), 'In the Matter of a General Inquiry under Section 47 of the Combines Investigation Act Relating to the Manufacture of Communications Equipment' (1978), exhibit T-4, table 8.

9 Securities and Exchange Commission, *Northern Telecom Form 10-K*, Commission file no. 1-7260, 2, 5. Bell Canada and affiliates accounted for approximately 68 per cent of all Canadian telephones.

10 Ibid. 4. These provisions exclude export sales.

11 RTPC, exhibit T-4, table 10. In February 1979 BC Tel announced that it had entered into an agreement with GTE to purchase both Automatic Electric (Canada) and Lenkurt (Canada) from GTE in exchange for shares in BC Tel.

12 Babe's original article also lists Manitoba Telephone System (MTS), Alberta Government Telephones (AGT), and Saskatchewan Telecommunications (Sask Tel) as the other major telephone companies in Canada.

13 See, for example, Charles Kennedy and A.P. Thirwall, 'Surveys in Applied Economics: Technical Progress,' *Economic Journal* 82 (March 1972): 17, 18, 21, 26.

14 Statement of John DesBrisay, Northern Telecom counsel, transcripts of *Restrictive Trade Practices Commission Inquiry into the Effects of Vertical Integration in Telecommunications* (28 November 1978), 112:17694.

15 As cited in Leroy Mantell, 'Some Estimates of Returns to Scale in the Telephone Industry,' *Digest of the Conference on the Economies of Scale in Today's Telecommunications Systems*, ed. Arthur Hall (Washington, DC: IEEE, 1973), 18–26.

16 Ibid.

17 Leonard Waverman, 'The Regulation of Intercity Telecommunications,' in *Promoting Competition in Regulated Industries*, ed. Almarin Phillips (Washington DC: Brookings, 1975), 219–20.

18 Ephraim Sudit, 'Additive Nonhomogeneous Production Functions in Telecommunications,' *Bell Journal of Economics*, 4 (Autumn 1973): 499–514.

19 Institute of Applied Economic Research, *A Study of the Productive Factor and Financial Characteristics of Telephone Carriers*, prepared for Department of Communications (Montreal, QC: Concordia University, 1977); Rodney Dobell et al., 'Telephone Communications in Canada: Demand, Production and Investment Decisions,' *Bell Journal of Economics* 3 (Spring 1972): 175–219.

20 CRTC, Telecom Decision CRTC 7-11, 'CNCP Telecommunications, Interconnection with Bell Canada' (17 May 1979), 199.

21 William Melody, 'Relations between Public Policy Issues and Economies of Scale'; and Arthur D. Hall, 'An Overview of Economies of Scale in Existing Communications Systems.' Both in *Digest of the Conference*, ed. Arthur Hall (Washington DC: IEEE, 1973), 39–47, 5–17.

22 The base year 1967 was selected for numerous reasons. First, Bell Canada used 1967 as its base year in studies on its own productivity. Second, in 1966 a new regulatory methodology regarding revenue requirements for Bell Canada and BC Tel was introduced whereby percentage return on total average capitalization replaced controlled earnings per share; hence, the post-1966 period is of greater applicability … [Other reasons are outlined in original article.]

23 W.E.G. Salter, *Productivity and Technical Change*, 2nd ed. (Cambridge: Cambridge University Press, 1966), 119–23; and John W. Kendrick, *Productivity Trends in the United States*, Economic Research Study No. 71, General Series (Princeton, NJ: Princeton University Press, 1961), 201.

24 Editor's note: A subsequent subsection titled 'Noncompensatory and

Lucrative Services' in Babe's original article has been omitted from this appendix.

25 John Kendrick and Daniel Creamer, *Measuring Company Productivity* (New York: The Conference Board, 1965); and Kendrick, *Productivity Trends.*

26 Alberta Government Telephones, 'Some Economic Aspects of Interconnection, *Alberta Government Telephones, Saskatchewan Telecommunications, and Manitoba Telephone System,* 'The Canadian Radio-television and Telecommunication Commission, between Canadian Pacific Limited and Canadian National Railway Company, Applicants, and the Bell Telephone Company of Canada, Respondent' (April 1978), 3.

27 Bell Canada, 'Memorandum on Productivity,' filed as Exhibit No. B-73-62 before the Canadian Transport Commission (1974).

28 See, generally, special issue of *Telecommunications Journal* 44 (March 1977).

29 Restrictive Trade Practices Commission, *Telecommunications in Canada, Part 3: The Impact of Vertical Integration on the Equipment Industry* (Ottawa: Supply and Services, 1983), 208.

30 Editor's note: In January 2009, Nortel Networks Corp. was officially granted bankruptcy protection.

PART THREE

Canadian Communication Thought

Introduction to Part Three

PAUL HEYER*

I first met Bob early in our respective careers when we were both on faculty in the Communication Studies Department at Simon Fraser University. Since that time we have had rather peripatetic careers, never managing again to be in the same place at the same time, save for the occasional conference. Nevertheless, I have been able to follow his contributions to the discipline through an impressive body of published work. Over the years we have also encountered a number of students, apparently just as mobile as we have been, who have been able to take courses with each of us. They told me about Bob's excellence as a teacher and how he imparted to them aspects of his research in progress before it would become a publishing fait accompli. With the results of some of that research now available in this volume, I was delighted when Edward Comor invited me to write the introduction to this section.

Early Babe, if I may use that phrase, worked primarily in the fields of political economy and policy. Indeed, he still resides there on occasion. More recent Babe, however, has become a major contributor to communication theory and history, especially the history of communication thought. The essays that follow attest to that interest and strongly emphasize the Canadian legacy. The selection on McLuhan derives from Babe's important but sometimes controversial book, *Canadian Communication Thought: Ten Foundational Writers*. I should add that the controversy derives not so much from the analysis the book provides, but from the selection of the particular ten and the criteria involved. This could be likened to major film critics compiling a list of the ten

* Wilfrid Laurier University

most important films. The lists will invariably differ, but not complete-ly. Few serious critics would absent from such a list Orson Welles's *Citizen Kane* (1941) or Jean Renoir's *Rules of the Game* (1939). Similarly, the consideration of Harold Innis (1894–1952) and Marshall McLuhan (1911–80) is a virtual given. After these inclusions, in both cinema and communication studies, the debate begins.

The opening essay in this section serves as an overture to the selections that follow, and as the title suggests, can be read as a kind of prequel to the aforementioned *Canadian Communication Thought*. It highlights five thinkers who have made major contributions to com-munication studies. According to Babe, they also happened to be 'the five foremost Canadian humanities and social science scholars writing in English in the twentieth century.' It is hard to fault this judgment. Somewhat more contentious is, apart from Innis and McLuhan, linking two of the others to a field, communication studies, with which they are not normally associated. Certainly George Grant is becoming increas-ingly acknowledged as an intellectual cousin to Innis, given his critique of technology, but Northrop Frye, a literary scholar, and C.B. Macpher-son, a philosopher, have not, as far as I am aware, had a noticeable influence on communication studies in Canada (when over the years I have seen communication researchers delve into literary theory, the source usually accessed has been Kenneth Burke, not Frye).

However, this is irrelevant to Babe's argument. His point, as I see it, is that if a tree falls in the forest – or in this case if a literary theorist or philosopher writes about issues that can inform another discipline – if we haven't yet done so, we should now listen to what they have to say. Frye, for example, had very Innis-like concerns with the implica-tions of oral versus written traditions; also, like Innis, he produced a critique of culture in which the concept of balance was used to measure the excesses of modernity. Similarly, Macpherson's notion of common versus private property has resonance with Innis's take on time-bias versus space-bias; his understanding of the relationship between the ownership of the means of production and its workers complements Innis's formulations on the centre/margins dialectic.

But what have these ideas to do with Canada besides emanating from scholars who were citizens of that country? This question is broached by Babe in a way that, although not directly influenced by the sociol-ogy of knowledge, seems usefully allied to that tradition, as does much of his recent work. Citing Seymour Lipset, along with Innis, Frye, and Grant, he makes comparisons between the American ethos, founded on revolution, emphasizing individualism and a distrust of government, with the alleged roots of the Canadian Weltanschauung, more collectivist and partial toward what government can do administratively on behalf of the people. Lipset's gloss is nonetheless challenged on two fronts: for the assumption that Canada is more elitist than the United States, and for his conflation of individualism and democracy.

Yet Canada's emphasis on collectivity and the common good, along with her lack of a revolutionary history compared to the United States, needs to be tempered in light of events seemingly ignored by Lipset, Innis, Grant, et al. Canada's history has been punctuated, if not by revolution, certainly by rebellions challenging its 'beneficent' social order. One need only recall the likes of Papineau, Riel, the post–Quiet Revolution rise of Quebec nationalism, and the ongoing struggle for First Nations rights and land claims. Perhaps it is relevant that the pantheon of critical humanities and social science thinkers cited, be they from the poorer rural margins like Innis, or urban savants like Frye and Grant, is primarily WASP – McLuhan's later conversion to Catholicism only seemed to make him more conservative – and with this ethnic privilege came blinders to the plight of racial and cultural minorities within the nation.

As for the American revolutionary tradition cited by Lipset, the term *revolution* is now just as likely in the United States to have connotations of Russia, China, and Cuba, or some third world country about to overthrow a dictatorship and nationalize its resources. While the United States loudly voices democracy and individual rights, her political economy has had a historical preference for dealing with stable regimes of whatever ilk. A democratic 'revolution' in Saudi Arabia, for example, would be most unsettling to American oil interests.

The Canadian intellectual tradition has also been characterized by other factors, as Babe points out, among them a more holistic and critical orientation, a concern with technology in its most inclusive sense – perhaps epitomized in McLuhan's reference to technology as an environment – and a dialectical approach emphasizing a clash or tension between opposites, a significant theme in the essays that follow. What is curious about the role of the last in Canadian intellectual history is how little it *seems* to owe to the tradition of Hegel and Marx, although Innis does give them a passing mention. In his *Harold Innis: A Memoir*, Eric Havelock notes that when the two of them were colleagues at the University of Toronto it was virtually forbidden to acknowledge the work of Marx, probably, I would surmise, because it must have seemed impossible at the time to separate Marxian theory from the Marxist politics that mutated from it.

The same situation existed in much of American social thought – Thorstein Veblen did effect a bow to Marx, but then sidestepped him. Modest shifts in attitude came with the influence of the Frankfurt school – Theodor Adorno and Max Horkheimer came to the country as refugees fleeing the Nazis – whose critical theory helped liberate Marx from the taint of communist totalitarianism, but they exerted little influence on Canadian intellectual life until the 1960s, and none at all on Canadian communication studies until recently.

Still, Innis managed to do some remarkable things with critical insights born of an intimacy with the land, the technologies that enabled nationhood, and his intellectual omnivorousness. Along with the first essay, the two subsequent entries in this section address his contribution. In 'Innis, Saul, Suzuki,' Babe makes intriguing connections between Innisian concepts and two high-profile Canadian thinkers who can be regarded as public intellectuals. Clearly there are overtones, if not a direct influence, of Innis's critique of culture in John Ralston Saul's arguments against the present tyranny of experts in the service of abstract systems and corporative language control. According to him, especially in his best-selling *Voltaire's Bastards*, the rise of reason leading to this situation can be traced back to the period 1530–1620. It might be worth noting that, given this assumption, the work of McLuhan could lend support to Saul's argument. This is the very period that, in *The Gutenberg Galaxy*, because of the full-fledged impact of moveable type printing, McLuhan associates with the rise of the nation state, quantification, modern science, and various forms of secular bureaucracy.

Although Saul's critique is well aimed, and indeed Innisian, as Babe contends, Saul's genealogy of the concept of reason and its implications can be questioned. A passage is quoted whereby Saul attributes the Holocaust to the application, within certain parameters, of rationality. This needs to be considered in broader context. Goya once titled an etching *The Dream of Reason Produces Monsters*. However, it was the unreasoning anti-Enlightenment dream, steeped in romantic nationalism, that gave birth to the Third Reich, a historical development that would have made cringe the Enlightenment philosophers whom Saul sees as unwitting culprits in the promulgation of what we now call instrumental rationality. For Voltaire, Diderot, Condorcet, & Co., one of reason's first principles is tolerance.

Innis's critique of modernity seems less ambitious but is more grounded in material conditions, more historically inclusive, and, for me, more telling. Monopolies of knowledge and subservience to the systems of corporatist bureaucracies existed before the Age of Reason. It was Benedictine monastic administrators in the Middle Ages, obsessed with the organization of daily labour, who put us on the clock, a point noted by Innis but explored more fully in Lewis Mumford's master work, *Technics and Civilization*. Earlier in history, the cult of the expert and the alliance for social control between powerful elites and the military were aspects of statecraft grounded in the organizational possibilities of writing. The electronic databases of corporate culture and governments today, Innis might say, are heir to the clay tablets and papyrus scrolls of antiquity.

For Innis, monopolies of knowledge seem an inevitable aspect of historical formation following the rise of civilization. With the establishment of print culture, which brought in its sway the Age of Reason, the old ecclesiastical monopolies were challenged, but new ones arose in their stead. This is where Saul extends Innis's argument in useful ways, but he sees origins at a point where Innis saw only another stage in the cyclical drama of history.

Following his discussion of Saul, Babe connects implications in the writings of Innis to explicit positions in the work of David Suzuki. Suzuki grounds his environmentalism in the ethos of indigenous peoples. Innis showed little interest in First Nations cultures, perhaps seeing them as doomed to extinction; there is a lament to that effect in his *The Fur Trade in Canada*. Despite having access to writings on Native Americans, such as the work of historian Francis Parkman and anthropologists Edward Sapir and Lewis Henry Morgan (who compared democracy among the Iroquois to the Greek example with which Innis was so enamoured), Innis based his model of a time-biased oral tradition on classicist accounts of Hellenic culture. Nevertheless, his critique of our lack of concern with continuity, and our 'present-mindedness,' dovetails, as Babe points out, with the more anthropologically informed ideas that Suzuki has been expounding for decades through a variety of media.

Although writing at a time when environmental issues were less urgent in the public mind than today, Innis does make a brief observation in that area in his *Essays in Canadian Economic History*. He points to the negative consequences that forestry has after an area is denuded and the camps are abandoned. But again this is in the form of a lament, whereas Suzuki's observations are a call to action.

In his essay 'Harold Innis and the Paradox of Press Freedom,' Babe tackles an aspect of Innis that most commentaries, including my own, have largely neglected. Historians of the press, especially in the United States, have also tended to overlook this contribution. Innis's observations on the subject are scattered over a number of his works. As with most of his writings they do not present an easy read. The collation here, with running commentary, is a significant step in helping potential readers access them.

Innis's arguments are complex and defy received wisdom. How did the transition to modernity, ushered in by print, bring with it new monopolies of knowledge as it was in the very process of shattering those of old? In what ways did the American Bill of Rights actually limit freedoms? How did new technologies relating to the press, from cheaper paper and the advent of the telegraph, to advances in the speed and capacity of the hardware, coupled with increased commercialization, diminish certain forms of 'news' while creating the illusion that the news being printed was representative of what was happening? These issues are examined in convincing fashion, starting with a discussion of how power and knowledge are not as synonymous as recent commentators – I would add to the list poststructuralists such as Foucault – have assumed.

To an Innisophile like myself, what Babe's analysis suggests is the value of bringing together and publishing in a single volume an edited selection of Innis's writings on the press – even more material in this area is available in his unpublished 'History of Communications' manuscript. Much of the argument presented here could serve as an extended introduction. The availability of such a text might complement, and perhaps even inform, those press critics McChesney, Chomsky, and Herman, who are cited at the outset of Babe's discussion.

Understandably, the longest essay in this section, given its scope, deals with the legacy of Marshall McLuhan, whom Babe contends is 'the most creative, imaginative scholar Canada has produced.' No argument there. Perhaps the case can be taken further. When, at the end of the millennium, *Time* magazine published a list of the 100 most influential thinkers of the twentieth century, the name McLuhan was conspicuously absent, leading to this writer's Quixote-like (one of McLuhan's favourite literary characters) letter of protest to the editor. One would think the *Time* selectors were still in a late 1970s early 1980s mode when, as Babe rightly points out, interest in McLuhan was at its lowest ebb – among some Canadian media scholars of my acquaintance at that time, his contributions were briefly resurrected so that they could be dismissed once and for all.

Babe notes how *Wired* magazine's 1996 canonization of McLuhan sparked a popular resurgence of interest in his ideas. However, in academe the tide began turning a decade earlier. Shaking off the hype that in the 1960s turned McLuhan from a private media scholar into a public media celebrity, scholars such as Daniel Czitrom, Joshua Meyrowitz, and Neil Postman began integrating his 'probes' into a variety of more contained and historically informed projects.

Of necessity, Babe must go over some well-trod territory, but in this extended essay, which provides book-like coverage, he has a knack for highlighting the essentials. I was especially pleased to read his comments on anthropologist Edmund Carpenter, my former teacher and a major McLuhan collaborator, whose importance is sometimes overlooked. And, in interfacing McLuhan with Macpherson, Frye, Suzuki, and postmodernism, as well as political economy, Babe provides an insightful commentary that can inform even the most knowledgeable McLuhanite.

If there is one area that I would like to have seen given a bit more consideration, it is the discussion of McLuhan's first book, *The Mechanical Bride*. James Carey once said of the Innis/McLuhan lineage, by drawing from Oscar Wilde's comment upon seeing Niagara Falls, that it would be more impressive if it ran the other way. Similarly, although McLuhan later dismissed the *Bride* in favour of a more formalist approach to media analysis, it should be viewed as a pioneering contribution to the field of critical cultural studies, along with Roland Barthes's oft-cited *Mythologies*, which dates from approximately the same period and shares certain similarities with the *Bride* (a decade later McLuhan and Barthes even discussed the possibility of a collaboration). As one of my graduate students once said after reading the *Bride*, 'Why did McLuhan stop there?' Well, he didn't. The point is not to do as he says in comments about which aspects of his work he considers most relevant, but to appropriate selectively from its entirety.

The final essay in this section deals with George Grant and expands upon points pertaining to his thought that were raised in the first entry. Grant's attempt to 'bring the darkness into the light as darkness' has led to a penetrating critique of mass culture and obsessive consumerism that is unfortunately little known outside of Canada. The parallels between Grant and Innis that were suggested earlier become increasingly apparent as Babe guides us through Grant's major works. Grant's fatalism, he tells us, need not engender resignation; it can help us understand what we should be doing. My reading is slightly different. From Grant, and Innis as well, I get a sense, not of resignation, or inferences regarding what should be done, but of a first call to an understanding of the things we should refrain from doing. To recycle and extend the words of another philosopher, David Hume, we cannot derive 'ought' from 'is,' but we may be able to discern ought not.

The legacy of Canadian communication thought increases in significance as we move into the new millennium. Innis's work, largely ignored in the decade following his death in 1952, is gradually finding an international audience. McLuhan's output has emerged from the black hole it entered shortly before and after his death in 1980 – his reputation today no longer eclipses a serious consideration of his ideas. Over the past generation, there has been no shortage interpreters of their work. Guilty as charged. The essays here, however, take such discussion to a new level. Employing intellectual history, the sociology of knowledge, and political economy, they expand our understanding of, not only Innis and McLuhan, but the contribution to communication studies of allied thinkers as well. In Robert Babe, Canadian communication thought has found a cartographer most worthy.

9 Foundations of Canadian Communication Thought

Canada has a rich heritage of communication thought. This paper relates and compares aspects of the thought of five foundational theorists – indeed, I would argue, the five foremost Canadian humanities and social sciences scholars writing in the English language in the twentieth century – to discern whether there exists a mode of communication study that may be termed 'quintessentially Canadian.' The theorists considered here are Harold Innis, George Grant, Marshall McLuhan, C.B. Macpherson, and Northrop Frye.

My choice of the last two may be somewhat surprising. The eminent University of Toronto political philosopher C.B. Macpherson, after all, never referred to himself as being a communication theorist. Nor do papers and books of renowned literary critic and theorist Northrop Frye appear on many reading lists of communication studies departments. Yet Macpherson's writings on property and political philosophy as mediating human relations form an important base upon which to build and should be recognized as such; likewise, Frye's proposal that verbal structures (stories, myths, poetry, scientific discourse, and so forth) mediate human relations qualify him, too, as being an innovative media theorist building a foundation for further developments in media and communication thought. Innis and McLuhan, after all, opened the way to considering *all* human artefacts as media of communication, inevitably 'biasing' relations between or among members of society; property and stories are among the most important artefacts in this context. These five writers, moreover, bring together for simultaneous consideration social science and humanities/cultural studies approaches, which are not always viewed as being complementary.

Canada as Milieu

According to the celebrated American sociologist Seymour Lipset, Canada is 'a more class-aware, elitist, law-abiding, statist, collectivity-oriented, and particularistic (group-oriented) society than the United States.'[1] These fundamental characteristics, Lipset continued, stem from 'the defining event' that gave birth to both countries, namely the American Revolution.[2] In Lipset's opinion, English Canada exists today because, over two hundred years ago, English-speaking peoples in the northern regions of North America rejected the 'liberal,' 'democratic' values of the American Declaration of Independence. Similarly, he opined, French-speaking Canadians under the sway of the clergy rejected the liberal, anti-clerical, democratic sentiments of the French Revolution. The result, he concluded, has been 'a conservative, monarchical, and ecclesiastical society' in the northern half of North America.[3]

Lipset is supported in these contentions by Harold Innis. In his 'Reflections on Russia,' Innis remarked, 'The Canadian has no revolutionary tradition – the influence of the Church in Quebec is that of pre-revolutionary France, the influence of the state in Ontario and in English-speaking provinces is that of the Loyalist – the counter-revolutionary of the American revolution. This is an island of counter-revolution in a world of revolutionary traditions.'[4]

Citing Northrop Frye, Lipset continued that a 'culture founded on a revolutionary tradition ... is bound to show very different assumptions and imaginative patterns from those of a culture that rejects or distrusts revolution.'[5] Americans, he suggested, look at governments through the eyes of the rebel; for them, governments are not to be trusted. For Canadians, on the other hand, lacking a revolutionary history, government is not deemed to be intrinsically hostile and so Canadians have tended to welcome government's provisioning of a greater range of services.

Not everyone would agree completely with Lipset's characterization of Canada, of course, particularly his claim that Canada is more elitist and less democratic than the United States. Slavery did not figure nearly as prominently in Canadian as in American history, after all, and disparities in wealth and income even today are much greater in the United States than they are in Canada, surely an indicator of a relative gap in U.S. democracy. One thinks perhaps that Lipset too readily accepts the American tendency to link individualism with democracy, and is forgetful of other, more communal notions.

Canadian political and moral philosopher George Grant has argued that, in eschewing revolution, Canadians retained roots in an older tradition of British conservatism, with the consequence that a greater sense of order and of the common good have prevailed in Canada than in the United States.[6] Grant's point is echoed by Gad Horowitz, who has suggested that Canada's social democratic/welfare state inclinations in the twentieth century arose from a tradition of British Tory conservatism.[7] More recently, John Ralston Saul proposed that the Canadian penchant for peaceful negotiation, egalitarianism, and collectivity stems from aboriginal roots.[8]

In any event, to the extent that concern for the collectivity has imbued the Canadian imagination more than the American, one could expect foundational Canadian communication theorists to show greater affinity than their American counterparts for what U.S. theorist James W. Carey has termed the 'culture as communication'. approach to communication studies, as opposed to the 'transmission model,' simply because the former is relatively more communal or collectivist and the latter more individualist and pragmatic.[9]

A further explanation for Canadians' concern for collectivity and the common good may be found in the geographic and demographic characteristics of the country. The bleakness of the Canadian landscape and the country's inhospitable climate are often cited as factors configuring the Canadian mind and artistic imagination. 'Nature is consistently sinister and menacing in Canadian poetry,' declared Northrop Frye.[10] Whereas Puritans migrating to the Thirteen Colonies described their new homeland in paradisiacal terms,[11] settlers in the northern half of North America, he attested, developed a 'garrison mentality,' by which Frye meant an image of themselves as collocations of people huddled in the wilderness for mutual support – an outlook markedly different from the rugged individualism typifying much of American thought. Even more fundamentally, Frye continued, the Canadian terrain engenders a 'double' vision: the bleakness of the landscape versus the imaginative purposefulness that people impute to it; the individual's struggle for survival versus the concomitant need for community; frontier versus farmland; wilderness versus metropolis, and so forth.[12] 'Double vision' is an aspect of what I will call here a dialectical cast of mind, or a dialectical imagination.

According to West Coast political analyst Herschel Hardin, however, the landscape provides but a superficial understanding of the Canadian identity, and to focus exclusively on that is sheer 'escapist fantasy.'[13] For Hardin, rather, the deeper contradictions concern (1) French versus English Canada, (2) the regions versus the federal centre, and (3) Canada versus the United States. Arthur Kroker, too, attributed the dialectical cast of Canadian thought primarily to the country's proximity to the United States,[14] as did novelist and poet Robin Mathews.[15]

The Canadian preoccupation with community in the face of isolation, regionalism, bilingualism, multiculturalism, and climatic adversity, and with maintaining an identity in the face of a powerful neighbour, may well have contributed also to what I have found to be a much greater concern for ontology in the mainstream Canadian discourse compared to the American. Ontology entails, for example, speculations or beliefs regarding the place of individuals and/or groups within the larger whole. It also relates to questions of natural law versus positive law, and to human nature. It inquires also into what is ultimately real – the reality behind appearances – and into the nature of time. Whereas American communication researchers, as Sandra Braman notes, typically avoid specifying or endorsing ontological positions,[16] in foundational Canadian communication thought such has not been the case; rather, the Canadian discourse is rife with explicitly ontological concerns. Canadians, after all, Margaret Atwood pronounced, have had as a central concern 'survival' – certainly an ontological question when considered in the abstract.

Furthermore, the Canadian communication discourse is more *critical* in Paul Felix Lazarsfeld's sense of the term. In a classic 1941 article, Lazarsfeld proposed that critical communication research differs in two basic ways from mainstream or 'administrative' research. First, referring specifically to increasing concentration of media control and the proliferation of techniques for manipulating large audiences, Lazarsfeld proposed that critical research 'develops a theory of the prevailing social trends.' Second, critical research presumes 'ideas of basic human values according to which all actual or desired effects should be appraised.'[17] Indeed it is from this notion of appraisal that the very name, *critical*, derives. Critical research, then, being evaluative, presumes enduring values (an ontological presupposition) whereby policies, activities, events, modes of human interaction, institutions, and so forth may be appraised, and serve also as goals toward which societies or individuals may aspire. Critical researchers, Lazarsfeld remarked, 'have the idea ever before them that what we need most is to do and think what we consider true and not adjust ourselves to the seemingly inescapable.'[18]

There are also other key points of departure: foundational Canadian communication thought is more holistic and humanities-oriented; it emphasizes dynamic change and exhibits a greater concern for equality than for 'effects.' It is more likely than mainstream American research to denigrate advertising, public relations, and media motivated primarily by profit. It exhibits stronger attachment to the maintenance of culture through time in the face of commercial, political, and technological pressures.

Canadian communication thought also emphasizes the importance, and the power, of the human imagination, and it studies how our imaginations are moulded, or at least influenced, by prevailing institutions, by predominant media of communication, by our stories or myths, by the arts, and by our educational systems. Canadian communication thought, then, focuses on media broadly defined, and on mediation, and on milieu – that is on how the technological and symbolic environments affect modes of interaction.

This concern for mediation and milieu stems undoubtedly from Canadian historical development, which is related partly to Canadian geography and demography. In a previous chapter it was noted that Canadian communication policy has often been driven by a presumed one-to-one correspondence between the development or deployment of technological means of communicating and national unity; this is the Canadian doctrine, or myth, of *technological nationalism*. But the Canadian scholarly discourse on media and technology has been, if anything, dialectical. Also as noted previously, some claim that technological endeavours like the CPR and broadcasting did not and could not create a nation, since nation pertains to outlook, history, values, and community, not merely the formation of a state – that is, the common governance of people living in a defined territory.[19]

Foundational Canadian communication theorists insist, further, that relations among people are mediated, by all sorts of human artefacts – institutions, philosophies, stories, myths, property law, and even by the pace of technological change. People are understood as living within milieux that bias or condition their perceptions and modes of interaction. Canadian communication theorists, furthermore, often inquire into who controls or affects the means of mediation, how that control is exercised, and for what (whose) purposes. This emphasis on control contributes to the political economy dimension characteristic of Canadian communication thought.

Dialectics

Space limitations dictate that not all the aforementioned commonalities of the foundational Canadian discourse and its distinctiveness from foundational American communication thought can be explored directly or in depth here. This paper therefore focuses on but one major difference – the role of dialectics in Canadian communication thought. Nonetheless, it is to be emphasized that many of the traits noted above are readily discernible in what follows, and indeed can be thought of as necessary concomitants (or even as characteristics) of dialectical modes of analysis.

Most importantly, dialectical concepts and processes entail the clash or tension of opposites, out of which issue either new syntheses or, at the very least, balance and continuing tension. Dialectical logic sees contradiction as the primary means whereby higher truths are attained, and deems standard (Aristotelian) logic to be unduly static and rigid. Dialecticians claim that events and indeed history are largely outcomes of contradictory forces.

A dialectical cast of mind is not common in Western social science where the goal is usually to detect linear, unidirectional causations (for example, 'effects research' in communication studies).[20] Nor are dialectical analyses typical in American thought in the humanities: powerful cultures, after all, encourage people to see things instrumentally, that is in terms of how power can be exercised effectively ('administrative research'); indeed, according to liberal/pluralist doctrine of the invisible hand (as developed prototypically by Adam Smith and John Rawls), analysts need not delve into contradictions and conflictual relations because, it is held, each person exercising her power and seeking her own interest contributes automatically, albeit inadvertently, to the 'common good.'

People at the margins, however, and Canada is, after all, marginal to the United States, can see things differently: unable to escape exposure to dominant discourses, they also understand that those discourses are not their own. When Harold Innis took up a teaching position in 1920 at the University of Toronto after studying at the University of Chicago, for example, he espied a dearth of materials dealing with Canadian economic history and adopted the position that economic models developed in older, industrialized economies should not be applied with impunity to emergent, peripheral ones. He therefore set about developing a 'philosophy of economic history or an economic theory suited to

Canadian needs.'[21] From the outset, then, Innis had a 'double vision,' which is to say a dialectical cast of mind, understanding the dominant discourse but realizing it was not his own.

Innis: The Dialectic of Space-Time

Running through both Innis's staples thesis and his media thesis are oppositions between periphery and centre, culture and empire, continuity and change, time and space. He saw markets and the price system not simply as givens, as do mainstream economists, but as instruments whereby dominant cultures 'penetrate' traditional ones and transform them into societies premised on present-mindedness, self-interest, money value, commodity exchange, materialism, and individualism. Through staples like fish, fur, timber, minerals, and wheat – which for mainstream economists are merely commodities and resources subject to and illustrative of the 'law of comparative advantage' – Innis linked modes of transportation, geography, social structure, culture, political organization, business and economic history, and most significantly relations between imperial centres and their colonial margins. Innis provided an interdisciplinary analysis of cultures in collision, of societies brought into contact (i.e., into communication) by the *media of staples*. Regarding the fur trade, for instance, he remarked, 'The history of the fur trade is the history of contact between two civilizations, the European and the North American ... Unfortunately the rapid destruction of the food supply and the revolution in the methods of living accompanied by the increasing attention to the fur trade by which these products were secured, disturbed the balance which had grown up previous to the coming of the European. The new technology with its radical innovations brought about such a rapid shift in the prevailing Indian culture as to lead to wholesale destruction of the peoples concerned by warfare and disease.'[22]

In his communication thesis, Innis turned from Canadian to world history. In place of staples he proposed that various means of inscription mediate human relations and thereby bias or help structure modes of human interaction. According to Innis, space-bound cultures use predominantly space-binding media – media that are light, transportable, easy to work with, and that have a large capacity to carry and store messages. Time-bound or traditional cultures, conversely, rely predominantly on time-binding media – media that are relatively difficult to use, difficult to transport, and enduring.

Innis proposed that in addition to attempting continuously to extend empire geographically, space-biased cultures 'spatialize' time, that is break it into discrete, uniform, measurable chunks that can be valuated in money terms. Like Lewis Mumford, Innis recognized that the mechanical clock is basic to this task. Through clocks, workers are summoned to factories and can be recompensed according to the 'time' they put in. 'Measurement of time,' he remarked, 'facilitated the use of credit, the rise of exchanges, and calculations of the predictable future essential to the development of insurance.'[23]

This is not, of course, the only possible conception of time. 'Time-bound' communities, by definition, are not likewise as engrossed in the moment. For them, time flows; human life is understood as 'a great stream of which the present is only the realized moment.'[24] Events are a succession of recurrences (the cycle of life), even though each instance may be charged with particular value and significance.[25] The biblical Book of Ecclesiastes captures well the conception of time as eternal recurrence:

A time to be born, and a time to die;
a time to plant, and a time to pluck up what is planted;
a time to kill, and a time to heal;
a time to break down, and a time to build up.

Just as space-bound cultures have a unique concern with time, so do time-bound cultures conceive space in a particular way. For them, space is neither unlimited nor something to be appropriated and annexed; rather, it is differentiated in terms of being sacred or profane. For time-bound cultures, spatial boundaries sustain community and a way of life. Space is where the community lives, where it maintains its connections with the past, and where its future unfolds – a conception totally at odds with the notion maintained by space-biased societies for whom the desire is predominantly to conquer new territories, create larger markets, and organize land into efficient configurations (factories, assembly lines, territorial divisions of labour, and so on). Space, like time, in other words, is commodified in space-biased cultures.

Particularly important for Innis as inculcators of space-biased consciousness in the twentieth century are mechanized (that is, mass) media. Newspapers, he maintained, played a large role in transforming the conception of time from that of continuity to sequential uniformity, and of space from concerns for locality to borderless land to be appropriated and organized through principles of commodity exchange. According to Innis, the telegraph and faster presses combined to give financial advantage to newspapers serving geographically extended markets with current 'news.'[26] Reliance on advertising added to these pressures, since advertisers are interested in fast turnovers. Hence, the 'bias' of newspapers was set: journalism came to be written 'on the back of advertisements'[27] and emphasized regionalism rather than localism, functioning in a manner destructive of 'time and continuity.'[28]

Change from one conception of time or of space to the other, according to Innis, typically is accompanied by conflict and struggle. The enclosure movement in England, the Oka crisis in Canada, Indonesia's genocidal treatment of the East Timorese, Innis would undoubtedly agree, were in essence struggles between adherents to rival conceptions of space and of time.

Innis insisted that a balance – between institutions, practices, and media exerting control as continuity through time, and ones endeavouring to extend control over space – is essential for stability. Undue emphasis on one mode of control or organization relative to the other inevitably leads to dis-organization.[29] For our present, space-biased era, Innis's plea for balance amounts, in essence, to 'a plea for time.' He wrote, 'The modern obsession with present-mindedness ... suggests that the balance between time and space has been seriously disturbed with disastrous consequences to Western civilization.'[30]

For Innis, however, a real sense of time is not simply to affirm that events and objects exist as a 'succession of particular states'; rather, it is to recognize, or believe, or have faith, that there exists 'a state of permanence beyond time.'[31] This is a question of ontology. A concern for time, according to Innis – the economic historian – therefore, is not the same as a concern for history. To the contrary! Whereas historical analyses imply that events are unique and that all things change, a concern for time entails a concern for what does not change. This is precisely George Grant's main theme and dialectic.

Grant: The Dialectic of Time

Just as Innis proposed that human artefacts, particularly modes of transportation, the means of inscription, and technologies for extracting staples, constitute milieux within which human interaction and social organization exist and are shaped, so too did political philosopher George Grant regard 'technology,' and particularly the pace of technological change, to be a general mediation decisively affecting modes of human interaction and the formation of values and onto-logical perspectives. Grant distinguished between 'antiquarian' and modern conceptions of time. By antiquity Grant meant civilizations prior to the rise of Western science, that is prior to 'the age of progress.' People of antiquity believed that meaning and value are intrinsic to the universe ('A time to be born and a time to die ...'). Accordingly, by repeating, imitating, and fulfilling divine acts as revealed in sacred stories and myths, people thought of themselves as participating in a fixed order of meaning and goodness. Actions not conforming to or recreating the sacred were of at best little significance to the ancients. In this regard Grant frequently pointed to Plato's conception of time, which he referred to as 'the moving image of an unmoving eternity.'[32] Through the doctrine of pure forms Plato maintained that the most real and perfect order is an ideal, incorporeal one. Although perfection, being an ideal, exists by definition in the immaterial realm of ideas, it nonetheless can have profound material consequences. As Grant expressed the point, 'The desire for good is a broken hope without per-fection, because only the desire to become perfect does in fact make us less imperfect.'[33]

However, Grant reflected, with the 'age of progress,' belief in a fixed order of goodness (what he termed 'mythic consciousness') all but disappeared. Attention came to be riveted on 'unique and irrevers-ible events,'[34] which is to say on 'history.' Modern people believe that humans make all meaning, that people create all value, and hence we are 'the measure of all things.' Grant termed this conception *time as his-tory*, meaning 'time-as-change.'

For Grant, 'continual technical achievement' has been the major agent in the transition to the modern conception of time. Technological change weakens people's sense of continuity and stability[35] and par-ticularly their belief in natural law, including their belief in the sanctity of human life. He maintained that positive (or legislated) law, devoid of considerations of natural law (that is, law intrinsic to the universe and extrinsic to human culture or consciousness), ultimately is tyranni-cal. That is because positive law is set by the most powerful in society, generally to suit themselves, and pari passu to the disadvantage of the weak. Grant prophesied, 'If tyranny is to come in North America it will come cosily and on cat's feet. It will come with the denial of the rights of the unborn and of the aged, the denial of the rights of the mentally retarded, the insane and the economically less privileged. In fact it will come with the denial of rights to all those who cannot defend themselves. It will come in the name of the cost-benefit analysis of human life.'[36]

Grant proposed further (as did Innis) that our technological order is sustained by the mass media, the arts, and the educational system, which together ensure that the antiquarian conception of time, community, equality, continuity, justice, and law remains largely unarticulated, leaving us thereby more or less oblivious to the prisons in which we live. For him, it is primarily by loving and by remembering the teachings of the ancients (that is by recovering a sense of time) that our best hope for freedom is to be found.[37]

Both Innis and Grant, then, were critical, holistic, dialectical, ontological thinkers. Both proposed strong connections between societal evolution and technological change, and both warned that society cannot survive if, in Grant's words, it puts 'its faith in techniques and not in wholeness.'[38] Like Innis, Grant railed at growing control over educational curricula by business interests and was appalled at the emphasis afforded narrow, technocratic instruction. Also like Innis, Grant lashed out at commercial media, viewing them as propaganda agents for liberal, capitalist modes of control. Innis and Grant alike dwelt on the dark side of liberalism and commodity exchange. Each thinker was deeply concerned that North America in general, and Canada particularly, was becoming increasingly depersonalized and alienating as a result of the growing predominance of these modes of thought and interaction. Canadian governments, they felt, were choosing power/objectivity/scientism/technology, over equality/love/community/continuity. Such choices, both scholars attested, were ripping apart the social fabric: 'Values' (how Grant hated that term; he felt it denoted something people create rather than something that is given) were being effaced or reconstituted in accordance with the nihilism of technological society.

Frye's 'Double Vision'

Similar themes recur throughout the immense corpus of writing of Northrop Frye. In *Fearful Symmetry*, his first book, Frye maintained that people generally adhere to or dwell in one or other of two 'cosmologies.'[39] One is the 'realist' or objectivist world view, which conceives the universe as existing independently of the thinker or observer. The task of knowing for those subscribing to this cosmology is to understand the world 'as it is.' This cosmology accords well with what Grant referred to as time as history, and to what Innis called space-bias. For Frye, however, this outlook is unduly unimaginative and ultimately, he declared (as did Innis and Grant), nihilistic. Untempered by the human imagination, scientism (what Frye also sometimes called 'the truth of correspondence') turns people into 'psychotic apes,'[40] that is animals possessing the powers to question and to reason, but bereft of answers to the most significant questions, like why we are here and who we are.

The other 'cosmology,' according to Frye, is imaginative, subjectivist, and mythological. This is the lived ontology of the poet William Blake and was adopted at times, too, by Frye. It is much the older of the two and in *Fearful Symmetry* said to be much the superior. There are, Frye acknowledged, many imaginative world views, but each one, he insisted, positions humans at the very centre of things. The earth, for example, according to mythopoeic understanding, was created for human enjoyment. When a person accepts that proposition, the environment immediately takes on 'a human shape.'[41]

In addition to close and obvious similarities between Frye's mythopoeic world view and both Grant's antiquarian notion of time and Innis's conception of time-bound cultures, all three theorists recommended 'balance.' Innis commended balance between time-binding and space-binding media of communication, and Grant between the modernist and antiquarian conceptions of time.[42] Likewise Frye extolled double vision – an ability to see simultaneously the fallen (material/fragmented) world and an unfallen (imaginatively united or reconstructed) one. Fallen, or normal vision, sees things 'as they are,' complete with antitheses, oppositions, struggles, fragmentations, and an absence of meaning. The imaginative vision, in contrast, transcends the absurdity or nihilism of fallen vision. The imaginative vision, however, must be kept in check by the 'truth of correspondence,' as otherwise people can lose all touch with reality.

However, in our era of science and technology, Frye felt that balance is particularly difficult to maintain. From a scientific point of view, he claimed, we know the universe is devoid of meaning or purpose, and hence science continually belies the myth of concern, that is intimations of meaning arising from and contained in human culture.[43] At the close of *The Modern Century*, for instance, Frye referenced Blake's dialectically opposite poems, 'The Tyger' and 'The Lamb' and declared in effect that, once enlightened by science, we can never return to mythopoeic consciousness: 'The child's vision [of the Lamb] is far behind us. The world we are in is the world of the tiger, and that world was never created or seen to be good. It is the subhuman world of nature, a world of law and of power, but not of intelligence or design. Things "evolve" in it.'[44]

In Frye's view, however, science too has mythic elements. Science spawns the myth of progress, for example, which he insisted has had particularly pernicious consequences. Developing out of science and technology and from Darwinian speculations regarding the origin of the species, the myth of progress has been used to 'justify' horrendous acts, even to the point of exterminating 'primitive' peoples. Frye was positively Innisian in the following excerpt: 'According to the myth of progress, history shows a progress from primitive to civilized states, which turns out on investigation to be a progress in technology, though it is often called science. If two cultures collide, the one that gets enslaved or exterminated is the primitive one.'[45]

Also, like Innis, Frye proposed that the means of message transmission have a bearing on the nature of the messages transmitted. In oral society, he suggested, the chief transmitters of culture are people with poetic and rhetorical skills, particularly the bards, prophets, and religious leaders. Reliant on memory, oral culture uses verse, formulaic units, stock epithets, and metrical phrases.[46] He characterized oral and early writing cultures as expressing themselves 'in continuous verse and discontinuous prose.'[47] Discontinuous prose consists of a series of disconnected but easily remembered proverbs or aphorisms: the Gospels of the New Testament, for instance. Continuity in verse is achieved by mnemonic devices such as rhythm and rhyme. A culture habituated to writing, on the other hand, tends toward 'continuous prose and discontinuous verse.' Continuous prose denotes continuity of ideas and logic, a requisite for the development of philosophy and history. Discontinuous verse means that poetry makes a break with continuous rhythms and rhymes and is intended more to be read than heard or memorized.

Frye contended that writing helps transform a society's myth of concern from the language of prescription ('thou shalt not ...'), and from stories recounting origins ('in the beginning ...'), to a more conceptual and propositional language.[48] People therefore begin to think less in terms of community and common heritage ('common good') and more in terms of an objectively given world. Indeed, Frye proposed that it was writing that gave rise to the 'truth of correspondence.' In part this was because authors and readers in a culture with writing are less reliant on memory since they can turn to documents, which can be cross-referenced, stored, and compared. As well, writing allows for greater abstraction and the induction of general principles (e.g., laws of nature).

Frye could be Innisian also in comparing old and new media. He remarked that media – developed primarily in the twentieth century, such as film, radio, and television – follow 'the imperial rhythms of politics and economics more readily than the regionalizing rhythms of culture.'[49] He remarked also that 'the fight for cultural distinctiveness ... is a fight for human dignity itself,'[50] the implication being that in homogenizing cultures mass media erode people's sense of uniqueness and hence sense of worth. Frye concluded, again in a manner worthy of Innis, 'The triumph of communication is the death of communication: where communication forms a total environment, there is nothing to be communicated.'[51]

Like Grant and Innis, Frye expounded upon the dialectic of time versus space. But unlike Grant, Frye was no Platonist, at least once he lost his early religious fervour. Frye, rather, followed Blake, whom he viewed as Plato's antithesis. He summarized, 'To Plato, whose Muses were daughters of Memory, knowledge was recollection and art imitation: to Blake, both knowledge and art are recreation.'[52]

McLuhan: Dialectic of Eye versus Ear

Marshall McLuhan self-consciously borrowed from Innis when he transmuted the dialectic of time/space into that of eye/ear. By focusing on sensory modes of message perception instead of biases inherent to different modes of message transmission, McLuhan went some distance in depoliticizing Innis. However, McLuhan's dialectic nonetheless can in part be recast into time/space, and hence re-politicized. This is because the eye orients receivers to objects in space, whereas the ear inclines people to the invisible and hence mystical, engendering community and intersubjectivity, also accentuating the importance of continuity.

Like Frye, McLuhan expressed a continuing concern for myth, although he differed fundamentally from Frye on the nature and role of myth in modern society. Frye, it will be recalled, maintained that myth is an imaginative construct imputing meaning to an otherwise meaningless universe. Psychologically, Frye claimed, we are driven to project our concerns onto the 'world of the tiger' in an effort to construct a 'home.' The purposes and meanings we construct, however, remain just that – imaginative constructions – which are continually in tension with, and belied by, the tiger (i.e., the 'truth of correspondence'). For McLuhan, by contrast, myth is not a flight from reality but is the highest form of truth. That is because myth generalizes the particulars.[53] Myths, in other words, affirm patterns or recurrences and set them out in the form of stories.

True to his pronouncements, McLuhan spoke and wrote in mythic terms: of King Cadmus and the dragon's teeth,[54] which he likened to letters of the alphabet chewing up oral culture; of Narcissus' self-absorption through bodily extension,[55] which he saw paralleling our own mesmerization with technological devices; and most fundamentally, albeit usually implicitly, the biblical story of the Fall and the coming of the New Jerusalem.[56] In adopting the position that myths are fundamentally true, McLuhan was much closer to the idealism and natural law position of George Grant and to Innis's conception of authentic time-bias than he was to Frye's existentialism.

Although eye/ear is a much less politicized mode of analysis than time/space, McLuhan nonetheless was aware of and in fact pointed to certain power dimensions of technological change. 'There can be no greater contradiction or clash in human cultures,' he pronounced, 'than that between those representing the eye and the ear.'[57] Moreover, McLuhan saw the innovator as a political force, since new technologies heighten people's awareness of their environment and hence lessen the 'taken-for-grantedness' of their surroundings; technological innovators and artists alike, in McLuhan's view, are therefore enemies of the established order, a notion not unlike Innis's conception of struggle by peripheral groups to wrest power from entrenched interests by developing new media to bypass established 'monopolies of knowledge.' McLuhan noted further that information speed-up makes porous previously well-defined borders. Historically the independence of villages and city states declined as information movement accelerated. McLuhan declared that when this happens, new centralist powers invariably take action 'to homogenize as many marginal areas as possible.'[58] Although he acknowledged that the wheel, roads, paper, money, and mechanical clock were important innovations accelerating transactions and thereby shifting power, the phonetic alphabet and typography for him were of utmost significance: 'The phonetic alphabet has no rival,' he insisted, 'as a translator of man out of the closed tribal echo-chamber into the neutral visual world of lineal organization.'[59]

Parallels between McLuhan's thought and Frye's are manifest. Both proposed, for instance, a golden age where meaning once abounded. Both contended that the rise of scientific objectivity banished this magical kingdom and cast humanity into a fragmented world. Whereas Frye proclaimed that, once removed from the garden (through the 'truth of correspondence'), people can re-enter only sporadically and temporarily by suspending disbelief as when reading a novel or viewing a play, McLuhan insisted that through electronics humanity re-enters the garden automatically. Since this is such a marked point of departure, let us pursue McLuhan's reasoning on this matter a bit further.

Although seldom if ever referring specifically to the term *dialectic* in reference to his own work, McLuhan was in fact the most dialectical of the writers surveyed here. In addition to counterpointing orality and literacy, ear and eye, acoustic and visual space, cool and hot media, figure and ground, and so on, his treatment of *chiasmus* well illustrates his penchant for dialectics. By *chiasmus* McLuhan meant that reversals occur when processes are taken to extremes. For example, virtue pushed far enough becomes a vice.[60] With regard to communications, the electric telegraph and ensuing electronic media have speeded up information movement to such an extent that there is now an implosion rather than an explosion: centres of power, according to McLuhan, no longer extend their reach as they did with 'mechanical' media like the printing press; rather, the movement with electronics is toward the negation of centres of power.[61] As in a pointillist painting, everyone and everything is increasingly understood as being related simultaneously in a complex system of mutual interdependence. The notion here is that the seeds of reversal are within every process, an idea McLuhan elaborated most fully in his *Laws of the Media*.[62]

With regard specifically to meaning and knowledge, information speed-up requires us to revert to mythic modes of information processing – that is, to pattern recognition – rather than dissecting bits of information and trying to discover causal connections. The reinstatement of myth – a renewed concern for the whole – re-establishes meaning in the electronic era, at least in McLuhan's opinion.

Macpherson's Dialectic of Property

Finally, C.B. Macpherson's dialectical analyses of property and political philosophy can likewise be understood as variations on Innisian themes of time-space. Macpherson defined property not as a thing but as an enforceable claim to some use or benefit. He also distinguished between property as a concept and property as an institution, arguing that these dual aspects are in continual interaction, either reinforcing or contradicting one another. 'What [people] see,' he wrote, 'must have some relation (though not necessarily an exact correspondence) to what is actually there'; he added, 'Changes in what is there are due partly to changes in the ideas people have of it.'[63] During times of stability, property as a concept and property as an institution are mutually supportive, the concept justifying the institution and the institution verifying the concept. During times of transition, however, conceptions of property inconsistent with the institution foreshadow change in the institution. Therefore, a good starting point for those interested in reforming property (i.e., changing social relations) is to challenge property's justificatory theories and its commonly accepted meanings.

Historically property has been conceptualized and institutionalized dichotomously: private property is the right to exclude others from some use or benefit, whereas common property is the right of an individual not to be excluded.[64] For example, the right to access streets and parks, according to Macpherson, is a property right possessed or claimed by individuals, but is common to all; in Canada, so is medicare and education up to and including the secondary level.

It is precisely because property can be set as either an enforceable right to exclude or as a right not to be excluded that Macpherson declared that property helps define and redefine relations among people. In our terms, property mediates human relations. To have property is to be able to participate in social/communicatory life; to have no property (no rights of access) is to be foreclosed from this. Property therefore signifies the selective protection of interests and thereby denotes the differential capacity to participate in social, economic, and communicatory life.

Macpherson emphasized that although both private and common property are created and enforced by the state or the community, these are rights of individuals (including corporations as 'artificial persons'). Macpherson wrote, 'In neither case does the fact that the state creates the right make the right the property of the state ... The state creates the rights, the individuals have the rights.'[65]

Through the ages property has been justified either as being necessary for people to realize their 'fundamental nature,' or as a 'natural right.' Disputes concerning what type of property is best, therefore, are usually couched in terms of 'human nature,' or with regard to what comprises a 'natural right' to property. Political philosophers such as John Locke, who supported *private* property, promoted a particular view of human nature – what Macpherson referred to as proprietary individualism, that is, a 'conception of the individual as essentially the proprietor of his own person or capacities, owing nothing to society for them. The individual [is] seen neither as a moral whole, nor as part of a larger social whole, but as an owner of himself.'[66]

Proprietary individualism means, further, that people are considered, and consider themselves to be, divisible, that aspects of the person (her skills and energy) can with equanimity be hived off and sold to others. Labour, therefore, can and should be sold in the marketplace as a commodity. Proprietary individualism, in brief, provides an ontological justification for the market economy and for human relations grounded on commodity exchange. It constitutes also a rationale for immense disparities among people in terms of their capacity to access the means of living.

In contrast to human nature as proprietary individualism, John Stuart Mill proposed that the human essence is that of exerter, enjoyer, and developer of capacities and skills. That conception of humanness, Macpherson declared, was endorsed by the ancients (Plato, Aristotle, the church fathers), but the market economy and its justificatory philosophy penetrated human consciousness to such a degree that this developmental view of human nature all but vanished. Utilitarians since the time of Jeremy Bentham have viewed the human essence as essentially a bundle of appetites demanding satisfaction. In our time, Macpherson wrote, 'the idea of man as activity rather than consumption' is what we need to retrieve.[67]

Common property, of course, is subversive of commodity exchange and the price system, both of which Innis associated with space-bound cultures. Common property, on the other hand, is consistent with Innis's notion of time-bound society, since time-bound society is communal and collective. Moreover, just as Innis detected a trend from time-binding to space-binding media of communication, so did Macpherson detect a movement historically from common property to private property, the latter being, in his view, 'largely an invention of the seventeenth and eighteenth centuries.'[68] Furthermore, Macpherson's dialectic concerning rival conceptions of human nature, namely people as infinite accumulators and consumers versus users and developers of their talents and capacities, is quite consonant with the space/time dialectic of Innis. Whereas Innis urged a balance between time-binding and space-binding media and so made 'a plea for time,' Macpherson likewise implored us to 'retrieve' the sense of people as doers and exerters of their capacities and urged a larger place for common property.

Moreover Innis and Macpherson had similar notions of mediation. Neither saw communication as merely the dispatching of messages by autonomous senders to recipients. Rather, senders, recipients, messages, and media for both these writers, as for the other theorists considered here, are simultaneously parts and products of an ongoing social/communicatory system. Hence if a message sender or receiver conceives herself to be an infinite acquirer and accumulator and acts accordingly, that is because the philosophical/propertied/communicatory order into which she was born and in which she lives tells her this is who she is and requires her to act accordingly. Material reality, then, from this perspective, in its foundations, is ideational, which is to say symbolic and communicatory.

Finally, it is in the context of mediation that asymmetric power relations are treated by both writers. Innis focused on relations between centre and periphery and ascribed these significantly but not exclusively to the means of inscription; Macpherson concentrated on relations between owners of the means of production and workers, and ascribed asymmetric power relations to the mode of property. Innis declared that relations between centre and margin, which is to say between space and time, must be readjusted to restore balance and prevent chaos; for Macpherson, the ratio between private property and common property must be altered to allow greater opportunity to individuals to fulfil their human potential and also to prevent environmental collapse.[69]

Macpherson discerned a 'race' between ontology and technology.[70] By ontology he meant the predominant conception, at any particular time, of the human 'essence.' By a race he implied not only that ontology and technology are both subject to change, but also that it really matters which changes the more quickly. Only if the conception of the human essence as doer, exerter, and developer of capacities replaces quickly the view of people as infinite desirers and accumulators can technological advance remain consistent with democratic freedoms.[71]

Conclusion

Having detected and summarized key themes and concerns that permeate the thought of these five foundational writers, let us conclude
briefly by addressing implications of their thought. The writers treated
here are virtually univocal in their condemnation of the market as the
chief means of organizing human activity, and by implication subordinating communication systems to commercial concerns. In the view
of these theorists, markets cause people to be unduly individualistic
in their actions and present-minded in their thoughts, whereas human
existence is radically contingent upon the actions of others and is seamless from past to future. The price system and the ensuing concerns for
economic power and efficiency, these theorists agree, tend to wipe out
the ethic of community.

These theorists also urge us to consider critically the communication
environment – the 'cultural ecology,' in McLuhan's words.[72] This environment is both technological and symbolic, and the authors propose
there is a close relation or interaction between these dual aspects of our
cultural ecology. By becoming more critically aware, they propose, we
may come to interpret matters differently, and then apply greater balance not only to our interpretations but also to our actions. The stakes
are high, all theorists agree.

It is important to emphasize that the field of questions raised by
these seminal Canadian communication theorists, as befits a dialectical
imagination, is completely different from those often taken to be the
founders of American communication thought – Lazarsfeld, Lasswell,
Lewin, Hovland, and Schramm. Perhaps it is more than coincidental
that raising important ontological questions and adopting dialectical
modes of analysis detract from the lustre of technological achievement
in the communication field, and from the free-flow of information –
both mainstays of the American discourse.

NOTES

1 Seymour M. Lipset, *North-American Cultures: Values and Institutions in
  Canada and the United States* (Orono: Borderlands Project, Canadian-Ameri-
  can Center, University of Maine, 1990), 2.
2 Ibid.

3 Ibid., 4.

4 Harold A. Innis, *Innis on Russia: The Russian Diary and Other Writings*, ed., preface William Christian (Toronto: Harold Innis Foundation, 1981), 74.

5 Lipset, *North-American Cultures*, 7.

6 George Grant, *Lament for a Nation: The Defeat of Canadian Nationalism* (1965; Ottawa: Carleton University Press, 1982).

7 Gad Horowitz, 'Tories, Socialists and the Demise of Canada,' *Canadian Dimension* 2, no. 4 (May–June 1965): 2.

8 John Ralston Saul, *A Fair Country: Telling Truths about Canada* (Toronto: Viking Canada, 2008).

9 James W. Carey, 'A Cultural Approach to Communication' (1975); repr. in *Communication as Culture: Essays on Media and Society*, 13–36. (Boston: Unwin Hyman, 1989).

10 Northrop Frye, *The Bush Garden: Essays in the Canadian Imagination* (Toronto: House of Anansi, 1971), 142.

11 R.B. Elder, *Image and Identity: Reflections on Canadian Film and Culture* (Waterloo, ON: Wilfrid Laurier University Press, 1989), 25.

12 Northrop Frye, *Divisions on a Ground: Essays on Canadian Culture*, ed. J. Polk (Toronto: House of Anansi, 1982), 49.

13 Herschel Hardin, *A Nation Unaware: The Canadian Economic Culture* (Vancouver: Douglas, 1974), 13.

14 Arthur Kroker, *Technology and the Canadian Mind: Innis, McLuhan, Grant* (Montreal: New World Perspectives, 1984), 8.

15 Robin Mathews, *Canadian Identity: Major Forces Shaping the Life of a People* (Ottawa: Steel Rail, 1988), 1.

16 Sandra Braman, 'Commentary,' in *Information and Communication in Economics*, ed. R.E. Babe (Boston: Kluwer, 1994), 101.

17 Paul F. Lazarsfeld, 'Administrative and Critical Research' (1941); repr. in *Mass Communication and American Social Thought: Key Texts 1919–1968*, ed. John Durham Peters and Peter Simonson (Lanham, MD: Rowman and Littlefield, 2004), 169.

18 Ibid.

19 Maurice Charland, 'Technological Nationalism,' *Canadian Journal of Political and Social Theory* 10 (1986): 196–220.

20 Everett M. Rogers, *A History of Communication Study: A Biographical Approach* (New York: Free Press, 1994).

21 Harold A. Innis, 'The Teaching of Economic History in Canada' (1929); repr. in *Essays in Canadian Economic History*, ed. Mary Q. Innis (Toronto, ON: University of Toronto Press, 1956), 3–16.

22 Harold A. Innis, *The Fur Trade in Canada: An Introduction to Canadian Economic History* (1930; Toronto: University of Toronto Press, 1962), 388.
23 Harold A. Innis, *The Bias of Communication* (1951; Toronto: University of Toronto Press, 1971), 72.
24 Ibid., 67.
25 Ibid., 66.
26 Ibid., 167–8.
27 Ibid., 186.
28 Ibid., 188.
29 Ibid., 64.
30 Ibid., 76.
31 Ibid., 89.
32 George Grant, *Philosophy in the Mass Age* (1959), repr., ed. W. Christian (Toronto: University of Toronto Press, 1995), 41.
33 Grant, *Time as History* (Toronto: CBC Learning Systems, 1969), 47.
34 Ibid., 21.
35 George Grant, *Technology and Empire* (Toronto: House of Anansi, 1969), 15.
36 George Grant, 'The Case against Abortion,' *Today* 3 (October 1981): 13.
37 Grant, *Time as History*, 49.
38 Grant, quoted in William Christian, *George Grant: A Biography* (Toronto: University of Toronto Press, 1993), 144.
39 Northrop Frye, 'Preface,' in *Fearful Symmetry: A Study of William Blake* (1947; Princeton, NJ: Princeton University Press, 1969), n.p.
40 Frye quoted in David Cayley, ed., *Northrop Frye in Conversation* (Toronto: House of Anansi, 1992), 53.
41 Frye, 'Preface.'
42 Grant found much merit in modern conceptions of time, law, and justice. He acknowledged that the freedom-to-do inherent in the modern conceptions had brought about multitudinous improvements – modern medicine and the plethora of labour-saving devices, for instance. No sane person could doubt this, Grant affirmed. That being the case, modern accounts of law and of justice *must* be true. Hence his dilemma. For while *both* modern and antiquarian accounts of time, law, and justice are true, Grant saw them to be mutually exclusive. In *Philosophy in the Mass Age* he expressed his perplexity by asking how these two 'true' accounts could even be 'thought together.' Difficulty there may be, Grant opined, but assuredly both *must* be thought since either one by itself is 'wholly unacceptable.' On the one hand, antiquarian conceptions of law and justice allow people to attribute horrendous conditions to the 'will of God'; on the other, 'the worst crimes

of the twentieth century have been perpetrated in the name of progress and man's right to make history.' George Grant, *Philosophy in the Mass Age*, 70–1.

43 Frye's 'science' may have been more of the nineteenth than of the twentieth century. According to Sir James Jeans, for example, from a twentieth-century perspective 'the universe begins to look more like a great thought than a great machine.' Quoted in A. Koestler, *The Roots of Coincidence* (London: Pan Books, 1972), 58.

44 Northrop Frye, *The Modern Century* (Toronto: Oxford University Press, 1967), 121.

45 Northrop Frye, *The Critical Path: An Essay on the Social Context of Literary Criticism* (Bloomington: Indiana University Press, 1971), 85.

46 Ibid., 39.

47 Ibid., 41.

48 Ibid., 43.

49 Frye, *Divisions on a Ground*, 38.

50 Ibid., 43.

51 Ibid., 38.

52 Frye, *Fearful Symmetry*, 85.

53 Marshall McLuhan, *The Gutenberg Galaxy: The Making of Typographic Man* (Toronto: University of Toronto Press, 1962), 25.

54 Marshall McLuhan and W. Watson, *From Cliché to Archetype* (New York: Pocket Books, 1971), 121–2.

55 Marshall McLuhan, *Understanding Media: The Extensions of Man* (New York: Mentor, 1964), 51 ff.

56 McLuhan interview with G.E. Stearn in *McLuhan: Hot and Cool* (New York: Signet Books, 1969), 261.

57 McLuhan, *Gutenberg Galaxy*, 68.

58 McLuhan, *Understanding Media*, 93.

59 Ibid., 93.

60 McLuhan and Watson, *Cliché to Archetype*, 165.

61 McLuhan, *Understanding Media*, 91–4.

62 Marshall McLuhan and Eric McLuhan, *Laws of Media: The New Science* (Toronto: University of Toronto Press, 1988).

63 C.B. Macpherson, ed., *Property: Mainstream and Critical Positions* (Toronto: University of Toronto Press, 1978), 1.

64 C.B. Macpherson, *Democratic Theory: Essays in Retrieval* (Oxford: Clarendon, 1973), 122–5.

65 Macpherson, *Property*, 5.

66 C.B. Macpherson, *The Political Economy of Possessive Individualism: Hobbes to Locke* (Oxford: Oxford University Press, 1962), 3.
67 Macpherson, *Democratic Theory*, 5.
68 Ibid., 122.
69 Macpherson, *Property*, 11.
70 Macpherson, *Democratic Theory*, 24.
71 Ibid., 63.
72 McLuhan, *Gutenberg Galaxy*, 35.

10 Innis, Saul, Suzuki

In the present chapter I focus on Innis's communication thesis and relate that to the thought of two of our eminent contemporaries, John Ralston Saul and David Suzuki. Although Innis died in 1952, his time-space media dialectic remains as pertinent as ever.

Harold Innis

For most of his career, Harold Innis was an economic historian specializing in Canada. He maintained that economic theory should be closely integrated with economic history, as history is the test of theory. His aim, therefore, was to develop a 'philosophy of economic history or an economic theory suited to Canadian needs.'[1] He identified three features as paramount in Canada's economic history – her trading dependence on other countries; her geography, particularly the inland water systems and Precambrian Shield; and the unique character of her natural resources or 'staples.' He saw technological developments, particularly in the fields of transportation and communication, as interacting with geography and staples to disrupt established patterns of social interaction. Tensions resulted, according to Innis, when groups controlling the technologies associated with staples entered traditional, time-bound cultures for resource extraction and purposes of trade.

A number of commentators, including Marshall McLuhan, Robin Neill, Barrington Nevitt, and Paul Heyer,[2] have noted close connections and similarities between Innis's staples (or economic history) and his media (or communication history) writings. According to Heyer, for example, studying the pulp and paper staple opened for Innis 'a door to the newly emergent field of communication studies; he simply followed pulp and paper through its subsequent stages: newspapers and journalism, books and advertising.'[3]

Innis's staples thesis anticipated and parallels his media/communication writings in other, more profound ways also. For example, as noted by Heyer, ocean transport favoured staples that are light and valuable (such as fur), whereas primary inland waterways favoured bulk commodities (like lumber and minerals), paralleling Innis's analysis of the physical properties of time-binding and space-binding communication media.[4] More remarkable still are the similarities in his treatments of power and culture. In his staples writings, the imperial centre (England, France, the United States), which exercised control over the trade in the predominant staple (fish, fur, lumber, mining, wheat), occupies a role equivalent to monopolies of knowledge in his media writings; moreover, a change in staple is accompanied by new patterns of political economic control. In the staples thesis, staples mediate relations between the imperial centre and the colonial margin as well as among people in the margin; over-specialization in extracting/harvesting any given staple skews ('biases') socio-cultural-economic development in the colony. In his communication books, the term analogous to staples is *media*. The 'bias' spoken of there occurs in terms of conceptions or understandings of time and space.

I propose that the Innisian tradition of media/communication analysis is a viable means of integrating critical political economy and critical cultural studies. The remainder of this chapter supports that position by examining, albeit briefly, works by two of Canada's most eminent contemporary writers, John Ralston Saul and David Suzuki. Both, I will argue, espouse a view of media/communication resembling that of Innis, and both seamlessly blend political economy and cultural studies.

John Ralston Saul

John Ralston Saul (b. 1947) is a distinguished essayist, award-winning novelist, and political philosopher who has ruminated for many years on epistemology, the nature of the Canadian state, the Enlightenment, and other matters. He is one of *Utne Reader's* 100 leading thinkers. Although there are but few allusions to Harold Innis in Saul's writings, he is certainly an admirer, describing the renowned economic historian and media theorist as 'the first and still the most piercing philosopher of communications.'[5]

There are striking similarities in the approaches of these two scholars. Consider the following: like Innis, Saul contrasts societies with memory ('time bound' in Innis's terms) to our own 'present-mindedness' (again, Innis's term). Indeed, Saul makes an Innisian 'plea for time' declaring, 'If you cannot remember, then there is no reality,'[6] and again, 'We are faced by a crisis of memory, the loss of our humanist foundation.'[7] He approvingly quotes Cicero: 'He who does not know history is destined to remain a child.'[8]

What has destroyed memory in our time, Saul maintains, is technocratic insistence on applying abstract models (he calls them 'structures,' 'systems,' and 'ideologies') to real-life situations. These systems, structures, models, or ideologies, he claims, are essentially ahistorical; they propose fixed relationships among key variables. Saul's claim here resonates completely with Innis's insistence that unique economies not be forced to fit into the preset, 'universal' categories and relationships of neoclassical economics, that instead economic theory unique to each region be developed on the basis of that region's economic history.

Each verbal structure (whether mainstream economics, accounting, political science, Marxist theory, even fascism), Saul writes, is an inflexible frame of reference that selects/bends/creates facts to fit its own internal logic. He attributes amorality on the part of today's elites ('technocrats') to an absence of memory, writing, 'The exercise of power, without the moderating influence of any ethical structure explains the institutionalization of state violence.'[9] Hence the importance of historical consciousness: 'Memory,' he writes, 'is always the enemy of structure';[10] this is because memory brings forth the details and the feelings that confound the strict logic that structures impose. The comments seem to accord well with the distress Innis exhibited in writing about the mechanization of knowledge and the growing ties between the universities and the military.

Like Innis, who compared and contrasted time-binding and space-binding media at various stages in the evolution of several civilizations, Saul investigates the history of Western civilization and proposes a 'great divide' between 1530 and 1620. At that point, he writes, 'Reason began, abruptly, to separate itself from and to outdistance the other more or less recognized human characteristics – spirit, appetite, faith and emotion, but also intuition, will and, most important, experience.'[11] Although the Age of Reason was promoted by Voltaire, Diderot, and others to challenge the existing 'monopoly of knowledge' based on superstition and arbitrary power, in the end, according to Saul, a new and equally if not more insidious monopoly of knowledge arose, this based on reason unmodified by humanist (or, in Innis's terms, 'time-binding') values, and this monopoly still dominates today. Saul explains, 'The twentieth century, which has seen the final victory of pure reason in power, has also seen unprecedented unleashings of violence and of power deformed. It is hard, for example, to avoid noticing that the murder of six million Jews was a perfectly rational act [given the "structure" within which the perpetrators acted] ... Reason is no more than structure.'[12]

Like Innis, Saul maintains that elites purposefully confuse illusion and reality. Innis was most concerned, of course, that media such as newspapers distort the life situation by neglecting time. For Saul, similarly, elites propagate misconceptions to the broader populace. For one thing, the world is presented, by Saul's account, not with the doubtful, sceptical mind of a Socrates, but through the template of unduly rigid, taken-for-granted models. He writes, 'Today's power uses as its primary justification for doing wrong the knowledge possessed by experts.'[13] Probably the most important falsity spread by elites today, however, in Saul's view, is denial of the existence of a 'public good' (a time-binding, communal concept in Innis's terms). Elites do this on the one hand by largely disregarding (neglecting to mention) the public or common good as it is seldom incorporated in their systems and models, and on the other by continually promoting its opposite – self-interest. Nowhere is the citizenry encouraged to adopt a 'disinterested' perspective from which to contemplate the larger well-being of society, Saul maintains.[14]

Like Innis, then, Saul focuses on *monopolies of knowledge* as a key to understanding control and governance in society. He writes, 'Power in our civilization is repeatedly tied to the pursuit of all-inclusive truths and utopias,' which is to say 'systems' or 'ideologies.'[15] And again, 'The possession, use, and control of knowledge have become [the elite's] central theme,' adding, 'However, their power depends not on the effect with which they use that knowledge but on the effectiveness with which they control its use.'[16] In Saul's view, like that of Innis, knowledge systems empower 'experts' versed in their application. Knowledge systems, for Saul, do not provide answers to society's pressing problems: precisely the opposite; they give rise to the most perplexing problems confronting us.

Like Innis, Saul sees communication media as linking elites and their monopolies of knowledge to the rest of society. However, whereas Innis looked to various modes of inscription and to electronic media as forging these links, Saul emphasizes language and the 'wordsmiths.' 'Language,' he writes, 'provides legitimacy.' 'So long as military, political, religious or financial systems do not control language, the public's imagination can move freely about with its own ideas. However, people in positions of responsibility, he adds, 'are rewarded for controlling language.'[17] Today, Saul sees two genres of languages in currency. One is 'public language' – 'enormous, rich, varied and more or less powerless';[18] this is the language of democratic 'wordsmiths' – those devoted to clarity and understanding. The other is 'corporatist,' the language of technocrats in business and government; their language is 'purposefully impenetrable to the non-expert';[19] it is *intended* to obscure.[20] In truly Innisian style Saul proclaims, 'The language attached to power is designed to prevent communication.'[21]

Monopolies of knowledge for Saul, as for Innis, do not go uncontested. Whereas Innis maintained that groups marginalized by lacking control over a society's predominant medium may contest power by introducing rival media, Saul maintains that there is a continuing dialectic between those who, through specialized vocabularies and mathematical complexities, would use language to obscure versus democratic forces using language to enlighten. In this regard Saul re-presents Innis's dialectic between the oral and written word. Innis maintained that democracy flourished in Greece when the oral dialectic and the written word were in healthy tension. That was because, Innis contended, the written word on its own stifles thought and freedom because readers are led step by step to the authors' preconceived conclusions. In his preface to *Empire and Communications*, Innis went so far as to write, 'All written works, *including this one*, have dangerous implications to the vitality of an oral tradition and to the health of a civilization.'[22] Saul presents a similar dialectic in his contrast of Socrates versus Plato: the former, 'oral, questioner, obsessed by ethics, searching for truth without expecting to find it, democrat, believer in the qualities of the citizen'; the latter, 'written, answerer of questions, obsessed by power, in possession of the truth, anti-democratic, contemptuous of the citizen.'[23] Whether or not one accepts fully Saul's depiction of Socrates and Plato, his position on orality and writing is quite in accord with Innis.

Innis was a 'modernist.' He never abandoned the quest for truth, which he believed had material grounding and could be tested through material evidence. The researcher, for Innis, ought always to try to take into account and compensate for her own biases when describing reality; but that truth exists and can be discerned, albeit incompletely as if through a glass darkly, never seems to have been in doubt for Innis. That belief, one senses, is belied in Saul's work by his quick dismissal of all systems of knowledge, presuming them to misrepresent lived conditions; indeed, Saul evinces certain characteristics often associated with postmodernism/poststructuralism.[24]

Saul is unique as a theorist insofar as his writings contain more than mere traces of poststructuralism, yet nonetheless he is able to incorporate astutely elements of political economy. He does this, in Innisian fashion, by elaborating a version of the dialectic of time versus space, by linking knowledge to power, and by focusing on the means of communication as a site in the struggle for power.

David Suzuki

Even more congruent to Innis's communication thesis are the media writings of broadcaster, author, geneticist, and environmentalist David Suzuki. Suzuki holds a PhD in genetics from the University of Chicago and was formerly professor at the University of British Columbia. While likely unconscious of Innis as an intellectual ancestor, Suzuki nonetheless consistently applies the Innisian time-space media dialectic in addressing people's relations with the environment. Whereas Innis illustrated that time-space media dialectic through myriad examples culled from world history, Suzuki does this by contrasting the mindsets of indigenous peoples with the modern West. Like Innis, Suzuki draws connections between differences in culture (conceptions of time, conceptions of space) on the one hand, and predominance of different media of communication, and patterns of their control (monopolies of knowledge), on the other. Let us begin by describing Suzuki's depiction of cultures in terms of conceptions of time.

Suzuki judges a society's conception of time to be 'one of the pillars of its worldview, its shared ideas and images that grant order and meaning to the universe.'[25] He repeatedly contrasts two disparate notions of time. One, termed the 'pre-scientific conception,' is similar to Innisian 'time-bias.' According to Suzuki, the 'pre-scientific mind,' which was widespread in Europe before Copernicus and still characterizes the mindset of many indigenous peoples about the globe, affirms the importance of continuity and in particular the dependence of succeeding generations on the actions of their forebears. Some variants of the pre-scientific mindset even endow humans with the responsibility of keeping the stars on their courses.[26] The pre-scientific mind also pays close attention to recurrent natural rhythms. Some of nature's cycles are held to be sacred and steeped in signs and significance, and people participate symbolically in these recurrences through rituals.

The media of communication that imbue pre-scientific peoples with mythic notions of time, Suzuki observes, have traditionally been songs, ceremonies, and stories.[27] For the Gitksan of central British Columbia, for example, each household is the proud heir of an *ada'ox* – the 'body of orally transmitted songs and stories that acts as the house's sacred archives and as its living, millennia-long memory of important events of the past' – an 'irreplaceable verbal repository of knowledge.' It consists in part of sacred songs believed to have arisen 'from the breaths of ancestors.' According to Suzuki and co-author Peter Knudtson, 'These songs serve as vital time-traversing vehicles. They can transport members across the immense reaches of space and time into the dim mythic past of Gitksan creation by the very quality of their music and the emotions they convey.'[28]

Cyclical time, Suzuki continues, bestows the notion that we are all parts of a seamless web of interconnectivity and interdependence through time and space – that we live in future generations and they in us.

The opposite conception of time, according to Suzuki, is the Western scientific tradition of 'time's arrow' – the idea that time is linear, sequential, and unidirectional.[29] This resembles Innis's depiction of time for space-biased societies. Suzuki writes that although science recognizes natural cycles and rhythms – the solar seasons, fluctuations of predator and prey populations, replication cycles of DNA – these expressions of cyclical time are conceived to exist only within the grander framework of linear time – for example, the relentless increase in entropy and linear chains of cause and effect.[30] Western notions of linear time, by marginalizing cyclical or mythic time, have helped demolish 'the intellectual and moral order of the Western world' as nothing is thought to remain the same;[31] thereby they have helped initiate the severe environmental problems we experience today.

For Suzuki, we in the West are beset by what Innis called 'present-mindedness.' We think little of the past and have few concerns over what may transpire in the distant future. Rather, he writes, the 'bottom line is often a weekly paycheque or an annual return on investment. Political reality is dictated by a horizon measured in months or a few years.' Indeed, 'linear time underlies our most cherished notions of "progress" – our collective faith in the inexorable, incremental refinement of human society, technology, and thought.'[32] This explains why it is difficult to mesh economic and political deadlines with nature's time needs.

Suzuki is also Innisian when he assesses the time-bias inherent to modern media. When he first became a broadcast journalist, he hoped he would enable viewers to experience nature in a way that would inspire them to love it. Later he understood that this could not be so: 'Now I realize that my programs, too, are a creation, not a reflection of reality ... Back in the editing room, hours of this hard-earned film are boiled down to sequences of sensational shot after sensational shot.'[33] He continues, 'What's missing in the filmed version of nature is time. Nature must have time, but television cannot tolerate it. So we create a virtual reality, a collage of images that conveys a distorted sense of what a real wilderness is like.'[34]

For Suzuki, the 'time-distortion' of modern media is not trivial. By instilling an impression that nature can move quickly, media cause people to harbour unrealistic expectations: 'Fish, trees or soil microorganisms don't grow fast enough for our speedy timeframe. But if the programs we create give an impression of a hopped-up nature, we might expect it to be able to meet our ever-faster needs.'[35] Suzuki suggests that although our rates of extracting resources – trees, fish, topsoil, clean water – are harmonious with the speed of our information technologies and the economy, they are certainly 'not in synch with the reproductive rates of natural systems.' He concludes, 'More and more our sources of information are no longer connected to the natural world and its limits.'[36]

Like Innis, who pleaded for 'balance' between time and space in order that society would neither become stagnant nor fall into chaos, Suzuki insists that we need to integrate these rival ways of understanding time. By conceiving time as a spiral, rather than as a circle or straight line, we could synthesize the cyclical or mythic with the linear, scientific notions, making us more aware than at present of the 'simultaneous spin of nature's seasons within time's trajectory,' a necessity, he concludes, if we are to survive.[37]

Suzuki, like Innis, connects control of media (political economy, monopolies of knowledge) to culture as manifested in conceptions of time. According to Suzuki, media are purposefully propagandistic in imparting a world view consistent with the short-term interests of their controllers. He explains, 'In our view, the media pour out stories that are full of assumptions and values in the guise of objective value-free reporting. Most programming on television simply takes for granted our right to exploit nature as we see fit, to dominate the planet, to increase our consumption, to create more economic growth, to dump our wastes into the environment. Few object to these assumptions because they are so deeply set in our culture that they are accepted as obvious truths. However, they are biases nevertheless. Yet the minute a natural history film takes a strong environmental position that questions these beliefs, it is immediately criticized and bombarded with the demand to present "the other side."[38]

The foregoing brief overview shows that the contemporary writings of David Suzuki and John Ralston Saul are largely congruent with and extensions of the mode of analysis inaugurated by Innis. Innis remains relevant in the new millennium, over a half century after his death.

NOTES

1 Harold A. Innis, 'The Teaching of Economic History in Canada' (1929); repr. in Innis, *Essays in Canadian Economic History*, ed. Mary Q. Innis (Toronto: University of Toronto Press, 1956), 3.
2 Marshall McLuhan, introduction to *The Bias of Communication* by Harold A. Innis (Toronto: University of Toronto Press, 1971); Robin Neill, *A New Theory of Value: The Canadian Economics of H.A. Innis* (Toronto: University of Toronto Press, 1972); Barrington Nevitt, *The Communication Ecology: Re-presentation versus Replica* (Toronto: Butterworths, 1982); Paul Heyer, *Harold Innis* (Lanham, MD: Rowman and Littlefield, 2003).
3 Heyer, *Harold Innis*, 30.
4 Ibid., 15.
5 John Ralston Saul, *Voltaire's Bastards: The Dictatorship of Reason in the West* (Toronto: Penguin, 1992), 53.
6 Ibid., 5.
7 Ibid., 70.
8 Ibid., 5.
9 Ibid.
10 Ibid., 14.
11 Ibid., 15.
12 Ibid., 16.
13 John Ralston Saul, *The Unconscious Civilization* (Toronto: House of Anansi, 1995), 43.

14 Ibid., 99.
15 Ibid., 18.
16 Saul, *Voltaire's Bastards*, 8.
17 Saul, *Unconscious Civilization*, 42.
18 Ibid., 46.
19 Ibid., 47.
20 Saul, *Voltaire's Bastards*, 8–9.
21 Saul, *Unconscious Civilization*, 54.
22 Harold Innis, *Empire and Communications* (1950; Toronto: University of Toronto Press, 1972), xiii. Emphasis added.
23 Saul, *Unconscious Civilization*, 55–6.
24 See Frank Webster, *Theories of the Information Society* (London: Routledge, 2002), 227–62.
25 Peter Knudtson and David Suzuki, *Wisdom of the Elders* (Toronto: Stoddart, 1992), 142.
26 David Suzuki and Amanda McConnell, *The Sacred Balance: Rediscovering Our Place in Nature* (Vancouver: David Suzuki Foundation and Greystone Books, 1997), 11.
27 Knudtson and Suzuki, *Wisdom of the Elders*, 145.
28 Ibid., 128.
29 Ibid., 143.
30 Ibid.
31 Suzuki and McConnell, *Sacred Balance*, 13.
32 Knudtson and Suzuki, *Wisdom of the Elders*, 143.
33 David Suzuki and Holly Dressel, *From Naked Ape to Superspecies: A Personal Perspective on Humanity and the Global Eco-Crisis* (Toronto: Stoddart, 1999), 79.
34 Ibid., 79.
35 Ibid.
36 Ibid.
37 Knudtson and Suzuki, *Wisdom of the Elders*, 145.
38 David Suzuki, *Metamorphosis: Stages in Life* (Toronto: Stoddart, 1987), 263.

11 Harold Innis and the Paradox of Press Freedom

You furnish the pictures and I'll furnish the war.
– William Randolph Hearst (1898, attr.)

Force and Knowledge

In the late 1940s and early 1950s economic historian Harold Adams Innis (1894–1952) – Canada's pre-eminent scholar of the twentieth century – helped inaugurate the now burgeoning field of media studies. According to American media scholar James W. Carey, Innis 'founded the modern studies that now exist under the banner of media imperialism.'[1] Likewise, Paul Heyer proposes that 'Innis should be considered the "father" of what has become known as "medium theory."'[2] Similarly, Marshall McLuhan attested that his own breakthrough book, *The Gutenberg Galaxy*, was but 'a footnote to the observations of Innis.'[3]

Surprisingly, given such resounding praise, Innis's work remains obscure. Among media scholars outside Canada, Innis's scholarship is for the most part unread and unacknowledged. In their recent historical surveys of radical mass media criticism, Scott and McChesney, for example, leave unmentioned one of the most original and trenchant critics of the U.S. press, Harold Innis.[4] Yet Innis, as will become increasingly apparent during the course of this article, brings much to the table that even celebrated critics of the press, scholars like McChesney, Chomsky, and Herman, do not offer – namely, a nuanced and detailed historical interleaving of technological/media change, shifts in political economic power, changes in culture, media messages, and monopolies of knowledge. After reading Innis, one would develop a much more nuanced understanding of the boosterism and jingoism of press coverage leading up to the U.S.-Iraqi wars than would otherwise be the case.

An essential key to understanding Innis's media writings generally, and his press criticism in particular, is his insistence, following the classical Greeks, on an opposition between power and knowledge.[5] A dialectic or contradiction between knowledge and power may seem quaint or out of place in contemporary mainstream Western culture. Indeed, the mainstream of Western thought seems still to adhere to the dictum of Francis Bacon (1561–1626) that 'knowledge itself is power.'[6] For Bacon, indeed, the precise purpose of science/knowledge is to increase human power over nature. In the same vein, contemporary society is often referred to, with great pride and approval, as the information society and the knowledge economy, implying still today a continuing congruence between knowledge and power, particularly as facilitated by new media of communication. Innis, though, saw things differently. He declared, 'Power and its assistant, force [are] the natural enemies of intelligence.'[7] And again, 'Force is no longer concerned with his [i.e., the scholar's] protection and is actively engaged in schemes for his destruction.'[8]

In his 1947 essay, 'Minerva's Owl,' Innis explained why he believed organized force strives to restrain scholarship and critical thought. He wrote, 'In the words of Hume: "As force is always on the side of the governed [due to vastly greater numbers], the governors have nothing to support them but opinion. It is, therefore, on opinion that government is founded; and this maxim extends to the most despotic and the most military governments as well as to the most free and most popular." The relation of monopolies of knowledge to organized force is evident in the political and military histories of civilization.'[9]

Consequently, according to Innis, political, military, and financial centres normally endeavour to control knowledge production and distribution. Thereby, they direct, bias, distort, or reconfigure 'knowledge.' Innis termed these power centres 'monopolies of knowledge.' He proposed further that a creative highpoint in the life cycle of civilizations occurs when each one enters its death throes, for it is then that organized force inadvertently loosens its grip, freeing knowledge workers to pursue truth, be creative, and engage in critical work. Innis wrote, 'With a weakening of protection of organized force, scholars put forth greater efforts and in a sense the flowering of the culture comes before its collapse. Minerva's owl begins its flight in the gathering dusk not only from classical Greece but in turn from Alexandria, from Rome, from Constantinople, from the republican cities of Italy, from France, from Holland, and from Germany.'[10]

Innis's 'Minerva's Owl' marks the only instance in which this seminal scholar invoked Greek mythology to help make a point,[11] the allusion well illustrating the influence upon Innis of several classicists at the University of Toronto. The owl, pet of the war goddess Minerva, is a metaphor for knowledge, whose flight represents 'the movement of the centre of Western civilization from one people and place to another.'[12] Normally, the owl is docile, meekly serving power and force as signified by Minerva. However, periodically, Minerva's grip is loosened, the owl is freed, but soon thereafter, according to Innis, it is forced to flee because the conditions supporting its existence are in decline. Although toward the end of a civilization, 'scholars put forth greater efforts and in a sense the flowering of the culture comes before its collapse,' the civilization does collapse, and scholarship in that location becomes more difficult or impossible. According to Innis, then, on the one hand, scholarship depends on force to ensure stability, but on the other, force erodes the integrity of scholarship.

According to Innis, another moment or opportunity of freedom for critical scholarship and for creative artistic endeavour occurs within a civilization when one mode of communication, normally introduced from the margin or the hinterland by groups aspiring to power, begins to challenge, eventually perhaps to supplant, the older medium. In *Empire and Communications* Innis surveyed civilizations, both ancient and modern, to show linkages among changing media, transformations in knowledge, and shifts in power, as illustrated by the following several, brief excerpts: 'The profound disturbances in Egyptian civilization involved the shift from absolute monarchy to a more democratic organization [coinciding] with a shift in emphasis on stone as a medium of communication or as a basis of prestige, as shown in the pyramids, to an emphasis on papyrus.'[13]

Regarding Babylon, 'A flexible alphabet in contrast with cuneiform and hieroglyphic or hieratic writing facilitated the crystallization of languages and favoured the position of cities and smaller nations rather than empires.'[14]

In Europe, 'The monopoly of knowledge built up under ecclesiastical control in relation to time and based on the medium of parchment was undermined by the competition of paper.'[15]

Later in Europe, another seismic shift occurred with the arrival of the printing press: 'Printing accentuated a commercial interest in the selection of books and the publisher concerned with markets began to displace the printer concerned with production. The monopoly of monasticism was further undermined. The authority of the written word declined. The age of cathedrals had passed.'[16]

But Innis was interested not only in civilizations of the past. In 'A Critical Review,' for example, he focused on the contemporary period of the late 1940s – the aftermath of the Second World War and the onset of the Cold War – to emphasize 'the suppression or distortion of culture, particularly through its influence on science.'[17] In fact, a careful reading of the foregoing statement reveals that Innis proposed a recursive relationship between culture and science. On the one hand, 'culture' (here, power centres) impinges upon science, distorting its findings; on the other, science biases, distorts, or suppresses culture.

To illustrate the first possibility, we could point to certain scientists in the employ of, for instance, tobacco companies or of certain oil companies, who for pecuniary reasons may have skewed 'findings' concerning health or environmental consequences of their sponsors' activities and products. Likewise, Christopher Simpson has documented how, for several decades beginning in the 1940s, main figures in U.S. media and communication scholarship had strong pecuniary links to the CIA and the U.S. military,[18] linkages that may well have induced these scholars not only to avoid but indeed to repudiate critical political economy in their theorizing.[19] On another front, Innis himself remarked that 'the bias of economics ... makes the best economists come from powerful countries,'[20] indicating that in his view mainstream economics favours the wealthy in their contestations with the poor. Innis also drew attention to the close conjuncture between science and the military, writing, 'The universities are in danger of becoming a branch of the military arm.'[21]

The paradox, and tragedy, of science, as Innis saw it, was that once science became free from the monopolies controlling time (a victory represented symbolically, perhaps, by Galileo's ultimate victory in his contestations with the church), it eventually succumbed to the monopolies controlling space (the military and commercial concerns): 'Science had gained in the escape from the monopoly of knowledge in terms of time but eventually lost in the development of knowledge in terms of space; an obsession with monopolies of space has been evident in the effects of militarism on geography.'[22]

Much more could and should be said about this aspect of Innis's political economy of knowledge thesis. Instead, however, I turn now to its reverse. According to Innis, the problem is not just that cultural/ political/economic power tends to guide, distort, or corrupt science and scholarship; the problem is also that science acts recursively on culture. He wrote, 'The impact of science on cultural development has been evident in its contribution to technological advance, notably in communication and in the dissemination of knowledge. In turn it has been evident in the types of knowledge disseminated; that is to say, science lives its own life not only in the mechanism which is provided to distribute knowledge but also in the sort of knowledge which will be distributed.'[23]

The manifestation, or material embodiment, of scientific knowledge in new technologies is obvious enough: the Internet, satellites, television, radio, and other 'mechanisms ... provided to distribute knowledge.' The very presence of such evolving infrastructure, irrespective of content or the ostensible 'messages,' may well have cultural consequences: for instance, the awe and esteem with which one regards science and large corporations. Innis's second point in the foregoing excerpt, however, namely that new media are inherently biased or selective in the types of messages/knowledge they transmit, is a more nuanced claim, and hence deserves elaboration. In his introduction to *Empire and Communications*, Innis summarized what has since become known as 'medium theory':

> The concepts of time and space reflect the significance of media to civilization. Media that emphasize time [continuity, duration] are those that are durable in character, such as parchment, clay, and stone. The heavy materials are suited to the development of architecture and sculpture. Media that emphasize space are apt to be less durable and light in character, such as papyrus and paper. The latter are suited to wide areas in administration and trade ... Materials that emphasize time favour decentralization and hierarchical types of institutions, while those that emphasize space favour centralization and systems of government less hierarchical in character. Large-scale political organizations such as empires must be considered from the standpoint of two dimensions, those of space and time, and persist by overcoming the bias of media which over-emphasize either dimension. They have tended to flourish under conditions in which civilization reflects the influence of more than one medium and in which the bias of one medium toward decentralization is offset by the bias of another medium toward centralization.[24]

Here Innis claims that by their intrinsic attributes (their heaviness and durability, but elsewhere also the extent to which they can store messages and their ease or difficulty in being encoded), media are intrinsically biased either toward supporting control through time (as exercised by religious leaders and others invoking custom, tradition, local culture, continuity, myth, collective memory, teleology), or control over space (as by large corporate businesses, government leaders, or the military, all of which are intent on administering large territories in the present). An alternative formulation of this space-time dialectic is being versus becoming.[25] Paper, for example, being lighter and more tractable than stone, and with the larger storage capacity, is the more space-binding of the two, emphasizing being in the present; paper in conjunction with the printing press is even more space-binding than paper in a manuscript culture. Furthermore, Innis declares that for a culture to flourish, time-bias and space-bias need continually to offset or counterbalance one another through rival media.

In Innis's mind, the space-bias of contemporary society (that is, an undue emphasis on being), is associated strongly with what he termed 'mechanized' media, and this space-bias, not being offset to any large extent by oral communication (Innis's favourite time-binding medium), causes difficulties of understanding. He stated unambiguously, 'The conditions of freedom of thought are in danger of being destroyed by science, technology, and the mechanization of knowledge, and with them, Western civilization.'[26] Innis, one might infer, adopted an apocalyptic view of Western civilization. Let's look in turn at each of the notions brought together in that condensed sentence.

Innis believed that the inventions of the mechanical printing press and the paper machine heralded a revolution in the mechanization of knowledge production and distribution.[27] He declared, 'We can conveniently divide the history of the West into the writing and the printing periods.'[28] Mechanization, he observed, gave rise to specialization, indeed to an 'obsession with specialization,'[29] and to the pursuit of economies of scale in knowledge production and distribution,[30] thereby inducing the arrival of the 'information industries.'[31] (Very likely this is the first time the term *information industries*, now a commonplace, was used). In referring to mechanization of knowledge and of media, Innis had in mind not only larger presses and larger print runs,[32] but as well larger class sizes in universities,[33] the use of mechanical instruments including books as teaching aids, which tend 'to emphasize the factual and the concrete [as opposed to] abstract ideas,'[34] the discouragement of oral dialogue and the concomitant decline of critical, creative thought,[35] insistence on the efficacy of formulaic knowledge,[36] and perhaps most importantly the undue emphasis on the present and the transitory ('present-mindedness').

In tying greater problems in understanding to the mechanization of media,[37] Innis made three major claims. One was at the international or cross-cultural level. Advances in communication, he claimed, decrease the ability of one culture or nation to understand or empathize with another. (How totally against the grain of the received wisdom of our day is that thought! We tend still to blithely indulge in the nostrums of the global village and greater understanding through international trade/communication.) Innis, however, pointed to, for example, 'the varied rate of development of communication facilities' as one source of cross-cultural tension.[38] Literate and less literate cultures grow apart; regions rife with instant messaging, we might speculate, become even more remote to countries lacking basic telephone service, and vice versa. But Innis goes further: 'The large-scale mechanization of knowledge is characterized by imperfect competition and the active creation of monopolies in language which prevent understanding and hasten appeals to force ... Application of power to communication industries hastened the consolidation of vernaculars, the rise of nationalism, revolution, and new outbreaks of savagery in the twentieth century.'[39]

Within cultures or countries, too, a proliferation of communicational activity breeds specialization and thereby differentiation, and hence segregation. Innis wrote, 'In the vast realm of fiction in the Anglo-Saxon world, the influence of the newspaper and such recent developments as the cinema and the radio has been evident in the best seller and the creation of special classes of readers with little prospect of communication between them.'[40] For Innis also, ease in transmission of scholarship fragmented the university; proliferation of disciplines, sub-disciplines, and specialties created 'congeries of hardened avid departments obsessed with an interest in funds in which the department which can best prove its superficiality or its uselessness is most successful.'[41] And again, 'Knowledge has been divided to the extent that it is apparently hopeless to expect a common point of view.'[42]

Innis also claimed, thirdly, that the mechanization and proliferation of media increase the difficulties of understanding at the level of the individual. There is, for example, an inordinate increase in the trivial. Innis declared, 'Mechanical devices become concerned with useless knowledge of useful facts.'[43] The trivial, for Innis, is virtually synonymous with 'present-mindedness.' Mechanized communication, he claimed, has virtually 'destroyed a sense of time.'[44] Innis cites Keynes's dictum – 'In the long run we are all dead'[45] – as indicating an obsessive present-mindedness on the part of even the most esteemed of scholars. Keynes basically claimed that 'we have little other interest than that of living for the immediate future.'[46] More generally, Innis maintained, 'work in the social sciences has become increasingly concerned with topical problems and social science departments become schools of journalism.'[47] For Innis, then, in scholarship as in popular culture, 'the balance between time and space has been seriously disturbed with disastrous consequences to Western civilization.'[48] (Regrettably, Innis did not live to see the advent of university courses celebrating 'popular culture' or the creation of 'cultural studies' departments, but one can imagine his consternation and the satirical bite of his ironic observations.)

Culture and education, Innis believed, ought properly to be concerned with 'the capacity of the individual to appraise problems in terms of space and time and with enabling him to take the proper steps at the right time.'[49] But in this, contemporary media and education fail us, and indeed it is here that the contradiction between true scholarship/creativity, or what Innis termed 'civilized culture' on the one hand, versus power and force on the other is most apparent. The state and business are focused on administering affairs in the present over vast geographic expanse. Innis commented, 'We are compelled to recognize the significance of mechanized knowledge as a source of power and its subjection to the demands of force through the instrument of the state ... Centralization in education in the interests of political organization has disastrous implications.'[50]

In summary, to consolidate and extend power, according to Innis, organized force dominates and thereby skews or distorts scholarship, education, science, and other knowledge generation/diffusion activities. Innis also insisted, however, that organized force normally controls as well what he sometimes termed 'the vernacular,' or what we might term popular culture. He wrote, 'The success of organized force is dependent on an effective combination of ... the vernacular in public opinion with technology [or media of communication] and science.'[51] Indeed, he claimed, once science had enfeebled the power of religion 'as an anchorage,' the state (and we could add corporations) became 'more dependent on cultural development.'[52] It is in the area of 'cultural development' that Innis's analysis and commentaries on the press become so poignant.

Law, Technology, and Press Freedom: Harnessing Science and the Vernacular

According to Innis, by controlling science, 'organized force' controls the trajectory of technological change, particularly innovations in the media of communication. In support of Innis's claim it may be recalled that the optical telegraph, radio, computers, satellites, and the Internet all came about through activity or funding of the military. Control over the media of communication is essential to those in power, in Innis's view (pursuant to Hume's axiom), because organized force cannot long continue to govern without the approval of the governed. Winning this approval, however, is contingent on maintaining control over the means of communication.

In this section I sketch out aspects of Innis's detailed depiction of technological change as it related to press systems and how that, in turn, relates to the structure of power. Three important areas in this regard were paper production, application of the telegraph to press systems, and increased speed of printing presses. In combination, these developments led to a revolution in the production and distribution of news, giving rise to a new 'monopoly of knowledge,' whose power was cemented in the United States by the Bill of Rights.

In Europe prior to the age of the electric telegraph and fast presses, interests associated with the landed aristocracy and the Crown endeavoured through censorship, licensing, taxation, grants of monopoly, and other means to curtail the emerging printing technologies from fostering and spreading dissent. In England, France, and elsewhere by the end of the sixteenth century, however, according to Innis, periods of book suppression 'were accompanied by the rise of news-letters which evaded censorship.' Innis continues, 'The extreme difficulties of the press were accompanied by the growth of advertising as a source of revenue, and it was significant that the first advertisements included books or products of the press, quack medicines, tea, chocolate ... Suppression of the printing of certain types of literature released the facilities for other types.'[53]

Suppression of radical thought was supplemented by efforts at cooptation. In the United States, for example, Jefferson, who championed small landowners as opposed to banking and commercial interests,[54] recognized the potential of the newspaper as 'an element of strategy.'[55] Jefferson not only encouraged the inauguration of the *National Gazette* (begun 21 October 1791) but also, through the grant of a monopoly of congressional news and a 'generous share of public printing,' persuaded the *National Intelligencer* to move from Philadelphia to Washington. In the 1820s, according to Innis, four of five members of President Andrew Jackson's Cabinet were 'experienced journalists.'[56] He continued, 'Other rewards of patronage to editorial partisans included government printing, advertising of letters on hand in post offices, and appointments to the post office involving the right to half the revenue from newspaper postage, the privilege of franking estimated to be worth four or five hundred dollars a year, the possibility of restricting newspapers with opposing views, exemption from military and jury service, and the advantage of early intelligence.'[57]

In 1791 the American Bill of Rights was enacted, which states, among other things, that 'Congress shall make no law ... abridging the freedom of speech, or of the press.'[58] For many, this provision established in law a basic democratic freedom. Innis, however, was of a different mind. He claimed that through devices like those enumerated above, the press remained (for a time) staunchly under political control and hence, it would seem, by decreeing freedom of the press, the dominant political interests of the day did not reduce and may even have enhanced for a time their freedom/power. In any event, for Innis, the legislation soon had consequences unforeseen by those enacting it: 'The full impact of printing did not become possible,' he wrote, 'until the adoption of the Bill of Rights in the United States with its guarantee of freedom of the press.'[59] By 'full impact,' Innis meant, in part, generation of a new monopoly of knowledge.

Technological Change and a New Monopoly of Knowledge

Exports of paper to the United States had a large impact on the development of the American newspaper industry. Newspapers in the American commercial centres before 1812 responded to the needs of business by running 'a large number of small advertisements,' often legal notifications. They enjoyed circulations, however, only in the hundreds. These 'broadsheets' endeavoured to conserve paper by reducing font sizes and trimming their physical dimensions.[60] According to Innis, by the 1830s, however, increases in supplies of wood pulp dramatically reduced the price of newsprint,[61] which, accompanied by technological advances in printing, gave rise to 'a new type of paper,' namely the penny presses, focused on mass circulation, on sensational news, and sustained by advertising directed toward 'consumers.'[62]

As newspapers gained circulation, they gained political clout. Rather than being dominated by political interests, as was the case in Jefferson's day, newspaper proprietors came to be highly influential in influencing public policy. One of their keenest interests, of course, concerned the price of newsprint. At the turn of the century, newsprint prices were increasing and newsprint companies were amalgamating, as evidenced by the formation in 1898 of the International Paper Company, composed of nineteen hitherto independent companies. Innis reports that 'with the enormous advantage of control over publicity,' newspaper owners exerted political pressures. To court press favour, Theodore Roosevelt launched a conservation campaign with the slogan, 'We are out of pulpwood,' while his successors, H.W. Taft and Woodrow Wilson, reduced and then finally removed tariffs on newsprint from Canada.[63] Moreover, appeals to the importance of a 'free press' blocked plans by the International Paper Company to acquire newspapers to secure markets for its output. 'Insistence on freedom of the press became a powerful factor in the defeat of newsprint producers.'[64]

Also central to the transformation of newspapers was the invention of the electric telegraph (circa 1837) and its application to journalism. This coupling, as had the lower price of newsprint, helped erode 'political control through the post office.' In this case, regional presses were freed from their dependence on the metropolitan press.[65] Innis, however, goes further: 'The telegraph destroyed the monopoly of political centres and contributed, in destroying political power, to the outbreak of the Civil War.'[66] This may seem extreme, but Innis observes repeatedly in his surveys of ancient and modern civilizations that changes in the mode of communication give rise to periods of instability, often accompanied by civil strife, as one monopoly of knowledge ebbs and a new one flows. In this instance, the monopoly of knowledge associated with land was challenged and defeated by interests centred on commercialism and finance. As Innis explains, 'Printing assumed mass production or reproduction of words and once it escaped from the pattern of the parchment manuscript it compelled the production of vast quantities of new material including material to meet the demands of science and technology. Improvements of communication hastened the development of markets and of industry.'[67] Thereby, 'a press less subservient to the political control of the Republican party followed the introduction of new inventions.'[68]

By Innis's account the invention of the telegraph and its application to journalism compelled newspapers 'to pool their efforts in collecting and transmitting news,'[69] leading in 1848 to the organization of what soon became the Associated Press, which in turn destroyed the 'parochial monopoly of New York papers.'[70] But the Associated Press itself, of course, became a concentrated news source and distribution system and helped to redefine the very notion of news. Interestingly, a Supreme Court decision establishing a property right in the news further entrenched AP's power,[71] although in another decision, *United States v. Associated Press*,[72] the same Court decreed, 'Freedom of the press from government interference under the first amendment does not sanction repression of that freedom by private interests ... Surely a command that the government itself shall not impede the free flow of ideas does not afford non-governmental combinations a refuge if they impose restraints upon that constitutionally guaranteed freedom.'[73]

The news cartel represented by the Associated Press and other ownership concentrations, although important, was not, however, what Innis had foremost in mind when he described the press as constituting a new monopoly of knowledge. Rather, in Innis's view, all presses – AP, Hearst, Pulitzer, the independents – in combination or as a totality, formed a new monopoly of knowledge in the sense of undue commercialism and an utter disregard of time in the sense of continuity and duration.

The third technological change (actually, a succession of changes) contributing to the transformation of the newspaper business and supporting a new monopoly of knowledge was the development of increasingly faster presses. 'With the linotype, advertisements could be changed daily and became a part of news.'[74] 'The cost of printing was vastly reduced with more efficient presses.'[75] Also important in the transformation of the newspaper were technological developments regarding the reproduction of illustrations and photographs, after the 1880s: 'Pulitzer's use of the cartoon had contributed to a quadrupling of circulation by the end of the first year. His success in increasing circulation with pictures was immediately followed by others. The multi-colour rotary press was introduced in the early nineties with pictures. By 1990 nearly all daily papers in the United States were illustrated.'[76]

Time-Space and the Monopoly of Knowledge

Innis noted that in holding down the price of newsprint and expanding circulation, newspapers favoured a 'marked extension of advertising.' In St Louis between 1875 and 1925, for example, newspapers reduced space allocated to news from 55.3 to 26.7 per cent, with a concomitant increase in the space devoted to advertising. For Innis, news for the 'cheap papers' was little more than 'a device for advertising the paper as an advertising medium.'[77] 'Freedom of the press,' as guaranteed by the U.S. Constitution, Innis observed dryly, narrowed the 'marketplace of ideas' because the industry began accommodating the interests of its advertisers.[78] For one thing, advertisers were interested in 'a constant emphasis on prosperity.' Moreover, muckraking in the financial field disappeared. And, beginning with Ivy Lee, PR professionals began 'disguising advertising material and planting it in unexpected places to be picked up as news.'[79] In brief, 'freedom of the press as guaranteed by the Bill of Rights in the United states [became] the great bulwark of monopolies.'[80] Attempts to increase circulation for advertisers, moreover, gave rise to comics, photos, and features, and 'a prevailing interest in orgies and excitement.'[81] According to Innis, 'The steadying influence of the book as a product of sustained intellectual effort was destroyed by new developments in periodicals and newspapers ... The Western community was atomized by the pulverizing effects of the application of machine industry to communication.'[82]

Arguably, these 'pulverizing effects' later contributed to the rise of a new 'philosophy' – namely, poststructuralism or postmodernism. It has been contended that Innis was a precursor or a forefather of post-structuralism[83] but, in fact, while anticipating it, Innis detested what he foresaw.

In Innis's view, a second unfortunate consequence of the Bill of Rights was a further supplanting of empathetic conversation by the 'cruelty' of mechanized communication.[84] He explained, 'The printing press and the radio address the world instead of the individual. The oral dialectic is overwhelmingly significant where the subject matter is human action and feeling, and it is important in the discovery of new truth but of very little value in disseminating it. The oral discussion inherently involves personal contact and a consideration for the feeling of others, and it is in sharp contrast with the cruelty of mechanized communication and the tendencies which we have come to note in the modern world.'[85]

A third contention was that, by empowering mechanized communication, the Bill of Rights fostered 'a narrowing of the range from which material is distributed and a widening of the range of reception, so that large numbers receive, but are unable to make any direct response.'[86] The right to freedom of speech specified in the Bill of Rights has been interpreted by the courts as an individual right to engage in personal conversation, not as a right of citizens to access media of communication owned by corporations. The freedom to publish affirmed in the Bill of Rights, therefore, is a right possessed by owners of the press to publish what they wish, and pari passu to exclude viewpoints and spokespersons as they see fit.[87] Hence, again, the Bill of Rights shored up the rights of the powerful and, at least relatively, reduced the rights of the general public. In a very real sense, the Bill of Rights reduced free speech; as Innis remarked, 'Those on the receiving end of material from a mechanized central system are precluded from participation in healthy, vigorous, and vital discussion.'[88]

Finally, and most importantly in Innis's view, as empowered by the Bill of Rights, the press developed into a new monopoly of knowledge in the service of space, to the preclusion of time. This is a continuing theme in Innis's work, and perhaps a few brief extracts will suffice to establish its central importance in his system of thought:

The influence of mechanization on the printing industry had been evident in the increasing importance of the ephemeral. Superficiality became essential to meet the various demands of larger numbers of people and was developed as an art by those compelled to meet the demands ... With these powerful developments time was destroyed and it became increasingly difficult to achieve continuity or ask for a consideration of the future.[89]

The overwhelming pressure of mechanization evident in the newspaper and the magazine has led to the creation of vast monopolies of knowledge of communication. Their entrenched positions involve a continuous, systematic, ruthless destruction of elements of permanence essential to cultural activity. The emphasis on change is the only permanent characteristic.[90]

In the United States the dominance of the newspaper led to large-scale development of monopolies of communication in terms of space and implied a neglect of problems of time.[91]

The Vernacular and the Scholarly

An undue focus on the problems of space ('present-mindedness') to the exclusion of time (continuity, the future) can have disastrous consequences. Ecologist David Suzuki reminds us that virtually all mainstream media neglected to cover the signing, in November 1992 by over half of the world's living Nobel laureates, of 'World Scientists'

Warning to Humanity,' a document that began starkly, 'Human beings and the natural world are on a collision course.'[92] Comments Suzuki, 'Half of all living Nobel prize winners suggesting that humanity could have as little as 10 years to avoid an absolute catastrophe are rated unworthy of reportage by media that obsessed for weeks and months, sometimes years over O.J. Simpson, Bill and Monica, Princess Diana, Michael Jackson, Martha Stewart, and Jennifer-Brad-Angelina.'[93]

Reading the foregoing excerpt from Suzuki's article, one might view popular culture as being on a collision course with scholarship/ science regarding time and space. Not, however, according to Innis. In Innis's view, popular culture and science, the vernacular and the scholarly, are usually cut from the same cloth and more often than not reinforce one another, emphasizing the present to the neglect of time both as duration and as a sense of the future. There being little contradiction between scholarship and popular culture, Innis believed, they comprise in combination the monopoly of knowledge of our day. Together they serve military and commercial force, and drive out understanding. One suspects that Innis would regard post-modernist/poststructuralist 'scholarship' as practised by the likes of Jean Baudrillard, Lawrence Grossberg, and Mark Poster as the apotheosis of present-mindedness and as harbinger of the collapse of civilization.

In the preface to *Changing Concepts of Time*, his final publication within his lifetime, Innis wrote, 'Intellectual man of the nineteenth century was the first to estimate absolute nullity in time. The present – real, insistent, complex, and treated as an independent system, the foreshortening of practical prevision in the field of human action, has penetrated the most vulnerable areas of public policy. War has become the result, and a cause, of the limitations placed on the fore-thinker. Power and its assistant, force, [are] the natural enemies of intelligence.'[94]

These are thoughts for our day – as America, for example, struggles with the fallout from its hasty ('present-minded') invasion of Iraq, and as the present-mindedness of consumerism takes a continuing, and deepening, environmental toll. Innis's basic constructs – time versus space, becoming versus being, knowledge versus force, monopolies of knowledge and the dialectics of power/technology/culture – all unfolded within a historical perspective that covers not just centuries but millennia – these are some of the riches that media scholars can recover through a perusal of the works of this neglected theorist.

NOTES

1 James W. Carey, 'Culture, Geography, and Communications: The Work of Harold Innis in an American Context,' in *Culture, Communication, and Dependency: The Tradition of H.A. Innis*, ed. William H. Melody, Liora Salter, and Paul Heyer (Norwood, NJ: Ablex, 1981), 80. Emphasis added.

2 Paul Heyer, *Harold Innis* (Lanham, MD: Rowman and Littlefield, 2003), 52.

3 Marshall McLuhan, introduction to *The Bias of Communication* by Harold A. Innis (1951; repr., Toronto: University of Toronto Press, 1971), ix.

4 Ben Scott and Robert W. McChesney, 'A Century of Radical Media Criticism in the USA,' in *Radical Media Criticism: A Cultural Anthology*, ed. David Berry and John Theobald (Montreal: Black Rose Books, 2006), 177–91; Robert W. McChesney and Ben Scott, ed., *Our Unfree Press: 100 Years of Radical Media Criticism* (New York: New Press, 2004).

5 Alexander John Watson, *Marginal Man: The Dark Vision of Harold Innis* (Toronto: University of Toronto Press, 2006), 313ff.

6 Francis Bacon, *Meditationes Sacrae* (1597) 'Of Heresies.'

7 Harold A. Innis, *Changing Concepts of Time* (Toronto: University of Toronto Press, 1952), xxvi.

8 Harold A. Innis, 'Minerva's Owl' (1947); repr. in *The Bias of Communication* (Toronto: University of Toronto Press, 1971), 30–1.

9 Ibid., 4.

10 Ibid., 5.

11 Watson, *Marginal Man*, 306.

12 Ibid., 308.

13 Harold A. Innis, *Empire and Communications* (1950; repr., Toronto: University of Toronto Press, 1972), 15.

14 Ibid., 43.

15 Ibid., 139.

16 Ibid., 143.

17 Harold A. Innis, 'A Critical Review' (1948); repr. in *The Bias of Communication* (Toronto: University of Toronto Press, 1971), 193.

18 Christopher Simpson, *Science of Coercion: Communication Research & Psychological Warfare 1945–1960* (Oxford: Oxford University Press, 1994).

19 See chapter 16 in this volume.

20 Innis, *Changing Concepts of Time*, 91.

21 Innis, 'Critical Review,' 195.

22 Harold A. Innis, 'The Problem of Space' (1951); repr. in *The Bias of Communication* (Toronto: University of Toronto Press, 1971), 129.

23 Innis, 'Critical Review,' 192.

24 Innis, *Empire and Communications*, 7.

25 Innis, 'Problem of Space,' 111.
26 Innis, 'Critical Review,' 190.
27 Innis, 'Minerva's Owl,' 27.
28 Ibid., 7.
29 Harold A. Innis, 'Industrialism and Cultural Values' (1950); repr. in *The Bias of Communication* (Toronto: University of Toronto Press, 1971), 139.
30 Harold A. Innis, 'Adult Education and Universities,' in *The Bias of Communication*, 205–6.
31 Harold A. Innis, 'Plea for Time,' in *The Bias of Communication*, 83.
32 Innis, 'Adult Education,' 206.
33 Innis, 'Critical Review,' 193.
34 Innis, 'Adult Education,' 204.
35 Innis, 'Critical Review,' 191; also, Innis, *Empire and Communications*, 138.
36 Innis, 'Plea for Time,' 86.
37 Innis, 'Minerva's Owl,' 31.
38 Ibid., 28.
39 Ibid., 29.
40 Ibid., 28.
41 Innis, 'Plea for Time,' 84.
42 Innis, 'Critical Review,' 190.
43 Innis, 'Adult Education and Universities,' 205.
44 Innis, 'Plea for Time,' 86.
45 J.M. Keynes, *A Tract on Monetary Reform* (London: Macmillan, 1924), 80.
46 Innis, 'Plea for Time,' 86.
47 Ibid.
48 Ibid., 76.
49 Ibid., 85–6.
50 Innis, 'Critical Review,' 195.
51 Innis, 'Minerva's Owl,' 5.
52 Innis, 'Problem of Space,' 130.
53 Innis, *Empire and Communications*, 150.
54 Innis, *Changing Concepts of Time*, 24.
55 Harold A. Innis, 'Technology and Public Opinion in the United States' (1949); repr. in *The Bias of Communication* (Toronto: University of Toronto Press, 1971), 157.
56 Innis, *Changing Concepts of Time*, 163.
57 Innis, 'Technology and Public Opinion,' 163–4.
58 Michael Emery, Edwin Emery, and Nancy L. Roberts, *The Press and America: An Interpretative History of the Mass Media*. 9th ed. (1954; Boston: Allyn and Bacon, 2000), 62.
59 Innis, 'Industrialism and Cultural Values,' 138–9.

60 Innis, 'Technology and Public Opinion,' 158.
61 Innis, *Empire and Communications*, 161.
62 Innis, 'Technology and Public Opinion,' 160.
63 Innis, *Changing Concepts of Time*, 75–6.
64 Ibid., 77.
65 Innis, 'Technology and Public Opinion,' 169.
66 Harold A. Innis, 'The Bias of Communication' (1949); repr. in *The Bias of Communication* (Toronto: University of Toronto Press, 1971), 59.
67 Innis, 'Industrialism and Cultural Values,' 138–9.
68 Innis, 'Technology and Public Opinion,' 174.
69 Ibid., 168.
70 Ibid., 178.
71 Ibid., 180.
72 326 U.S. 1 (1945).
73 Qtd in Innis, *Changing Concepts of Time*, 58.
74 Innis, *Bias of Communication*, 174.
75 Innis, *Changing Concepts of Time*, 75.
76 Ibid., 75.
77 Innis, 'Technology and Public Opinion,' 162.
78 Innis, 'Industrialism and Cultural Values,' 139.
79 Innis, *Changing Concepts of Time*, 81.
80 Ibid., 94–5.
81 Innis, 'Plea for Time,' 78.
82 Ibid., 79.
83 Andrew Wernick, 'No Future: Innis, Time Sense and Postmodernity,' in *Harold Innis in the New Century*, ed. Charles R. Acland and W. Buxton (Montreal and Kingston: McGill-Queen's University Press, 1999), 261–80.
84 Innis, 'A Critical Review,' 191.
85 Ibid.
86 Innis, *Changing Concepts of Time*, 89.
87 Myles Ruggles, *Automating Interaction: Formal and Information Knowledge in the Digital Network Economy* (Cresskill, NJ: Hampton, 2005).
88 Innis, *Changing Concepts of Time*, 89.
89 Ibid., 82.
90 Ibid., 11.
91 Innis, *Empire and Communications*, 170.
92 Union of Concerned Scientists, 'World Scientists Warning to Humanity,' actionbioscience.org. http://www.actionbioscience.org/environment/worldscientists.html.
93 David Suzuki, *Time to Change* (Toronto: Stoddart, 2006).
94 Innis, *Changing Concepts of Time*, xxvi.

12 The Communication Thought of Herbert Marshall McLuhan

I have no theories whatever about anything. I make observations by way of discovering contours, lines of force, and pressures. I satirize at all times, and my hyperboles are as nothing compared to the events to which they refer ... My canvasses are surrealist, and to call them 'theories' is to miss my satirical intent altogether.

— McLuhan to W. Kuhns (1971)

Herbert Marshall McLuhan was born in Edmonton, Alberta, on 21 July 1911, and grew up in Winnipeg, Manitoba. Radio broadcasting was in its infancy in the 1920s, but even then McLuhan was fascinated by electric communication. He built a crystal set to which he and his brother listened each evening while drifting off to sleep.[1]

In 1934 McLuhan was awarded a MA in English from the University of Manitoba. The next year, pursuing a second MA at Cambridge, he became imbued with the writings of T.S. Eliot, Ezra Pound, Wyndam Lewis, and James Joyce – none of whom evidently merited a place on the curriculum at Manitoba. McLuhan particularly loved Joyce's wordplay and the manner in which that poet/novelist required readers to tease out meanings from words, often neologisms, by their context and by applying the reader's own insights and experiences. Joyce abandoned linear narrative in favour of a multilayered mode of exposition, and this, too, enthralled McLuhan. Of Joyce, McLuhan declared, '[He is] probably the only man ever to discover that all social changes are the effect of new technologies ... on the order of our sensory lives.'[2]

Also at Cambridge McLuhan attended lectures by, among others, I.A. Richards, a pioneer of 'practical criticism.' Richards maintained that words derive meanings from context and are best understood in terms

of 'effects,' often subliminal, as opposed to their 'content' or dictionary definitions. Richards also discussed at length the theory of metaphors and their relation to contextual meaning.[3] Richards's influence
is apparent even in the opening sentence of McLuhan's first scholarly
publication, an essay on G.K. Chesterton, which refers to 'the meaning
and effect' of that author's work.[4] In his mature scholarship McLuhan
applied 'practical criticism' to artefacts other than literary works – to the
wheel, for example, and the electric light bulb, furniture, clothing, and
the printing press. He argued that all artefacts have 'effects' on people's
psychologies and on their interpretative processes. In endeavouring to
discern these effects, McLuhan was inspired also by F.R. Leavis, whom
he also heard lecture at Cambridge. In *Culture and Environment* Leavis
applied techniques of literary criticism to the social environment.[5]

In 1936 McLuhan was hired as a graduate teaching assistant in the
English Department at the University of Wisconsin, where immediately
he set out to familiarize himself with popular culture – sports, comics,
music, advertising, news of the day – a strategy for developing rap-
port with students. This research and activity led directly to McLuhan's
first (and to some, his best) book, *The Mechanical Bride*, published several years later. It was also at Wisconsin that McLuhan converted for-
mally to Catholicism.[6] As a convert, he was devout and attended Mass
virtually every day for the rest of his life. McLuhan recognized, but
only occasionally admitted, that religious zeal undergirded his media
studies.[7]

The following year he moved to Saint Louis University, a Catholic
institution, but returned to Cambridge on a year's leave of absence in
1939 for doctoral studies; he received his PhD in 1943 for a dissertation
on Thomas Nash, thereby solidifying his reputation as a literary scholar of the Elizabethan period.[8] In 1944 he accepted an appointment at
Assumption College, now part of the University of Windsor (Ontario).
Two years later he moved to St Michael's College at the University of
Toronto, whereupon he wrote to his friend and former student Walter
Ong, 'So Walter, I must regard this move as a permanent one.'[9] And so
it proved.

Like a number of Canadian communication theorists, McLuhan was
born an outsider, and in several respects he remained one.[10] McLuhan
maintained that only 'outsiders' *really* understand their culture or environment: 'The poet, the artist, the sleuth – whoever sharpens our perception tends to be antisocial; rarely "well-adjusted," he cannot go along
with currents and trends. A strange bond often exists among antisocial

types in their power to see environments as they really are. This need to interface, to confront environments with a certain antisocial power, is manifest in the famous story, "The Emperor's New Clothes."[11]

McLuhan saw himself very much as poet, artist, and sleuth. And 'superior' is also an apt term for his self-appraisal. In an interview he once intoned, 'The road to understanding media effects begins with arrogant superiority; if one lacked this sense of superiority – this detachment – it would be quite impossible to write about them.'[12]

The Mechanical Bride was published in 1951. In the original edition it sold but a few hundred copies. However, it well exemplifies his scholarly stance. There McLuhan wrenched artefacts of commercial culture from their normal context and subjected them to critical scrutiny and commentary.

McLuhan's critics sometimes point to a disjuncture between his *The Mechanical Bride* and the works that followed,[13] an observation, incidentally, with which McLuhan concurred. Whereas the critics suggested that pecuniary considerations may have guided McLuhan's later, less critical scholarship, McLuhan's explanation was simply that his first tome had been a misguided attempt to preserve the book culture in an electric age.[14]

McLuhan's next milestone, *Explorations*, a journal he co-edited with anthropologist Edmund Carpenter, was published between 1953 and 1959. It, too, attained scant distribution, but according to James Carey was at the time nonetheless 'influential among ... a small group of academics.'[15] Readers included Susan Sontag, Jacques Derrida, Claude Lévi-Strauss, and Roland Barthes.[16] The journal proposed that 'revolutions in the packaging and distribution of ideas and feelings modified not only human relations but also sensibilities ... We are largely ignorant of literacy's role in shaping Western man, and equally unaware of the role of electronic media in shaping modern values.'[17]

In these two highly condensed sentences we find McLuhan's basic thesis: that media, whether print or electronic, modify both individuals and cultures by reshaping ideas and perception, that media 'massage' users imperceptibly, and that culture has become a product or commodity. Writing in *Explorations* were such luminaries as Siegfried Giedion, Northrop Frye, David Riesman, Karl Polanyi, and Robert Graves.

In 1963, the University of Toronto established the Centre for Culture and Technology to induce McLuhan to stay in Canada. The seminars at the 'coach house,' as the headquarters were fondly called, became renowned. Guests included John Lennon, Yoko Ono, Buckminster Fuller, Glenn Gould, Pierre Elliot Trudeau, and Edward Albee. Derrick de Kerckhove, who studied under McLuhan in the late 1960s, recalled that as a teacher McLuhan endeavoured to equip students to deal in new ways with information they already had. Nor would McLuhan close an argument; his probes and aphorisms were intended to stimulate students into thinking things out for themselves.[18]

McLuhan's most notable scholarly milestones were *The Gutenberg Galaxy* (1962), and, most eventfully, *Understanding Media* (1964). In 1965 the American public relations firm Gossage & Feigen, seeing in McLuhan mass marketing possibilities, contracted with him and proceeded to make him a celebrity.[19] In the same year journalist Tom Wolfe published a highly influential essay, 'What If He Is Right?' in *New York* magazine. McLuhan's writings soon attracted commentators the likes of Raymond Williams, Kenneth Burke, Kenneth Boulding, George Steiner, Susan Sontag, and Theodore Roszak. Although many were detractors, the attention further propelled McLuhan into stardom; he became a media guru, appeared on television talk shows, advised politicians on their images, and was quite simply the most famous academic in the world. Over the next few years some dozen other volumes appeared embossed with his signature, many co-authored.

The secondary literature on McLuhan and his work also became substantial and is still growing. Most notably [as of the year 2000] he is the subject of two major biographies, a book of reminisces by some seventy acquaintances,[20] and several collections of critical essays.[21] As part of a nineties McLuhan renaissance, *Wired* magazine named him its 'Patron Saint.'[22]

When McLuhan burst into public prominence in the mid-1960s, he was, in Northrop Frye's phrase, 'caught up in the manic-depressive roller coaster of the news media': 'hysterically celebrated in the sixties,' all but ignored in the seventies and eighties.[23] Indicative of the obscurity into which he fell is Bruce Powe's reminiscence that in 1978–9, the last year he taught his once-popular seminar at the coach house at the University of Toronto, he achieved an enrolment of but six students. Cardboard boxes filled with remaindered copies of *The Executive as Drop-Out* and *From Cliché to Archetype* littered the classroom.[24]

In the 1990s, however, there was a resurgence of interest in McLuhan and, if anything, he was accorded greater scholarly respect than ever before. Perhaps electric technology had penetrated the academic mind sufficiently to make his ideas seem less outrageous. McLuhan scholar Glenn Wilmott has suggested that the rise of poststructuralism as an academic stance in the postmodern age sufficiently 'problematized' objectivity, empiricism, rationalism, specialized knowledge – the critical values previously invoked to dismiss McLuhan – making him now more academically acceptable.[25]

In 1979 McLuhan suffered a stroke that left him virtually speechless. His former colleague Edmund Carpenter recounted touchingly, 'I immediately went to see him. He stood before the fireplace, next to [his wife] Corrine, looking much the same as when we'd first met, but now no words came & his hands flew about in frustration. Corrine took them & held them before her. "Tell me, Marshall. I can understand you. I can tell Ted." She looked into his eyes & he smiled & they both laughed, holding hands, and this was communication even more dazzling than that first day.'[26]

McLuhan died on 31 December 1980.[27] On his tombstone, in 'digital-analogue typeface,' is the inscription, 'The Truth Shall Make You Free.'[28]

Four Influences

Apart from poets and literary critics noted above, who had major influence on McLuhan, there were others, too, who should be mentioned. One was Lewis Mumford. His *Technics and Civilization* appeared in 1934 and was one of the first books to emphasize the interplay of technology and culture. Although in subsequent works Mumford dismissed the thesis advanced there, namely that electricity is an organic, egalitarian, decentralizing technology that fosters community and reverses the fragmenting effects of industrial technology, McLuhan embraced it and continued to promote it all of his scholarly days.[29]

Important also to McLuhan's development was the Swiss historian of architecture Siegfried Giedion, author of *Space, Time and Architecture* (1954) and of *Mechanization Takes Command* (1948). The latter book's subtitle, *A Contribution to Anonymous History*, captures well Giedion's contention that the meaning of history arises from and is revealed by 'humble objects.'[30] Giedion saw mechanization as an extension, indeed a supplanting, of the hand.[31] He maintained also that industrialization 'mechanized' consciousness: it split thought from feeling – a most precarious condition in a time when the technological means of doing things have attained such immense power. For civilization to survive, Giedion warned, intellect and emotion must be reintegrated. McLuhan extended Giedion's thought by viewing various media of communication, particularly the printing press, as mechanizing human relations.

And, like Giedion, McLuhan argued that mechanical innovations fracture thought from feeling.[32] He also saw the inorganic (i.e., the technological) as melding with the organic so as to utterly transform human nature – creating a 'new' (i.e., prosthetic) man. McLuhan referred often to the myth of Narcissus to emphasize that, in being mesmerized by their technological extensions, people become oblivious to the effects that technological extensions have on them.

A third figure to note was classicist Eric Havelock. Born in England in 1903 and educated at Cambridge, Havelock taught at the University of Toronto between 1929 and 1947. With other classicists at the University of Toronto in the 1940s, Havelock is credited with helping inspire Innis's communication thesis, and indeed Havelock's 1951 tome, *The Crucifixion of Intellectual Man*, is acknowledged in the preface to Innis's last book, *Changing Concepts of Time*. After leaving the University of Toronto, however, Havelock developed themes parallel to those of McLuhan. McLuhan referred often to Havelock's *Preface to Plato*, which he regarded as being very supportive. For McLuhan, Havelock was the first classicist to have made a careful investigation of how the phonetic alphabet created disequilibrium in the ancient world.

Finally, a word on Innis. McLuhan often described himself as being a 'disciple of Harold Adams Innis.' However, although they were for several years contemporaries at the University of Toronto, Innis and McLuhan hardly knew one another: as late as December 1948 McLuhan still misspelled Innis's name,[33] and only in 1951 did he begin reading anything by that great political economist. Upon learning that Innis had placed *The Mechanical Bride* on his syllabus, however, McLuhan decided he should learn more about such a person, and turned immediately to 'Minerva's Owl,' where he found instant recognition – so much so that McLuhan referred to his *The Gutenberg Galaxy* as being but a 'footnote to the observations of Innis.'[34]

One thing about Innis's work that resonated with McLuhan was its style. McLuhan saw Innis as an artist: 'Without having studied modern art and poetry, he [Innis] yet discovered how to arrange his insights in patterns that nearly resemble the art of our time [the poetry of Baudelaire and the paintings of Cézanne, for instance]. Innis presents his insights in a mosaic structure of seemingly unrelated and disproportioned sentences and aphorisms ... He expects the reader to make discovery after discovery that he himself had missed.'[35]

McLuhan added, 'How exciting ... to encounter a writer whose every phrase invited prolonged meditation and exploration.'[36]

McLuhan was also impressed by Innis's method. In his view, Innis did not investigate in detail the *content* of structures – for example, the types of books in the ancient libraries, or the *nature* of the philosophies, religions, and sciences of antiquity. Rather, it was the *existence* of libraries, or the predominance of religious belief per se that Innis deemed important. McLuhan concluded that Innis 'invites us ... to consider the formalities of power exerted by these structures in their mutual interaction.'[37]

Furthermore, McLuhan lauded how Innis painstakingly catalogued details from which 'leapt' conclusions based on 'the sudden realization of a pattern';[38] McLuhan thereafter recommended 'pattern recognition' as a means of coping in an era of information overload.

Finally, and most importantly, McLuhan accepted wholeheartedly Innis's main claim that culture, society, and civilization change in tandem with changes in the media of communication. It has been suggested that McLuhan's famous aphorism and axial principle, 'The medium is the message,' was formulated while reading Innis's introduction to *Empire and Communications*,[39] which would certainly affirm McLuhan's indebtedness to Innis. We will see below, however, that McLuhan reworked, indeed inverted, Innis's explanation of the nature of the interaction between media and society. For that reason particularly, McLuhan's collaborator and close friend Edmund Carpenter has suggested that Innis's influence on McLuhan has been overstated.[40]

Literary Criticism Approach to Media Studies

McLuhan's media studies, he acknowledged, derived from and extended his literary work.[41] In particular, he applied the techniques and concepts of literary criticism to the non-verbal world. McLuhan justified these procedures with the claim that language often 'evokes' objects and situations that are themselves non-verbal, and by contending that the 'interplay' works both ways. He declared, 'We are taking for granted that there is at all times interplay between these worlds of *percept* and *concept*, verbal and nonverbal. Anything that can be observed about the behavior of linguistic cliché or archetype can be found plentifully in the nonlinguistic world.'[42]

The terms *percept* and *concept* figure prominently in McLuhan's work. His associate and co-author Barrington Nevitt, interpreting McLuhan, defined *percepts* as 'the raw sensory data of human experience generated by direct encounter with existence.'[43] *Concepts* are 'replays of percepts,' that is abstractions formed from experiencing similar percepts. Being abstractions, concepts are verbal, whereas percepts are non-verbal.

McLuhan claimed, further, that since language is a technology (i.e., an artefact and a means of doing things), it can properly be compared to other artefacts or technologies, again justifying his practice of applying the tools of literary criticism to the non-verbal world.

We turn now to some of the ways whereby McLuhan applied techniques and concepts of literary criticism to non-verbal artefacts, bearing in mind that for McLuhan all artefacts are 'media' – because they 'extend' the human organism.

Archetype and Cliché

McLuhan cited approvingly Northrop Frye's definition of *archetype* as a recurring form in literature that becomes recognizable on account of repetition. Archetype, therefore, is 'a form of cliché.'[44]

Unlike Frye, however, McLuhan applied the literary notions of cliché and archetype to the material or non-verbal environment. Every innovation, he averred, recalls an older form (a former cliché), and in so doing becomes an archetype. He provided several examples: A flagpole flying a flag is a present-day commonplace or cliché, but in recalling ('retrieving') a spear with a banner it becomes an archetype.[45] Likewise an electric circuit is a current cliché but is an archetype when feeding an electric log fire.[46]

New media for McLuhan are 'new clichés' whose first effect is to liquidate or scrap the clichés (media) of previous cultures and environments. McLuhan noted that there is consequently a tendency for a sense of absurdity or alienation to arise during times of rapid technological change – what Frye had called the 'alienation of progress.' The secondary effect of new media, however, is to retrieve ancient, broken, and fragmented clichés, 'making them transcendental.'[47]

McLuhan believed that artists also help re-establish a sense of equanimity in times of rapid change. Poets like Eliot and Joyce, he claimed, drew upon the fragments of both cultures past and present to construct archetypes as a way of patterning the human condition, thereby restoring for audiences a sense of meaning and stability. McLuhan repeatedly invoked the line from Eliot's *The Wasteland*, 'These fragments I have shored against my ruins,' to indicate the artists' endeavours in this regard.

But even here McLuhan was dialectical. For if archetypes can restore meaning by retrieving past forms, they can also lull audiences into quiescence.[48]

Clichés, too, he saw dialectically. Although normally they are 'dull habituation,' with but slight modification they can function as 'probes'[49] or stimuli, inducing thought and discovery. His revised aphorism, 'The medium is the massage,' for example, in recalling but differing slightly from the original, becomes a probe.

Late in his career McLuhan amplified his analysis of cliché and archetype to arrive at four 'laws of the media.' He set them out as combined propositions and questions:

- What does the artefact enhance or intensify or make possible or accelerate?
- If some aspect of a situation is enlarged or enhanced, simultaneously the old condition or unenhanced situation is displaced thereby. What is pushed aside or obsolesced by the new 'organ'?
- What recurrence or retrieval of earlier actions and services is brought into play simultaneously by the new form?
- When pushed to the limits ... the new form will tend to reverse what had been its original characteristics. What is the reversal potential of the new form?

McLuhan insisted that this 'tetrad of effects' is simultaneous, not sequential: 'All four aspects are inherent in each artifact [or medium] from the start.'[50] The automobile, for instance, (1) *enhances* privacy (alone at a drive-in movie; going outside to be alone), (2) *renders obsolete* the horse and buggy, (3) *retrieves* the knight in shining armour and the countryside, and (4) *reverses* into traffic jams.[51] The telephone (1) *enhances* dialogue, (2) *renders obsolete* privacy by eroding barriers between physical spaces, (3) *retrieves* instant access to users, as in a tribal village, and (4) *reverses* into the mythic world of discarnate, disembodied intelligences ('the sender is sent').[52] Money (1) *enhances* or speeds up transactions, (2) *renders obsolete* haggle and barter, (3) *retrieves* the potlach in the form of conspicuous consumption, and (4) pushed to its limit disappears into credit and the credit card, that is *reverses* into an absence of (tangible) money.[53]

McLuhan even claimed that 'all our artifacts are in fact words,'[54] although a better rendering would perhaps have been 'signs.' To justify that claim, McLuhan coined a pun: 'All of these things [artefacts, words] are the outerings and utterings of man.'[55] He noted further that in some traditional societies 'speech and weaving are synonymous'[56] in the sense that stories are told through the patterns woven into fabrics. But perhaps most profoundly, he argued that each 'tetrad,' being the potential, inherent action or power of an artefact, is in fact that object's 'word or *logos*.'[57]

Metaphors

Another literary convention that McLuhan applied to the world of material artefacts was the *metaphor*. The term comes from the Greek *metapherein*, meaning 'to carry across or transport.' McLuhan remarked that only with the advent of the telegraph did information become separated from material media such as stone, papyrus, and paper; previously, 'communication' had been linked to roads, bridges, sea routes, rivers, canals, and other means of *carrying across*. Hence, McLuhan concluded, for communication media, 'the notion of metaphor was apt.'[58]

In the age of electricity, moreover, McLuhan continued, *media as metaphor* regains cogency, but now what the media translate or carry over are *users*: 'In this electric age we see ourselves being translated more and more into the form of information, moving toward the technological extension of consciousness.'[59]

More generally he declared, 'All media are active metaphors in their power to translate experience into new forms. The spoken word was the first technology by which man was able to let go of his environment in order to grasp it in a new way ... Just as a metaphor transforms and transmits experience, so do the media.'[60]

For McLuhan, when we use the telephone, *we* are transported, angelically, without bodies, to distant locations. When we use television, *we* are grafted into the logic of the medium that is our prosthesis. It goes almost without saying that McLuhan used metaphors and analogies continuously to explain or illustrate his position on media.

Symbols

McLuhan maintained that people often confuse objects with symbols, and he took exception particularly to Northrop Frye's definition of symbol as 'any unit of any work of literature which can be isolated for critical attention.'[61] McLuhan insisted that the Greek *symballein* meant 'throwing together.' The concept of 'symbol,' therefore, is structural, denoting the juxtaposing of things. He wrote, 'A kettle is not a symbol unless related or juxtaposed with stove, or pot, or food. Things in isolation are not symbols. Symbolism as an art or technique meant precisely the breaking of connections.'[62]

McLuhan borrowed from the symbolist poets, who intentionally broke commonplace associations and constructed new ones. In his figure/ground analysis, for instance, McLuhan imaginatively wrenched out of normal context *figures* and focused attention on normally taken-for-granted *grounds*.

Myth

Like Frye, Innis, and Grant, McLuhan proposed that essentially there are but two modes of discourse – the linear, logical mode as practised in Western scientific and philosophical thought, and the mythic. *Myth*, he declared, characterizes the thought and expression of preliterate cultures, is narrative in form, and encapsulates timeless as opposed to particularistic human drama. Given information over-abundance and speed-up due to electric technology, he proposed (and in this he differed from Frye and Innis) that people turn again to mythic modes of understanding: 'When man is overwhelmed by information,' he expounded, 'he resorts to myth; myth is inclusive, time-saving, and fast.'[63] Elsewhere he wrote, 'Myth is a succinct statement of a complex social process.'[64]

Again, McLuhan spoke and wrote in mythic terms: most fundamentally, albeit implicitly, about the biblical story of the Fall and New Jerusalem. Let us pause, then, and see how that narrative structures McLuhan's media theory.

According to McLuhan, there was once a golden age of manuscript culture when all the senses were in balance. Thought at that time was not divorced from feeling since literate people still participated in oral dialogue. On the other hand, through literacy they had attained a sense of logic and an appreciation of objectivity and so were able to ward off preliterate superstition. Upon developing the printing press, however, people became alienated from their now increasingly objectified and fragmented world. (McLuhan's justification for making these assertions is addressed in the next section). However, the good news is that through electronics people can now anticipate the prospect of being reunited and becoming whole once more. In an interview McLuhan exclaimed, 'The Christian concept of the mystical body – all men as members of the body of Christ – this becomes technologically a fact under electronic conditions.'[65]

On the other hand, McLuhan definitely had a dialectical cast of mind, and so he also warned that the *global village* (his metaphor for an electronically interconnected world) is a dangerous, undesirable, claustrophobic, and possibly totalitarian place in which to live: 'The more you create village conditions, the more discontinuity and division and diversity. The global village absolutely insures maximal disagreement on all points. It never occurred to me that uniformity and tranquillity were the properties of the global village. It has more spite and envy.'[66]

This and other warnings respecting the trials and tribulations inhering in the global village can be likened to prophecies concerning the plagues of the Apocalypse, destined to occur prior to the New Jerusalem.

Media and Perception

Whereas the Western scientific world view, at least until the beginning of the twentieth century, maintained that objects and forces have identities in and of themselves and that language ought ideally to have the exactitude of 'one word, one meaning' in order properly to represent these things, McLuhan opined differently. He contended that words, *like all else*, derive meaning primarily from context.

It follows, therefore, that we cannot expect McLuhan to remain completely consistent in his use of key terms such as *visual* and *acoustic*. And indeed he was not. At times these terms refer literally to sensory perception by the eye and ear respectively, but at others to rather generic modes of cognition and ways of processing data. Hence, flickering television images, paintings by Seurat, mosaics, symbolist poetry, cartoons, and ideographs, although sensed by the eye, are not 'visual' according to McLuhan: they lack continuity and/or high definition and require people to experience them *as if* by hearing or touch; in these instances, often unconsciously, viewers add information to what they actually receive visually. McLuhan therefore termed these audile-tactile media. This seemingly outrageous proposition should become less outlandish after we have further reviewed McLuhan's work. For the present, however, it is sufficient to emphasize that in reading McLuhan one must always be on guard for shifting meanings and indeed for multiple levels of meaning.

The Sensorium

McLuhan insisted that each sense interacts with and hence is modified by the others.[67] Recalling Thomas Aquinas, he proposed the notion of the *sensorium* to denote senses in interaction. At any given time, the sensorium will be characterized by a particular ratio or proportion among the various senses. Some individuals or cultures afford greater emphasis to hearing, for example, others to sight. Ratios among the senses tend to be stable for a given time and place, but when shifts occur, 'massive' changes for individuals and for the society result.

Eye and Ear

It is something of an understatement to say that McLuhan drew attention to differences between the eye and the ear as modes of apprehending the world. The eye, he claimed, perceives, or perhaps more accurately creates, *visual space*, which he described as connected, linear, and serial. We look at one thing at a time, in sequence, and think of there being continuity, connectedness, or relatedness among the things we view. Visual space, therefore, is continuous, can be filled up with objects, and in that sense is undifferentiated or homogeneous; in our culture kilometres, for instance, measure distances irrespective of time (epoch), location, and what different spaces may contain.

Furthermore, visual space is infinitely divisible and extensible.[68] When using the eye, therefore, there is a tendency to think of things as comprising parts, giving rise to a propensity for dissection as a mode of inquiry. Objects are always in front of and seemingly detached from the viewer, giving rise also to the notion of 'objectivity,' a premise or goal upon which much of Western science has been based. Nonetheless, and somewhat paradoxically, McLuhan emphasized, each spectator has a distinct point of view or perspective, helping explain also the rise of individualism and the fragmentation of society into specialties.

The ear by contrast, according to McLuhan, is attuned to or creates *acoustic space*, which is neither connected nor continuous. Silences, rhythms, and a potpourri of sounds incessantly fragment or differentiate acoustic space. The auditory world therefore can be full of surprises, some calamitous, others serendipitous: 'To the blind all things are sudden,' McLuhan often remarked.[69] Furthermore, acoustic space is characterized by simultaneity, as when musical instruments combine symphonically; audition generally occurs within the context of multiple sounds and other sensory impressions, including visual ones, unlike reading, where sight alone is used. In combination, these multiple sensory impressions affect interpretation. In auditory space the hearer is always at the centre of things, not in front of them; sound surrounds. Moreover, sounds penetrate and resonate with interiors, whereas vision takes in surface phenomena only. Objectivity, therefore, has little meaning in an acoustic world: indeed, to use acoustic information, positivistic science must first convert it through instrumentation into visual information.

According to McLuhan, part of the explanation for the *apparent* objectivity of sight versus the subjectivity inherent to sound (and touch) is that the gaps or intervals are obvious enough with touch and sound, but less so with vision. Sometimes, however, gaps in visual space *are* manifest: 'Darkness is to space what silence is to sound, i.e., the interval,' McLuhan pronounced.[70] Darkness encourages people imaginatively to visualize or 'fill in' what might be there. McLuhan attested that mosaics therefore are visual equivalents of sound and touch since their components are separated by darkness, and viewers need to establish connections or patterns.

Epistemology and Ontology of Visual and Acoustic Space

Whereas vision usually gives the sensation of there being no gaps, for McLuhan this is a false impression; he maintained that normally there are neither *logical* nor *causal* connections between or among items in visual space, merely proximities. Advertisers well know that by carefully arranging objects, connections are created in viewers' minds between the product and the scene, no matter how ludicrous.

McLuhan traced distinctions between logic and analogy as modes of thought to differences between the properties of visual and acoustic space. He contended that logic derives from the (illusion of) connectedness of visual space, whereas analogy derives from gaps inherent to audile/tactile space. It is from gaps or intervals, not connections, that knowledge of proportions, and hence analogies stem. It is worth quoting McLuhan at length on this important insight: 'Perhaps the most precious possession of man is his abiding awareness of the analogy of proper proportionality, the key to all metaphysical insight and perhaps the very condition of consciousness itself. This analogical awareness is constituted of a perpetual play of ratios: A is to B what C is to D, which is to say that the ratio between A and B is proportioned to the ratio between C and D, there being a ratio between these ratios as well. This lively awareness of the most exquisite delicacy depends upon there being no connection whatever between the components. If A were linked to B, or C to D, mere logic would take the place of analogical perception.'[71]

Theory of Media

McLuhan's media theory stems in large part from his analysis of perception and his concern for effects. Media, he declared, may extend or amplify one or other of the senses, increasing thereby the relative importance of that perceptor in the sensorium.

McLuhan's media analysis, however, was not confined to extensions of the senses. He was concerned also with media that extend other parts of the body. The wheel, for example, extends or amplifies the leg, just as the axe extends the hand and clothing the skin. Likewise, a chair 'outers' the human posterior. According to McLuhan, *all artefacts* extend some aspect of the person, and therefore mediate human relations, making *all artefacts* media of communication: It is through our 'outerings,' as well as our 'utterings,' that we meet.

Moreover, human extensions interact bidirectionally with their environs. On the one hand the environment 'selects' or favours certain extensions while rendering others obsolete. On the other, the environs comprise, in part, the human extensions previously selected. Environs, too, mediate human relations.

Although McLuhan considered all artefacts to be bodily extensions, and therefore as constituting media, he indeed afforded considerably greater attention to those extending or amplifying the senses. These, he attested, directly affect perception and consciousness. Moreover, he distinguished particularly between media that emphasize the simultaneity of hearing versus those that amplify the sequential logic of the eye. Furthermore, McLuhan distinguished between 'hot' and 'cool' media. *Hot* media, like radio and the movies, extend a single sense in high definition. High definition is the state of being well filled with data. Hot media, therefore, are low in audience participation. For McLuhan, print normally is a hot medium, although he certainly understood Innis, Joyce, Eliot, and other modernist writers as being 'cool.' A *cool* medium, then, is low in definition (for example, a voice over the telephone or a cartoon), requiring the recipient to fill in or supplement the information that is provided.[72] McLuhan's distinction between hot and cool media parallels Frye's dichotomy of the truth of correspondence versus mythopoeic consciousness, and more generally between the ontologies of scientific objectivity versus social construction.

Tribal cultures, in McLuhan's view, use predominantly cool media. When confronted with hot media, cultures based on cool ones tend to collapse: 'A tribal and feudal hierarchy of a traditional kind collapses quickly when it meets any hot medium of the mechanical, uniform, and repetitive kind. The medium of money or wheel or writing, or any other form of specialist speed-up of exchange and information, will serve to fragment a tribal structure.'[73]

However, at the extreme, the converse is true, 'A very much greater speed-up, such as occurs with electricity, may serve to restore a tribal pattern of intense involvement such as took place with the introduction of radio in Europe ... Specialist technologies detribalize; the nonspecialist electric technology retribalizes.'[74]

For media that extend either the eye or the ear, then, at the limit there is a reversal (chiasmus). Vision normally is associated with continuity and connectedness, and therefore fosters logic (rationality), empiricism, and narrative. By contrast tactility and hearing, which are associated with intervals, support paradox, dialectic, intuition, aphorism, pun, and complementarity. However, when pushed to the extreme (as in a literate culture dominated by the printing press), vision causes fragmentation; in high definition, vision permits and encourages division, subdivision, and classification.[75] Furthermore, as noted above, it affords the sighted person a distinct point of view, giving rise to specialist knowledge, another form of fragmentation.[76] Tactility, likewise, at the extreme leads to fragmentation, but for a different reason: 'At [the audile-tactile] end of the sensory spectrum, individuality is created by the interval of tactile involvement ... Intense individuality is even more characteristic of the nonliterate population depicted by Dickens or Al Capp than it is of the consciously cultivated individuality of the highly literate.'[77]

A recurring theme of McLuhan, what we might call his principle of inversion or reversal, is that 'every process pushed far enough tends to reverse or flip suddenly; this is the *chiasmus pattern*, perhaps first noted by ancient Chinese sages in *I Ching: The Book of Changes*.'[78]

Media Analyses: Spoken Language

For McLuhan, language is an amplification of mental processes. He wrote, 'Language does for intelligence what the wheel does for the feet and the body; it enables [people] to move from thing to thing with greater ease and speed and ever less involvement.'[79] He also declared, 'Language is ... man's greatest and most complex artifact.'[80]

McLuhan thought of spoken language as being one of the very first 'mass media.' Citing his associate Edmund Carpenter, he wrote, 'In the oral tradition, the myth-teller speaks as many-to-many, not as person-to-person. Speech and song are addressed to all.'[81]

We see here that McLuhan's conception of orality aligns more closely with that of Frye than Innis. As Carey points out, for McLuhan orality 'is deeply informed by a liturgical sense of chant and memory rather than [as is the case of Innis] a political sense of discussion and debate.'[82]

By McLuhan's account, in oral cultures people live in the simultaneous, all-inclusive world of acoustic space. This means, among other things, that preliterate people apprehend interdependencies readily;[83] they have, in other words, an implicit ecological understanding. On the other hand, simple causality tends to elude them: failure to strike a prey for an ear-oriented person is a sure sign of cosmic displeasure, not poor marksmanship.[84]

McLuhan saw a world of difference between spoken and written language. Every word a person utters (and 'outers'), he wrote, 'extends or involves all of his sensory life.'[85] By comparison other media, including written language (but excluding computers), are 'specialist extensions.'

Spoken words fly by through time; they are not materially embedded so as to take up visual space. Paradoxically, however, spoken words are more concrete in meaning and 'evoke things directly.'[86] Speech, then, is 'resonant, live, active'; it is, according to McLuhan, a 'natural force.'[87] In oral cultures speech is always associated with power: the Book of Genesis, for instance, begins with pronouncements that God spoke and things came to be; Adam named the animals and attained power over them.

Writing

Since writing makes the thought world visible, it makes the eye predominant over the ear. Consequently, writing causes cultures to move from acoustic to visual space. This movement has both benefits and costs. On the one hand, predominance of the eye enables the detached, objective, logical, and experimental world view of science to take hold. Moreover, visual detachment via the written page gives people 'the power of the second look,' permitting them to escape the uncritical, superstitious, and emotionally involved life.[88] On the other hand, by deepening dependence on the eye, literacy causes thought to separate from feeling, alienation being the alter ego of objectivity. Writing causes organic tribal society to fragment into specialties and individualism.

All modes of writing, of course, emphasize the eye, and to that extent have similar effects. McLuhan, however, contrasted ideograms with the phonetic alphabet and typography, claiming that ideographs are 'totally different.' For McLuhan, ideographs are 'complex Gestalts' that do not separate meaning from sight or from sound, and that involve 'all the senses at once.' McLuhan's associate, Barrington Nevitt, explained that Chinese ideographic writing, for example, entails simultaneity, not merely sequence (as does alphabetic writing). The Chinese figure for 'east,' for instance, combines signs for tree and sun (themselves pictograms) indicating that at sunrise the sun is tangled in a tree's branches. For 'red,' Chinese writing combines abbreviated pictures of rose, iron rust, cherry, and flamingo.[89]

Phonetic writing, in contrast, is merely (but powerfully) 'a visual code for speech.' McLuhan maintained that the alphabet 'dissociates or abstracts not only sight and sound, but separates all meaning from the sound of the letters.'[90] The letter sequence c-o-w, for instance, derives meaning from linguistic convention only; considered separately, the letters (and their associated sounds) are meaningless. Moreover McLuhan saw the alphabet as wiping out non-alphabetic modes of discourse – both indirectly, by facilitating the issuance of military orders across vast tracts of space and thereby enabling strong cultures to dominate, and perhaps efface, weaker ones, and directly by enfolding non-alphabetic languages into itself. Pictographic and ideographic modes of writing require many signs, and are quite unwieldy; the phonetic alphabet, in contrast, has few letters and so can easily encompass pictographic languages. The translation of ideographic languages into the phonetic alphabet, therefore, is a one-way street: 'The alphabet cannot be assimilated; it can only liquidate or reduce.'[91]

Likewise manuscripts provided only a foretaste of the transformative effects of the printing press and moveable type. Although centuries of predominance of manuscripts assuredly did diminish the importance of the ear compared to what it had been in oral culture, according to McLuhan manuscripts nonetheless were 'highly tactile'; consequently, there was no split of the visual from the 'audile-tactile complex.'[92] All that changed in the sixteenth century, however, with Gutenberg's invention: moveable type 'split vision and tactility asunder,' the two modes of perception thereafter going 'their divergent ways to set up the rival empires of Art and Science.'[93]

Typography for McLuhan caused an utter change of consciousness. In manuscript culture, since readers were imbued with senses other than sight, the notion of a single 'literal meaning' never arose. 'To the oral man,' McLuhan declared, 'the literal is inclusive, contains all possible meanings and levels [e.g., allegorical and metaphorical as well as literal meanings].'[94] From the sixteenth century on, however, readers felt 'impelled to separate level from level, and function from function, in a process of specialist exclusion.'[95]

McLuhan made the same distinction by contrasting 'light on' (literal meaning) versus 'light through' (allegorical or metaphorical meaning). Light through implies that the spectator is glimpsing a portion of complex reality *through* (or with the aid of) a text, whereas 'light on' presumes the text is all there is to see.[96] In terms of visual arts the equivalent distinction is between a stained glass window and a realistic painting.

McLuhan saw other consequences flowing from moveable type. The printing press, he speculated, was probably the first instance of a reduction of a handicraft into mechanical terms. Not only was print 'the first mass-produced thing,' it was also the first 'uniform and repeatable "commodity."' He added, the 'assembly line of movable types' foreshadowed and made possible 'a product that was uniform and as repeatable as a scientific experiment; such a character does not belong to the manuscript.'[97]

The linearity of type, moreover, helped ingrain 'lineal, sequential habits.' But most importantly, print relegated 'auditory and other sensuous complexity to the background.'[98] 'Objectivity means leaving out all modes of awareness except the visual.'[99]

Furthermore, print is associated with changes in the perception of time and space. Time as duration, that is as something that happens between two points, arose with writing and the clock.[100] Time came to be 'measured not by the uniqueness of private experience but by abstract uniform units.'[101] Likewise typography converted sacred spaces into merely profane ones. 'A "sacred" universe,' he wrote, 'is one dominated by the spoken word and by auditory media; a "profane" universe, on the other hand, is one dominated by the visual sense.'[102] He added, 'For medieval man, as for the native, space was not homogeneous and did not contain objects. Each thing made its own space, as it still does for the native (and equally for the modern physicist).'[103]

Electric Media

For hundreds of thousands of years, from the invention of the wheel to the birth of the electric telegraph, media were 'mechanical' – that is, they extended only a part of the body and hence induced detachment, fragmentation, objectivity, specialization, detribalization, and individuality. The mechanical era thus was one of 'explosion' and fragmentation. With electric circuitry, however, there was a reversal – an 'implosion.' Electric media merge individuals and environment into an interdependent, simultaneous system whereby the 'globe [becomes] no more than a village.'[104] Individualism is superseded by communitarianism; an ecological understanding replaces instrumentalism; systems theory predominates over linear cause-effect. Electric technologies amplify not select body parts, but extend and 'outer' the entire central nervous system. The result is to 'involve us in the whole of mankind and to incorporate the whole of mankind in us.' Through electronics we approach a state of cosmic consciousness where each person is, and knows herself to be, part of everyone else. It is no longer possible to adopt the 'aloof and dissociated role of the literate Westerner.'[105]

Stated otherwise, electric technologies – some more than others – reassert the primacy of acoustic space, albeit now on a global scale. Even television, McLuhan claimed, bears the properties of an audile-tactile medium. One basis for this claim was the blurriness of the television image; McLuhan claimed that the TV picture, based on dots and lines, requires viewers to 'fill in' the missing information, just as they do in acoustic space. A second and more convincing explanation concerns information speed-up and abundance. With information overload, old strategies for attaining knowledge and making sense of the world – isolating a structure or institution, studying it in detail and making either logical or causal connections among its parts – no longer suffice. We are required instead to *make* sense of the superfluity of information by detecting patterns, intuiting resonances, and comprehending the pressures that various blocks of information and their originating structures bring to bear on one another, because in principle no connections exist except those we forge. The receiver must, in other words, adopt once more mythic modes of understanding and become an artist – creating 'mosaics' from the unrelated bits.

Art and Artists

By McLuhan's account, people are normally blithely unaware of the media's *massage*, that is of media effects; generally, we are too preoccupied with the individual messages that media deliver to notice their broader ramifications. 'The "content" of a medium,' McLuhan disclosed, 'is like the juicy piece of meat carried by the burglar to distract the watchdog of the mind.'[106]

McLuhan contended further that media users are the 'servo-mechanisms' of evolving technology. He wrote that users are the veritable 'sex organs of the technological world,'[107] just as bees are the sex organs of the plant world; 'to behold, use or perceive any extension of ourselves in technological form is necessarily to embrace it.'[108] Citing both William Blake and the Old Testament psalmist, McLuhan proposed that we 'become what we behold.'[109] In another formulation he charged that users are the real content of a medium, because media not only enfold (surround) users, but more importantly shape them in ways consistent with the media's logic. In the case of the phonetic alphabet and typography, for example, users become logical, linear, fragmented, detached, empirical, and objective; with television, however, they become analogical, intuitive, involved, affective, communal.

Being a servo-mechanism, of course, is the apotheosis of un-freedom. And it is precisely at this point that McLuhan called upon the artist as saviour. 'The serious artist,' he declared, 'is the only person able to encounter technology with impunity, just because he is an expert aware of the changes in sense perception.'[110] He declared further, 'The job of the artist is to keep people tuned to the present and if you're going to tune their sensibilities and their perceptions you have constantly to rearrange the focusing of their perceptions. The artists' job is to make it new at all times, not for the sake of novelty but for the sake of relevance … If you want to tune in on your time and know where it's at, the artists' new rhythms, new images will show you how.'[111]

Method of the Artist

Normally, since the environment is background, it is of low intensity or low definition. We tend therefore to pay it little attention. However, a storm in nature or a polluting smokestack suddenly raises our environs to high intensity and we cannot avoid noticing that. Technological change, likewise, can push the fabricated environment into high definition or high intensity, and it is then that a reversal, or chiasmus, occurs. When an environment is pushed to high intensity and thereby becomes an object of attention, it becomes in effect 'an anti-environment,' assuming thereby the character of 'an art object'[112] on account of the attention it engenders. 'Anti-environments,' according to McLuhan, are *figures* to environments, and as such they enable people to perceive their *ground*, that is their accustomed environment, with greater clarity. Intensification of an environment (i.e., turning a portion of the environment into an 'art form') is in McLuhan's opinion the principal strategy used by artists to increase awareness.

In *Through the Vanishing Point*, McLuhan with Harley Parker demonstrated how poets and visual artists through the ages have constructed counter environments to increase awareness. Using his pointillist technique, Seurat, for instance, painted *light through*, 'making paint itself the [apparent] light source';[113] Seurat, according to McLuhan, thereby anticipated the electric age since, in confronting thousands of tiny dots, the spectator is placed as if in acoustic space, where there is no single point of view. Likewise cubism, which depicts objects simultaneously from many different angles, dropped entirely 'the illusion of perspective in favor of instant sensory awareness of the whole.'[114] In literature, Eliot's *The Waste Land*, Wyndam Lewis's *The Apes of God*, Joyce's *Finnegan's Wake*, and the entire Theatre of the Absurd[115] create anti-environments to the accustomed literary forms, again anticipating the electric age.

McLuhan saw himself, of course, as an artist, and he consistently adopted tactics analogous to those of the artist. In the preface of *The Mechanical Bride*, for instance, he announced he would wrench out of the everyday context typical commercial imagery (our accustomed 'ground') to induce concentrated attention.[116] Likewise, in *The Gutenberg Galaxy*, he eschewed the logical, linear mode of presentation ('ground') typifying print in favour of a mosaic style consisting of brief sections headlined by a principal thought; undoubtedly McLuhan intended thereby to represent through a printed form information speed-up in an electric environment.

McLuhan's Political Economy

At times, for instance when discussing the role of artists and advertisers and the blind spots of liberal economics, McLuhan was seminal in political economic analyses. At other times, however, his aphorisms simply denied the existence of asymmetries in the distribution of power and revealed antipathy to major political economic concerns. This section explores the paradoxical nature of McLuhan's political economy.

Artists and Advertisers

An incisive insight into political economy emerges from McLuhan's treatment of artists and advertisers. The true artist, he contended, like the inventor, is an 'ultimate enemy' of established power. The artist causes perceptions to change, thereby enabling people to see things as they really are. Similarly inventors create products and processes that, by transforming environments, increase awareness.[117] Awareness for McLuhan is always an enemy of established power.

McLuhan was cognizant, however, that capitalist economies tend to domesticate artists and their works. He asked, 'If it is true that the artist possesses the means of anticipating and avoiding the consequences of technological trauma, then what are we to think of the world and bureaucracy of "art appreciation"? Would it not seem suddenly to be a conspiracy to make the artist a frill, a fribble, or a Milltown?'[118]

McLuhan also recognized that those artists who do fulfil their function must often pay a high price in terms of forgone wealth. Many 'artists,' therefore, choose to work for advertising agencies and public relations firms. McLuhan was consistent throughout his career in critiquing such 'fallen' artists and their works. In *Understanding Media*, for instance, he remarked, 'Ads are not meant for conscious consumption. They are intended as subliminal pills for the subconscious in order to exercise an hypnotic spell.'[119]

In *From Cliché to Archetype*, likewise, he cautioned that in an age of electricity much greater power accrues to advertisers than hitherto on account of a reversal between product and information. He wrote, 'As the economy moves more and more into the electrical orbit of programmed information, production is oriented increasingly toward service. Hardware becomes software. This process appears sufficiently in the world of advertising. As the means of advertising have greatly enlarged, the images created by advertising become an ever larger portion of the needs and satisfactions of the public. Eventually, people could look to the ad image as a world in itself.'[120]

McLuhan perceived that the mass media generally have become little more than vehicles for advertisers: 'The film medium,' for instance, is now a 'monster ad for consumer goods. In America this major aspect of film is merely subliminal ... In fact, the movie is a mighty limb of the industrial giant.'[121]

Technological Change

McLuhan also frequently drew attention to power dimensions of technological change. As noted, he ascribed to the innovator a role in democratizing society by heightening the public's awareness of its environment. He proposed also other political-economic dimensions to technological change. He remarked, for instance, that 'lack of homogeneity in speed of information movement creates diversity of patterns in organization ... Any new means of moving information will alter any power structure whatever.'[122] That principle, he continued, holds true both within cultures and organizations, and between/among them. Regarding intra-organizational conflict, he asserted, technologically based discrepancies can cause collapse.[123] Hierarchies, for example, can be rent asunder as the free flow of information increases. Regarding intercultural communication, information speed-up makes porous previously well-defined borders; historically the independence of villages and city states declined as information movement speeded up. McLuhan declared that as information movement accelerates, new centralist powers invariably take action 'to homogenize as many marginal areas as possible.'[124] Although he acknowledged that the wheel, roads, paper, money, and the mechanical clock were important innovations accelerating transactions and thereby shifting power, for him the phonetic alphabet and typography were of greatest importance.

On the other hand, McLuhan proposed that at some point a reversal (chiasmus) occurs – a most un-Innisian, un-political economy proposition. For McLuhan, the electric telegraph and ensuing electronic media have speeded up information movement to such an extent that there is now an implosion. Rather than centres of power extending their reach as they did with 'mechanical' media, the trend with electronics is toward the negation of centres of power; as in a pointillist painting, everyone and everything is increasingly understood as being related simultaneously to all else in a complex system of mutual interdependence.

It is precisely at this point, then, that McLuhan abandoned the realism/materialism of political economy in favour of an idealism denying asymmetries in power. Evidently it did not occur to him that even in an age of electronics, technologies can be associated with a particular ruling class, or as Innis would put it, with a particular monopoly of knowledge.

Critique of Liberal Economics

In *The Mechanical Bride* McLuhan satirized liberal economists' faith in the price system and the 'invisible hand.'[125] Mainstream economics, he judged, gives short shrift both to conflict and to power. Although eschewing the thoroughly class-based critical analysis typifying Marxism, McLuhan's early and later work alike are rife with insights on how everyday business practices conflict fundamentally with democratic values and with the broader public interest. Advertising, news, public relations, and 'entertainment' for McLuhan are all instruments whereby corporations lull audiences into somnambulism, or worse seduce them into compliance.

Furthermore, McLuhan charged, mainstream economics presumes incorrectly that products merely insert themselves into existing environments. In reality, products create new environments[126] and thereby utterly transform the cultural, social, and psychological fabric of life. Paralleling the political economy of Dallas Smythe, McLuhan even regarded time spent with media as unpaid *work*, a notion far removed indeed from economic orthodoxy. 'Newspaper reading,' he advised, is 'a form of employment ... All media that mix ads with other programming are a form of "paid" learning.'[127]

McLuhan averred that 'work' does not exist in a non-literate world: the primitive hunter or fisher 'worked' no more than does the poet, painter, or thinker of today, because *the whole person* was engaged in the activity. 'Where the whole man is involved,' McLuhan insisted, 'there is no work.' Work for McLuhan, then, is synonymous with the division of labour and the specialization of functions celebrated by Adam Smith as the means for increasing the wealth of nations. Division of labour for McLuhan, however, is part and parcel of the fragmentation characteristic of visual space.

However, McLuhan enthused, fragmentation ends with the predominance of electric media and the ensuing speed-up of information. In the electronic global village, everyone is once again a hunter and gatherer – albeit now of information rather than of food: 'Today, information-gathering resumes the inclusive concept of "culture," exactly as the primitive food-gatherer worked in complete equilibrium with his entire environment.'[128] Becoming 'totally involved in our roles,' we have a renewed dedication and commitment 'as in the tribe.'[129] (Here again, McLuhan's inclination for hyperbole and mythic depiction is evident, even when critiquing the hyperbole of the 'invisible hand').

The McLuhan Paradox

The corpus of McLuhan's writings is like a minefield, sown not only with serious, indeed profound insights, but also with satirical, hyperbolic bombs, making him an author difficult to systematize or summarize. Moreover, McLuhan contended that the content of any text, including his own, is the reader, implying that certain ideas and assertions can be taken seriously by some commentators and be dismissed by others merely as 'probes,' satire, or hyperbole. McLuhan certainly was paradoxical and ironic, and intended his terms, ideas, and claims not to be interpreted 'literally,' but to be construed with multiple levels of meaning, indeed as forming 'anti-environments,' which could mean that his statements may connote the opposite (chiasmus) of what they apparently say.

When, then, if ever, can McLuhan be taken at face value, as meaning precisely what he said? Was it when he affirmed his Catholicism and declared that electronics makes imminent on earth the mystical body of Christ? Or was it when he admitted that he was resolutely opposed to all innovation, to all change, and urged people turn off all the buttons and leave things alone for a while? Was it when he claimed to be a value-free scientist,[130] simply observing and describing what was going on? Or when he intimated he was an artist, exploring, making probes, creating anti-environments to shock people into awareness?

Perhaps all of these McLuhans, and others, are equally true – and false. It is a principle of systems theory that when a researcher changes levels of analysis, everything she surveys changes too. (Atoms of hydrogen and oxygen, studied separately, for example, have properties very different from when they combine to form molecules of water, a higher-level or more complex system.) McLuhan insisted that he was a systems analyst, addressing the interactions of large structures and how they mutually transform one another. Perhaps in his mind, at the highest level of Being, the contradictions that he displayed and seemed to embody are resolved.

McLuhan's inconsistencies are nowhere more apparent than in his evaluations of television and the world ushered in by that medium. One side of McLuhan reviled television. As a parent he limited his children to about one hour of viewing a week. As a grandparent he told his son Eric that television is 'a vile drug which permeates the nervous system especially in the young.'[131] In an interview with G.E. Stearn, published three years after *Understanding Media*, he pronounced, 'Most media ... are pure poison – TV, for example, has all the effects of LSD.'[132] On the other hand, McLuhan did not become a media celebrity by castigating the idiot box. To the contrary, he proffered a utopian vision of a 'retribalized' humanity, of universal harmony, and the emergence of a 'collective consciousness.'

Yet a further way of understanding the McLuhan paradox is by again invoking the myth of Minerva's owl. In opening *The Gutenberg Galaxy*, McLuhan maintained that we in the modern West 'are experiencing the same confusions and indecisions which [the Elizabethans] had felt.' We, like they, are living 'simultaneously in two contrasted forms of society and experience.'[133] Living in paradoxical times cannot help but result in paradoxical scholarship – and give rise to immense creativity!

According to Isaiah Berlin, 'Few new truths have ever won their way against the resistance of established ideas save by being overstated.'[134] Perhaps McLuhan agreed with that proposition. In any event, he practised hyperbole and in so doing drew attention to his key thesis that modes of communicating affect social organization through shifts in perception.

McLuhan and Canadian Communication Thought

Despite being world renowned, McLuhan was quintessentially a *Canadian* communication scholar. The terms, methods, and concerns we have identified with Canadian communication thought abound in McLuhan's writings – the dialectical method, holism, ontological concerns, historical study, critical approaches, mediation, change, and transformation. To attempt to draw out all the parallels and differences with the other theorists would require another chapter at least. Here comparisons and contrasts with Innis, Macpherson, and Frye are undertaken, but even given that limitation the analysis must remain partial.

McLuhan and Innis

McLuhan accepted and elaborated upon Innis's main claim that changes in the means of communication lie at the very heart of civilizational change. Moreover, McLuhan seized upon and developed into a leitmotif Innis's remark that writing causes the eye to substitute for the ear.[135] To that extent at least, we may say that Innis and McLuhan were of one mind. We noted previously as well an affinity of style and similarity in scope of these eminent scholars.

In important respects, however, McLuhan departed from, even inverted (chiasmus again) Innis's work. Whereas Innis arrayed media along a spectrum of time-bias–space-bias, McLuhan distinguished media as to their relative audile-tactile versus visual properties. Whereas Innis emphasized that media are extensions of message *senders* and analysed the implications of that, particularly with regard to the exercise of power through time or across space, McLuhan drew attention to media as extensions of the sensory apparatus of message *recipients*, and on how media alter perception. Whereas Innis insisted that a medium's effects depend upon the context, and even then it creates only tendencies, McLuhan frequently was more deterministic, even referring to people as servo-mechanisms of technological change. Innis's approach was inextricably bound up with political economy, but McLuhan's was tied most directly to individual and social psychology, and to literary studies; by downplaying the importance of messages and message senders, McLuhan deflected attention from power considerations.

There is also a marked difference between Innis and McLuhan with regard to the linearity of their analyses. Adopting the stance of literary critic, McLuhan applied the rhetorical term *chiasmus* to media to indicate that at high intensity there is a reversal in a medium's effects. Innis, to the contrary, never argued that a space-binding medium pushed to the limit becomes time-binding! The divergence between Innis and McLuhan in this regard probably has something to do with their differing religiosities: Innis, the agnostic brought up in a strict Baptist faith, envisaged the collapse of civilization on account of an ever-increasing present-mindedness due to the lack of balance between space-binding and time-binding media; McLuhan, devoutly Catholic but likewise apocalyptic, saw in technology the means of redemption and the possibility, even inevitability, of returning to an unfallen state.[136]

Of course every medium, by definition, brings sender and receiver into contact and hence each medium is simultaneously an extension of sender *and* receiver. A microphone, for instance, serves to augment the voice of the speaker but also to intensify the hearing capacity of the listener, as does a hearing aid. The fact that media are simultaneously extensions of both senders and receivers, and serve to bring them together into a communicating system, could indicate that the analyses of Innis and McLuhan are both partial and that they can profitably be combined to attain an enlarged, more holistic understanding.

But combining Innis and McLuhan is no easy task. Although their depictions of tribal and literate cultures were consistent, there is a perplexing antithesis regarding electronics. Do electronic media augment and heighten the space-binding properties of print, as Innis suggested, or do they amplify the audile-tactile sensibilities associated with time-bound tribalism, as McLuhan claimed? Innisian analysis suggests that with electronics there will continue to be increased global hegemony on the part of a shrinking number of power centres, and possibly the collapse of civilization as all sense of permanence, commonality, and continuity is destroyed. From McLuhan, on the contrary, we learn that electronics will recreate on a global scale the harmony and balance purported to exist in manuscript society. (However, as noted previously, McLuhan was not consistent in making these predictions, and at other times prognosticated a bleak future, one not inconsistent with Innis's dark vision.)

McLuhan and Macpherson

Macpherson's notion of people as doers, exerters, and developers of capacities and talents finds parallel in McLuhan's depiction of the artist. For McLuhan, the artist is society's innovator who constructs antienvironments whereby the general populace can come to understand better their condition. Whereas Macpherson's hope was that everyone, given improved property relations, could become an 'artist' in McLuhan's sense, McLuhan proffered no such hope: artists, for him, are seldom well-adjusted people; they are, rather, the tiny enlightened minority functioning on the margins of society, and it was these very characteristics that accounted for their insight and understanding.

Macpherson and McLuhan were alike in maintaining that human nature evolves and is malleable. For Macpherson, however, human nature is affected primarily by the institution of property and by the accompanying philosophical/propaganda discourses 'justifying' the mode of property at any given time. McLuhan, in contrast, looked to the 'extensions of man' (of which the mode of property is undoubtedly one, but certainly one among many others) as fixing human nature; McLuhan's analysis, therefore, was much less politicized than Macpherson's.

Both scholars thought that people in present society are alienated from themselves, their environments, and each another. Whereas Macpherson attributed this condition to the mode of property and supportive ideologies, McLuhan attributed alienation to the mode of communication, particularly the phonetic alphabet and the printing press. The two theorists were alike also in presenting an alternative, more organic vision, founded in Macpherson's case on common property, and in McLuhan's by the commonalty induced by electronic modes of communication. In both cases the organic society entails 'retrieval' of things lost: the wisdom of the ancients concerning human nature and common property in the case of Macpherson, and simultaneous, 'acoustic' space and mythic consciousness in the opinion of McLuhan.

McLuhan and Frye

McLuhan's thought begs comparison with that of Frye. For one thing, both were literary theorists and were contemporaries at the University of Toronto. Periodically they referred in their writings to one another, usually critically. Most significantly, both centred their communication thought on a theory of perception.

McLuhan and Frye agreed there are two competing 'cosmologies,' what we can loosely term science and arts, or realism versus the mythopoeic. McLuhan and Frye agreed further that since knowledge comes from perception, and since sense organs feed information to the mind, knowledge is derived from mental experience. In addition, both Frye and McLuhan insisted that without the application of the human imagination to sensory data, the world is fragmented; stated otherwise, the connections or meanings forged are imaginative products of human construction. Both recommended, finally, a 'double vision.' Single vision for McLuhan was when one sense overpowers the others; for Frye, single vision was scientific, unimaginative, sight-based knowledge.

Where McLuhan and Frye parted company was with regard to what they attributed the ascendancy of one or other of these world views at any given time or place. For Frye, the mythopoeic world view marked an attempt by people to make themselves at home in a universe devoid of meaning; furthermore, he claimed, the mythopoeic world view is continually challenged in our era by science (the truth of correspondence). For McLuhan, in contrast, it was not a struggle between the reality principle and mythic invention; for him, in fact, myth is a high – indeed the highest – form of truth, because, like scientific theory, myth generalizes recurrences and particulars. For that reason he continually referred to ancient myths – of Narcissus and Cadmus, for example – as they have applicability to and do illustrate our present condition.

In a sense what myths accomplish in Frye's thought, sensory extensions do for McLuhan. Frye argued that people view the world through stories, that myths and literature affect how people experience their environment and thereby how they act upon it. McLuhan on the other hand argued that our sensory extensions bias our perceptions and thereby our understanding and hence affect our actions.

Frye and McLuhan both sought transcendence. For Frye, however, transcendence was a fiction, a delusion, a social construction; by suspending disbelief one can enter for a time mythic worlds where nature has a human face and there is meaning to existence – but only for a time, since Frye understood science and technology as standing against and subverting these imaginary worlds with the harsh existential truth that there are in nature no connections, no meanings. McLuhan, conversely, ascribed no ultimate tension or conflict to science and technology; for McLuhan, technology is *the means* of reunification, the way whereby humanity will approach the godhead.

Frye and McLuhan both argued for balance. In Frye's case, the balance was between science and arts, a balance when achieved he termed 'the educated imagination.' The balance McLuhan recommended, by contrast, was between eye and ear, a balance he referred to as 'common sense.' McLuhan's balance was not that people might escape reality, but that they might approach it more closely. In that regard he forwarded a role for the creative artist that was remarkably different from Frye's. McLuhan declared that the artists' job is to tune people's sensibilities to the present, make audiences aware of their condition, so that we might either adjust to altered circumstances, or counter and attempt to neutralize those conditions. There is no notion whatsoever in McLuhan's work of the artist helping audiences escape the anxiety of harsh reality – except when his discussions turn to advertising. McLuhan viewed advertisers as fallen artists who beguile. The two scholars agreed, however, that critical awareness is a requisite to self-defence against the machinations of advertisers and public relations professionals.

Frye assented to McLuhan's characterizations of oral versus literate cultures but did not attribute the differences to extensions of the eye or ear. For Frye, rather, it was more a question of information storage, objectification, and abstraction. The ability to store knowledge outside the human mind through writing frees people to create new and more abstract knowledges and gives rise to the notion that knowledge can be objective. These thoughts are not inconsistent with McLuhan's, but neither are they McLuhanesque.

Frye did dispute, however, McLuhan's distinction between linear and sequential media. Frye claimed that *all* media, whether oral, written, or electronic, are *both* linear *and* simultaneous, albeit in different stages. He wrote, 'The act of reading, or its equivalent, consists of two operations that succeed one another in time. We first follow the narrative, from the first page or line to the last: once this pursuit of narrative through time is complete, we make a second act of response, a kind of *Gestalt* of simultaneous understanding, where we try to take in the entire significance of what we have read or listened to. The first response is conventionally one of the listening ear, even if we are reading a written text. The association of the second response with visual metaphors is almost inevitable.'[137]

Simultaneous response for Frye entails comparing the position forwarded by the message sender with other evidence or knowledge, and involves an evaluation.

Frye argued further that the *new* 'oral' (i.e., electronic) media, compared to print, actually *increase* the purely linear (or uncritical) response. This is due in large measure to the fact that electronic media do not allow time for critical reflection: 'Far from encouraging a shift from linear and fragmented to simultaneous and versatile response, the electronic media have intensified the sense of a purely linear experience which can only be repeated or forgotten.'[138]

But here, as in other matters, Frye could be inconsistent, or, as he might prefer, 'dialectical.' He wrote also that media such as film and television reassert properties of the oral tradition and of poetry by 'presenting things in terms of symbol and archetype,'[139] and that they thereby retrieve such non-linear modes of thought as astrology, Tarot cards, and the *I Ching*.[140] This all sounds highly McLuhanesque!

McLuhan, for his part, did not refrain from critiquing Frye and charged that his famous colleague's theory of genres ignored all media but print. 'In this century,' McLuhan admonished, 'the effect of nonprint media on literature has been as extensive as it has been on psychology and anthropology,' and he concluded pointedly that 'by ignoring the oral tradition of both preliterate and postliterate cultures, Professor Frye sets up a system of classifications that apply [only] to a recent segment of human technology and culture – a segment that is rapidly dissolving.'[141]

Finally, Frye and McLuhan each presented a dialectic of media and society. For Frye, technology empowers even as it alienates; media erode critical consciousness even as they entertain; they inform even as they increase the power of the advertiser and the public relations professional; they decrease privacy and imprison audiences even as they empower them. McLuhan likewise, as we have seen, entertained sharply dichotomous images of the global village.

McLuhan's Thought for the Twenty-First Century

Ecology

McLuhan's mode of media analysis opens the way for a new environmentalism. Consider first his notion of the global village. As ecologists Paul and Anne Ehrlich remark, most people still don't realize that humanity has become a truly global force, interfering in a very real and direct way in many of the planet's natural cycles.[142] McLuhan's key construct, the global village, should, therefore, be helpful in increasing ecological awareness.

It is not only by emphasizing globalism, however, that McLuhan helps foster environmentalism. He does this implicitly also through his notion of shifting sensory ratios. In this regard I again cite the Ehrlichs: 'People are sight-oriented animals and have relatively poorly developed chemosensory abilities. Toxification of the planet might be much more obvious to dogs, which live in a world shaped to a greater extent by their sense of smell. One can barely imagine how we would perceive changes in our environment if, like some fishes, we oriented to it primarily by detecting distortions in electrical fields, or if we responded primarily to sonar returns as bats do.'[143]

McLuhan's insistence that we recognize patterns in a fast changing world, rather than seeking to understand fragments, is also in accord with ecological understanding. David Suzuki, for example, remarks that scientists usually 'focus on parts of nature, attempting to isolate each fragment and control the factors impinging on it,' thereby attaining only a 'fractured mosaic of disconnected bits and pieces, whose parts will never add up to a coherent narrative.'[144] McLuhan and Suzuki are like-minded in recommending that we should supplement fragmented knowledge with mythic narrative. Suzuki, of course, insists that the 'new' narrative or myth encourage ecological balance.

McLuhan knew his thought had ecological dimensions. He saw people and their artefacts as being in dynamic interaction and indeed termed his mode of analysis an 'ecological approach.'[145] He affirmed further, 'The electric age is the age of ecology. It is the study and projection of the total environment of organisms and people, because of the instant coherence of all factors, made possible by moving information at electric speeds ... Our ecological approach is paleolithic. It assumes total involvement in process rather than fragmentation and detachment.'[146]

Postmodernism

In some respects McLuhan was a postmodernist before the term had even been coined. This helps explain both the opprobrium he experienced at the apex of his career from many entrenched scholars, and the renewed interest and heightened favour that his work currently enjoys. His writings have, if not inspired, then at least been 'warmly regarded' by such key postmodern theorists as Jean Baudrillard, Charles Jencks, and Mark Poster.[147] McLuhan's stance on the relativity and subjectivity of meaning, his disregard for scientific absolutes, his insistence that readers actively engage with texts, and his anti-authoritarianism resonate with the postmodern mind.

This is not to say that McLuhan anticipated accurately all elements of our day. Thirty some years after publication of *Understanding Media*, his prognostication concerning the demise of the automobile is yet to be fulfilled. Nor do we notice a rise in communitarian sentiments in an electronic information age as a reading of McLuhan would lead us to expect. It is indeed the failure of this last-mentioned prediction to be fulfilled – if anything, the trend has been in the opposite direction and our era is aptly described as being neoliberal or neoconservative – that requires us to inquire again into McLuhan's truncated political economy.

Truncated Political Economy

McLuhan paid more attention to political economy than is commonly recognized. His *The Mechanical Bride* and *Culture Is Our Business*, along with passages in other works, demonstrate a keen understanding that business interests have taken over cultural production and shaped it to their pecuniary ends. He understood also that modern media crush indigenous cultures, and at times he displayed an awareness and concern regarding the totalitarian possibilities of electronic media. McLuhan's contributions to political economy are real and should be celebrated.

Yet political economy certainly was not McLuhan's forte – his explanation of how viewers, readers, and audiences participate in the construction of meaning being a case in point. As present-day analysts with a stronger political economy bent insist, there is a class- or wealth-based dimension to interpretation insofar as it involves struggles among variously positioned groups possessing, implicitly or explicitly, different class interests, and there is hegemony whereby oppressed groups come to understand their circumstances as elites would have them to do. Of this, McLuhan remained largely oblivious.

Likewise, his insistence that 'the medium is the message' is quite antithetical to political economy. For if it is merely the existence or non-existence of a medium that matters most, media owners and programmers are absolved of responsibility for content. (McLuhan had not assumed that position in *The Mechanical Bride*; there, he set out to combat the influence of advertising messages through an innovative mode of cultural criticism.)

Moreover, McLuhan insisted that television is not a visual medium, a contention absurd on the surface and one that minimizes certain political-economic aspects of media practice. According to environmental writer and media analyst Alison Anderson, for example, 'television *is* a visual medium' nonpareil, and hence 'the availability and quality of pictures is of much ... importance.' She continues, 'Certain environmental issues receive more television news coverage than others because of their visual qualities ... Environment stories really need good pictures ... Global warming is very difficult because you can't actually see global warming.'[148] Activist groups such as Greenpeace have gone to great lengths, some even life-forfeiting, to concoct great visuals for the nightly television news.[149] All of this escapes McLuhan on account of his insistence that television is an audile-tactile medium.[150]

Moreover, even the closest reading of McLuhan's texts will not uncover treatment of key political-economic trends and issues linked to proliferating global communications: for example, global divisions of labour and the ever-increasing predominance in world commerce of transnational corporations, decline in national sovereignty, and heightening disparities between rich and poor. All these trends are dependent upon, or can be explained in part by, proliferating media interconnected globally; none are captured by the phrase 'the global village.' A much clearer picture of present-day political economy can be attained by reading McLuhan's mentor Harold Innis, or his contemporary Dallas Smythe.

Nevertheless, it is also to be affirmed that Marshall McLuhan remains the most creative, imaginative scholar that Canada has produced. His immense contribution to Canadian and world communication thought is increasingly recognized, and deservedly so. By juxtaposing his thought alongside that of other key writers, a truly comprehensive understanding can be achieved.

NOTES

1 Maurice McLuhan, interview, 'Marshall McLuhan: What If He Is Right?' *Ideas*, CBC Radio, 17 November 1980.

2 Marshall McLuhan and Quentin Fiore, *War and Peace in the Global Village* (New York: Bantam Books, 1968), 4.

3 Don Theall, *The Medium Is the Rear View Mirror: Understanding McLuhan* (Montreal and Kingston: McGill-Queen's University Press, 1971), 12.

4 Marshall McLuhan, 'G.K. Chesterton: A Practical Mystic,' *Dalhousie Review* 14, no. 4 (January 1936): 455.

5 Philip Marchand, *Marshall McLuhan: The Medium and the Messenger* (Toronto: Random House, 1989), 35.

6 W. Terrence Gordon, *Marshall McLuhan: Escape into Understanding* (Toronto: Stoddart, 1997), 74.

7 Marshall McLuhan, 'Interview with Gerald Emanuel Stearn,' in *McLuhan: Hot and Cool*, ed. Gerald Emanuel Stearn (New York: Signet Books, 1969), 261.

8 At St Louis, one of his students was Walter Ong, who became an eminent medium theorist.

9 Qtd in Gordon, *Marshall McLuhan*, 135.

10 Liss Jeffrey, 'The Heat and the Light: Towards a Reassessment of the Contribution of H. Marshall McLuhan,' in 'The Medium's Messenger: Understanding McLuhan,' special issue, *Canadian Journal of Communication* (December 1989), 7–8.

11 Marshall McLuhan and Quentin Fiore, *The Medium Is the Massage* (New York: Bantam Books, 1967), 88.

12 McLuhan, 'Interview with Stearn,' 284.

13 James P. Winter and Irving Goldman, 'Comparing the Early and Late McLuhan to Innis's Political Discourse,' in 'The Medium's Messenger: Understanding McLuhan,' special issue, *Canadian Journal of Communication* (December 1989): 92–100; see also Dennis Duffy, *Marshall McLuhan* (Toronto: McClelland and Stewart, 1969), 11–12.

14 McLuhan, 'Interview with Stearn,' 261. See also Duffy, *Marshall McLuhan*, 11.

15 James W. Carey, 'Marshall McLuhan: Genealogy and Legacy,' *Canadian Journal of Communication* 23, no. 3 (1998): 296.

16 Edmund Carpenter, 'That Not-So-Silent Sea,' *Canadian Notes & Queries* 46 (Spring 1992): 3–14.

17 Marshall McLuhan, 'Introduction,' in *Exploration in Communication*, ed. Edmund Carpenter and Marshall McLuhan (Boston: Beacon 1960), ix.

18 Another of his students records McLuhan as saying, 'A good teacher won't just offer his students a package, but a do-it-yourself kit. He will put himself into a point of awareness. He will force him out of his previous modes of thinking. A good teacher saves you time.' Qtd in B.W. Powe, *A Climate Charged* (Oakville, ON: Mosaic, 1984), 28.

19 Carpenter, 'That Not-So-Silent Sea,' 7.
20 Barrington Nevitt and Maurice McLuhan, *Who Was Marshall McLuhan?* (Toronto: Stoddart, 1994).
21 For example, Raymond Rosenthal, ed., *McLuhan: Pro and Con* (Baltimore: Pelican Books, 1969); and Stearn, *McLuhan: Hot and Cool.*
22 *Wired Magazine,* January 1996.
23 Northrop Frye, 'Across the River,' in *Divisions on a Ground: Essays on Canadian Culture,* ed. J. Polk (Toronto: House of Anansi, 1982), 37.
24 Powe, *A Climate Charged,* 19–20.
25 Glenn Willmott, *McLuhan, or Modernism in Reverse* (Toronto: University of Toronto Press, 1996), xii.
26 Carpenter, 'That Not-So-Silent Sea,' 21.
27 Matie Armstrong Molinaro, 'Marshalling McLuhan,' in 'Marshall McLuhan,' special issue, *Antigonish Review* 74–5 (1988): 92–5.
28 W. Terrence Gordon, *McLuhan for Beginners,* illus. Susan Willmarth (New York: Writers and Readers Publishing, 1997), 134.
29 See Paul Grosswiler, *Method Is the Message: Rethinking McLuhan through Critical Theory* (Montreal: Black Rose Books, 1998), 9–10. See also James W. Carey, 'The Roots of Modern Media Analysis: Lewis Mumford and Marshall McLuhan' (1980); repr. in *James Carey: A Critical Reader,* ed. Eve Stryker Munson and Catherine A. Warren, 34–59 (Minneapolis: University of Minnesota Press, 1997).
30 Siegfried Giedion, *Mechanization Takes Command: A Contribution to Anonymous History* (New York: Oxford University Press, 1948), v.
31 Ibid., 5–6.
32 These thoughts also are present in Innis.
33 Marshall McLuhan, 'Letter to Lewis Mumford, December 5, 1948,' in *Letters of Marshall McLuhan,* ed. Matie Molinaro, Corrine McLuhan, and William Toye, 208 (Toronto: Oxford University Press, 1987).
34 Marshall McLuhan, introduction to *The Bias of Communication* by Harold A. Innis (Toronto: University of Toronto Press, 1971), ix.
35 Ibid., vii. Also Marshall McLuhan, foreword to *Empire and Communications* by Harold A. Innis (Toronto: University of Toronto Press, 1972), v–xii.
36 McLuhan, introduction, ix.
37 Ibid., ix–x.
38 A. John Watson, 'Harold Innis and Classical Scholarship,' *Journal of Canadian Studies* 12, no. 5 (Winter 1977): 46.
39 Molinaro, McLuhan, and Toye, *Letters of Marshall McLuhan,* 219–20.
40 Carpenter, 'That Not-So-Silent Sea,' 11–12.
41 McLuhan, 'Interview with Stearn,' 261.

42 Marshall McLuhan and Wilfred Watson, *From Cliché to Archetype* (New York: Pocket Books, 1971), 20. Emphases added.
43 Barrington Nevitt, *The Communication Ecology: Re-presentation versus Replica* (Toronto: Butterworths, 1982), 176.
44 McLuhan and Watson, *Cliché to Archetype*, 118.
45 Marshall McLuhan and Bruce R. Powers, *The Global Village: Transformations in World Life and Media in the 21st Century* (New York: Oxford University Press, 1989), 16.
46 McLuhan and Watson, *Cliché to Archetype*, 21.
47 Ibid., 118.
48 Ibid., 16.
49 Ibid., 121.
50 Marshall McLuhan and Eric McLuhan, *Laws of Media: The New Science* (Toronto: University of Toronto Press, 1988), 98–9.
51 Ibid., 148.
52 Ibid., 153.
53 Ibid., 99, 106, 107.
54 McLuhan and Powers, *Global Village*, 7.
55 Ibid.
56 Ibid.
57 Ibid.
58 Marshall McLuhan, *Understanding Media: The Extensions of Man* (New York: Mentor, 1964), 91.
59 Ibid., 64–5.
60 Ibid., 64, 66.
61 Qtd in McLuhan and Watson, *Cliché to Archetype*, 36.
62 Ibid.
63 McLuhan, 'Interview with Stearn,' 273.
64 Marshall McLuhan, *The Gutenberg Galaxy: The Making of Typographic Man* (Toronto: University of Toronto Press, 1962), 25.
65 McLuhan, 'Interview with Stearn,' 261.
66 Ibid., 272.
67 Marshall McLuhan, *Counterblast* (Toronto: McClelland and Stewart, 1969), 60.
68 See Nevitt, *Communication Ecology*, 149–53.
69 For example, McLuhan, *Counterblast*, 41.
70 Marshall McLuhan and Harley Parker, *Through the Vanishing Point: Space in Poetry and Painting* (New York: Harper and Row, 1968), 97.
71 Ibid., 240.
72 McLuhan, *Understanding Media*, 36.
73 Ibid., 38.

74 Ibid.
75 McLuhan and Parker, *Through the Vanishing Point*, 222.
76 Ibid.
77 Ibid.
78 Marshall McLuhan and Barrington Nevitt, *Take Today* (Don Mills, ON: Longman, 1972), 3–4.
79 Ibid., 83.
80 McLuhan and Watson, *Cliché to Archetype*, 55–6.
81 E.S. Carpenter, *Explorations* 9 (1960), extracted in McLuhan, *Gutenberg Galaxy*, 66–7.
82 Carey, 'Marshall McLuhan,' 294.
83 McLuhan, *Gutenberg Galaxy*, 63.
84 Duffy, *Marshall McLuhan*, 23.
85 Ibid.
86 McLuhan, *Counterblast*, 79.
87 McLuhan, *Gutenberg Galaxy*, 19.
88 McLuhan and Nevitt, *Take Today*, 39–40.
89 Nevitt, *Communication Ecology*, 59.
90 McLuhan, *Gutenberg Galaxy*, 47.
91 Ibid., 50.
92 Ibid., 56.
93 Ibid., 81.
94 Ibid., 111.
95 Ibid.
96 Ibid., 106.
97 Ibid., 125.
98 Ibid.
99 McLuhan and Nevitt, *Take Today*, 141.
100 McLuhan, *Understanding Media*, 134.
101 Ibid., 135–6.
102 Ibid., 144.
103 Ibid., 149.
104 Ibid., 20.
105 Ibid.
106 Ibid., 32–3.
107 Ibid., 196.
108 Ibid., 55.
109 Ibid., 32–3.
110 Ibid., 33.
111 Maurice McLuhan, interview, 'Marshall McLuhan, What If He Is Right?'

112 McLuhan and Parker, *Through the Vanishing Point*, 247.

113 Ibid., 181.

114 McLuhan, *Understanding Media*, 28.

115 McLuhan and Watson, *Cliché to Archetype*, 152.

116 Marshall McLuhan, *The Mechanical Bride: Folklore of Industrial Man* (1951; repr., Boston: Beacon, 1967), v–vi.

117 McLuhan and Nevitt, *Take Today*, 95.

118 McLuhan, *Understanding Media*, 71.

119 Ibid., 202–3.

120 McLuhan and Watson, *Cliché to Archetype*, 201.

121 McLuhan, *Understanding Media*, 257.

122 Ibid., 92.

123 Ibid.

124 Ibid., 93.

125 McLuhan, *Mechanical Bride*, 139–40.

126 McLuhan and Nevitt, *Take Today*, 59.

127 McLuhan, *Understanding Media*, 185.

128 Ibid., 130.

129 Ibid., 129.

130 'If a doctor, surgeon or scientist,' said McLuhan, 'were to become personally agitated about any phenomenon whatever, he would be finished as an explorer or observer. The need to retain an attitude of complete clinical detachment is necessary for survival in this kind of world.' McLuhan, 'Interview with Stearn,' 280.

131 Marchand, *Marshall McLuhan*, 61.

132 McLuhan, 'Interview with Stearn,' 286.

133 McLuhan, *Gutenberg Galaxy*, 1.

134 Qtd in Paul Heyer, *Communications and History: Theories of Media, Knowledge and Civilization* (New York: Greenwood, 1988), 125.

135 For example, Harold Innis, *Empire and Communications* (1950; repr., Toronto, ON: University of Toronto Press, 1972), 41, 81.

136 See, for example, David F. Noble, *The Religion of Technology: A Divinity of Man and the Spirit of Invention* (New York: Penguin Books, 1997).

137 Northrop Frye, *Words with Power* (Toronto: Penguin, 1990), 69. See also Northrop Frye, *The Critical Path: An Essay on the Social Context of Literary Criticism* (Bloomington: Indiana University Press, 1971), 43.

138 Frye, *The Critical Path*, 43.

139 Ibid., 145.

140 Ibid.

141 McLuhan and Watson, *Cliché to Archetype*, 87.

142 Paul R. Ehrlich and Anne H. Ehrlich, *Betrayal of Science and Reason: How Anti-Environmental Rhetoric Threatens Our Future* (Washington DC: Island, 1996), 14.

143 Ibid., 43.

144 David Suzuki and Amanda McConnell, *The Sacred Balance: Rediscovering Our Place in Nature* (Vancouver: Douglas and McIntyre, 1997), 15.

145 McLuhan, *Counterblast*, 33.

146 Ibid., 36, 33.

147 Grosswiler, *Method Is the Message*, 4.

148 Alison Anderson, *Media, Culture and the Environment* (New Brunswick, NJ: Rutgers University Press, 1997), 121–2.

149 Stephen Dale, *McLuhan's Children: The Greenpeace Message and the Media* (Toronto: Between the Lines, 1996).

150 See also David L. Altheide, *An Ecology of Communication: Cultural Formats of Control* (New York: Aldine De Gruyter, 1995).

13 Red Toryism: George Grant's Communication Philosophy

Although virtually unknown abroad, within Canada George Grant, who died in 1988, remains by far the best known of indigenous philosophers. His fame arose not solely from the quality of his prose. Grant appeared frequently on radio and television, and indeed two of his books under review here (*Philosophy in the Mass Age* and *Time as History*), as well as David Cayley's interviews, were originally prepared for broadcast on CBC radio. Together with *Lament for a Nation*, these short works provide a fine introduction to, and résumé of, the thought of this distinguished Canadian philosopher, communication scholar, and critic of technology.

For some, George Grant was paradoxical as a political/existentialist philosopher and communication theorist. On the one hand, he was a self-proclaimed 'conservative,' in the sense of one who desires to retain or retrieve what is good. His philosophic Platonism, his religious convictions, and his Canadian nationalism all point to the aptness of the term *conservative* when applied to Grant. On the other hand, Grant was also a socialist since, in his view, pursuit of the eternal good, adherence to natural law, and preservation of Canadian nationhood all imply, and require, collective action, communal sensibilities, and activist governments. After all, what is a socialist, Grant asked, but one who wishes in the name of some higher, collective good to use government to curb the excesses of individual greed?

While *Lament for a Nation*, published originally in 1965, is by far Grant's most famous and celebrated work, there is much more in his writings than expressions of concern for the survival of his country. In fact, given the full breadth of his work, Canada can be seen, allegorically, as an archetype of the crises all people face in an era of rapid technological change. Grant's work, therefore, should be of considerable interest to readers worldwide.

Broadcaster David Cayley opens *George Grant in Conversation* with a masterful, forty-five-page synthetic overview of Grant's thought. Here Cayley also deftly estimates the influence on Grant of major thinkers. For instance, Grant once referred to the writings of conservative political philosopher Leo Strauss as being for him a 'high blessing.'[1] For Cayley, however, although Strauss certainly once tipped a debate Grant had in his own mind on a crucial issue, Grant was anything but an acolyte: the two differed fundamentally on the role of the United States in the world (Grant saw the United States as imperialist and the principal cause of homogenization of cultures) and regarding the goal of equality upon which Grant placed very high value. Likewise, with respect to Heidegger, who influenced Grant's thinking on technology, Cayley relates that Grant periodically turned a small photograph of that German existentialist to the wall, depending on how he happened to feel about 'the old bastard' that day.[2]

Following the introductory essay, *In Conversation* presents interviews with Grant edited by Cayley. These are useful not only for summarizing, clarifying, and tying together Grant's thought in a dialogic setting, but also, on occasion, they cause Grant to expand upon certain controversies, such as the content of natural law.[3]

Philosophy in the Mass Age was Grant's first major work. Its eight lectures were intended to introduce moral philosophy to a general radio audience. Here Grant challenges Western notions of progress and affirms the importance of philosophy in assisting people to comprehend and act properly in their world. Reminiscent of Jacques Ellul, Grant claims that mass production and its techniques penetrate 'all the moments of our work and leisure – that is ... our total lives.'[4] Embedded in the techniques of massification, he continues, is an ethic of domination, whether over nature or over other people, making necessary an intensive search for a new or renewed moral philosophy so that we may be able once again to distinguish good from less than benign uses of power.

Despite its extreme importance, however, Grant continues, society inhibits that search: 'Every instrument of mass culture is a pressure alienating the individual from himself as a free being.'[5] For one thing, people in mass society find increasingly that responsibility for their lives resides with the whole system, rather than with the individual, seemingly negating the usefulness of individual searches. For another, in mass society, reason itself becomes primarily an instrument to control nature and to adjust the masses to what commercial society requires of them. That means that thought not serving the dominant interests 'is sneered at as "academic,"' and that people, therefore, are strongly induced to 'educate themselves to get dominance over nature and over other men,' rather than on how to inquire into the nature of right and wrong.[6]

In addition to the eight lectures exploring various aspects of moral philosophy (including chapters on mythic and modern consciousness, natural law, history as progress, Marxism, and American morality), the 1995 edition of *Philosophy in the Mass Age* presents for the first time a transcription of a ninth broadcast in which Professor Grant responded to questions from listeners.

Lament for a Nation can be understood at two levels. The first is one of grieving over the passing of the very possibility of Canada. 'To be a Canadian,' Grant maintained, once meant a desire to build a community with a stronger sense of the common good and of public order than was possible with American individualism.[7] That vision for Grant disappeared with the electoral defeat in 1963 (hard on the heels of the Cuban Missile Crisis) of the Conservative government of John Diefenbaker over the issue of nuclear warheads on Canadian soil. According to Grant, in yielding on that issue, Canada became 'like fish left on the shores of a dying lake,' the very element required for its continuance, namely a sense of justice and morality in the face of the technological imperative, having disappeared.[8] However, even Diefenbaker's populism and small-town private enterprise ideology, Grant felt, would have been insufficient to save Canada in any event. What was needed, rather, was a large dose of socialism. Curtailing the civil service as Diefenbaker had done, Grant observed, strengthened the power of *private* governments, namely the corporations; such strengthening must be anti-nationalist because corporations (increasingly) are transnational.[9]

The second level at which *Lament for a Nation* can be understood concerns a fundamental questioning of the nature of human existence in technological society. The Canadian quandary for Grant was a particular instance of a broader confrontation that all people are experiencing. 'A society dominated by corporations,' he argued, 'could not vote for an independent defence policy,' or indeed for anything else of substance. After all, Grant asked, 'where can people learn independent views, when newspapers and television throw at them only processed opinions' acceptable to the power elite?[10] The capitalist ethic of profit-making, Grant insisted, infuses virtually all mass communication.[11]

Extending the argument, the unceasing and unmitigated ethic of profit seeking is but a particular manifestation of the will to power. Will to power, a Nietzschean notion, Grant observed, gives primacy to conquering human as well as non-human nature. By exercising control over heredity, over the human mind, and over society, 'man will conquer and perfect himself.'[12] Liberalism for Grant 'is the perfect ideology for capitalism [as] it demolishes those taboos that restrain expansion.'[13]

In Time as History, perhaps his densest work, Grant again 'brushed against the writings of Nietzsche' because, according to him, that nihilistic philosopher 'thought the conception of time as history more comprehensively than any other thinker.'[14] Grant defined 'time as history' as an apprehension of 'the absence of any permanence in terms of which change can be measured or limited or defined.'[15] The opposite conception, as Grant noted in *Philosophy in the Mass Age*, had been the Platonic vision of 'history as the moving image of an unchanging eternity.'

In an age of technological progress, which is to say in an era where time is conceived as history, 'horizons' (that is, frameworks and perspectives, including most importantly the notion of God) become 'simply the creations of men.'[16] Whereas in the past people thought that their horizons were true statements about reality, affirming, for example, that ultimate reality is reason or love, time as history teaches us that 'horizons are not discoveries about the nature of things, [but rather merely] express the values which our tortured instincts will to create.'[17] At the heart of this existentialist dilemma are science and technology, which have created the awareness or belief that our horizons are mutable. 'Indeed,' Grant declared, 'the idea of time as history was more shaped in response to the progressive sciences than by anything else.'

There is also, however, according to Grant, a grievous error in our thinking about science and technology that exacerbates the problem. Science and technology are often conceived as standing outside the moral order, scientists simply finding out things pre-existing in the order of nature that their pure curiosity leads them to discover, implying that it is up to us to decide whether the knowledge gained will be used for good or for ill. This common attitude, Grant emphasized, is quite mistaken since science combines willing with reasoning.[18] By engaging the will, science cannot be absolved from the moral dilemmas it raises.

The relevance of Grant's (and Nietzsche's) questions/analyses remains with us and, if anything, increases in a period now driven by a neoconservative or neoliberal policy agenda. Canada, for example, having entered a North American Free Trade Agreement, is currently dismantling or reducing in the name of deficit reduction venerable and self-defining social programs that hitherto had helped provide a semblance of equity and justice. Other countries are doing the same, premised on a 'New World Order' of unencumbered product and capital flows. Likewise, new communication technologies – from global satellite systems and fibre-optic cable networks to 'information highway initiatives' – are part and parcel of 'globalization' (more properly called 'corporatization'), further homogenizing cultures and centralizing geopolitical control within transnational companies. Moreover, environmental crises are becoming ever more acute as species are annihilated at a truly alarming rate, as deforestation and desertification spread, as ozone depletion increases, as global warming accelerates, and as ground and lake water become further contaminated – all outcomes of the exercise of human will upon nature in the absence of much recognition of an intrinsic value to non-human forms of life.[19]

As well, heightening competition and the increased commodification of ever-more aspects of social life magnify gaps between rich and poor, both internationally and domestically. Furthermore, techniques of control (advertising, public relations, human relations, propaganda, reproductive technologies, and so forth), when coupled with the ethic of greed, erode respect by power elites for those upon whom power is exercised. Middle- and upper-middle-class Canadians seem hardly to blink nowadays at the growing immiseration of the less well-to-do, whether in countries like East Timor or at home where approval ratings for cut-and-slash governments remain high. As Grant remarked so presciently over twenty-five years ago, 'The present darkness is a real darkness ... The sun is hidden by the clouds and the usefulness of our ancient compasses has been put in question.'[20]

Grant has been criticized for being unduly pessimistic, and it is easy to see how a reader could come away with that impression. Grant's intention as a philosopher, after all, was that of 'bringing the darkness into light as darkness.'[21] What enabled him to do this consistently for so many years, however, was his deep conviction, acquired while in England during the midst of the Second World War, that beyond the seeming maniacal chaos and apparent relativity of time and space, 'there is order.'[22] Ultimately, therefore, Grant wrote from a foundation of great hope.

He has also been charged with providing few solutions to the profound problems he raised. To 'lament,' after all, is to imply that it is already too late to do much. After exquisitely unfolding Nietzsche's thought, for instance, Grant confined his counsel to an admonishment to remember what had been handed to us from older traditions, particularly from the Jews and the Greeks, and to sift 'by loving and thinking' their truth from their error, thereby opening ourselves up 'to the whole.' Grant himself assessed, however, that 'this is to say very little.'[23] One might wish that he had been able, or had been more inclined, to couple his deep analyses and profound faith with plans for action. While Grant was himself a social activist in the sense that he devoted his life to teaching and writing about injustices, inconsistencies, and moral dilemmas pervading our society, in only calling his readers and listeners to remember, to think, to love, and to believe (important as these are), he may in the end have inspired passivity among his readers.

The paradox of Grant is yet deeper. On the one hand, he always insisted that it truly matters what one does, that each individual ultimately is responsible for his or her own moral comportment. On the other, 'necessity' and 'fate' are recurrent, albeit sometimes implicit, themes in his writings. Fatalism would seem to detract from the significance of human action. Grant's penchant for fatalistic interpretations was perhaps ultimately the source of his apparent lack of revolutionary zeal.

Nonetheless, for readers able to retain a spirit of hope and activism in the face of Grant's evident fatalism, the writings of this brooding philosopher of modernity can be of immense aid for comprehending our time, and inferentially at least for pointing us toward what we should be doing.

NOTES

1 David Cayley, ed., *George Grant in Conversation* (Toronto: House of Anansi, 1995), 3.
2 Ibid., 26.
3 Ibid., 67–70.
4 George Grant, *Philosophy in the Mass Age* (1959; repr., ed. W. Christian, Toronto: University of Toronto Press, 1995), 4, 5.
5 Ibid., 8.

6 Ibid., 10.
7 George Grant, *Lament for a Nation: The Defeat of Canadian Nationalism* (1965; repr., Ottawa: Carleton University Press, 1995), 12.
8 Ibid., 25.
9 Ibid., 18.
10 Ibid., 57.
11 Ibid., 61.
12 Ibid., 67.
13 Ibid., 47.
14 George Grant, *Time as History* (1969; repr. ed., intro. by William Christian, Toronto: University of Toronto Press, 1995), 57.
15 Ibid., 37.
16 Ibid., 40.
17 Ibid.
18 Ibid., 25–6.
19 David Suzuki, *Time to Change* (Toronto: Stoddart, 1994).
20 Grant, *Time*, 68–69.
21 Cayley, *George Grant*, 171.
22 Ibid., 49.
23 Grant, *Time*, 68–9.

PART FOUR

Cultural Ecology and the Political Economy of Knowledge

Introduction to Part Four

HANNO HARDT*

The intersection between culture and economics remains one of the most important locations for the study of the social and political conditions of society. For many years, Robert Babe has defined this location and offered explanations that enhance our understanding and promote thinking about its practical consequences. He has done so with a grounding in the history of numerous efforts in economics and cultural studies, for instance, to come to terms with the underlying idea of communication as an existential force in the ecological life of society. Indeed, a consideration of specific economic and cultural practices is inconceivable without a grasp of the range of theories and practices of communication that have marked the development of particular world views.

Thus, approaching this section from the rich perspectives of communication and cultural studies (in the United States) offers insights into the potential of interdisciplinary scholarship. But it also reminds the reader of the need for a radical critique of the dominant economics paradigm and the dominant theory of media and communication. Babe's contribution to this task goes a long way to help explain the current conditions, grounded in history as a pertinent method of analysis and knowledge of the ideological constraints visible in U.S. scholarship in communication studies, in particular.

These issues are much older, however, and while they define the historical context of the field, they remain ignored or neglected, as Babe notes. In fact, the rise of the social sciences in the United States and Europe coincided with the rising concerns about industrialization,

* University of Iowa and University of Ljubljana

urbanization, and the impact of technology on transportation and information. More specifically, it was a time when U.S. scholarship drew on the insights of historical scholarship in the social sciences, and political economy in particular, to help analyse the consequences of modernization. The latter involved the rejection of divine order explanations and a turn to notions of the individual and society as foundations of a modern understanding of political economy. Babe's work continues in this historical tradition with its roots in nineteenth-century German political economy, followed by a holistic, humanistic approach that resurfaced with the contributions of the Frankfurt school and British cultural studies. Thus, he considers communication as imbedded in a broad, Anglo-German philosophical context of constructing an ecological world view.

The work of Karl Knies (1821–98) in Germany reflects this perspective and confirms the centrality of communication in a theory of society. His studies of transportation and telegraphy placed the notion of communication (and the press) within a general framework of historical inquiry into the economic life of society, realizing at the time that political economy could never be complete in itself. Breaking down the isolation of individuals, communication becomes the central process in the formation and development of society.

For Knies, and other German political economists of his generation, the interdependence of the economic and cultural spheres of society provides the foundation of a comprehensive theory of society in which communication constituted the binding force.

Thus, Albert Schäffle (1831–1903) relies on the production and dissemination of ideas as a building block in his organismic theory of society, while Karl Bücher (1847–1930) addresses communication in the context of an economic theory of Western development. Both work within a historical-cultural framework in which the organization of society rather than the individual was the focal point of economic activities. Knies, in particular, together with Wilhelm Roscher (1817–94), Bruno Hildebrand (1812–78) and Gustav von Schmoller (1838–1917) represent the historical school of political economy, where notions of 'process' and 'growth' and the idea of 'change' played a major role.

During the twentieth century, the German historical tradition was continued by others, including Max Weber (1864–1920) and Ferdinand Tönnies (1855–1936). Together with Werner Sombart (1863–1941), they consider the role of the press and public opinion and the rise of advertising in capitalism.

A generation of American students of political economy in Germany consequently established their own theoretical positions upon returning to the United States. They included Henry C. Adams (1851–1921), Richard T. Ely (1854–1943), Edmund J. James (1855–1925), Roland Falkner (1866–1940), Henry R. Seager (1870–1930), Frank A. Fetter (1863–1949), and Simon Patten (1852–1922). The last, in particular, addresses the importance of communication in society as a major force, able to provide an atmosphere of understanding and cooperation to become a key ingredient in the shift from individual to social control, which rests on opinion and suggests the importance of understanding the development of ideas.

In later years, Albion S. Small (1854–1926) and Edward A. Ross (1866–1951) provide links between sociology and economics in the United States and address the centrality of communication in the growth and development of society. Their work was rarely acknowledged as part of an intellectual history of the field and seems to have played no major role in the development of modern communication studies. The latter had separated from sociology (or economics) under the influence of practical considerations regarding journalism and the older academic tradition of speech and rhetoric.

Although Harold A. Innis (1894–1952) addresses the impact of communication on economics and makes a significant contribution to the historical-cultural tradition in the Canadian context, his work remains obscure, rarely acknowledged or pursued by other economists of his generation in the United States. Instead, American communication scholarship recognizes the importance of his approach to the study of communication, especially after the publication of *Empire and Communications* (1950) and *The Bias of Communication* (1951), and individual scholars like James Carey (1935–2006) integrate his thinking into their own historical-cultural approach to rethinking the role of communication and media in contemporary society.

At this point the work of Robert Babe becomes an important link between the historical record of economic thought in the United States and Germany, for instance, and the interdisciplinary nature of communication and cultural studies, whose future theoretical and practical relevance will depend on realizing and acting on the consequences of his insights.

In this light, Babe's turn to a critical analysis of economic thought for an explanation of the current bifurcation between cultural studies and political economy provides an opportunity for reviewing the relations between culture and economy through, among other mediations, the notion of price (money) as a medium of communication.

Georg Simmel's (1858–1918) *Philosophy of Money* (1907) furnishes an explanation of the social meaning of money, determining relations of domination and providing the means to overcome individual limitations. Babe examines the symbolic power of money, prices, and commodity exchange vis-à-vis issues of communication and the potential of an ecological world view, in which production as communication becomes a predominant force in the life of modern societies. His first essay in this section serves as an important reminder of the intellectual roots of economic thought, including issues of exchange and their creative potential for understanding the complexity of the notion of communication itself.

Babe's commitment to history as a source of explanation for contemporary issues of new media and communication is demonstrated in his work with the Canadian tradition of communication scholarship, and the contributions of Harold Innis, in particular. He concentrates on the potential threat of modern media of communication with their tendency to increase delusion and remove people from direct experiences of culture and nature, for instance, while the consequences of a digital media environment offer insights into the role of communication as information in a 'space-bound' world. The significance of Babe's examination, however, remains the fact that he has turned his attention to creative, intellectual efforts outside the field to suggest the wider, indeed ecological implications for an Innisian approach, in which knowledge as power employs media as central agents of diffusion and control.

In his critique of the neoclassical treatment of information, Babe engages this key concept in communication studies in a close reading, suggesting not only its interdisciplinary importance, its nature as a public good, but also alluding to the dire consequences of its increased commodification. His solution emerges from a turn to the political economy of information and communication grounded in the work of Innis, Dallas Smythe (1907–92), and Kenneth Boulding (1910–93). In other words, Babe uses a dialectic constellation, which shifts from the immaterial conception of information and the determinism of neoclassicism to notions of evolution or transformation and, therefore, uncertainty in understanding the political economy of information and communication. The latter is grounded in a conception of human interaction, in which communication means power and where culture and society are binding forces.

The result is a dynamic model of social communication that supports his formulation of an ecological project. Moreover, from this ecological understanding of culture – stemming from Babe's rejection of mainstream economics and, indeed, poststructuralist ontologies – in this section we see him embrace a material essence that most social scientists continue to ignore: what environmentalists call 'ecosystems.' To quote him directly, 'It is not simply the disappearance of species valued for themselves that is at issue, ... extinctions weaken the very fabric of life.'[1]

Media play a major role in the sustained discourse of society, as Babe realizes in his discussion of paradigm shifts and the established order. He turns to the historical development of mainstream media studies (including communication and cultural studies) and provides a critical analysis of its scholarship under shifting material conditions to document the neglect of political economy aspects of the field. Indeed, U.S. communication studies has historically supported the dominant ideology, embracing a specific idea of democracy and reinforcing existing systems of power, beginning with the influence of the Chicago school on the role of the social sciences in modern society.

Subsequently cultural studies, imported from the United Kingdom, undergo radical changes in the process of adaptation, with the neglect of power and class, in particular, and political economy as a method of inquiry.

Babe returns to the value-laden idea of the modern economic discourse to establish the importance of information and communication and, therefore, the centrality of communication studies as an interdisciplinary component in the forging of a new economics paradigm, in which information provides the basis for a sharing of knowledge and is recognized as a common good. At the same time, he constructs an argument for establishing and reinforcing the place of political economy in the arsenal of cultural studies, concluding that the 'renowned split between political economy and cultural studies has been, in a sense, a distraction, a diversion, a *faux* debate.'[2]

Indeed, the intellectual ties between sociology (and, therefore, the study of media and communication) and economics in the United States had been close with the emergence of institutional economics in the 1920s and 1930s. Thorstein Veblen (1857–1929) comes to mind as a critic of traditional economic theory and a contributor to new theoretical formulations with the rise of the social, the emphasis on community and communication, and the dynamic nature of the cultural environment as a major element of economic life. Furthermore, as Babe

recognizes, Theodor Adorno and Max Horkheimer 'laid the foundation for a cultural studies rife with political economy considerations.
For these authors, to adequately understand culture it is insufficient
merely to depict general relations between various cultural products ...
and social life. Rather, one needs to explore how cultural products help
organize society (allocate leisure time and promote passivity and conformity in audiences, for example), and address in detail the production, reproduction, distribution, exchange, and consumption of cultural
commodities.'[3]

At the same time, the search for a response to the (mostly) German
influence on the development of the social sciences in the United States
ended in the reign of empiricism, behaviourism, and scientism. The
result was the type of communication research associated with the
Lazarsfeld tradition, while mainstream economic thought turned to
information and the consequences of its dissemination.

Throughout his work (in this section) Babe demonstrates the need
for changing perspectives and incorporating positions, whose details
emerge from the history of economic thought, social and technological
progress, and the associated intellectual discourse. Indeed, he succeeds
in pitting the ideas of Harold Innis, in particular, against the dominant
paradigms to conclude that a much older generation of scholars had
been able to identify the major flaws of a narrow conceptualization
of information and communication (here in the context of economic
thought). By doing so, he confirms not only the relevance of Innis in
the twenty-first century, but makes a strong argument for the uses of
history in explanations of contemporary issues.

In the meantime, cultural studies and its older companion, communication and media studies, linger. While the former is seeking to
escape a routinized approach to issues of culture and society, the latter negotiates a safe return to the primacy of empiricism reminiscent
of the 1950s. However, in what must be one of the great, if not tragic,
ironies in modern intellectual history, Babe recognizes that American
cultural studies strayed far from its holistic foundations. Under these
circumstances, Babe's arguments regarding the centrality of communication and information in progressive thought may serve as a reminder
that the substance of communication studies, once defined by early
sociology, redirected by the empirical tradition represented by Wilbur
Schramm (1907–87) and Paul Lazarsfeld (1901–76), and subsequently
claimed by cultural studies and literature, may once again be applied
more creatively by yet another interdisciplinary interest located in the

work of political economists. His insights provide a relevant critique of American cultural studies and its impact on understanding communication. As such they are a meaningful addition to the critical literature on communication studies in the United States.

In fact, addressing the conditions of communication as a vital social, cultural, economic, and political process has always been the task of relevant disciplines beyond communication studies. The history of philosophy, for instance, is filled with scholarly inquiries about the nature of language and communication. Other disciplines followed as they developed and expanded their intellectual territories. Communication studies, on the other hand, has not been recognized as a discipline in its own right, nor has it actively sought an interdisciplinary existence beyond its adoption of social scientific methodologies. David Riesman (1909–2002) has characterized the dilemma of the field as being plagued by an intimidation of adventurous research in a methodological monoculture, while Tönnies once derided any attempts in Germany to establish a separate science of the press, suggesting that media studies are in the purview of sociology.

Although the field of communication and media studies had been temporarily inhabited by scholars from other disciplines, their efforts have had limited effects on theorizing communication and media. More typical have been brief encounters with the field on issues of media and communication before important contributors moved on, among them, for instance, Harold Lasswell (1902–78), Carl Hovland (1912–61), Kurt Lewin (1890–1947) and Lazarsfeld, in pursuit of their specific disciplinary interests. In fact, one could argue that their work confirmed the principal location of media and communication in the respective disciplines, such as political science, psychology, and sociology.

In light of these historical developments of communication and media studies in the United States, and the intellectually tedious performance of cultural studies, the task of integrating communication and media theoretically in social, economic, cultural, or political processes, supported by 'adventurous' research, falls to the respective disciplines and their demonstrated awareness of the centrality of communication in their own pursuit of understanding and theorizing their respective domains.

The essays in this section provide a rich example of a historically grounded effort to address the potential of a political economy of communication and media and by doing so raise questions about the conditions of communication studies / cultural studies regarding any exploration of alternative explanations, including the role of economic thought.

Situated historically, Babe's work reflects and revives key aspects of the German, British, and Canadian traditions, reminding us that empiricism and specialization have in some significant ways limited our capacities going forward. The critiques and analyses presented in these chapters are examples of what can be gained (analytically and culturally) by applying an ecological and dialectical approach to the political economy of knowledge.

NOTES

1 See p. 323.
2 See p. 378.
3 See p. 369.

14 Economics and Information: Toward a New (and More Sustainable) World View

Economists regard markets as information-generating, -distributing, and -processing systems. Markets produce information in the form of prices. Prices, economists believe, are money indicators of relative social value that, when combined with knowledge possessed by parties prior to exchange, normally suffice to coordinate smoothly the activities of multitudinous economic agents.

Mainstream (neoclassical) economists acknowledge that economic agents enter markets possessing certain types of non-price knowledge. Households, for example, know both their own 'initial holdings of goods (including labor power),' as well as 'the satisfactions [they] can derive from different combinations of goods acquired and consumed.'[1] Firms, likewise, know the technological alternatives available to transform inputs into outputs.[2] The only additional information required of households and firms for an efficient distribution of resources, according to economic orthodoxy, is that of market price.

The conception of price as information, however, demands closer scrutiny. In a classic article formulating the notion, F.A. von Hayek defined *market price* as 'a numerical index [attached to each kind of scarce resource and final output] which cannot be derived from any property possessed by that particular thing, but which reflects, or in which is condensed, its significance in view of the whole means-ends structure.'[3]

For von Hayek, then, as for other economists sharing the tradition, price is condensed information issuing from the exchange relations of myriad economic agents. As von Hayek further explained, 'In any change [an economic agent] will have to consider only these quantitative indices (or "values") in which all the relevant information is concentrated; and by adjusting the quantities one by one, [the household or firm] can appropriately rearrange [its] dispositions without having to solve the whole puzzle [i.e., the economy-wide input-output matrix] ab initio.'[4]

Parties to transactions, then, tend not to know, nor need they know, the panoply of factors giving rise to relative prices. All that is required, according to von Hayek and neoclassicism, is knowledge of 'how much more or less difficult to procure [preferred items] have become compared with other things.'[5] And that type of information, economists aver, is generated and distributed automatically by market activity in the form of prices.

Externalities

In *Principles of Economics* (first published in 1890) Alfred Marshall opened a door for economists to consider economy-ecosystem interactions. He introduced the term *external economies* to denote benefits to third parties that are unmediated by the price system but result from production or consumption activities of buyers and sellers.[6] In *The Economics of Welfare* (1920), A.C. Pigou, a disciple of Marshall, broadened the Marshallian notion to encompass also *external diseconomies*, that is, third-party costs. Smoke from a factory, for instance, Pigou elucidated, imposes harms on bystanders in terms of 'injury to buildings and vegetables, expenses for washing clothes and cleaning rooms, expenses for the provision of extra artificial light, and in many other ways.'[7] In all such instances, Pigou advised, welfare could be increased by governments taking measures to narrow the gap between 'marginal social net product' and 'marginal private net product.'[8] To accomplish this he proposed applying per unit taxes and subsidies.

For neoclassical economists, *externalities* (the modern term denoting both external economies and external diseconomies) result from (and indeed may even be defined in terms of) inaccurate or incomplete information. As we have seen, for 'normal' commodities and activities (i.e., those presumed to have no important third-party effects), economists contend that prices are normally sufficient to ensure optimum decision-making, both on the part of economic agents considered individually, and for the economy overall. Given externalities, however, market price is acknowledged to be inappropriate since people not participating in a particular commodity exchange are by definition nonetheless affected by the transaction, with the result that some benefits or costs are omitted in deriving the 'condensed' information that represents that particular commodity, hence distorting its perceived 'significance in view of the whole means-ends structure.'

The neoclassical response to the informational dilemma posed by externalities has been to urge price adjustments so that prices more accurately represent system-wide costs and benefits. Two general modes of implementing price adjustments have been proposed. One is creation of transferable property rights in previously non-commodified costs and benefits so that these, too, may bear a price and thereby affect the prices of the commodities or activities previously characterized by externalities. Firms, for example, could be required to buy rights to pollute from those affected by the pollution.⁹ A major disadvantage to this approach, recognized by neoclassicists, concerns the high transaction costs if third parties are numerous and/or spatially dispersed, as is often the case with pollution. The second approach, entailing fewer transaction costs, is to impose per unit taxes, provide per unit subsidies, or perhaps set prices directly through a regulatory board, in order to adjust market prices. The disadvantage of this latter method, according to neoclassicists, concerns the difficulty if not indeed the impossibility of determining 'correct' prices.¹⁰ Variants of cost/benefit analysis, none very satisfactory, have been proposed to try to cope with this problem.¹¹

Despite difficulties, neoclassicists remain adamant that the 'solution' to environmental crises lies in price adjustments, whether implemented through commodification of currently non-commodified harms and benefits, or through taxes, subsidies, and price regulation designed to alter market prices. In both cases, the recommended action contemplates a market-based 'solution' to ecosystem problems. Proponents evidently are confident that prices can, in principle, adequately condense and transmit any and all information required for sound decision-making.

Prices as Externality

It is, to say the least, ironic that mainline economists put such great stock in market solutions to rectify ecosystem crises when these very crises have arisen in the first place on account of burgeoning market-place activity – particularly since the price system is inherently silent with regard to the appropriate scale of marketplace activity vis-à-vis ecosystem vitality.¹² It is also ironic, if not indeed altogether quite perverse, that economists maintain that adjusted price information will remedy the informational problem designated as 'externalities.' First, as discussed immediately below, information *means* externality; externalities result from the very properties of information. Second, as discussed in the following section, prices and commodity exchanges, as highly reductionist forms or modes of information/communication, actually induce a lack of caring for our natural environment.

Properties of information inconsistent with commodity treatment, making information per se a significant source of externality, have been noted elsewhere.[13] Briefly, information is rooted in the shape, or form, or structure, or pattern of matter/energy. Information derives from the organization or patterning of matter or energy. Different substances, even human memories, can be shaped to convey or hold the 'same' forms, and these forms can be present at many locations at the same time. As Kenneth Boulding was fond to remark, 'When a teacher instructs a class, at the end of the hour presumably the students know more and the teacher does not know any less ... What the student gains the teacher does not lose.'[14] This 'public good' character of information – or at least of the 'form' element of the dialectic of information (matter-in-form) – is precisely what makes shared culture and community possible. Economists today, however, are seemingly oblivious to the fact that the teaching/communicating process, as Boulding noted, is utterly unlike the mode of commodity exchange since, in the act of communication, information/knowledge does not 'change hands.' Stated another way, there is little or no incremental cost in diffusing information widely, making all attempts to commodify information by restricting access to it ('privatizing' it), such as through copyright, signal scrambling, or user fees, economically dubious – even by the criteria set forth by neoclassical economics.

Already, therefore, we have pinpointed severe inconsistencies in the neoclassical program and in the Western economic enterprise of promoting environmental health by 'internalizing externalities' through price adjustments. Externalities are deemed by neoclassicists to result from the conveyance of inadequate or inaccurate price information. By correcting price information, neoclassicists maintain, a more desirable allocation of resources will result. But information, including price information, is inconsistent with the commodity mode on account of information's dialectical character (matter-in-form). Economists cannot with consistency recommend enfolding greater and greater aspects of life within the ambit of commodity exchange when the very means recommended for such enfolding (i.e., improved price information) is inherently inconsistent with commodity treatment and with the methodologically individualist mode of analysis typifying economics.

The problem, however, is yet more severe.

The Semantics of Prices

Apart from general properties of information that point to an omnipresence of 'externalities,' more perplexing still are semantic properties of prices. The concern here is that price, as a particular mode of information/communication, alters perception in ways that are fundamentally anti-environmental (and anti-community as well). Price, I will argue, cannot even in principle connote information sufficient and suitable for decision-making consistent with guarding ecosystem health. Before embarking, therefore, on even greater commodifications in the name of preserving ecosystem vitality, the semantic properties of this 'key symbol' of pecuniary cultures need to be scrutinized closely.[15]

Prices are, in essence, names for objects, processes, and relationships. As names, prices both connote and transform social meaning. When prices are applied to components of the ecosystem, these components are transformed into commodities, that is, into 'containers of exchange value,'[16] and hence are made to seem as being substitutable for all other commodities. According to neoclassical theorist Joseph Stiglitz, for example, 'natural resources are basically no different from [i.e., are infinitely substitutable for] other factors of production.'[17] Indeed, nature (usually termed 'land') in neoclassicism is viewed as being but a commodity, almost infinitely substitutable for capital and labour, and as consisting of elements (namely, the panoply of natural resources) that are in turn almost infinitely substitutable one for another. From the premise of infinite substitutability, neoclassical statements such as 'the world can, in effect, get along without natural resources' ineluctably follow.[18]

Neoclassicists fell into the error of infinite substitutability by reducing all economic information to that of price and all economic communication to that of commodity exchange. Prices seem to turn guns into butter, butter back into guns, land into capital, and capital back into land. Infinite bidirectional transformations posited by neoclassicism assume away, in other words, 'time's arrow,' that is, history and the unidirectional flow of time. Money, by ostensibly providing the common denominator (or common 'name') for all things, creates an illusion of virtually limitless, bidirectional substitutability, obscuring such ecological realities as limits and thresholds.

A threshold denotes a point of no return, a place where bidirectional substitutions are no longer possible. Events have finality once a threshold is crossed. Likewise, limits are not normally congruent with the logic of the price system since, at a limit, there is no option as to the direction in which to proceed. Ecologists, of course, posit the existence of limits and thresholds: niches become filled; species become extinct; emissions from radioactive substances can never be reversed; people die. In accordance with the entropy law,[19] production leads to exponential increases in waste, straining the regenerative capacity of natural cycles.[20] Time in the real world, in other words, is not bidirectional, and hence prices mislead by indicating infinite bidirectional substitutability/reversibility.

In other traditions, as noted by Daly and Cobb, life has been ascribed as having intrinsic value: 'Existence in general, and especially life,' they write, 'are to be affirmed in themselves.'[21] Not so, however, for the price system or for neoclassicism. Prices depict all value as relative: value in the price system consists solely of potential for trade, this being substitutable for (or transformable into) so much of that. Being worth something on its own merits (i.e., intrinsic value) is totally antithetical to the semantic meaning of prices, and therefore to neoclassicism.

Indeed, neoclassicism and the price system, as systems of information, knowledge, and communication, also utterly efface intimations of uniqueness and sacredness, as these too imply an absence or inappropriateness of substitutes, which is to say an inappropriateness of price. Absence of price, by neoclassicism's logic, however, means an absence of value. For neoclassicism, conservation of a pristine forest is senseless since, qua forest, it has no commodity exchange value. On the other hand, viewed from the standpoint of being a supply of newsprint, the forest can be 'valuable' indeed.

Markets, therefore, as information-generating and communication systems, by precluding vital concepts like uniqueness, sacredness, intrinsic value, thresholds, limits, and history, are fundamentally at odds with sustainable development and, in consequence, with long-term human survival. The price system, as a mode of encoding information and communicating knowledge, stands at the very heart of the environmental crisis.

Commodity Exchange as Communication

Commodity exchange is certainly one mode of communication. As such it has far-reaching consequences relevant to economy-ecosystem interaction. Most of the social effects of commodity exchange are invisible to neoclassicism, however, since neoclassicism can envisage no other communicatory mode with which to compare.

Marx is well known, among other things, for remonstrating how commodity relations alienate people from one another, that is, how markets inhibit and destroy fully textured communication. Less well known, yet prophetic, was his analysis of how commodity relations alienate people from nature. Under systems of private property and ubiquitous commodity exchange, Marx maintained, people relate to nature 'in the mode of possession, of having and grasping';[22] people also come to think of nature as dead and submissive to their whims and demands.[23]

Economic historian Karl Polanyi deepened and extended Marx's analysis of alienation, showing how commodity treatment of land and the resulting alienation from nature further estrange people from one another. Polanyi wrote, 'The economic function is but one of many vital functions of land. It invests man's life with stability; it is the site of his habitation; it is a condition of his physical safety; it is the landscape and the seasons. We might as well imagine his being born without hands and feet as carrying on his life without land. And yet to separate land from man and organize society in such a way as to satisfy the requirements of a real-estate market was a vital part of the utopian concept of a market economy.'[24]

More recently, interrelations among commodification, alienation from nature, and breakdown of human community have been afforded extended treatment by Daly and Cobb.

Communication through commodity exchange leaves parties to transactions untouched.[25] The whole point of commodity trade is to exchange equivalents. The focus is entirely on the items being exchanged, as opposed to relations among those doing the exchanging. Since each party to commodity exchange has something the other party wants, and since each wants to retain as much as possible of what he or she already has, there is therefore as well an element of conflict to all commodity exchange, further alienating parties participating in this mode of communication.

'Land,' analogously, can be perceived and treated as being a 'party' to commodity exchange. In return for fertilizer, water, pesticides, and other capital items, land 'trades' crops that bear a cash value. According to utilitarian principles of individual maximization, the party 'trading' with land will endeavour to minimize expenses (i.e., retain as much as possible of what he or she already has) consistent with exacting what land has to offer, so as to maximize present values, given time constraints, discount rates, time horizons, and so forth. Affording land no intrinsic value, however, means that a land's qualities not passing through markets receive no attention from those engaging in market activity. Present benefits, moreover, receive greater weight than future costs, so that over-cultivation leading to desertification, or the burning of rain forests in favour of short-term agriculture, may seem 'rational' from a profit-maximizing perspective. Instrumentalist or commodity-type treatment, furthermore, displaces and obscures other modes of interaction whereby land 'communicates' with humans – for instance, by providing a sense of individual identity and helping constitute human community.

Instrumental, commodity treatment of land is deadly since our actual relationship with land is that of reciprocal communion. Some forty-five years ago, Norbert Wiener expressed as elegantly and lucidly as anyone humanity's intimate relationship with land, writing, 'The pattern maintained by ... homeostasis ... is the touchstone of our personal identity. Our tissues change as we live: the food we eat and the air we breathe become flesh of our flesh and bone of our bone, and the momentary elements of our flesh and bone pass out of our body every day with our excreta. We are but whirlpools in a river of ever-flowing water. We are not stuff that abides, but patterns that perpetuate themselves.'[26]

How can we objectify and represent ecosystem elements solely by price, and reduce our interactions with the ecosystem to the mode of commodity exchange, to the mode of 'having and grasping,' when it is 'flesh of our flesh and bone of our bone,' when we are part of it, and it of us?

The Ecosystem as Communicatory

Within most organizations – whether organisms, households, firms, or ecosystems – communication seldom assumes the mode of quid pro quo such as typifies commodity exchange. In organisms, for instance, the various bodily members, such as eye and ear, complement one another to create and maintain the higher-level system. Likewise in healthy firms and households, members relate to one another not through quid pro quo analogous to commodity exchange, but rather through cooperation and complementarity. Likewise for ecosystems.

From an eco-centred perspective, there are no divisions; all things are inextricably interlinked, not so much as substitutes as neoclassicists contend, but rather as interdependent and interacting components of larger systems. We are all parts of something larger, and we are all in continuous communion with this larger entity, and thereby necessarily with one another as well. This communion between us and our environment and hence with our fellow living creatures is what neoclassicists refer to as 'externalities,' and what ecologists refer to as 'ecosystems,' and this is precisely what economists strive to commodify, to internalize, and to privatize.

Since interdependence among ecosystem components can seldom be reduced to the quid pro quo typifying commodity exchange, it follows that the information passing among components cannot appropriately take the form of prices, since price has meaning only when things are substitutable for one another (this being equivalent to so much of that). Price information, then, is clearly inappropriate when the concerns are with complementarities, with cooperation, with symbiosis, with synergy, with empathy, with system-component relations – an array of communicatory modes far exceeding what is normally considered by economists, yet ones essential to non-market organizations including ecosystems.

Economics versus Communication Studies as World Views

From these brief remarks essential features of an alternative world view, more congenial than neoclassicism to the prospect of survival in the twenty-first century, emerges. This alternative centres on information and communication, but not in the neoclassicists' restricted sense. Information and knowledge structures, rather, are to be viewed as defining or helping to provide meaning to material reality. These structures evolve incrementally and often unpredictably. Since they can be, and often are, shared, they imply and induce collective, communal modes of living, hence giving heightened presence to gift, as opposed to commodity exchange relations. Information and knowledge as central organizers also imply systems theory and methodologically collectivist modes of analysis, in contrast to markets and the current emphasis on methodological individualism. Moreover, information and knowledge imply connectivity to the past as well as to the future, contrasting with the economists' present-mindedness.

Theorists [particularly those discussed herein and in Part One] espousing conceptions of information/communication that are more realistic and expansive than those hitherto characterizing mainstream economics have much to contribute to a large range of matters not previously thought of as being in the domain of communication studies, not the least of which is environmental practice. Much more promising than orthodox economics as an inclusive mode of analysis, then, is that branch of political economy focusing on information, knowledge, media, and communication. The political economy of media and communication acknowledges that signs and symbols do not and should not always take the form of price, and that modes of interacting are far more variegated than the mode of commodity exchange. The stakes involved in changing the world view – at the highest levels of decision-making as well as in the rank and file of society – are great indeed. In the words of David Suzuki, 'It's a matter of survival.'

NOTES

1 Kenneth J. Arrow, 'The Economics of Information,' in *The Computer Age: A Twenty-Year View*, ed. Michael Dertouzos and Joel Moses (Cambridge, MA: MIT Press, 1979), 313.
2 Ibid., 314.
3 F.A. von Hayek, 'The Use of Knowledge in Society,' *American Economic Review* 35 no. 4 (September 1945): 525.
4 Ibid.
5 Ibid.
6 Alfred Marshall, *Principles of Economics: An Introductory Volume*. 8th ed. (1890; London: Macmillan, 1947), 266.
7 A.C. Pigou, *The Economics of Welfare*. 4th ed. (1920; London: Macmillan, 1932), 184.
8 Ibid., 131–5.
9 See, for instance, Ronald Coase, 'The Problem of Social Cost,' *Journal of Law and Economics* 3 (1960): 1–44.
10 William J. Baumol and Wallace E. Oates, 'The Use of Standards and Prices for Protection of the Environment,' in *The Economics of the Environment: Papers from Four Nations*, ed. Peter Bohm and Allen V. Kneese, 161–73 (London: Macmillan, 1971).
11 Samuel Chase, ed., *Problems in Public Expenditure Analysis* (Washington DC: Brookings, 1968).
12 Herman E. Daly and John B. Cobb Jr, *For the Common Good: Redirecting the Economy toward Community, the Environment, and a Sustainable Future* (Boston: Beacon, 1989), 58–61.
13 See chapter 1.
14 Kenneth E. Boulding, *The Image: Knowledge and Life in Society* (1956; Ann Arbor: University of Michigan Press, 1961), 35.

15 Alan Dyer, 'Making Semiotic Sense of Money as a Medium of Exchange,' *Journal of Economic Issues* 23, no. 2 (June 1989): 503.

16 Ibid., 505.

17 Joseph E. Stiglitz, 'A Neoclassical Analysis of the Economics of Natural Resources,' in *Scarcity and Growth Reconsidered*, ed. V. Kerry Smith (Baltimore, MD: Johns Hopkins University Press, 1979), 64.

18 R.M. Solow, 'The Economics of Resources or the Resources of Economics,' *American Economic Review* 64, no. 2 (May 1974): 10.

19 Nicholas Georgescu-Roegen, *The Entropy Law and the Economic Process* (Cambridge, MA: Harvard University Press, 1971).

20 Tryve Haavelmo and Stein Hansen, 'On the Strategy of Trying to Reduce Economic Inequality by Expanding the Scale of Human Activity,' in *Population, Technology, and Lifestyle: The Transition to Sustainability*, ed. Robert Goodland, Herman E. Daly, and Salah El Serafy (Washington DC: Island, 1992), 38–51.

21 Daly and Cobb, *For the Common Good*, 104.

22 Howard L. Parsons, ed., *Marx and Engels on Ecology* (Westport, CT: Greenwood, 1977), 18.

23 Ibid., 17.

24 Karl Polanyi, *The Great Transformation: The Politics and Economic Origins of Our Time* (1944; Boston: Beacon, 1957), 178–9.

25 Lewis Hyde, *The Gift: Imagination and the Erotic Life of Property* (New York: Vintage Books, 1979).

26 Norbert Wiener, *The Human Use of Human Beings: Cybernetics and Society* (1950; repr., New York: Avon Books, 1967), 130.

15 Innis, Environment, and New Media

Canadian communication thought began with Harold Innis (1894–1952). Innis, of course, lived prior to the onset of the modern environmental movement, often ascribed to publication in 1962 of Rachel Carson's *Silent Spring*. Hence there are few direct allusions in Innis's work to the human impact on the environment's capacity to sustain life. His concern, rather, was largely confined to the recursive impact of culture on material surroundings, and of material surroundings on culture.

In this regard, Innis developed two 'theses' – *the staples thesis* to which he devoted the largest portion of his career, and the *communication thesis* on which he spent the last few years of his life. Innis's staples and communication theses are consistent insofar as both denote bidirectionality among the material environment, human thought, and human activity in the context of political/economic power and control. It is the communication thesis, however, that concerns us here.

Innis's communication thesis essentially involves a triangulation among a medium, its 'bias,' and social organization. Commentators on Innis, however, have taken diverse points of view regarding his conception of media. Edward Comor, citing Innis's 1946 book, *Political Economy in the Modern State*, proposes that Innis 'recognized organisations, institutions, and technologies as "communication media" in that they constitute core structures through which people interact and history unfolds.'[1] Others, however, date Innis's communication writings to publication in the early 1950s of *The Bias of Communication* and *Empire and Communications*, and maintain that his concept of media was much narrower – comprising orality, modes of inscription, and electronic means of relaying messages.[2]

In this latter regard, it was Innis's position that the physical properties of media (their weight or mass, their durability, their tractability, their capacity to store information) make them biased toward either time or space. Media that are intractable (stone carvings), are difficult to transport, durable, and possess limited capacity to store information he deemed 'time-binding,' as they intrinsically support and induce time-bound cultures, characterized as being ceremonial, communitarian, hierarchical, in tune with custom and tradition, religious, and geographically confined. Media that are easy to use and transport, that are not durable, and that have abundant capacity he called 'space-binding,' as they give rise to, and support, space-bound cultures, characterized by Innis as secular, present-minded, and intent on territorial expansion and administration of vast territories.[3]

Any medium that predominates in a society at a given time, according to Innis, is controlled by that society's elite. Time-bound societies are controlled by elites who exert control by means of 'time'; that is, they are 'custodians' of time and invoke tradition, a sense of the sacred, natural (or divine) law, and make appeals to the collectivity as such. Space-bound societies, by contrast, are controlled by elites exercising influence over 'space'; these are the 'administrators' who frame and enforce positive (secular) laws, who engage in and control markets and the price system, who advertise, and who educate for the exigencies of ever-changing job markets.

For Innis, in order for a group to exercise control through time or over space, it must control the media of communication predominant at that time, and the properties of those media must be in accordance with the 'bias' of the society. For example, hieroglyphics carved in stone favoured a priesthood ruling a time-bound society, whereas newspapers with advertising, being readily disposable and published with frequency, support changes in fashion, current affairs, marketing, and administration over a wide area, and hence empower business leaders and regional/national governments. Space-binding media are inherently weak in providing continuity or a sense of local identity, but facilitate governance and administration over large territories, and help create a common, indeed 'global,' economy and culture.

The issue of power and control in Innis's writings, however, is yet more subtle. The arrival of new media, according to Innis, engenders a struggle for ascendancy, not only among groups of people, but among types of knowledge. Innis saw *opinion* – that is control over people's thoughts and perceptions – not *force*, as the ultimate means of social control.

Regarding 'opinion,' however, Innis gave much less emphasis to biased news reports than to the unobtrusive indoctrination of complete mindsets. Most generally and significantly, he viewed as powerful those who inculcate in people's minds one or another conception of time, and one or another conception of space – even to the point that these become the common sense of an era. Specifically, Innis proposed at least three remarkably different conceptions of time: social or organic (cyclical) time, differentiated or punctuated linear time, and undifferentiated mechanical time. Oral/tribal society, and societies influenced by time-binding modes of inscription, Innis maintained, tend to view time organically or cyclically.

Knowledge in oral society is handed down through poetry, song, story, and myth from generation to generation; such knowledge is meant to apply to all times. Likewise, stone inscriptions endure for centuries, and in societies relying on this medium, knowledge will change but slowly. Such knowledge is not inconsistent with the sciences; according to Innis, 'The discovery of periodicity in the heavens [in Babylon] enormously strengthened the position of religion in its control over time and continuity.'[4]

However, more tractable forms of writing (paper, for example) helped change the conception of time. In positing a unique day as being of extraordinary importance, he maintained, the Romans fostered the belief that time comprises not just cycles but also sequences of single, sometimes unique and extraordinary, moments.[5] This conception, he added, 'contribute[d] to the growth of Roman law notably in contracts';[6] contracts record specific acts as taking place or to take place at a given point in time. This conception of time is what George Grant termed 'time as history'[7] and differs remarkably from mythic or cyclical time as eternal recurrence.

This notion of time as unstoppable sequence, albeit punctuated by distinct moments, continued for many years, but became a stepping stone to time as undifferentiated sequence. According to Innis, business requires that time be conceived as a 'ceaseless flow of mechanical time.'[8] The length of contracts, the number of hours worked, the interest accrued, and the rents due are all based on durations of time irrespective of differentiated 'moments' that might take place within the specified intervals. Innis noted, too, that 'the establishment of time zones facilitated the introduction of uniformity in regions.'[9] James Carey has written a remarkable essay, in the vein of Innis, on the electric telegraph as a medium changing people's conception of time toward undifferentiated sequence.[10]

Control of space for Innis had at least two meanings. Most simply, in modern society, ownership of land and articles occupying space are associated with power and control. Imperial rulers and giant corporations, in this sense, obviously 'control space.' But even more basically, control over space means control over how people understand and conceptualize space. People in time-bound cultures conceive space in ways very different from those in space-bound cultures. For the former, space is neither unlimited nor something to be appropriated and annexed; rather, it is bounded and needs to be protected (i.e., nurtured, sustained). Space is where the community lives, where its roots are, how it maintains its connections with the past, and where its future will unfold. Land is to be cared for as one would care for a gift[11] that has been inherited and will be passed on. The words now quoted, ascribed to Chief Seattle, propose, in effect, an absence of private ownership over space:

> How can one buy or sell the air,
> The warmth of the land?
> That is difficult for us to imagine.
> If we don't own the sweet air
> And the bubbling water,
> How can you buy it from us?
> ...
> The wind that gave
> My grandfather his first breath
> Also received his last sigh.
> And the wind also breathes life into our children.
> All things are bound together.
> All things connect.
> What happens to the Earth
> Happens to the children of the Earth.
> Man has not woven the web of life.
> He is but one thread.
> Whatever he does to the web,
> He does to himself.[12]

In space-bound cultures, the view of land is quite different. There, the desire is to conquer new territories, create larger markets, and organize land into efficient configurations (factories, assembly lines, territorial divisions of labour, and so on).[13] Space, like time, becomes commodified in space-biased cultures.

Innis viewed various media in terms of a continuum from highly time-biased (orality, stone and chisel) to highly space-biased (daily press, radio). For him there were, in principle, no gaping discontinuities. However, some following Innis's path – Marshall McLuhan and Walter Ong, for example – distinguished broadly among three epochs of human civilization, each anchored by a predominant mode of communication: orality, writing, and electronic communication. Within the era of writing, moreover, major discontinuities were proposed with the introduction first of the phonetic alphabet and, again, with the inception of the printing press.[14] More recently some have suggested that we have entered yet another era, that of digital communication, thought to be as distinct from the analogue era of electronic communication as was typography from manuscript culture in the era of writing.[15] Some attention has been paid to applying principles and modes of analysis developed by Innis to this digital age.[16]

Innis had grave misgivings with regard to what he perceived as an uninterrupted introduction, especially since the late nineteenth century, of increasingly space-biased media. Whereas over the course of human history he saw time- and space-binding media oscillating with one another in influence, and hence periodically achieving dynamic balance, in the modern era the trend for him has been largely toward ever-increasing space-bias – with dire consequences for Western civilization. Hence, Innis made 'a plea for time,' which for him meant greater emphasis on the oral dialectic as a means of counterbalancing the space-bias of mechanized communication.

Dire consequences for Innis, evidently, were solely at the social plane, as he afforded scant attention to environmental outcomes. He envisaged disruption of community, the lapse of democracy, augmentation of empire, the curtailment of free thought, and the collapse of values and of peace as concomitants of unmitigated space-bias, but regrettably he did not expound on the implications of space-bias for the capacity of the cycles of nature to sustain life.

In this chapter I now explore two themes. First, I apply Innis's communication thesis to environment or ecology; I ask, in other words, what can be said regarding the trend toward increasingly space-biased media with respect to the capacity of the environment to sustain life. Second, I explore the newest phase of electronic media, namely the digitalization of communication, within Innis's framework, again with a view to teasing out implications for environmental well-being.

Innisian Bias and the Environment: Present-Mindedness

One of the characteristics of space-bound cultures, according to Innis, is 'present-mindedness,' which he defined, in part, as a 'lack of interest in problems of duration.'[17] Innis ascribed the rise of present-mindedness in Western civilization particularly to 'the bias of paper and printing.'[18] News caters to 'excitement: a prevailing interest in orgies,'[19] and helps increase circulation and advertising, which, he declared (quoting Wyndam Lewis), 'dwells in a one-day world.'[20] Those controlling the press system, he maintained, have little interest in continuity; rather, they strive to increase hedonism and consumption, and the one-day lifespan of their chosen medium is well suited to those goals.

Present-mindedness, or living for the moment with little consideration of past or future, is of course hostile in the extreme to environmentalism. At one time fish at the Grand Banks off Newfoundland, for example, were so plentiful that they 'could be scooped out of the sea with buckets.'[21] As Clive Ponting notes, however, 'There was no attempt to limit catches and all the attention was devoted to increasing the effectiveness of exploitation; fish numbers fell in area after area and as they did so the fleets turned to catching younger and immature fish, which only exacerbated the problem.'[22] Today, of course, the Newfoundland cod fisheries are dead.

'Present-mindedness' and the concomitant anti-environmentalism characterizing space-bound cultures are to be contrasted with the view of time and the generally benign concomitant environmental practices of time-bound cultures. According to Chief Oren Lyons of the Onondaga, 'We are looking ahead, as is one of the first mandates given to us as chiefs, to make sure that every decision we make relates to the welfare and well-being of the seventh generation to come, and that is the basis by which we make decisions in council. We consider: will this be to the benefit of the seventh generation? That is a guideline.'[23]

Clive Ponting, likewise, remarks that hunter-and-gatherer groups all over the world, by and large, 'lived in close harmony with the environment and did minimal damage to natural ecosystems.' He adds, 'There is also evidence that some of these groups did try to conserve resources in the interest of maintaining subsistence over a long period.'[24]

Present-mindedness was evident in the recent debate in North America over the Kyoto Protocol to lessen greenhouse gas emissions. In March 2001, American President G.W. Bush announced that the United

States, which had been a major force in drawing up the Kyoto treaty in 1997, would not ratify it; Bush called the treaty 'economically irresponsible.' He claimed that ratification would cost the U.S. economy $400 billion and 4.9 million jobs.[25] Later, Bush unveiled his Clean Skies plan, which linked reductions in greenhouse emissions to growth in GNP.[26] The United States accounts for about 25 per cent of the world's human-made carbon-dioxide emissions. In Canada, too, the federal government faced, but withstood, enormous pressure from business and provincial governments not to ratify the Protocol. During the intense period of the debate (from 2 September 2002 to 6 December 2002) the *Globe and Mail*, arguably the most influential paper in the country, virtually barred its environmental reporters, Martin Mittelstaedt and Alana Mitchell, from writing on the issue (Mittelstaedt informed this author that the *Globe*'s editorial board decided that Kyoto was a political and an economic story, not an environmental one)[27] – an indication indeed of a monopoly of knowledge in action.

Collapse of the Local

The printing press, and particularly the newspaper, in Innis's view, not only served to help increase present-mindedness, but also lessened attachments to the local. This is because space-binding media tend to efface local cultures and thereby land is conceived increasingly in utilitarian (market-based) terms. Innis noted that, historically, the state 'has been interested in the enlargement of territories and the imposition of cultural uniformity on its peoples,'[28] and consequently it encouraged the spread of literacy. Likewise the daily press, enjoying economies of scale, developed news to market not just regionally, but nationally and internationally.[29]

In time-bound societies, of course, land was viewed very differently. According to Karl Polanyi, 'Land [was] tied up with the organizations of kinship, neighborhood, craft and creed – with tribe and temple, village, gild, and church.'[30] Land, in other words, served many vital functions apart from an economic one: 'It invest[ed] man's life with stability; it [was] the site of his habitation; it [was] a condition of his physical safety; it [was] the landscape and the seasons.'[31] According to David Suzuki, likewise, time-bound cultures almost universally have maintained a strong feeling-bond for the land: 'Universally, the key to [Native] perspectives is rootedness to the land, a profound sense of interconnectedness with all animate and inanimate objects around.'[32]

What becomes of environmentalism when a feeling-bond for land is lost, when land is conceived not so much as a home but as a resource to be exploited, or as a marketable commodity to be bought and sold? One response is to list recent environmental catastrophes: Chernobyl, Three Mile Island, Bhopal, *Exxon Valdez*.[33] In all these instances, and countless lesser ones, there was little or no feeling-bond for the land on the part of those responsible for the damage.

Delusion

In his essay 'A Plea for Time' Innis wrote, 'As modern developments in communication have made for greater realism they have made for greater possibilities of delusion.' He continued, 'We are under the spell of Whitehead's fallacy of misplaced concreteness; the shell and pea game of the county fair has been magnified and elevated to a universal level.'[34] In 'A Critical Review,' likewise, he lamented that 'the conditions of freedom of thought are in danger of being destroyed by science, technology, and the mechanization of knowledge, and with them, Western civilization.'[35]

The theme that modern media of communication, on account of their ostensible realism, increase the possibilities and likelihood of delusion, has been taken up by many writers, including Roland Barthes,[36] Susan Sontag,[37] Walter Lippmann,[38] Daniel Boorstin,[39] and Jean Baudrillard.[40] When people lived close to nature, their knowledge of nature was direct; they were generally highly informed of the state of their natural environment, at least locally. Suzuki insists that traditional knowledge, gleaned over thousands of years by people deeply embedded within nature, is often profound. Those people 'looked with wonder, awe, and passion, and what they acquired was critical for their very survival.'[41] Through their stories, which incorporated these observations, they transformed the 'awesome physical dimensions of the cosmos into experiential ones.'[42] The Kayapó of the Amazon, for example, have intricate knowledge expressed in their songs and stories about the needed helpfulness of red ants in growing the domesticated manioc plant. Modern biologists refer to this as *co-evolution*. Suzuki comments, 'Modern anthropology has not always been eager to acknowledge the profound ecological insights poetically expressed in many Native myths, songs, and stories ... Native myth has not seriously been studied as a transmitter of encoded ecological knowledge.'[43]

By contrast, in cultures bound together by technologically sophisticated media of communication, people's experience of nature is most often indirect – mediated by these technological extensions. Innis suggested that our conception of reality is distorted in favour of space at the expense of time, which environmentally could mean, for example, that our attention is directed to the burgeoning diversity of consumer goods and styles, even while we lose sight of the dwindling number of organic species. Our health, erroneously, is understood to be bound up with growth in GNP and exports of commodities, as opposed to biodiversity, the purity of air and water, and the state of the land. Media of communication can create powerful illusions, like the magician, diverting our attention from things that matter onto the inconsequentials.

And in this they have been hugely successful. 'Cutting-edgers' today, according to pollster Michael Adams, 'have no interest in ideals, ethics or societal issues ... Life for them is an unending exploration of all the micro-pleasures the world has to offer them.'[44]

Breakdown of Community

In Innis's view, 'The Western community was atomized by the pulverizing effects of the application of machine industry to communication.'[45] He made this claim for a number of reasons. First, by neglecting time, media by definition neglect cultural heritage, which binds people together. In place of heritage, media emphasize 'hedonism,' which for Innis is akin to 'the atomization of society.'[46] Furthermore, media tend effortlessly to cross community and political boundaries, increasing nationalism during the Second World War perhaps, but weakening community in the sense of personal loyalties.[47]

The question here becomes whether community based on contiguity is necessary for, or contributes to, environmental health. Many would answer affirmatively and the economists' notions of externalities and public goods can be invoked to substantiate that response. An *externality exists* when one person's or corporation's manufacture or use/consumption of a good affects the welfare of other parties; a *public good* is defined as one whose use or enjoyment by one person does not decrease the use or enjoyment of it by others. Modern economic thinking concentrates on individual acts of exchange, production, and consumption, and proposes that externalities and public goods are exceptions, not the rule. To argue otherwise would basically transform 'economics' into 'ecology,' the major premise of the latter being that interdependence is rife among communities of organisms and of organisms with their environment.[48]

One 'public good,' for which there can be no market price, is biodiversity. Arne Naess, founder of deep ecology, wrote, 'Diversity enhances the potentialities of survival, the chances of new modes of life, the richness of forms.'[49] David Suzuki goes even further, noting that life was instrumental and indispensable in creating the conditions necessary for life and remains indispensable for maintaining life: 'Life is not a passive recipient of these elemental gifts [air, water, earth, fire],' he writes, 'but an active participant in creating and replenishing them.'[50]

In explaining this seeming paradox Suzuki refers, for example, to *the metabolic cycle* whereby the food of all living creatures is the organic materials of the previously living, *the hydraulic cycle* whereby living entities absorb, store, and release vast quantities of fresh water, thereby shaping weather and climate, and *the cycle of oxygenation* whereby plants convert the energy in sunlight into storable chemical energy through photosynthesis and release oxygen into the atmosphere. There are also cycles of sulphur and phosphorous. According to Niles Eldredge, curator at the American Museum of Natural History, 'Life is part of [a] cyclical process – at once utterly dependent on the availability of such vital commodities as carbon, oxygen, sulfur, and phosphorous – and at the same time, taking an active role in producing or otherwise making these elements available.'[51]

It is for this reason, among others, that species' extinctions in our day are so tragic. It is not simply the disappearance of species valued for themselves that is at issue, but even more significantly extinctions weaken the very fabric of life. Suzuki writes, 'Each species that disappears tears at that fabric of life a little, changing forever the configuration among the remaining species. While for a time the fabric can withstand the disappearance of various strands without losing its integrity, at some point there can result a tragic collapse.'[52]

According to the United Nations Environmental Programme, 'Global biodiversity is changing at an unprecedented rate, the most important drivers of this change being land conversion, climate change, pollution, unsustainable harvesting of natural resources and the introduction of exotic species.'[53] Whereas the rate of extinctions during the past 600 million years averaged perhaps one species per year, present extinction rates are much higher – according to biologist Bruce Coblentz, perhaps hundreds or even thousands of times higher. Estimates are that currently as many as five plant species *per day* become extinct; extinction rates of animal species are greater still. Humans for millennia have been associated with extinctions, but in the past the main factor was over-hunting. That cause, although still important today,[54] has been superseded by habitat destruction – not only through the 'clearing' and draining of land for cities, agriculture, and fuel, but as well on account of pollution, global warming, and the introduction of competitive species. According to the U.N. Food and Agricultural Organization, in the 1990s there was a 2.2 per cent loss of global forested area, a major factor in species extinctions. Also significant in loss of biodiversity, however, has been a 27 per cent decline in the 1990s in the world's coral reefs, attributable to warming of the seas and their related acidification.

From one standpoint – the predominant one in our space-bound culture – each individual organism simply draws elements needed for survival (air, water, nutrition) from its environment. Western philosophical individualism recognizes this truth and amplifies it in describing the struggle for survival of individual organisms and, indeed, of entire species. Charles Darwin and his popularizers (Herbert Spencer and Julian Huxley) went a long way in ingraining this idea into Western consciousness. This individualist (i.e., space-biased) understanding, however, masks the greater truth – namely the 'public good' character of biodiversity.

Biodiversity is, indeed, a 'public good' in the classic sense of the term. One person's or species' benefit from biodiversity does not subtract from other people's or other species' benefit. This, however, means that there can be no market value (or exchange price) for biodiversity. Indeed, markets exist only because, and as long as, the level of biodiversity is sufficient to sustain human life! That being the case, it is ludicrous even to attempt to *impute* a 'market value' for biodiversity.

Biodiversity will be preserved, then, not because of market valuations, but because of bonding, or a sense of community – of people one for another and with all life. But, according to Innis, it is precisely this sense of commonality or community that the price system and other space-biased media penetrate and break down.

People in technologically advanced societies generally live under the delusion that humanity has escaped or is escaping the natural world, and in the process we lose sight that biodiversity is a public good. We inhabit air-conditioned houses, move about in climate-controlled malls, enjoy rounds of golf on perfect lawns, turn a tap to attain water of any temperature, buy meat in cellophane-wrapped styrofoam containers, turn night into day with the flick of a switch, and communicate instantaneously over vast spaces. Attaining these creature comforts through the exercise of our technologically derived powers has meant we have, abandoned the confines of local ecosystems in favour of regional, national, and, indeed, global economies. What we generally fail to remember, though, is that in so doing, we have not only constructed a mega-ecosystem, but also that we remain as dependent on biodiversity as ever; it is just that the scale of things has grown so immense that our life support now is primarily beyond our direct perception.

The air conditioners, jet airplanes, packaged food, and so forth, too, are 'media' of communication in the Innisian sense as they (implicitly or silently) propagate space-biased conceptions of time and of space. As consumers we are immensely attracted to our conveniences and comforts and, hence, *we* are complicit in our own indoctrination into a space-biased world view. Such is the profundity of our tragedy. As Edward Comor suggests, 'An Innisian perspective (like the Gramscian concept of hegemony) is in fact so very powerful *because* people are active participants in forging their own biases; hence, we're talking about "suicide" rather than "murder"!'[55]

Digital Media

I turn now to the second question. Do digital media – that is the coupling of communication and computers in message construction, distribution, and reception – 'bias' communication in a unique way, or do they simply extend and deepen yet again the space-bias of modern life? In other words, are digital media qualitatively new, in the way that some view the printing press as being a marked departure from manuscripts, even though both are a mode of writing? Here I explore some of the implications of analogue/digital dichotomy, particularly as it relates to environmental well-being.

Digitalization Magnifies Space-Bias

That digital media are even more space-biased than analogue media is easy to see. First, consider *ease of transport*. Analogue media attenuate in transmission, and both the signal plus the encroaching noise are amplified when extending the distance covered. Digital media, by contrast, can be regenerated at each retransmission node, giving them expanded geographic coverage. Moreover, digitalization enhances portability in terms of size and weight. A digitalized set of encyclopedias can be carried effortlessly in a shirt pocket, and indeed downloaded wherever there is a telephone line (and, increasingly, even where there is not).

Digitalized movies can carry subtitles in many languages, making cultural borders increasingly permeable.

Digitalization *is easy to work with*. The present author was never able to master the relatively simple skill (compared to, say, stone engraving) of the typewriter, but can produce elegantly appearing typed pages with a word processor. Digitalization has increased the ease and lowered the cost of video/image production and enhanced significantly the ease of replication – as the sound-recording industry and copyright police are well aware.

Digitalization has expanded *storage capacity* beyond the wildest expectations of previous generations, whose records consisted of paper-based files. Not only is capacity expanded, but documents can actually be located in a matter of seconds.

And, of course, digital media are intended to be *evanescent* regarding messages. It takes but a click of a mouse to realign the electrostatic charges on a carrier (hard drive, rewritable CD, USB memory stick, etc.). This is not to say that digital media are not useful in archiving; they certainly are. But the medium itself is designed to be used over and over again with different messages – unlike a stone engraving, or even a sheet of newsprint.

This all seems eminently clear. The more intriguing question, perhaps, is whether the digital mode bears distinctions from analogue media other than heightened space-bias, which likewise may have environmental implications.

Environment as Information

Shannon and Weaver were among the early theorists of digitalization, developing in 1949 their 'mathematical theory of communication' [see chapter 1]. They defined *information* in the context of selecting choices from an array of predetermined and known possibilities, and *the quantity* of information as the logarithm to base 2 of the number of available choices. Digitalization, as we understand the term today, however, goes far beyond Shannon and Weaver's limited perspective. Any and all information that could previously be transmitted electronically can now be transformed or translated for purposes of transmission or manipulation into sequences of binary digits.

Author Katherine Hayles attributes to Shannon and Weaver the common conceptualization today of information 'as an entity distinct from the substrates [or media] carrying it.'[56] Hayles explains that from Shannon and Weaver's formulation it 'was a small step to think of information as a kind of bodiless fluid that could flow between different substrates without loss of meaning or form.'[57] Such is precisely what is meant by the term *convergence*.[58]

At the very time Shannon and Weaver were purporting to measure information by counting the number of binary digits required to recast messages into the digital mode, other theorists were de-materializing information. In *The Human Use of Human Beings* (1950) cyberneticist Norbert Wiener, for example, maintained that organisms can be viewed, metaphorically, as *messages*. 'To describe an organism,' he explained, 'we do not try to specify each molecule in it, and catalogue it bit by bit, but rather to answer certain questions about it which reveal its pattern.'[59] Organisms, including human organisms, for Wiener, are *patterns*, which is to say *information*; only secondarily are they material.

Another who viewed information as essentially immaterial was Kenneth Boulding, a contemporary of Wiener, Shannon, and Weaver. Boulding declared that, due to its immateriality, information is unconstrained by the laws of physics, and in particular by the laws of thermodynamics. The first law states that matter-energy can neither be created nor destroyed; the second (the 'law of entropy') that matter-energy in a closed system continually degrades into less complicated (i.e., less differentiated) states. Due to its 'immateriality,' information/knowledge, in Boulding's eyes, is 'primal' to evolutionary processes. Knowledge alone, he maintained, is what can really increase without limit:

> The through-put of information in an organization involves a 'teaching' or structuring process which does not follow any strict law of conservation even though there may be limitations imposed upon it. When a teacher instructs a class, at the end of the hour presumably the students know more and the teacher does not know any less. In this sense the teaching process is utterly unlike the process of exchange which is the basis of the law of conservation. In exchange, what one gives up another acquires; what one gains another loses. In teaching this is not so. What the student gains the teacher does not lose. Indeed, in the teaching process, as every teacher knows, the teacher gains as well as the student. In this phenomenon we find the key to the mystery of life.[60]

At this point, however, it seems advisable to qualify Boulding's remarks. Although from one point of view information can be thought of as being *epiphenomenal* to matter and energy, information *is* nonetheless dependent upon matter-energy: information is the shape or pattern that matter or energy assumes and to which meaning is imputed by recipients sensing the shape or pattern. Information is not the matter-energy itself, but relates to the form of the matter or energy. Without matter or energy, however, there is no shape, and hence no information. This is why I have come to the position that it is more accurate to think of information as being *dialectical* (matter-in-form, with interpretation) than it is to declare information as being *epiphenomenal*.

This distinction makes a huge difference. As Boulding remarked, matter-energy *is* subject to the two laws of thermodynamics, and indeed, entropy is defined as the inevitable lessening of differentiation (i.e., loss in information, or complexity of form) of matter or energy. Information, therefore, is not as far removed from the laws of thermodynamics as Boulding seems to indicate. While Boulding and his students assuredly departed his lectures much enriched, all continued to produce entropy simply by living, learning, and eventually dying.

Yet another who celebrated the purported immateriality of information was Marshall McLuhan. Although McLuhan wrote before digital communication was all-pervasive, he anticipated our digitalized era. When we view television, he claimed, we (or our minds) are transported, angelically, without bodies, to distant locations. When we use television, likewise, we are grafted into the logic of the medium, which is our prosthesis. In *Understanding Media*, he wrote, 'By putting our physical bodies inside our extended nervous systems by means of electric media, we set up a dynamic by which all previous technologies that are mere extensions of hands and feet and teeth and bodily controls – all such extensions of our bodies, including cities – *will be translated into information systems.*'[61]

Digitalization, in brief, seems to be helping to construct a new Platonic era, as opposed to the perhaps undue materialism of the scientific revolution. Information and pattern today, it can be argued, are becoming increasingly more important to our way of thinking than mere matter or substance. There are many indicators of this, apart from the phenomenon of convergence and declarations of notable theorists reviewed above. A few examples follow

The Image and Public Relations

The importance of image and public relations, of course, preceded the digital era.[62] Nonetheless, given digital technologies, what had previously been taken as a stencil from the real (e.g., a photograph) now becomes what Jean Baudrillard has called 'a copy without an original.' In sound recordings, duets with a long-deceased crooner are forged; in television news clips, billboard advertisements for competing television networks are electronically expunged; in movies, human actors can interact with digitally constructed animations and dead stars can spring to life. The pattern or the image seemingly takes precedence over material reality.

Revivifying Extinct Species

Popularized by *Jurassic Park*, the perception grows that conserving or preserving the informational or genetic sequences of species is almost as good as conserving the species themselves.

Cloning, Genetic Engineering, and Designer Babies

In *From Chance to Choice: Genetics & Justice* the authors write, 'Scientific knowledge of how genes work will empower human beings to cure and prevent diseases; it may also let us shape some of the most important biological characteristics of the human beings we choose to bring into existence.'[63] Humans become 'texts' to be authored through the manipulation of genetic information.

Copyrighting and Patenting of Genetic Sequences

This, of course, represents the ultimate frontier of what Innis referred to as the 'penetrative powers of the price system.' Vandama Shiva has written a series of books on inequities to the third world attributable to the patenting and copyrighting of life forms.[64]

Cyborgs

Defined as the seamless intermeshing of human and intelligent machine, cyborgs are exemplified by 'virtual reality' devices where demarcations between bodily existence and computer simulations are blurred if not eliminated.[65]

Information Economy / Post-industrial Society

Decisive in proposing that Western societies have entered a new era – one based on knowledge or information – were Fritz Machlup and

Daniel Bell. Machlup's 1962 book, *The Production and Distribution of Knowledge in the United States,* was seminal in conceiving information and/or knowledge production, processing, and distribution as important economic activities.[66] Even more influential, though, was Daniel Bell. He proposed that for *pre-industrial societies* the major resource is land and the major output is food and other agricultural products; for *industrial societies* the key resource is machines or capital, and the key outputs are factory-produced commodities; but for modern, *post-industrial societies,* the key resource is knowledge or information, and the characteristic outputs are informational.[67]

Each of the foregoing privileges a disembodied or abstract form of information over its substance or material embodiment. Extended essays on the anti-environmental implications of each of the foregoing points could be written. Here I turn instead, however, to an amazing essay by two neoclassical economists, Chandler Morse and Harold Barnett, who took the Neoplatonic conception of information to its ultimately absurd, yet logical, conclusion. They argued that *no effort* should be made toward conservation since anything and everything, comprising identical subatomic particles can (in the future) be reconstituted out of basic elements: They wrote, 'Advances in fundamental science make it possible to take advantage of *the uniformity of energy matter,'* making it feasible, 'without preassignable limit, to escape the quantitative constraints imposed by the character of the earth's crust ... Natural resource building blocks [are now] to a large extent atoms and molecules,' rendering, in their view, conservationist practices and the naturalist ethic of previous eras anachronous and perverse.[68]

Centuries ago, settlers in North America viewed their new homeland as virtually infinite – this on account of the low population, the huge geographic expanse, and the richness of wildlife and resources. As late as 1854, a resident of New York State could write, 'There would be days and days when the air was alive with [passenger pigeons], hardly a break occurring in the flocks for half a day at a time. Flocks stretched as far as a person could see, one tier above another.'[69] Flocks reportedly were so thick the sky was darkened. Today, of course, the birds that once numbered perhaps 5 billion are extinct. Herds of bison, too, which may have reached 60 million until Europeans began exploiting them for meat and hides, by 1890, had dwindled to a few hundred and were virtually extinct.

Extinctions, pollution, environmental disasters and near disasters, images of the solitary Earth taken from the moon, and *Silent Spring* by

Rachel Carson, did much to begin shifting the conception of the planet from that of limitless frontier to finite and endangered spaceship, beginning particularly in the 1960s. There is ample indication, however, that today conceptions of information and knowledge are shifting back our notion once more to that of infinite Earth. Consider, for instance, the remarks of Julian Simon as another leading apostle of the doctrine of the infinite Earth: 'The first three chapters [of his book] offer a mind-boggling vision of resources: the more we use, the better off we become – and there's no practical limit to improving our lot forever. Indeed, throughout history, new tools and new knowledge have made resources easier to obtain. Our growing ability to create new resources has more than made up for temporary setbacks due to local resource exhaustion, pollution, population growth, and so on.'[70]

According to this view, information and knowledge are unconstrained. Hence, so too is the economy, and beyond that the Earth. This view, however, is premised on a Platonic conception of information, not a materialist one, and it is argued here, the digitalization of information/communication contributes to this view. Meanwhile, extinctions increase exponentially, and the web of biodiversity contracts.

Conclusions

'Innisian bias' in our day means that space supersedes time as a principle and a means of social organization and control. Space-bias, I have argued here, is much less conducive to ecological balance and sustainability than is time-bias. For a number of reasons, any increase in the space-bias of media predominant in society can be expected to result in increased deterioration of the environment's capacity to sustain life.

A general thrust, unfortunately, of digital media is to increase and deepen space-bias, and for that reason alone digital media can be expected to deepen ecological crises. Although, to be sure, anti-globalization activists like Maude Barlow write glowingly of uses that can be made of the Internet to unite and keep informed dispersed groups in their struggles against spaced-biased policies,[71] nonetheless the overwhelming trend surely is toward greater global concentration of media and heightened use of media to administer laws, security, surveillance, funds, market demand, production, distribution, and other requirements of 'space-bound civilization.' The melding of the Worldwide Web with global banking alone is sufficient to indicate the much-enhanced space-bias that digital media present. This being the case, the conclusion inevitably follows that digital communications deepen and extend the anti-environmental thrust of previously existing space-binding media.

However, digital media do something more. They help foster a mindset that information is immaterial and that information matters more than matter. In the spirit of Innis, we might say that digital information biases not only space over time, but also the immaterial over the material (and paradoxically so, given that Innis associated time-bias with religion, which addresses the unseen) – and that, too, has grave implications regarding how we care for the environment. Moreover, digital media help reinvigorate the doctrine of the infinite Earth, a posture toward nature that is anti-environmental in the extreme.

Innis wrote, 'Each civilization has its own methods of suicide.'[72] Let us hope that ours is not through digital communication.

NOTES

1 Edward A. Comor, 'Historicising Internet Developments through the Political Economy of Harold A. Innis,' Annual ISA Conference, Chicago, February 2001.

2 For example, James Carey, 'Harold Adams Innis and Marshall McLuhan,' *Antioch Review* (Spring 1967): 5–31.

3 Harold Innis, 'The Bias of Communication' (1949); repr. in *The Bias of Communication*, intro. by Marshall McLuhan (Toronto: University of Toronto Press, 1971), 33–64.

4 Harold Innis, 'The Problem of Space' (1951); repr. in *The Bias of Communication*, (Toronto: University of Toronto Press, 1971), 99.

5 Innis, *The Bias of Communication*, 69.

6 Ibid.

7 George Grant, *Time as History* (Toronto: CBC Learning Systems, 1969).

8 Innis, 'Plea for Time,' in *The Bias of Communication*, 74.

9 Ibid.

10 James W. Carey, 'Technology and Ideology: The Case of the Telegraph,' in *Communication as Culture: Essays on Media and Society*, ed. James W. Carey (Boston: Unwin Hyman, 1989), 201–30.

11 Lewis Hyde, *The Gift: Imagination and the Erotic Life of Property* (New York: Vintage, 1979).

12 Chief Seattle, 'How Can One Sell the Air?' in *Environmental Discourse and*

Practice: A Reader, ed. Lisa M. Benton and John Rennie Short (Oxford: Blackwell, 2000), 12–13.

13 David Harvey, *The Condition of Postmodernity* (Oxford: Blackwell, 1990), 232.

14 Marshall McLuhan, *The Gutenberg Galaxy: The Making of Typographic Man* (Toronto: University of Toronto Press, 1962).

15 For example, N. Katherine Hayles, *How We Became Posthuman: Virtual Bodies, in Cybernetics, Literature, and Informatics* (Chicago: University of Chicago Press, 1999); also Michael E. Hobart and Zachary S. Schiffman, *Information Ages: Literacy, Numeracy, and the Computer Revolution* (Baltimore, MD: Johns Hopkins University Press, 1998).

16 Catherine Frost, 'How Prometheus Is Bound: Applying the Innis Method of Communications Analysis to the Internet,' *Canadian Journal of Communication* 28, no. 1 (2003): 9–24; Heather Menzies, 'The Bias of Space Revisited: The Internet and the Information Highway through Women's Eyes,' in *Harold Innis in the New Century: Reflections and Refraction*, ed. Charles Acland and W. Buxton (Montreal and Kingston: McGill-Queen's University Press, 1999), 322–38; Ronald J. Deibert, *Parchment, Printing, and Hypermedia: Communication in World Order Transformation* (New York: Columbia University Press, 1997).

17 Innis, 'Plea for Time,' 76.

18 Ibid.

19 Ibid., 78.

20 Ibid., 79.

21 Clive Ponting, *A Green History of the World: The Environment and the Collapse of Great Civilizations* (New York: Penguin Books, 1991), 175.

22 Innis, 'Plea for Time,' 175–6.

23 Oren Lyons, 'An Iroquois Perspective,' in *Environmental Discourse and Practice: A Reader*, ed. Lisa M. Benton and John Rennie Short (London: Blackwell, 2000), 15.

24 Ponting, *Green History*, 32.

25 Tom Cohen, Associated Press, 'Canada Ratifies Kyoto Protocol following Months of Debate,' *Environmental News Network*, 17 December 2002.

26 'Backgrounder: The Kyoto Protocol, Canada and Kyoto,' CBC News, 23 September 2002.

27 Robert E. Babe, 'Newspaper Discourses on Environment,' in *Filtering the News*, ed. Jeff Klaehn (Montreal: Black Rose Books, 2006), 187–222.

28 Innis, 'Plea for Time,' 76.

29 Ibid., 78.

30 Karl Polanyi, *The Great Transformation: The Political and Economic Origins of Our Time* (1944; Boston: Beacon, 1957), 178.
31 Ibid.
32 David Suzuki and Keibo Oiwa, *The Japan We Never Knew: A Journey of Discovery* (Toronto: Stoddart, 1996), 85.
33 Mitchell Thomashow, *Ecological Identity: Becoming a Reflective Environmentalist* (Cambridge: MIT Press, 1995), 2.
34 Innis, 'Plea for Time,' 82.
35 Innis, 'A Critical Review,' *Bias of Communication*, 190.
36 Roland Barthes, *Mythologies* (New York: Hill and Wang, 1957).
37 Susan Sontag, *On Photography* (New York: Farrar, Straus and Giroux, 1973).
38 Walter Lippmann, *Public Opinion* (New York: Macmillan, 1922).
39 Daniel J. Boorstin, *The Image: A Guide to Pseudo-Events in America* (New York: Atheneum, 1978), especially chap. 5.
40 Jean Baudrillard, *Simulations*, trans. Paul Foss, Paul Patton, and Philip Beitchman (New York: Semiotext[e], 1983).
41 Suzuki and Oiwa, *Japan*, 82.
42 Peter Knudstson and David Suzuki, *Wisdom of the Elders* (Toronto: Stoddart, 1992); 49.
43 Ibid., 55.
44 Michael Adams and Christine de Panafieu, 'God Is Dead? "Whatever,"' *Globe and Mail*, 16 June 2003.
45 Innis, 'Plea for Time,' 79.
46 Ibid., 80.
47 Ibid., 81.
48 Ponting, *Green History*, 11.
49 Arne Naess, 'The Shallow and the Deep, Long Range Ecology Movements: A Summary,' *Inquiry* 16 (1973): 95–100.
50 David Suzuki and Amanda McConnell, *The Sacred Balance: Rediscovering Our Place in Nature* (Vancouver: Douglas and McIntyre, 1997), 124.
51 Niles Eldredge, *Life in the Balance: Humanity and the Biodiversity Crisis* (Princeton, NJ: Princeton University Press, 1998), 160.
52 Suzuki and McConnell, *Sacred Balance*, 124–6.
53 United Nations Environment Programme, *Global Environment Outlook 3: Past, Present and Future Perspectives* (London: Earthscan), 121.
54 See, for example, Alana Mitchell, 'Few of World's Large Fish Remain, Study Says,' *Globe and Mail*, 15 May 2003.
55 Edward A. Comor, personal correspondence, 13 July 2003.
56 Hayles, *How We Became Posthuman*, xi.
57 Ibid.

58 See chapter 7.

59 Norbert Wiener, *The Human Use of Human Beings: Cybernetics and Society* (1950; repr., New York: Avon Books, 1967), 129.

60 Kenneth E. Boulding. *The Image: Knowledge and Life in Society* (1956; Ann Arbor: University of Michigan Press, 1961), 35.

61 Marshall McLuhan, *Understanding Media: The Extensions of Man* (New York: Mentor, 1964), 64.

62 See, particularly, Stuart Ewen, *PR! A Social History of Spin* (New York: Basic Books, 1996).

63 Allen Buchanan, Norman Daniels, Daniel Wikler, and Dan W. Brock, *From Chance to Choice: Genetics & Justice* (Cambridge: Cambridge University Press, 2000), 1.

64 Vandama Shiva, *Monocultures of the Mind* (London, UK: Zed Books, 1993); Vandama Shiva, *Stolen Harvest* (Cambridge, MA: South End, 2000); Vandama Shiva, *Tomorrow's Biodiversity* (New York: Thames and Hudson, 2000).

65 Hayles, *How We Became Posthuman*, 3.

66 See chapter 1.

67 Daniel Bell, 'The Social Framework of the Information Society,' in *The Computer Age: A Twenty-Year View*, ed. M. Dertouzos and J. Moses, 163–211 (Cambridge, MA: MIT Press, 1979); Fritz Machlup, *The Production and Distribution of Knowledge in the United States* (Princeton, NJ: Princeton University Press, 1961).

68 Harold Barnett and Chandler Morse, *Scarcity and Growth: The Economics of Natural Resource Availability* (Baltimore, MD: Johns Hopkins University Press, 1963), 10, 11. Emphasis added.

69 Qtd in Ponting, *Green History*, 168.

70 Julian Simon, *The Ultimate Resource 2*, rev. ed., with appreciation by Milton Friedman (Princeton, NJ: Princeton University Press, 1996), 73.

71 Maude Barlow, *The Fight of My Life* (Toronto: HarperCollins, 1998), 219.

72 Harold Innis, 'Industrialism and Cultural Values' (1950; repr. in Harold A. Innis, *The Bias of Communication*, Toronto: University of Toronto Press, 1971), 141.

16 The Political Economy of Knowledge: Neglecting Political Economy in the Age of Fast Capitalism (as Before)

In some ways postmodernist/poststructuralist thought is the ontology best supporting and depicting today's fast capitalism. Fast capitalism denotes, after all, an increasing volume, speed, and territorial expanse of digitalized communication networks, a reduced time for product cycles, accelerating speeds of style and model changes, and perhaps most importantly imagery embedding mythic meanings onto the banality of mass-produced consumer items. Postmodernist/poststructuralist thought, likewise, addresses and presumes the fluidity, speed, exponential growth in, and easy transformation of symbolic structures in a digital age.

Many maintain that postmodernist/poststructuralist thought, which began entering the mainstream of many American disciplines in the early 1980s, constitutes a huge break from the modernist and Enlightenment traditions.[1] In a number of ways this is true. The Enlightenment presumed, for example, that a material reality exists, independent of human thought, about which, nonetheless, humans can learn by applying the scientific method of induction and deduction. For postmodernists, by contrast, human culture is all-encompassing; we cannot stand outside culture.

However, I argue here, since fast capitalism is still capitalism, one can expect also to find deep-seated continuities between postmodernist thinking, especially as it becomes increasingly mainstream, and what went before. For, as political philosopher C.B. Macpherson insisted, mainstream discourses normally support or 'justify' the prevailing political-economic order.[2] Indeed, for Macpherson, such is the primary purpose of mainstream political philosophies and other scholarship in the humanities.

Although the innovators of postmodernist discourses may very well have understood their project as constituting a radical break with the past, and although contemporary critical postmodernists may intend their work to challenge existing power structures, norms, and received wisdoms, postmodernist thought can also, I will argue, be turned rather easily into a paradigm propping up established power, war, gross inequality, and other forms of injustice.

I begin this paper by focusing on mainstream American media/communication/cultural studies scholarship as they evolved over the last hundred years, to demonstrate the veracity of Macpherson's insight regarding dominant discourses sustaining established power. In so broad a survey I can, of course, touch but briefly on key phases, but the upside is that clear patterns, indeed constancies, emerge. The period certainly witnessed dramatic changes in the predominant means of mediated communication – from local to regional and then to national press systems, the rise of cinema and broadcasting, and more recently, the inauguration of computer communications, digitalization, and the Internet. Moreover, modes of transmission significantly expanded in capacity and in distance capability, with digital communication satellites being perhaps the apotheosis of that trend. For these reasons alone one could expect to find major revolutions in mainstream media/cultural studies scholarship.

But, to repeat, the fast capitalism of today is still capitalism, and if mainstream scholarship in the social sciences and humanities tends to support prevailing structures of political-economic power, then deepseated constancies over time should be evident in that scholarship – despite fundamental changes in the modes of communication. I argue here, then, that as the predominant media of communication evolved from print, to film/broadcasting, to today's globalizing, digitalized electronic communication, so too did mainstream scholarship in cultural and media studies, *but in ways that consistently ignored or 'justified' the neglect of political economy*, which is to say that this scholarship abstracted from or otherwise dismissed the existence and/or importance of disparities in communicatory power. At each stage, moreover, as I will point out, mainstream paradigms were belied by both real world events and practices, and by marginalized scholarship, making all the more convincing the political economy of knowledge thesis developed here.

The continuous neglect of political-economic aspects of information, media, communication, and culture is evident, despite the fact (or more accurately, one suspects, *due* to the fact) that communication and

culture have long been central to American wealth generation, governance, and foreign policy. Before documenting the argument, then, it
is worthwhile speculating on reasons for this continuous inattention.
To focus, for example, on asymmetries internationally in communicatory and cultural power would be also to put into question, at least
implicitly, the legitimacy or justness of those asymmetries, whereas to
ignore them, obscure them, or to deem them insignificant makes seem
more apt 'free trade' in cultural 'commodities' – a mainstay certainly
of the official, 'liberal' American paradigm. Similarly, to draw attention to domestic media ownership concentrations and to the role of
advertising in filtering news and other content would be to raise grave
doubts about the state of American democracy. As enlarged upon
below, through much of the last century there was a cosy, even sym-
biotic, relationship between the most eminent of media scholars and
the U.S. military/corporate complex. One might say that, all too often,
and whether inadvertently or not, mainstream American media scholarship served as a cover for American media power, domestically and
internationally.

Today, in the age of fast capitalism, the political-economic stakes
of influencing or controlling communication and culture are growing
exponentially. By the same token, the neglect of political economy by
mainstream scholarship becomes all the more severe. It is in this context
that an appraisal of postmodernist/poststructuralist scholarship needs
to be undertaken, for, by extrapolating past experience, one can foresee
a pronounced tendency for postmodernist thought, as it becomes ever-
more mainstream, to likewise aid and abet domination by the political-
corporate elite.

The Chicago School in the Age of Print

Standard histories of American communication/media studies begin
by referencing the 'Chicago school' of John Dewey, Robert Park, and
Charles Cooley.[3] For some intellectual historians, the Chicago theorists
were foundational; for others, they were but precursors, or even merely
'forefathers of the forefathers.'[4] But virtually unanimously, the Chicago
theorists are seminal.

In the early decades of the twentieth century, Dewey, Park, and
Cooley inquired broadly from humanist perspectives into the role of
media in American society. They viewed society as an organism whose
citizens are bound together through networks of transportation (lik-

ened to blood vessels) and communication (likened to nerves). They were progressivist theorists speculating on how technological change, particularly emerging media of communication, could and would enlighten citizens, foster community, and increase democracy. According to Dewey, 'The Great Society created by steam and electricity may be a society, but it is no community ... Communication alone can create a great community.'[5]

Indeed, Dewey seemed to hold to a doctrine of inevitable human betterment through technological change. Technologies, he opined, are instruments to solve problems, and as the problems change, so do the instruments. Through this doctrine of *instrumentalism*, he gave short shrift to other possibilities – to domination and subordination through technological means, for instance, and to the possibility of ecosystem collapse. The chief failing of the Chicago school, according to Daniel Czitrom, was its 'refusal to address the reality of social and economic conflict in the present.'[6] Tellingly, Dewey's plans for *Thought News* – a newspaper that 'shall not go beyond the fact; which shall report thought rather than dress it up in the garments of the past,' and that would use philosophic ideas as 'tools in interpreting the movement of thought; which shall treat questions of science, letters, state, school and church as parts of one moving life of man'[7] – never came to fruition.

The naive technological optimism of the Chicago theorists is difficult to comprehend, given the uses to which media were then being put. In 1917, for example, acting on the advice of Walter Lippmann, the Wilson Administration created the Committee on Public Information (CPI) as the government's propaganda arm during the Great War. CPI produced hundreds of ads promoting the war effort and pressured newspapers into giving it free advertising space. Each week CPI sent ideas and captions for cartoons to some 750 political cartoonists. It distributed thousands of official news releases and war-related public interest stories. It even published its own newspaper.[8] Meanwhile, the commercial press was 'continually silenced by orders and prosecutions'; war critics were arrested, 'often without warrants, hustled off to jail, held incommunicado without bail.'[9]

The war years were, in fact, not exceptional. They were, rather, fulfilling a nascent 'control revolution'[10] that began prior to the turn of the century through image-based advertising of addictive and non-addictive branded products. According to T.J. Jackson Lears, print advertisements presented 'a nether realm between truth and falsehood ... The world of advertisements gradually acquired an Alice-in-Wonderland quality.'[11]

Writing contemporaneously with the Chicago school was Dewey's former student and arch nemesis, journalist Walter Lippmann. In his influential 1922 tome, *Public Opinion*, Lippmann argued that most of us, most of the time, live in a 'pseudoenvironment,' defined as the 'way in which the world is imagined ... a hybrid compounded of "human nature" and "conditions."'[12] On the one hand, Lippmann proposed, people inadvertently construct pseudoenvironments by unconsciously imposing stereotypes and preconceptions onto the reality around them; on the other, pseudoenvironments can also be purposefully fabricated for popular consumption by media practitioners skilled in manipulating symbols.[13]

Through his notion of pseudoenvironment, Lippmann foreshadowed postmodernist constructs like simulacra and hyperreality. He also was a precursor of the 'crisis of democracy' position, as forwarded decades later by Zbigniew Brzezinski[14] and the Trilateral Commission,[15] and arguably as responded to by neoconservative governments through trade agreements[16] and anti-terrorism legislation.[17] For Lippmann, democracy had turned a corner (he called it 'a new image of democracy') as experts now garnered popular consent for their policies by skilfully manipulating pseudoenvironments while leaving untouched the popular illusion that citizens are in charge of their destinies. Lippmann saw these deceptions as necessary for governance in the modern age, and thereby he helped inspire, or at least 'justify,' the public relations / image-manufacturing industries.

A major problem in openly constructing pseudoenvironments along the lines suggested by Lippmann, of course, concerns the distaste many Americans felt and feel regarding oligarchy and being manipulated; as Lippmann remarked: 'The desire to be the master of one's own destiny is a strong desire.'[18] A second difficulty would be the incredulity of audiences. Better, then, to construct pseudoenvironments surreptitiously. One way of doing this is to incorporate into them the fiction that democracy persists, that people remain in control. It is in this context that the second generation of media scholars, led by such towering figures as Paul Felix Lazarsfeld and Elihu Katz, can be interpreted.

Lippmann's work constituted an advance over the Chicago school in the sense that political economy was a cornerstone of his analysis. However he was also, in another sense, a regression whose anti-democratic, elitist position was in sharp contrast with the democratic spirit of Dewey and his colleagues. Lippmann in his own way, moreover, was every bit as naive as the Chicago school; while convinced that cultures (pseudoenvironments) can and must be manufactured by elites, to secure popular consent, until his later years Lippmann guilelessly presumed that the policies made possible thereby would be largely beneficent and centred on the common good. Only the prolonged war in Vietnam dissuaded him of that hallucination.[19]

Era of Movies and Broadcasting: The Empirical School

The Chicago theorists' influence waned by the early 1930s. It became increasingly difficult to sustain a posture of inevitable progress through advancing technology in the face of the First World War's devastations, the use of media for advertising, public relations and propaganda, and the onset of the Great Depression. Not to be discounted, as well, was the impact of Lippmann's *Public Opinion*. Reviewing the book in 1922, Dewey himself declared, 'The manner of presentation is so objective and projective, that one finishes the book almost without realizing that it is perhaps the most effective indictment of democracy as currently conceived ever penned.'[20]

In the 1930s, therefore, born out of the government's psychological warfare activities of the First World War, a less idealistic, more pragmatic paradigm of media studies came to the fore.[21] The emerging literature eschewed speculating on how media would contribute to community, democracy, enlightenment, and human betterment, to focus instead on persuasion, psychological manipulation, and marketing. The Second World War, likewise, was a boon to the new breed of media researchers, many of whom were complicit with the U.S. government's propaganda activities during and continuing after that war. Christopher Simpson lists the following, among others, as eminent American communication/media scholars working for or with the U.S. military on psychological warfare during the Second World War: Hadley Cantril, Ithiel de Sola Pool, Leonard Doob, George Gallup, Louis Gutman, Carl Hovland, Harold Lasswell, Paul Felix Lazarsfeld, Daniel Lerner, Rensis Likert, Leo Lowenthal, Robert Merton, Elmo Roper, Wilbur Schramm, Edward Shils, Frank Stanton[22] – a virtual *Who's Who* of American communication studies.

Given connections with the U.S. military, and their focus on persuasive communication,[23] it might at first seem surprising that the sole media 'law' these researchers devised was the 'law of minimal effects' as 'discovered' by Lazarsfeld. Arguably, his *The People's Choice* (1944) and its main finding concerning 'minimal effects'[24] responded, albeit implicitly, to (1) concerns raised by the Payne Fund Studies (1920s) on the deleterious effects of movies on children (sleep disturbance, negative influences on attitudes and behaviour, emotional stimulation, presentation of non-mainstream moral standards), (2) continued overt domestic as well as foreign propaganda and psychological warfare, including but certainly not limited to Hitler's use of sound and light to mesmerize a nation, and (3) the panic generated by Orson Welles's 1938 Halloween radio adaptation of 'War of the Worlds.'[25] All these, if not neutralized, could either undermine belief in the existence of American democracy in an age of media manipulation, or lead to restrictions on the freedom of media owners and advertisers, or both.

Lazarsfeld (1901–76) was a Viennese social psychologist who emigrated to the United States in the 1930s. His major research interest was marketing, and he set up both the Princeton Office of Radio Research (1937) and the Columbia University Bureau of Applied Social Research (1939) to further his studies. Lazarsfeld's bureaus received funding from the Rockefeller Foundation (as means to launder funds from the CIA[26]), the radio networks, newspaper publishers, marketing firms, and polling companies. He and his associates investigated questions such as audience demographics, satisfactions that audiences attain from radio, and correlations between audience tastes and social stratification. Large portions of Lazarsfeld's research was intended to aid media companies gain audiences and help advertisers and public relations firms become more adept at moulding audience tastes and opinions. Lazarsfeld was, then, an empirical social scientist whose mission was, one might say, to help elites structure pseudoenvironments and ascertain their effectiveness in shaping behaviour and opinion. Indeed, Lazarsfeld coined the term *administrative research* to denote the type of work he performed and to distinguish that from *critical research*.[27] 'More than anyone else,' writes Czitrom, Lazarsfeld 'shaped the field of communications research in the next decade.'[28] Hanno Hardt agrees: 'Under Lazarsfeld's leadership communication research in the United States [became] a formidable enterprise which was deeply committed to the commercial interests of the culture industry and the political concerns of government.'[29]

The People's Choice, Lazarsfeld's seminal study, investigated voter intention and behaviour in the context of election propaganda concerning the 1940 presidential election. Lazarsfeld and co-authors Bernard

Berelson and Hazel Gaudet claimed that 'activation' of latent predispositions and 'reinforcement' of pre-existing attitudes were the main consequences of election publicity. Significantly, Lazarsfeld and associates maintained that only 'conversion' from prior intentions should be considered important in terms of media effects, and since conversion was barely evident in their panel studies the authors concluded that media effects 'are really quite limited.'[30] For four decades thereafter, according to Chaffee and Hochheimer, '"limited effects" was a major defence of owners of new media technologies, including television, from government regulation in the United States.'[31]

In addition, in *The People's Choice*, Lazarsfeld et al. developed the 'two-step flow' model of mass communication, elaborated later in *Personal Influence* by Lazarsfeld and Elihu Katz.[32] That model proposed that the attitudes of most people are not influenced directly by media, but rather by opinion leaders with whom they are in personal contact. Mainstream media scholarship seized that premise, modifying it, however, in even more distinctly anti–political economy ways. Soon there appeared the *multi-step model* of diffusion, as forwarded by researchers such as Everett Rogers and Floyd Shoemaker.[33] The new model proposed that 'the ultimate number of relays between the media and final receivers is variable,'[34] which is to say that general audiences were hypothesized as being even further removed from direct media influence than had been proposed by the two-step flow.

As well as suiting the needs of the broadcasting and motion picture industries, the law of minimal effects was consistent with the democratic aspirations of the American citizenry. Even though millions of dollars were spent each year on media advertising and PR with the intent of affecting audience behaviour and understanding, solace for democrats could be found in the 'law of minimal effects' and in the two-stage/multi-stage flow as these, supposedly, kept citizens in charge of their destinies despite persuasion and attempted manipulation at every turn. The minimal effects model also played into the hands of U.S. foreign and trade policy in countervailing cultural protectionists around the world, including UNESCO. More on this below.

The People's Choice suffered from major methodological flaws. First, misconstruing 'activation' and 'reinforcement' as being of little significance was one major shortcoming: reinforcing the status quo and generating active support, after all, are *desiderata* from the standpoint of governing elites. Second, a large proportion of the interviewees in fact stated that media were the single most important influence on their voting intentions, not 'opinion leaders,' a finding that Lazarsfeld duly reported but overlooked in drawing conclusions. Perhaps most significantly, however, to derive a 'law' of media effects based on a panel study carried out in Erie County, Ohio, during a lopsided election campaign is, to say the least, overdrawn. Nonetheless, Lazarsfeld's conclusion remained for decades the received wisdom in media studies, with Joseph Klapper's *The Effects of Mass Communication* (1960) perhaps marking 'the watershed.'[35]

The 'law of minimal effects' was in effect an umbrella term, a prophylactic, under which ongoing research into how the public's beliefs and perceptions can be manipulated was carried out. Notable among that research activity were Carl Hovland's studies. During the Second World War funding came from the U.S. military, and after the peace from the Rockefeller Foundation. According to Lowery and DeFleur, between 1946 and 1961 Hovland's team conducted over fifty experiments on how opinions and beliefs can be modified by persuasive communication.[36] Wilbur Schramm, for one, has judged that Hovland's findings completely contradicted Lazarsfeld's law of minimal effects, stating, 'Experimental research on opinion change showed that one-third to one-half of an audience is significantly affected by even a single exposure to a persuasive message.'[37] Significantly, in their commentary introducing this research, Lowery and DeFleur assert, 'Once new principles [of persuasion] were uncovered, they could then be used by pragmatic, innovative Americans to make a better world for everyone … There was much work to be done by social and behavioral scientists. The world was still filled with prejudice, discrimination, and bigotry. And now that nuclear weapons were a reality, the task of improving relationships between peoples seemed more urgent than ever. Badly needed, for example, was a better understanding of how people's beliefs, attitudes, and behavior could be modified in socially approved ways through carefully designed persuasive communication.'[38] (As if the general public were responsible for the introduction, proliferation, and deployment of nuclear weapons!)

Other mainstream research programs during this period pertained to content analyses of propaganda (Harold Lasswell), survey techniques and the measurement of public opinion (George Gallup, Elmo Roper), audience and market research (Lazarsfeld), and decision-making in small groups (Kurt Lewin). Although variegated, the research had commonalities: it was positivist and empirical, it was methodologically individualist, and it focused on means of changing attitudes/behaviour/

beliefs. It was, one might say, *in direct contradiction to the 'law of minimal effects.'*

The 'law of minimal effects' was belied not only by ongoing research, but also by practices and premises of media companies. Broadcasters sold advertising, for example, on the basis that 'activation' was an important and sought-after consequence of media exposure; corporations hired PR professionals to 'reinforce' corporate images as well as to 'convert' audiences during periods of crisis management – the Rockefeller interests' media activities following the Ludlow Massacre being seminal in this regard.[39] From the 1930s through the 1960s, moreover, an intense multimedia campaign of anti-communist indoctrination was waged on domestic audiences by the U.S. government and media corporations, entailing censorships, persecutions of media celebrities and academics, and the production/distribution of anti-communist materials in the guises of entertainment and 'news,' all on the presumption that media have strong effects.[40]

The period also saw the rise of an oppositional, albeit marginalized, communication scholarship. In 1948, Dallas Smythe began teaching the first course on the political economy of communication, although discretion dictated that for several years the course bear the title 'The *Economics* of Communications.'[41] In the course Smythe focused primarily on electronic communication. Over time he was joined at Illinois by critical scholars George Gerbner (in 1956) and Herbert Schiller (in 1960), and a coherent oppositional, albeit marginal, American critical media studies scholarship was born. Gerbner, particularly, challenged directly the 'law of minimal effects.' He maintained that in contemporary society people attain their identities not from their families, schools, churches, and communities, but from 'a handful of conglomerates who have something to sell.' He claimed further that people who watch large amounts of television are more likely to believe that the world is mean and violent, and he backed these contentions up with prodigious empirical studies.[42] In congressional testimony of 1981 he declared, 'Fearful people are more dependent, more easily manipulated and controlled, more susceptible to deceptively simple, strong, tough measures and hard-line postures. They may accept and even welcome repression if it promises to relieve their insecurities. That is the deeper problem of violence-laden television.'[43]

Although the minimal effects model declined by the 1960s as the result of methodological problems, overdrawn conclusions, and conflicting evidence (such as provided by Hovland), another theory that had been waiting in the wings since the 1940s – namely *uses and grati-fications* – promptly took its place, becoming 'one of the most popular theories of mass communication.'[44] As noted by Wimmer and Dominick, uses and gratifications focused attention on audience members, as opposed to message senders,[45] or indeed, for that matter, on messages.[46] Christopher Simpson attributes the rebirth of 'uses and gratifications' to a 1959 paper by RAND Corporation researcher W. Phillips Davison;[47] in any event, by 1968 and publication of *Television in Politics: Its Uses and Influences* by Blumler and McQuail,[48] 'uses and gratifications' was mainstream.

Unlike minimum effects, 'uses and gratifications' did not deny the possibility of profound consequences of media on audiences; what it did assert, rather, was that consequences are anticipated and actively sought out by audiences in light of pre-existing needs and desires.[49] Once again, audiences remain in control, at least according to mainstream theory, denying political economy concerns.

Sponsors of research into persuasive communication understood 'uses and gratifications' at a more pragmatic level. To affect or control public attitudes and behaviour, message senders (moulders of pseudoenvironments) must first offer audiences something they need or desire. According to the 'uses and gratifications' school, uses of television programming include attaining information, gaining a sense of personal identity (as through role modelling), facilitating social interaction, and being entertained.[50] Each of these 'uses,' however, has major, albeit underemphasized – even unacknowledged – political economy implications: 'Attaining information,' for example – undoubtedly a goal of newspaper readers and many television viewers – poses the question of what news/information is made available to these inquiring minds and what is not – questions addressed with telling results in analyses of news content by such marginalized political economists as Edward S. Herman and Noam Chomsky.[51] As Walter Lippmann remarked, 'News and truth are not the same thing, and must be clearly distinguished; the function of news is to signalize an event, the function of truth is to bring to light the hidden facts.'[52] One of the factors causing a divorce between news and truth, Lippmann proposed, is the control exercised over reporters by media owners,[53] who in turn are responsive to desires of advertisers, both individually and as a system. Decades after Lippmann's *Public Opinion* was published, Chomsky and Herman denoted advertiser control as one of several 'filters' through which news must pass prior to publication. All these areas, and more, that are of concern to political economists and are obscured by focusing merely on the 'uses and gratifications' of audiences.[54]

Likewise, 'attaining a sense of personal identity' – another 'use and gratification' – is loaded with unacknowledged political-economic import. It is surely a goal of much advertising to set forth models of comportment; when audiences seek out and find role models in the media, they become complicit to their own political-economic control – the very definition of *hegemony*. Critical researchers George Gerbner and associates responded with 'cultivation research,' which studies 'how exposure to the world of television contributes to viewers' conceptions about the real world.'[55] For Gerbner, cultivation was all about social control by elites to benefit elites. It constituted, in essence, empirical analyses of the successes/limitations of Lippmann-styled pseudoenvironments. Gerbner's major finding was that heavy users of the medium are more likely to accept as real television's depiction of social life than are light users.

From a 'uses and gratifications' perspective, audiences also use media to provide bases for conversation and social interaction, or use media as a substitute for real-life interactions. From a political economy perspective, however, as Walter Lippmann emphasized, it is very much in the interest of elites that the general public interpret the social, political, and economic environment in ways conducive to preserving and extending elite authority, and one marvellous way of instituting this form of social control is by providing topics for daily conversation (an O.J. Simpson or Michael Jackson trial, say, or continually fretting over 'weapons of mass destruction'). Even better is if audiences forego conversations altogether, relying instead on media 'friends' for their 'socializing.' Near the end of his life, wartime propagandist John Grierson reflected on the immense propaganda potential of television, coupling as it does the audience's desire to be 'cosy' with prodigious powers of suggestion. He asked, 'Where more notably than in the home does the power of suggestion operate?'[56]

Although 'uses and gratifications' peaked by the 1980s, the doctrine may be thought of as constituting but one stream of a much broader and still contemporary anti-political economy doctrine, namely the 'active audience.' In the opening chapter of the revised edition of *The Process and Effects of Mass Communication* (1971), Wilbur Schramm immodestly claimed he had been first, way back in 1952, to suggest that audiences are 'highly active, highly selective ... manipulating rather than being manipulated by a message – a full partner in the communication process.'[57] Schramm added that his original article 'How Communication Works' was intended to be 'a reaction against ... the irrational fears of propaganda being expressed in the early 1950s.'[58] He continued, 'The unsophisticated viewpoint was that if a person could be reached by the insidious forces of propagandas carried by the mighty power of the mass media, he could be changed and converted and controlled. So propaganda became a hate word, the media came to be regarded fearfully, and laws were passed and actions taken to protect "defenseless people" against "irresistible communication."'[59] Schramm is as much as admitting that his research program was designed to neutralize or abolish the political economy of media.

The doctrine of active audiences expanded significantly over ensuing years – to such a point, indeed, that according to some contemporary proponents everyone is capable of construing his or her unique meanings from media texts.[60] Media presentations for these theorists are likened to Rorschach tests. As Paul Cobley summarizes, 'The crux of the issue is whether there are as many possible readings of a text as there are readers, or whether there may be a small number of "correct" or "legitimate" readings of a text (or even just one "correct" reading) ... For [Stanley] Fish, the reader supplies everything; this is because there can be nothing that precedes interpretation. As soon as human beings apprehend an item in the world they have already embarked on a process of interpreting it. There can be no "given" as such.'[61]

Emphasizing active audiences, again, reduces the possibility of political economy for, as the Mattelarts ask, 'What is the point in dwelling on unequal exchange of television programmes and films on the international audiovisual market if the power of meaning lies in the hands of the consumer?'[62]

Like 'uses and gratifications,' the doctrine of the 'active audience,' too, *can* be made compatible with political economy, even though advocates associated with the doctrine failed to do this. In England, Stuart Hall, for instance, suggested that the 'codes' readers bring to texts are as important as the texts themselves and that codes are class-based. Hall did not dispute that there is a dominant meaning (a 'preferred reading') to texts; to the contrary, he maintained that meanings are to be struggled over and thereby he related codes or 'readings' to political economy.[63]

Media Transfer Model

In official policy circles, the United States for decades has championed an international 'free flow' of information, albeit a 'free flow' encumbered by stringent copyright, and has justified that position with two principal contentions. First, it has claimed that 'free flow' of information and individual liberty in accessing informational artefacts are the sine qua non of democracy and of individual liberty / human rights; emerging media, viewed from this perspective, are 'technologies of freedom'[64] – certainly not instruments of oppression, domination, empire, and control. Second, in international fora, the United States claims that informational artefacts are and should be recognized as being merely economic commodities, produced and consumed for no purposes other than to satisfy consumer wants ('consumer sovereignty') and to earn pecuniary rewards for rights' holders; hence these artefacts are/should be subject to international trade rules as enforced by the World Trade Organization and other bilateral/multilateral trade arrangements, as opposed to policies of cultural organizations like UNESCO.[65]

It is evident that the 'law of minimal effects' and the doctrine of 'active audiences' (if understood as being devoid of political-economic considerations) could go a long way toward countering international concerns over America's media dominance. Even more effective, though, would be a doctrine positively promoting global media expansion. Such was the political-economic import of the 'media transfer model' as developed and promoted by luminaries like Elihu Katz, Wilbur Schramm, Lucien Pye, Daniel Lerner, and Ithiel de Sola Pool – all bankrolled by the U.S. military and CIA.[66] MIT's de Sola Pool, for example, insisted that 'where radio goes, there modernization attitudes come.'[67] Radio audiences in third world countries, according to these theorists, after being continually exposed to Western media, will wish to imitate modern (i.e., Western) attitudes and behaviour and cast off obsolete indigenous customs that inhibit economic expansion. The loss of customs and traditions that this entails is much to be desired, in the view of these authors. Alienation and dislocation, loss of referents, social and cultural upheaval, loss of sovereignty and extension of American influence were concomitants largely unmentioned by these media transfer theorists.

More recently, in a rare but deservedly renowned public utterance, State Department officials cast a rather different light on America's cultural exports and, by implication, on the media transfer model. Characterizing media exports as 'soft power' (defined as 'the ability to achieve desired outcomes in international affairs through attraction rather than coercion'),[68] Nye and Owens deemed this form of power to be as important as armaments in America's quest for world domination,[69] perhaps explaining, too, why so much of the innovation in communication media over the past hundred years – radio, satellites, computers, the Internet – is traceable to the U.S. military.[70]

Controversies surrounding 'free flow' versus 'cultural imperialism' are, of course, decades old,[71] even leading the United States and the United Kingdom to withdraw, for a time, from UNESCO,[72] as they were losing the battle there (and subsequently to fight their cause instead through international trade agreements and institutions such as the World Trade Organization). This is not the place to recount those prolonged and bitter disputes, except to note that disagreements persist to the present: virtually unilaterally, in October 2005, the United States argued and voted against UNESCO's Convention on Cultural Diversity.[73]

Poststructuralist Cultural Studies

Through foundational texts by writers like E.P. Thompson, Raymond Williams, and Richard Hoggart [as discussed at greater length in chapter 17], political economy was initially a mainstay – even the driving force – of British cultural studies.[74] Likewise did foundational Canadian cultural/media theorists, beginning with Harold Innis, who linked time/space bias of media with monopolies of knowledge, emphasize political-economic aspects of culture. However, as Sardar and van Loon remark, 'Questions of power and politics, class and intellectual formation, so fundamental to the British exponents of cultural studies, lost their significance in the United States.'[75]

Intellectual historian Richard E. Lee dates the inception of *American* cultural studies to a 1966 international conference at Johns Hopkins University, entitled 'Criticism and the Sciences of Man / Les Langages critiques et les sciences de l'homme.'[76] It was there that Paul de Man (1919–83), newly arrived at Yale, listened to a lecture by Jacques Derrida, and the Yale school of deconstruction was born.[77] Deconstruction, through de Man's influence, became 'profoundly conservative.'[78] For de Man and the Yale poststructuralists, there were 'no facts, only interpretations; no truths, only expedient fictions,' and these axioms were applied not only to literature but to the human sciences.[79]

Poststructuralism spread rapidly in the United States: from literary studies at Yale to sectors of virtually all the humanities, including media and communication studies. Elsewhere [in the next chapter], I address critically the work of two American proponents of postmodernism/poststructuralism in media/cultural studies: Lawrence Grossberg and Mark Poster. Here, though, it is worthwhile noting Poster's declaration that poststructuralism 'is a uniquely American practice,' that the writings of such seminal French poststructuralists as Derrida, Baudrillard, Lyotard, and Foucault 'have far greater currency in the United States than in France.'[80] This contention, if correct, supports the main argument developed here, namely that mainstream scholars in the United States particularly, especially in media and communication studies, have a marked proclivity to marginalize political economy.

In what sense and in what ways, though, are poststructuralism and political economy antithetical? Briefly, by emphasizing culture and language as makers of 'reality,' or the unavoidable lens through which reality is interpreted, poststructuralists deny the objectivity or the 'truths' proposed by Enlightenment rationality. Mark Poster writes, 'Language no longer represents a reality, no longer is a neutral tool to enhance the subject's instrumental rationality: language becomes or better reconfigures reality ... Electronic communication systematically removes the fixed points, the grounds, the foundations that were essential to modern theory.'[81]

But if 'reality' is merely a fabrication of language, then the concerns raised by such seminal modernists as Marx, Durkheim, Thoreau, and their successors are likewise mere linguistic fabrications, mere 'phantasmagoria,' bearing no necessary relation to material existence. Indeed, the very criteria whereby social arrangements are to be judged (equity, human dignity, environmental health, peace) become mere linguistic constructs. As Frank Webster remarks, 'Postmodernists' emphasis on differences – in interpretation, in values – is in close accord with the abandonment of belief in the authentic.'[82] Quoting Michel Foucault, he adds, 'Postmodernists believe that "each society has its regime of truth, its general politics of truth: that is, the types of discourse which it accepts and makes function as true." In such circumstances postmodern thinkers perceive themselves to be throwing off the strait-jacket of Enlightenment searches for "truth," emphasizing instead the liberating implications of *differences* of analysis, explanation and interpretation.'[83]

But it is hard to do political economy if one is preoccupied with celebrating differences in analysis, in explanation, and in interpretation.

Indeed, from this postmodernist/poststructuralist perspective, political economy would be but one more of the 'grand narratives' to be dismissed.

Moreover, postmodernist thought, if bereft of political-economic considerations regarding power centres structuring language, diffusing messages and censoring texts, in effect takes the position that 'pseudoenvironments' (or, in Baudrillard's term, 'simulacra') are all there is and all there can be. Lippmann, one senses, would be delighted. The PR agencies and other spinners and fabricators are now absolved from not only the intent to deceive, but from deception as well.

The conservative bent of poststructuralism is well illustrated by comparing the early and late writings of Jean Baudrillard. According to Poster, arguably a disciple of Baudrillard, Baudrillard initially set out to 'extend the Marxist critique of capitalism to areas that were beyond the scope of the theory of the mode of production'; later, he abandoned Marxism to take up a 'semiological model [as a way to] decipher the meaning structure of the modern commodity.'[84] Ensuing from this transition, Poster advises, Baudrillard developed the notion of '"hyperreality" [as] the new linguistic condition of society, rendering impotent theories that still rely on materialist reductionism or rationalist referentiality.'[85] In brief, Baudrillard was initially a materialist grounded in the Marxist tradition, albeit one endeavouring to extend that tradition to encompass the consumer society, and ended up as a poststructuralist for whom materialist and rational/logical explanations were 'impotent.'

When the real and the fictitious, the objective and subjective, become merely 'entangled orders of simulation ... a play of illusions and phantasms,'[86] there is little possibility for political economy. Baudrillard himself recognized this, stating, 'Power, too, for some time now produces nothing but signs of its resemblance ... Power is no longer present except to conceal that there is none.'[87] He continued, 'Is any given bombing in Italy the work of leftist extremists, or of extreme right-wing provocation, or staged by centrists to bring terror into disrepute and to shore up its own failing power, or again is it a police-inspired scenario in order to appeal to public security? All this is equally true, and the search for proof, indeed the objectivity of the fact does not check this *vertigo of interpretation*. We are in a logic of simulation which has nothing to do with a logic of facts and an order of reasons.'[88]

If 'the reality principle' is in its death throes, and if the 'vertigo of interpretations' now dwarfs facts, how can one possibly pursue justice? It would make much more sense simply to luxuriate in the consumer society and forge whimsical interpretations of media-concocted phantasms – according to Frank Webster, a common postmodernist recommendation.[89]

In this brief overview of aspects of intellectual history we have discovered several ironies and paradoxes: mainstream U.S. communication studies was born out of CIA and military funding, but issues of communicatory power (political economy) were continuously ignored in the mainstream literature; eminent media scholars engaging in psychological warfare and media propaganda avowed allegiance to a 'law of minimal effects'; America's most distinguished journalist self-avowedly attempted to save democracy by counselling elites to manufacture pseudoenvironments; authorities proclaimed in their books that authors provide little more than Rorschach tests for their readers. In such a bizarre context, is it not easy to accept that poststructuralists like Poster, drawing on Baudrillard, positioning themselves as egalitarians striking out at authority, in fact serve established power (whether by design or by inadvertence) by reducing the accountability with which power is wielded?

Summary

Although there were remarkable changes in the modes of communicating from the early 1900s to, say, the 1980s, accompanied by equally momentous changes in media theorizing by mainstream American scholars (identified here as writers most frequently cited in histories of media/communication thought), there was at least one notable constancy: the avoidance of political economy. To avoid political economy in media scholarship is to draw attention away from disparities in communicatory power and from uses to which that power is put. Some of the theorists reviewed here may honestly have believed that these issues are insignificant; others may, perhaps, more consciously have played into the hands of powerful message senders. Irrespective of motivation, the consequence in each case has been the same: mainstream American media scholarship 'justified,' through inattention, gross disparities in communicatory power.

NOTES

1 Frank Webster, *Theories of the Information Society* (London: Routledge, 1995), 163–75.

2 C.B. Macpherson, *Property: Mainstream and Critical Positions* (Toronto: University of Toronto Press, 1978), 11–12.

3 For example, James W. Carey, 'The Chicago School of Communication Research,' in *James Carey: A Critical Reader*, ed. Eve Munson and Catherine Warren, 14–33 (Minneapolis: University of Minnesota Press, 1997); Daniel Czitrom, *Media and the American Mind: From Morse to McLuhan* (Chapel Hill: University of North Carolina Press, 1982), 91–121; J.G. Delia, 'Communication Research: A History,' in *Handbook of Communication Science*, ed. Charles R. Berger and Steven Chaffee, 20–98 (Newbury Park, CA: Sage, 1987); Hanno Hardt, *Critical Communication Studies: Communication, History & Theory in America* (London, UK: Routledge, 1992), 42–76; Everett Rogers, *A History of Communication Study: A Biographical Approach* (New York: Free Press, 1994).

4 Wilbur Schramm, *The Beginnings of Communication Study in America: A Personal Memoir* (Thousand Oaks, CA: Sage, 1997), 107.

5 John Dewey, *The Public and Its Problems* (Chicago: Swallow, 1927), 98, 141.

6 Czitrom, *Media and the American Mind*, 112.

7 From an 1892 advertisement announcing its imminent publication. In Brian A. Williams, *Thought and Action: John Dewey at the University of Michigan* (Ann Arbor: Bentley Historical Library, University of Michigan, 1998), 30.

8 Stuart Ewan, *PR! A Social History of Spin* (New York: Basic Books), 111–13.

9 Charles A. Beard and Mary Beard, *The Rise of American Civilization* (New York: Macmillan, 1927), 640.

10 James Beniger, *The Control Revolution: Technological and Economic Origins of the Information Society* (Cambridge, MA: Harvard University Press, 1986).

11 T.J. Jackson Lears, 'From Salvation to Self-Realization: Advertising and the Therapeutic Roots of the Consumer Culture 1880–1930,' in *The Culture of Consumption*, ed. Richard Wightman Fox and T.J. Jackson Lears (New York: Pantheon, 1983), 21.

12 Walter Lippmann, *Public Opinion* (1922; repr., New York: Free Press, 1965), 17.

13 Ibid., 133.

14 Zbigniew Brzezinski, *Between Two Ages: America's Role in the Technetronic Era* (New York: Viking, 1970). Brzezinski, with David Rockefeller, was co-founder in 1973 of the Trilateral Commission.

15 Michel Crozier, Samuel Huntington, and Oji Watanuki, *The Crisis of Democracy* (New York: New York University Press, 1975). Regarding the United States, the Report declared,
    Some of the problems of governance in the United States today stem from an excess of democracy ... Needed ... is a greater degree of

moderation in democracy. In practice, this moderation has two major areas of application. First, democracy is only one way of constituting authority, and it is not necessarily a universally applicable one. In many situations the claims of expertise, seniority, experience, and special talents may override the claims of democracy as a way of constituting authority ... Second, the effective operation of a democratic political system usually requires some measure of apathy and noninvolvement on the part of individuals and groups. In the past, every democratic society has had a marginal population, of greater or lesser size, which has not actively participated in politics. In itself, this marginality on the part of some groups is inherently undemocratic, but it has also been one of the factors which has enabled democracy to function effectively. Marginal social groups, as in the case of the blacks, are now becoming full participants in the political system. Yet the danger of overloading the political system with demands which extend its functions and undermine its authority remains. (113–14).

16 See, for example, Maude Barlow and Tony Clark, *MAI* (Toronto: Stoddart, 1997).

17 According to the *Globe and Mail*, 'The Department of Homeland Security, along with the Patriot Act, effectively suspended the rule of law in the United States – citizens can now be searched or arrested without a warrant, imprisoned without trial, tried by secret military tribunal, tortured or executed in secrecy. Their phones can be tapped, mail read, Internet monitored, and what they read at or borrow from the library can be analyzed for signs of deviancy. The guarantees of personal liberty in the Constitution have been trampled over. Between 30,000 and 40,000 people have been detained or harassed under the Patriot act, and precious few charges involving actual terrorism have been laid as a result.' Paul William Roberts, 'The Flagging Empire,' *Globe and Mail*, 10 September 2005.

18 Lippmann, *Public Opinion*, 195.

19 D. Steven Blum, *Walter Lippmann: Cosmopolitanism in the Century of Total War* (Ithaca, NY: Cornell University Press, 1984), 9.

20 John Dewey, 'Review of Public Opinion by Walter Lippmann,' *New Republic* 30 (1922): 286–8.

21 Christopher Simpson, *Science of Coercion: Communication Research & Psychological Warfare 1945–1960* (Oxford: Oxford University Press, 1994), 16.

22 Ibid., 26–29.

23 Ibid., 52.

24 Paul F. Lazarsfeld, Bernard Berelson, and Hazel Gaudet, *The People's Choice* (New York: Duell, Sloan and Pearce, 1944).

25 See Shearon Lowery and Melvin DeFleur, *Milestones in Mass Communication Research*, 2nd ed. (New York: Longman, 1988), 31–103.
26 Simpson, *Science of Coercion*, 81.
27 Paul F. Lazarsfeld, 'Remarks on Administrative and Critical Research' (1941; repr. in *Qualitative Analysis: Historical and Critical Essays*, 157–67, Boston, MA: Allyn and Bacon, 1972). The term *critical* was coined by Max Horkheimer in a 1937 article, 'Traditionelle und Kritische Theorie'; see Rogers, *History of Communication Study*, 110.
28 Czitrom, *Media and the American Mind*, 129.
29 Hardt, *Critical Communication Studies*, 114.
30 Lowery and DeFleur, *Milestones*, 102.
31 Steven H. Chaffee and John L. Hochheimer, 'The Beginnings of Political Communication Research in the United States: Origins of the "Limited Effects" Model,' *Mass Communication Review Yearbook*, ed. Michael Gurevitch and Mark R. Levy (Beverly Hills, CA: Sage, 1985), 5:75.
32 Elihu Katz and Paul F. Lazarsfeld, *Personal Influence: The Part Played by People in the Flow of Mass Communication* (1955; repr., New York: Free Press, 1964).
33 Everett Rogers and Floyd Shoemaker, *Communication of Innovations: A Cross Cultural Approach* (New York: Free Press, 1971), chap. 6.
34 Stephen Littlejohn, *Theories of Human Communication*, 4th ed. (Belmont, CA: Wadsworth, 1992), 351.
35 Stephen H. Chafee and John L. Hochheimer, 'The Beginnings of Political Communication Research,' in *Mass Communication Review Yearbook*, ed. M. Gurevitch and M.R. Levy (Sage, CA: Beverly Hills, 1985), 5:95.
36 Lowery and DeFleur, *Milestones*, 138.
37 Wilbur Schramm, *The Beginnings of Communication Study in America: A Personal Memoir*, ed. Steven H. Chaffee and Everett M. Rogers (Thousand Oaks, CA: Sage, 1997), 101.
38 Lowery and DeFleur, *Milestones*, 137.
39 Ewen, *PR!* 78–83; Howard Zinn, *A People's History of the United States* (1980; New York: HarperPerennial, 2005), 355–57.
40 Michael Barson, *Better Dead Than Red* (New York: Hyperion, 1992); Richard A. Schwartz, *Cold War Culture: Media and the Arts, 1945–1990* (New York: Checkmark Books, 1998).
41 John Lent, 'Interview with Dallas W. Smythe,' in *A Different Road Taken: Profiles in Critical Communication*, ed. John A. Lent (Boulder, CO: Westview, 1994), 43. Emphasis added.
42 See Michael Morgan, ed., *Against the Mainstream: The Selected Works of George Gerbner* (New York: Lang, 2002).
43 As quoted in Associated Press, 'George Gerbner, Studied TV Culture,' *Washington Post*, 2 January 2006.

44 Littlejohn, *Theories*, 364. 'Uses and gratifications' constituted a portion of Lazarsfeld's research whose aim was to help media interests gain audiences.
45 Roger D. Wimmer and Joseph R. Dominick, *Mass Media Research*, 8th ed. (Belmont, CA: Wadsworth, 2005), chapter 18.
46 Littlejohn, *Theories*, 364.
47 Simpson, *Science of Coercion*, 91.
48 Jay Blumler and Denis McQuail, *Television in Politics: Its Uses and Influences* (London, UK: Faber and Faber, 1968); see also Jay Blumler and Elihu Katz, eds., *The Uses of Mass Communication* (Beverly Hills, CA: Sage, 1974).
49 Elihu Katz and Michael Gurevitch, 'Uses of Mass Communication by the Individual,' in *Mass Communication Research: Major Issues and Future Directions*, ed. W.P. Davidson and F. Yu (New York: Praeger, 1974), 12.
50 Daniel Chandler, 'Why Do People Watch Television?' Aberystwyth University, http://www.aber.ac.uk/media/Documents/short/usegrat.html.
51 Edward S. Herman and Noam Chomsky, *Manufacturing Consent: The Political Economy of Media* (New York: Pantheon, 1988).
52 Lippmann, *Public Opinion*, 226.
53 Ibid., 227.
54 Indeed, another such concept – 'consumer sovereignty' – stems from the similarly depoliticized discourse of neoclassical economics.
55 James Shanahan and Michael Morgan, *Television and Its Viewers: Cultivation Theory and Research* (Cambridge: Cambridge University Press, 1999), 7.
56 John Grierson, 'Learning from Television' (1963; repr. in *Grierson on Documentary*, ed. Forsyth Hardy, London: Faber and Faber, 1979), 210–19.
57 Wilbur Schramm, 'The Nature of Communication between Humans,' in *The Process and Effects of Mass Communication*, ed. Wilbur Schramm and Donald F. Roberts (Urbana: University of Illinois Press, 1971), 8.
58 Ibid.
59 Ibid. In the opening chapter of his original 1954 edition, Schramm writes that *The Process and Effects of Mass Communication* was a response to the USIA's need to train some of its 'new employees in the field of research and evaluation.' See Schramm, foreword in *Process and Effects*.
60 Stanley Fish, *Is There a Text in This Class? The Authority of Interpretive Communities* (Cambridge, MA: Harvard University Press, 1980). See also, Anthony Easthope, *Literary into Cultural Studies* (London, UK: Routledge, 1991), 47–51.
61 Paul Cobley, 'Interpretation, Ideation and the Reading Process,' in *The Communication Theory Reader*, ed. Paul Cobley (London: Routledge, 1996), 405, 406.
62 Armand Mattelart and Michèle Mattelart, *Theories of Communication* (London: Sage, 1995), 125.

63 Stuart Hall, 'Encoding/Decoding,' in *Culture, Media, Language*, ed. Stuart Hall, Dorothy Hobson, Andrew Lowe,.and Paul Willis (London: Hutchinson, 1980), 128–38.

64 Ithiel de Sola Pool, *Technologies of Freedom* (Cambridge, MA: Harvard University Press, 1983).

65 Sandra Braman, 'Trade and Information Policy,' *Media, Culture and Society* 12 (1990): 361–85.

66 de Sola Pool, Lerner and Schramm, all exponents of the 'media transfer model,' for decades undertook research for the CIA through the CIA-funded Center for International Studies at MIT. Schramm, according to Everett Rogers, was a part-time CIA campus informant. Dallas Smythe concurs, writing that Schramm filed surreptitious reports on Smythe's activities at the University of Illinois during the 1950s and 1960s. See Robert Babe, *Canadian Communication Thought: Ten Foundational Writers* (Toronto: University of Toronto Press, 2000), 115. Among Schramm's publications was the co-authored book, *The Reds Take a City* (New Brunswick, NJ: Rutgers University Press, 1951); material in his seminal *The Process and Effects of Mass Communication* (1954) was prepared initially as training materials for U.S. government propaganda programs. Turning to another foundational researcher, Daniel Lerner was a towering figure behind the *media as development* paradigm; by allowing modern media and their consumerist messages into 'developing countries,' modernization would occur rapidly through the demonstration effect and the desire to emulate the West, or so he argued. See Lerner, *The Passing of Traditional Society: Modernizing the Middle East* (New York: Free Press, 1958). These thoughts were taken up by, among others, Schramm, Rogers, and de Sola Pool. Even into the 1990s de Sola Pool was posthumously championing 'free flow' for giving (international) audiences what they want. See Ithiel de Sola Pool, *Technologies without Boundaries: On Telecommunications in a Global Age*, ed. Eli M. Noam (Cambridge, MA: Harvard University Press, 1990).

67 Ithiel de Sola Pool, 'Communication and Development,' in *Modernization: The Dynamics of Growth*, ed. M. Weiner (Washington DC: Voice of America, 1966), 106–10; as quoted in Gerald Sussman and John Lent, 'Introduction: Critical Perspectives on Communication and Third World Development,' in *Transnational Communications: Wiring the Third World*, ed. Gerald Sussman and John A. Lent (Newbury Park, CA: Sage, 1991), 5–6.

68 Joseph S. Nye and William A. Owens, 'America's Information Edge,' *Foreign Affairs* (March/April 1996): 20–36.

69 Ibid., 20.

70 Armand Mattelart, *Mapping World Communication: War, Progress, Culture,*

trans. Susan Emanuel and James A. Cohen (Minneapolis: University of Minnesota Press, 1994), 3–121.

71 Kaarle Nordenstreng and Herbert I. Schiller, eds., *National Sovereignty and International Communication: A Reader* (Norwood, NJ: Ablex, 1979); UNESCO, *Many Voices, One World,* McBride Commission Report (Paris: UNESCO, 1980).

72 William Preston, Edward S. Herman, and Herbert I. Schiller, *Hope and Folly: The United States and UNESCO 1945–1985* (Minneapolis: University of Minnesota Press, 1989).

73 United Nations Educational, Scientific and Cultural Organization, *Convention on the Protection and Promotion of the Diversity of Cultural Expressions* (Paris: United Nations, 2005), http://unesdoc.unesco.org/images/0014/001429/142919e.pdf.

74 Ziauddin Sardar and Borin Van Loon, *Introducing Cultural Studies* (Cambridge, UK: Icon Books, 1999), 58; Graeme Turner, *British Cultural Studies: An Introduction* (Boston: Unwin Hyman, 1990), 41–84.

75 Sardar and Van Loon, *Introducing Cultural Studies,* 58.

76 Richard E. Lee, *Life and Times of Cultural Studies: The Politics and Transformation of the Structures of Knowledge* (Durham, NC: Duke University Press, 2003).

77 Other prominent members of the Yale school of deconstruction included Harold Bloom, Geoffrey Hartman, and J. Hills Miller.

78 Lee, *Life and Times,* 156.

79 Ibid., 154.

80 Mark Poster, *Critical Theory and Poststructuralism: In Search of a Context* (Ithaca, NY: Cornell University Press, 1989), 6.

81 Mark Poster, 'The Mode of Information and Postmodernity,' in *Communication Theory Today,* ed. David Crowley and David Mitchell (Stanford, CA: Stanford University Press, 1994), 176.

82 Webster, *Theories,* 173.

83 Ibid., 167–8.

84 Mark Poster, introduction to *Jean Baudrillard: Selected Writings,* ed. Mark Poster (Stanford, CA: Stanford University Press, 2001), 1.

85 Ibid., 2.

86 Ibid., 23.

87 Ibid., 45, 46.

88 Ibid., 31. Emphasis added.

89 Webster, *Theories,* 167–8.

17 Cultural Studies, Poststructuralism, Political Economy*

So play the chords of love, my friend
Play the chords of pain
If you want to keep your song
Don't, don't, don't, don't play the chords of fame.
— Phil Ochs (1970)

What Is Cultural Studies?

John Hartley begins his book on the history of cultural studies with the following, possibly perplexing, observation: 'There is little agreement about what counts as cultural studies ... The field is riven by fundamental disagreements about what cultural studies is for, in whose interests it is done, what theories, methods and objects of study are proper to it, and where to set its limits.'[1]

Some definers of cultural studies cast their nets far and wide. An entry in Wikipedia, for instance, suggests that cultural studies 'combines political economy, communication, sociology, social theory, literary theory, media theory, film/video studies, cultural anthropology, philosophy, museum studies and art history/criticism to study cultural phenomena in various societies.'[2] Likewise, Blundell, Shepherd, and Taylor remark that among the 'resources' available to cultural studies are 'the disciplines of English literature, sociology, communication, anthropology, linguistics and various forms of semiology, film and tel-

---

* Adapted from Robert E. Babe, *Cultural Studies and Political Economy: Toward a New Integration* (Lanham, MD: Lexington Books, 2009).

evision studies, and, more recently, art history and musicology.' They continue, 'Cultural studies takes these resources, interrogates them, adapts them to the task at hand, and interpellates them within its own continuously developing theoretical matrices.'[3] Richard Johnson apparently agrees, declaring that cultural studies is both winnower and scavenger, 'stealing away the more useful elements [of other disciplines] and rejecting the rest.'[4] Blundell, Shepherd, and Taylor claim that writing histories of cultural studies or describing its 'schools' is quite difficult, that really 'the most that is possible are accounts from various practitioners, each account being informed by the practitioner's own biography and relation to cultural studies.'[5] Likewise, Sardar and Van Loon declare, 'Cultural studies is ... a collective term for diverse and often contentious intellectual endeavours that address numerous questions, and consist of many different theoretical and political positions.'[6] In brief, according to the foregoing, cultural studies is difficult to pin down and hence to analyse or critique.

In this chapter, however, I propose that cultural studies is not nearly as formless or inchoate as these excerpts indicate, that its main fissures are readily identifiable. One major fissure is between cultural materialism and poststructuralism. *Cultural materialism* was how the inaugurators of British cultural studies (Raymond Williams, Richard Hoggart, and E.P. Thompson) envisaged the emerging field as they set out to understand and describe working-class culture as a 'full rich life,'[7] including but not limited to language practices and literature. Cultural materialism was also implicit in how the Frankfurt school, represented in this chapter by Max Horkheimer and Theodor Adorno, inaugurated their style of cultural studies through the construct of the *culture industry*. Poststructuralist cultural studies,[8] on the other hand, particularly as it developed in the United States, focuses on the language component of culture to such an extent that it often seems to address little else. The emphasis on language, and the denial that language can represent material reality, constitutes fundamental differences in ontology between cultural materialism and poststructuralism.

There are other points of departure between cultural materialism and poststructuralist cultural studies, too, such as macro versus micro views and long-term versus short-term concerns. As inaugurated by Raymond Williams and other British theorists, cultural studies was to be holistic ('macro') and take into account long-term trends.[9] By contrast, according to contemporary American poststructuralists Lawrence Grossberg and Janice Radway, 'Cultural studies is committed to the radically contextual [i.e., micro], historically specific [i.e., short-term] character not only of cultural practices but also of the production of knowledge within cultural studies itself.'[10] These terms, *radically contextual* and *historically specific*, accurately describe poststructuralist cultural studies' emphasis on specific occurrences as opposed to general or abstract structures that influence, or even determine, specificities.[11]

Again, in a more recent formulation, in his capacity as editor of the journal *Cultural Studies*, Grossberg declared cultural studies to be 'a *radically contextual* practice of the *articulation* of knowledge and power.'[12] *Articulation*, in fact, is a key element in poststructuralists' arsenal of analytical tools and hence warrants some attention here. Articulation alludes to what is taken to be the pliable and essentially fluid nature of structures. The concept has been associated particularly with Grossberg's mentor, Stuart Hall. In an interview with Grossberg, Hall remarked that he liked using the term because of its double meaning. On the one hand, Hall noted, *articulation* means 'to utter or speak forth,' thereby connoting 'language-ing.' On the other, it means 'joining temporarily,' as when a truck (or 'lorry') is connected to a trailer. 'The two parts are connected to each other,' Hall explained, 'but through a specific linkage that can be broken.'[13] As easily, and even more appropriately, however, Hall might have used a linguistic example in place of the truck-trailer analogy, for instance when the letters *s-c-h* are brought together with other letters to spell *school*, are 'de-articulated' to form such words as *secondary, classroom*, and *honours*, and are 're-articulated' for *schlock*. Or when a noun is articulated with an adjective and a verb to form a sentence. In any event, *articulation* in poststructuralist cultural studies illustrates well the linguistic bent and is to be viewed as a major point of departure from both cultural materialism and political economy, both of which assume that structures in the material world are not nearly as transitory or pliable as is evidently presumed by poststructuralism.

Finally, another and related difference between cultural materialism and poststructuralist cultural studies concerns the status of *the dialectic*. The very name *cultural materialism* (and indeed the title of one of Williams's books, *Problems in Materialism and Culture*) indicates dialectical interplay and tension between material conditions and (among other things) language practices. In contrast, poststructuralists insist we reject dialectical thinking; in poststructuralist Mark Poster's words, we must shift our attention from action in the material world to language,[14] and again, 'As we bid farewell to the proletariat we must close the books on a whole epoch of politics, the era of the dialectic and the class struggle.'[15] Poster claims that we are so irretrievably caught up in language that we can never fathom the complexities of the material world, and we might as well simply accept that and focus our attention exclusively on language. In brief, he rejects dialectical interaction between language and the non-linguistic realm. For Grossberg, likewise, *articulation* takes the place of the dialectic in social studies.

Another split within cultural studies is between *critical* and *celebratory* cultural studies. At issue here is the treatment of power. Celebratory cultural studies proposes either that message recipients make their own meanings (the 'active reader' thesis) or that people select cultural products from a vast array of possibilities to best satisfy their pre-existing wants and needs ('uses and gratifications') – or, setting theory aside, that media products are just plain fun. By contrast, *critical* cultural studies emphasizes asymmetries and injustices in the distribution of communicatory/cultural power, focusing particularly on power possessed by elite message producers. Although poststructuralists often view their work as being critical,[16] in fact it often merges with celebratory cultural studies by unduly proposing radical interpretive freedom and variants of uses and gratifications theory, particularly the purported capacity of media users to easily reconstruct identities.

Today, exponents of poststructuralist cultural studies often write as if *their* presumptions and *their* modes of analysis encompass the entire cultural studies field. Notwithstanding the fragmentation noted above of cultural studies, when poststructuralist cultural studies scholars denigrate political economy, as they are wont to do, they usually do so as if they were speaking for the entire field. Arguably, the differences between poststructuralists and political economists today, however, are no greater than differences between poststructuralists and cultural materialists; indeed, I contend, the differences are identical! So, when poststructuralists like Lawrence Grossberg, Angela McRobbie, Mark Poster, Jean Baudrillard, and others point to irreconcilable differences between cultural studies and political economy,[17] one should be aware that really they are representing only their particular (poststructuralist) mode of cultural studies, not the entire field.

A main thesis of this chapter is that a momentous change occurred when poststructuralism displaced cultural materialism as the predominant cultural studies paradigm and that this change is the source of the split between contemporary cultural studies and political economy.[18] The present chapter explores the origins and foundations of cultural studies and establishes the initial unity with political economy, the implication being that for cultural studies and political economy to be reintegrated there must be a resurgence in the original cultural studies paradigm, namely cultural materialism, and a waning of poststructuralist cultural studies.

It is of some urgency to overcome the split, to reconcile or reintegrate political economy and cultural studies. On the one hand, to study culture without taking into account either the influence of the political-economic base or the political-economic consequences of cultural activities is to be naive in the extreme. These oversights, moreover, can cause one to misconstrue oppression as pluralism, persuasion as democracy, and elite control as popular freedom. They also can entail a flight from lived conditions into the safe haven of language or discourse, making thereby the pursuit of social justice (as but one example) impossible. Mark Poster, for instance writes, 'It becomes increasingly difficult, or even pointless, for the subject to distinguish a "real" existing "behind" the flow of signifiers.'[19] He continues, 'The tendency in poststructuralism is therefore to regard truth as a multiplicity, to exult in the play of diverse meanings, in the continual process of reinterpretation, in the contention of opposing claims.'[20] Obviously, it becomes impossible to even conceive of social justice in these circumstances.

On the other hand, to over-emphasize the political-economic determinants to the neglect of human volition and interpretive freedom is also detrimental. Denying or belittling human agency is tantamount to denigrating human dignity and is to understate the possibility of social reform.

This chapter argues that there is a balance, a dialectical middle ground, that must be sought after, achieved, and maintained. And that middle ground is precisely what the foundational writers featured in this chapter – Theodor Adorno and Raymond Williams – achieved through their *cultural materialism*. And that balance is precisely what was lost in cultural studies' poststructuralist turn.

To see how cultural studies was conceived at its beginnings, then, I propose two major points of origin. One is Britain, where Raymond Williams turned from literary analyses of 'great works' to critical appreciations or 'readings' of everyday life. Stuart Hall, Lawrence Grossberg, and many others have nominated Raymond Williams, along with Richard Hoggart and E.P. Thompson, as inaugurators, certainly, of *British* cultural studies. A second point of origin is the Frankfurt school and in particular Theodor Adorno. Terry Eagleton, a former student of Raymond Williams, wrote, 'It was the Frankfurt School which first turned serious attention to mass culture, and so lies at the origin of what is known today as Cultural Studies.'[21] Other points of origin, too, can be identified. Particularly compelling are the fascist prison cells where Antonio Gramsci was incarcerated from 1926 to 1937. Raymond Williams regarded Gramsci's work on hegemony as 'one of the major turning points in Marxist cultural theory.'[22] Today, Gramsci's term *hegemony* is virtually a household word. His contributions to cultural theory are undoubtedly seminal and highly significant. While Gramsci's work is not considered further here, it is clear that fuller consideration would assuredly support, not refute, the main thesis: in its beginnings cultural studies was fully integrated with, and not antithetical to, political economy.

Raymond Williams (British Cultural Studies)

Raymond Williams (1921–88), a self-proclaimed 'Welsh European' (as opposed to an English subject or person of British ancestry),[23] is the most renowned of the three founders of British cultural studies. According to Graham Murdock, 'Raymond Williams ... did more than anyone else to map out the terrain that cultural studies would come to occupy.'[24] Like Hoggart and Thompson, Williams believed that democracy requires that working-class culture be authenticated. Williams authored over twenty scholarly books, some seven novels, several plays, and was editor or co-editor of numerous other volumes.[25] His first book, *Culture and Society 1780–1950*, published in 1958, is the second chronologically of the three founding texts of British cultural studies.

Cultural and Society traces changes in the meaning of culture gleaned from the writings of a succession of British authors over a period of 170 years. Williams's objective was to develop 'a new general theory of culture' by interrelating all of culture's major elements[26] – *industry, democracy, class*, and *art* – to show that as these changed, so did the meaning of culture.[27] Political-economic concerns, then, are built into the very core of Williams's theory of culture. Indeed, he declared, 'The development of the word *culture* is a record of a number of important and continuing reactions to these changes in our social, economic, and political life';[28] and again, 'Our meaning of culture is a response to the events which our meanings of industry and democracy most evidently define.'[29] For Williams, *culture* is 'a special kind of map by means of which the nature of the changes [including political-economic changes] can be explored.'[30] For example, when traditionalists equate culture with elitist ('high') culture,[31] they are being anti-democratic, for the implication is that working people are inferior and hence incapable of participating wisely in political affairs. This class bias, according to Williams, infused the schools, which he thought normally reinforced existing social relations.[32]

A virtue of T.S. Eliot's famous but otherwise conservative essay *Notes towards the Definition of Culture* (1948), according to Williams, is its treatment of culture not just as elite culture, but also as 'a whole way of life.'[33] Eliot pronounced that 'culture includes all the characteristic activities and interests of a people: Derby Day, Henley Regatta, the twelfth of August,[34] a cup final, the dog races, the pin table, the dart board, Wensleydale cheese, boiled cabbage cut into sections, beetroot in vinegar, nineteenth century Gothic churches, and the music of Elgar.'[35]

This notion of culture as a whole way of life, which Williams appropriated, did not originate with Eliot, however. Williams understood that it had already become commonplace within anthropology and sociology, and that it may even be traced to such literary theorists as Coleridge (1772–1834) and Carlyle (1795–1881). As compared to those literary conservatives,[36] however, Williams's innovation was to apply this broad conception of culture as an antidote to elitist schools of thought. It is true, Williams affirmed, that as a result of its historically subservient position, the working class had not (yet) contributed substantially to culture in the restricted sense of a body of imaginative and intellectual 'works.' But then, for him, 'a culture can never be reduced to its artifacts while it is being lived.'[37] What the working class *had* accomplished, and magnificently so, was the creation of institutions based on a collectivist view of society: trade unions, the cooperative movement, a political party. And this, too, is culture – albeit in the broader and deeper sense of 'a whole way of life.'[38]

Moreover, Williams noted, working-class people often engage in a wide range of 'skilled, intelligent, and creative activity,' such as gardening, carpentry, metal working, and politics, which not only give pleasure but also improve community life. From the contemptuous eye of the highly literate, such activities are likely be scorned. But for Williams (displaying a high degree of reflexivity), the contempt of the highly literate 'is a mark of the observers' limits, not those of the activities themselves.'[39] Indeed, he maintained that the highly literate are 'deluded' when they judge the quality of life by the standard of great literature: 'The error resembles that of the narrow reformer who supposes that farm labourers and village craftsmen were once uneducated, merely because they could not read.'[40]

Rather than seeking out and documenting 'proletariat literature' or other working-class 'works,' Williams proposed it would be better to focus on 'alternative ideas of the nature of social relationship.'[41] Whereas *individualism* is the hallmark of bourgeois social relationships, and *service* (or noblesse oblige) characterizes an authoritarian, aristocratic, protective stance, Williams claimed we can 'properly associate' the following with the working-class conception of social relationship: communism, socialism, cooperation, community, solidarity, and neighbourhood. Each of these terms connotes a conception of society as neither neutral (as in the bourgeois or liberal view), nor protective (as in the paternalistic conception), but rather as 'the positive means for all kinds of development, including individual development.'[42]

Like Hoggart, Williams was at pains to distinguish between popular culture as transmitted by mass media and authentic working-class culture: 'We cannot fairly or usefully describe the bulk of the material produced by the new means of communication as "working class culture,"' he insisted. 'For neither is it by any means produced exclusively for this class, nor, in any important degree, is it produced by them.'[43] Williams and Hoggart both saw commodified entertainment, rather, as eroding authentic working-class culture.

Williams dated the onset of commercialized culture, particularly the routine commodification of literary works, to the late eighteenth century. In support of this claim he cited Adam Smith, who not only noted the narrow, class-based origin of most cultural works (an observation having affinity to Innis's monopolies of knowledge), but who also may be regarded as anticipating Gramsci's notion of *hegemony*.[44] For Williams, however, Smith's remarks were most notable for depicting conditions whereby artists' works were 'purchased, in the same manner as shoes or stockings.'[45] The commodification of cultural production, Williams added, 'followed inevitably from the institution of commercial publishing.'[46]

For Williams, the commodification of cultural artefacts caused a rift in conceptions of both art and the role of the artist. In the period of the romantics (Blake, Shelley), genuine art was viewed as issuing from the superior imagination and as being a vehicle for the perfection of humankind. Art produced for the marketplace, on the other hand, stems merely from 'the calculating faculty.'[47] From this distinction, it was not a huge leap for literary critics such as F.R. Leavis and Matthew Arnold to set 'high' art (as appreciated by the elite) against 'low' art (or 'art' for the plebs). For Williams, however, that distinction bore all sorts of anti-democratic ramifications, which he set out to rectify, his method being, essentially, to recast the notion of culture from *culture as art* into the axiom, *culture as a whole way of life*.[48]

In this foundational cultural studies book, and consistently with his interweaving political economy, Williams acknowledged that 'the dominant class can to a large extent control the transmission and distribution of the whole common inheritance.' He explained, 'A tradition is always selective, and there will always be a tendency for this process of selection to be related to and even governed by the interests of the class that is dominant. These factors make it likely that there will be qualitative changes in the traditional culture when there is a shift of class power.'[49] Williams also insisted, however, that 'communication is not only transmission; it is also reception and response.'[50] In this, as in so many other ways, he advanced a unity between what are now known as cultural studies and political economy. Regarding transmission, he stated that 'any governing body will seek to implant the "right" ideas in the minds of those whom it governs.' But he then quickly qualified that observation by noting that interpretation by message receivers depends not only upon their skill with the language but as well on their 'whole experience,' adding, 'Any real theory of communication is a theory of community.'[51] At first blush this latter claim might seem to be in accord with the hypothesis of radical interpretive freedom as advanced by active reader theorists and poststructuralism; Williams, however, as noted in greater detail below, made a significant qualification: he viewed interpretive freedom as being constrained by class.

Williams's version of cultural studies, as inaugurated in his foundational book, differs markedly from contemporary poststructuralist cultural studies in several other ways, too. Many poststructuralists today claim that meaning is in language, that one can never escape language to get at the 'real' state of affairs, or indeed that no 'real' exists beyond language. For Williams, however, changes in the meanings of words (for instance, in such words as *culture, industry, art,* and *democracy*), and the invention of new words, are responses to changes in the lived conditions. Indeed, for him, changes in the meanings of words constitute 'a record' of reactions to changes in social, economic, and political life. That record, therefore, becomes a type of 'map' guiding explorations into the nature of those changes.[52] Among the words originating in the 'decisive period' from 1750 to 1850, are '*ideology, intellectual, rationalism, scientist, humanitarian, utilitarian, romanticism, atomistic, bureaucracy, capitalism, collectivism, commercialism, communism, doctrinaire, equalitarian, liberalism, masses, medieval* and *medievalism, operative* (noun), *primitivism, proletariat* (a new word for 'mob'), *socialism, unemployment, cranks, highbrow, -isms,* and *pretentious.'*[53]

According to Williams, moreover, words and concepts developed in previous times cannot be applied with equanimity or without modification to current situations. Meanings change as lived experience changes; there is interaction between language and lived conditions.[54] Williams's emphasis on language reflects his vocation as an English professor, an orientation he certainly shared with contemporary poststructuralists. However, by insisting on a two-way interaction between language and material conditions, he was far removed from contemporary poststructuralism.

Culture and Society was first in what can now be regarded as a family of books, others including *The Long Revolution* (1961), *Keywords* (1976), *Problems in Materialism and Culture* (1980), and *The Year 2000* (1983). The later tomes further clarified and extended the author's position regarding interdependencies between culture and political-economic conditions and trends. Elsewhere I have addressed matters raised but left underdeveloped in *Culture and Society* but dealt with more extensively in his later books – treatments of the 'mass,' the relation between base and superstructure (economic determinism), and technological determinism.[55]

Theodor Adorno (Frankfurt School)

Through their concept of *the culture industry* (that is, enterprises engaged in the mass production, reproduction, and distribution for profit of cultural artefacts),[56] Theodor Adorno and Max Horkheimer laid the foundation for a cultural studies rife with political-economic considerations. For these authors, to adequately understand culture it is insufficient merely to depict general relations between various cultural products (say, musical genres) and social life. Rather, one needs to explore how cultural products help organize society (allocate leisure time and promote passivity and conformity in audiences, for example), and address in detail the production, reproduction, distribution, exchange, and consumption of cultural commodities.[57]

In what follows I summarize Adorno's seminal contributions to a nascent political economy of media as contained in his foundational cultural studies texts. Although often writing with regard to media products of the 1940s and earlier, the connections he forged between cultural production and power remain as pertinent as ever. The goal here is not to canvass the full corpus of Adorno's work.[58] Rather, the point is simply that in formulating and forwarding *the culture industry* as an important analytical category, Adorno (with Horkheimer) helped introduce a political economy mode of media analysis, major aspects of which were later elaborated by successor political economists, and he did so in such a way as to integrate what are today regarded as critical political economy and cultural studies.

Commodification of Culture

In his 1944 essay with Horkheimer entitled 'The Culture Industry' (published in English in 1977), and in articles compiled posthumously as a book bearing the same title, Adorno claimed that cultural production had by then become an industrial process akin to other industrial processes. The 'culture industry,' like other industries, he proposed, produces and purveys commodities for profit in response to market conditions, including revenues, costs, market structures, marketing/ advertising, competition, and so on. For Adorno, 'Culture now impresses the same stamp on everything; films, radio and magazines make up a system which is uniform as a whole and in every part.'[59]

Adorno is sometimes criticized for insisting that the culture industry produces sameness in cultural commodities. Postmodernists, particularly, point to the seemingly enormous range of cultural commodities from which individuals can select to construct and reconstruct personal 'identities.'[60] However, as noted by Stephen Crook, using mass-produced commodities to construct 'identities' or 'lifestyles' actually entails a good deal of conformity, and hence this practice can be understood as affirming Adorno's essential position. 'The successful adoption of a lifestyle is only possible, only recognizable as such on the basis of conformity,' Crook writes. Indeed, he goes further to suggest that 'postmodernizing change might be seen as intensifying, rather than relaxing, pressures toward dependency and conformism through the demand for information.'[61]

For Adorno, the culture industry has become a 'totality' through which 'the whole world is made to pass,'[62] so much so that it now controls both 'high' and 'low' art, obscuring or effacing demarcations that for centuries had delimited the two.[63] In previous eras, according to Adorno, high art served the noble function of critique by providing 'negative knowledge of the actual world.'[64] (Prime examples of this, one might interject, were the Dadaist painters and sculptors of the 1920s in Weimar Germany, prior to the tight state control under fascism of art for propagandistic purposes.[65]) Fulfilling the important role of critique was possible, according to Adorno, only because and to the extent that artists are free from pressures to conform. To be sure, in both the Middle Ages and the Renaissance there had often been a 'unity of style,' as influenced by the respective structures of social power. Nonetheless, Adorno insisted, the truly great artists frequently transcended conformist pressures. However, contemporaneous with the rise of mass media, which is to say with the birth of the culture industry, 'high art' became transformed. Retaining still perhaps vestiges of its venerable critical function, high art now, for the most part, reveals 'obedience to the social hierarchy'; it has become little more than mere style.[66] Contemporary high art is renowned less for its 'autonomous essence,' or for its 'own specific content and harmonious formation,' than for its money value attributable to its role as status symbol.[67] Adorno and Horkheimer summarized, 'The prestige seeker replaces the connoisseur ... No object [today] has an inherent value; it is valuable only to the extent that it can be exchanged.'[68]

'Low' or popular art likewise is diminished, in Adorno's view. No longer the authentic voice of working people, low art has been taken over and commodified by the culture industry. Through easy replication, mass distribution, and centralized administration, mass culture is packaged 'as a commodity for narcissistic consumption,'[69] depriving individuals 'from coming to consciousness of themselves as subjects.'[70]

Dialectic of Art

Music, like all art, for Adorno, is intrinsically dialectical. On the one hand, music is 'the immediate manifestation of impulse'; on the other, it is 'the locus of its taming.'[71] By expressing impulse, for instance, impulse is 'tamed.' The 'disciplining function' of music has long been known. But, in the age of the culture industry, the contradictions are taken to a new level. When working people made their own music, it rebelled against conventions and oppression through 'impulse, subjectivity and profanation'; when music is produced by the culture industry, however, 'the listener is converted, along his line of least resistance, into the acquiescent purchaser ... Representatives of the opposition to the authoritarian schema become witnesses to the authority of commercial success.'[72] Music complements the reduction of people to silence, filling 'the pockets of silence that develop between people moulded by anxiety, work and undemanding docility.'[73]

Adorno and Horkheimer chose the term the culture industry, rather than mass culture, to emphasize that non-elite culture for the most part no longer arises spontaneously from the grass roots; nor is it to be understood as the contemporary form of popular culture.[74] Rather, they insisted, the outputs of the culture industry are consciously and purposefully manufactured by elites whose intent is to make money.[75] Whereas authentic popular culture, for Adorno, is not merely rebellious but is also an 'expression of suffering and contradiction [whereby people attempt] to maintain a grasp on the idea of the good life,'[76] productions from the culture industry falsely insist that 'the good life' is attainable here and now, that by conforming to the consumptionist ethic happiness is available immediately.

Control of Consciousness

In his analysis of the astrology column of the Los Angeles Times, Adorno pointed to its essentially conservative ideology, its justifying of the status quo, and its promulgating social conformity.[77] The column implicitly urged readers to adjust themselves 'to the commands of the stars at given times,' emphasizing thereby 'the individual's powerlessness' in the face of cosmic design, which the column compensated for 'with suggestions of unexpected good fortune, assistance and the like.'[78] Adorno's editor, J.M. Bernstein, adds, 'What holds for astrology exemplifies the culture industry generally from advertising to film and television.'[79]

As a means of promoting conformity, Adorno and Horkheimer remarked that radio was clearly an advance over the telephone, as it turns 'all participants into listeners ... No machinery of rejoinder has been devised.'[80] (Since Adorno's time, of course, talk radio – ostensibly a two-way forum – has become the rage; arguably listeners who call in, however, are often little more than sounding boards for the radio host.) For Adorno and Horkheimer, technological innovations of all sorts, not just mass media, deepen elite control over society: 'A technological rationale is the rationale of domination itself.'[81]

Curtailing controversy by controlling discussion of basic issues is not the only means whereby the culture industry strengthens the already powerful. Also important is the diversionary function of entertainment. According to Adorno and Horkheimer, in what might be seen as an unduly puritanical declaration but one nonetheless pinpointing an important elite strategy and typical audience response, 'Pleasure always means not to think about anything, to forget suffering even where it is shown. Basically it is helplessness. It is flight; not, as is asserted, flight from a wretched reality, but from the last remaining thought of resistance. The liberation which amusement promises is freedom from thought and from negation.'[82]

Moreover, according to Adorno, the culture industry constructs reality for its audiences. Referring to the movies of the 1940s (but anticipating by decades the enculturation studies of George Gerbner and colleagues), Adorno and Horkheimer remarked on 'the old experience of the movie-goer, who sees the world outside as an extension of the film he has just left ... The illusion [prevails] that the outside world is the straightforward continuation of that presented on the screen.'[83] Adorno later qualified these remarks, writing, 'What the culture industry presents people with in their free time ... is indeed consumed and accepted, but with a kind of reservation, in the same way that even the most naïve theatre or filmgoers do not simply take what they behold there for real ... It is not quite believed in. It is obvious that the integration of consciousness and free time has not yet completely succeeded.'[84]

Adorno and Horkheimer suggested also that the leisure industry prolongs and extends work because 'entertainment' often attunes workers into fitting the requirements of capitalist society.[85] Adorno gave sports as an example, speculating that the physical exertion and 'functionalization' of the body in team activity subtly train people into modes of behaviour required by the workplace.[86] 'Sports,' he wrote, 'is not play but ritual in which the subjected celebrate their subjection; they parody freedom in their readiness for service, a service which the individual exacts from his own body.' The athlete, he continued, plays the role of the master by inflicting on his 'slave' (his own body) 'the same injustice he has already endured at the violent hands of society.'[87] Sports as indoctrination has been the subject of several studies since the time of Adorno.[88] More generally, Adorno thought that experiences of mass culture are 'inevitably after-images of the work process itself ... so profoundly does mechanization determine the manufacture of leisure goods.'[89]

Furthermore, Adorno claimed that centralized administration had transformed mass culture 'into a medium of undreamed of psychological control.'[90] This it accomplished through positive and negative messages, prescriptions, taboos, schemata, and stereotypes. Stereotypical images and schematized themes, Deborah Cook explains, enlarging on Adorno, 'prevent individuals from thinking beyond the given.'[91] She claims Adorno was among the first to compare the products of the culture industry with Nazi propaganda, arguing that in both cases stereotypes and schemata play upon the emotions and irrational impulses of mass audiences in order to undermine their critical and rational thought.[92]

For Adorno, products of the culture industry are layered with meanings, with the hidden layers often being the more important as they bypass the defences of consciousness.[93] He wrote, 'Probably all the various levels in mass media involve *all* the mechanisms of consciousness and unconsciousness stressed by psychoanalysis.'[94] Layers of meanings, indeed, constituted one of several portals whereby Adorno introduced Freudian categories into his analysis. Whereas layers of meaning are used by the culture industry to 'handle' audiences, multiplicity of meanings also implies that the culture industry can never take for granted the effects intended for audiences.[95]

Matters for Adorno, however, are yet more complex. For example, whereas 'heterodox ideology' is often used by the culture industry to attract interest, in the end orthodoxies are invariably promoted. Often the more sensationalist a newspaper is, for example (the *Toronto Sun*, perhaps?), the more conservative its orientation. Adorno remarked that tabloid newspapers often use excesses to attract circulation, but in the end affirm a conventional 'moral of the story.'[96] Likewise, many feature films today contain 'excesses' to attract audience interest, but in the end they support existing distributions of political and economic power (*Pearl Harbor, Armageddon*, and *Independence Day*, for example). (It is also likely, however, that a critical mainstream cinema is much more evident in our day than it was in Adorno's – *Fahrenheit 911, The Corporation, Blood Diamond, Syriana, Manufacturing Consent* being prime examples).

Political Economy of Art and Knowledge

While cultural monopolies may appear to be strong, according to Adorno and Horkheimer, in fact they are weak: they 'cannot afford to neglect their appeasement of the real holders of power if their sphere of activity in mass society ... is not to undergo a series of purges.'[97] The authors here may have had in mind purges against critical artists in Nazi Germany (Bertoldt Brecht, Fritz Lang, the Berlin Dadaists and Expressionists, for instance), but closer to home they became only too familiar with American intolerance during the Red Scare of the 1950s and beyond.

In addition to political/military repressions and pressures, of course, there are also the corporations – what Raymond Williams termed 'extra-parliamentary formations of political and economic power,'[98] which include the great financial institutions and transnational corporations. Indeed, Horkheimer and Adorno provided a rudimentary description of the entanglement of cultural monopolies and larger political-economic structures: 'The dependence of the most powerful broadcasting company [NBC] on the electrical industry [GE], or of the motion picture industry on the banks, is characteristic of the whole sphere, whose individual branches are themselves economically interwoven.'[99] In making these claims Horkheimer and Adorno were prescient, as one of the major activities of present-day critical political economy is mapping lines of control over concentrated media by advertisers and large industrial structures, by the military, and by governments.[100]

Adorno wrote also of 'servile intellectuals'[101] who downplay the control aspects of the culture industry and celebrate instead its fun and democratic veneer. *Uses and gratifications* theorists, for example, insist that audiences, not media companies, are in control as audiences purportedly select from a vast array of media offerings in accordance with their pre-existing needs and preferences (the doctrine of consumer sovereignty). One such 'need' is to be entertained, and we just saw Adorno's riposte to that. Another is to perceive order or pattern in an otherwise chaotic existence. Adorno acknowledged that need, too, but claimed the media's *covert* response is to inculcate ideology. He explained, 'The concepts of order which it [the culture industry] hammers into human beings are always those of the status quo. They remain unquestioned, unanalysed and undialectically presupposed ... The power of the culture industry's ideology is such that conformity has replaced consciousness.'[102]

In the face of all this, Adorno contended, the public remains largely placid. Although not unaware of the deceptions inherent in the proffers of the culture industry, he suggested, people tend to view the fleeting gratifications as adequate compensation.[103] On the other hand, as noted previously, he also claimed that people's 'deep unconscious mistrust' keeps them from construing the world entirely in accordance with the culture industry's representations.[104]

The Poststructuralist Turn (American Cultural Studies)

As noted in chapter 16, *American* cultural studies began in 1966. At the heart of the breach between political economy and poststructuralist cultural studies today is a difference in ontology attributable to that poststructuralist turn. To establish this point, I focus here on a written debate (1996) between Nicholas Garnham, representing political economy, and Lawrence Grossberg, representing poststructuralist cultural studies. Here are the pertinent passages:

> GARNHAM: The rejection of false consciousness within cultural studies goes along with the rejection of truth as a state of the world, as opposed to the temporary effect of discourse. But without some notion of grounded truth the ideas of emancipation, resistance, and progressiveness become meaningless. Resistance to what, emancipation from what and for what, progression toward what?[105]
>
> GROSSBERG: Thus the category of false consciousness returns – actually it has never left political economy. According to Garnham, without such a notion (and the related notion of truth), intellectuals have no valid role. And cultural studies of course rejects such notions.[106]

According to poststructuralists, 'truth' is always, and is merely, a matter of interpretation, whether on the part of an individual or as a consensus attained through social interaction. Truth is not to be discovered, but simply invented, constructed, interpreted, or agreed to – for a while. The same poststructuralist doubts apply to 'authenticity.' In a world overcome by simulations, hyperrealities, copies without originals and radical freedom to interpret, the notion of authenticity has no place, poststructuralists maintain. There are many 'truths,' on every issue, none more valid than any other. And these 'truths,' moreover, are quite provisional, merely awaiting reinterpretation. Hence, regarding cultural studies itself, Grossberg declared, 'The fact that cultural studies starts with a particular position cannot define its future – that is indeed one of its peculiarities and strengths.'[107]

Critical political economy, on the other hand, is by definition an evaluative discipline; it judges events and conditions by *values* deemed to have some philosophical, experiential, or moral grounding. It is a scholarly discipline dedicated to the pursuit of social justice. Pursuing social justice in the material world, however, is impossible if one accepts the poststructuralist position that there is now a rupture between language and material reality, for if we are trapped within language, as is contended, we can know nothing of our material conditions. If we can know nothing of the material world, it follows that we cannot pursue social justice, except perhaps through 'language-ing' and linguistic 'articulations.'

Furthermore, there is the related poststructuralist proposition that in the contemporary (postmodern) era of simulacra and articulations, both cause and effect (causation) and rationality (logic) are anachronistic baggage. According to Mark Poster, for example, 'Linearity and causality are the spatial and temporal orderings of the now by-passed modern era.'[108] But if an effect has no cause or causes, there can be no (efficacious) policies, which is again tantamount to dismissing the pursuit of social justice, which is the heart of political economy. And if rationality (logic) is dead, so too must all scholarship be, such as political economy, which is based on reason.

In the form of a question, Grossberg briefly set out the terms whereby he could envisage closer collaboration of cultural studies with political economy. 'The question,' he wrote, 'is whether it is possible to have a political economy theorized around *articulation* rather than strict determination or necessity.'[109] (Note that Grossberg chose not to say 'theorized around interpretation rather than truth or authenticity,' although that would have represented his position equally well.) Grossberg defined *articulation* as 'the production of identity on top of differences, of unities out of fragments, of structures across practices,' adding that 'articulation links this practice to that effect, this text to that meaning, this meaning to that reality, this experience to those politics; and these links are themselves articulated into larger structures, etc.'[110] More briefly, according to Grossberg, articulation is *'the production of the real.'*[111] Likewise, Grossberg's mentor, Stuart Hall, has described articulation as the forging of a whole or a structure out of parts, parts that 'are related as much through their differences as through their similarities,' adding that these parts inevitably relate to one another in terms of dominance and subordination.[112]

These declarations and definitions imply that there are few if any limitations with regard to what can be joined, few or no irreversibles, few bonds that cannot be broken, few constraints on creating and disassembling structures. Articulation implies *enormous freedom to do*.

The foregoing declarations and definitions, then, certainly do not call attention to disparities across sectors of society or among individuals in their relative capacities *to do*. Nor do they even hint at the capacity of some to prevent others from doing. Articulation is the joining of structures, but who or what does the joining, and for that matter the disassembling, and why these structures, and with what consequences? Can a merger between two companies really be equated to combining the letters t and o to form a new structure, to?[113] Or hooking a trailer onto a truck?

In the debate, Garnham maintained that in the absence of a truth somehow grounded outside of discourse, notions of 'emancipation, resistance, and progressiveness become meaningless ... Resistance to what,' he asked, 'emancipation from what and for what, progression toward what?'[114] These are, indeed, fundamental questions. For a political economist, understanding and describing what exists is the first step on the road to reform. For poststructuralists, evidently, in contending that we are trapped within language, saying ('articulating' or 're-articulating') something is the best we can do.

Conclusion

The renowned split between political economy and cultural studies has been, in a sense, a distraction, a diversion, a *faux* debate. Attracting so much attention on account of the bitterness exuding from the combatants, the hostilities have diverted analysts from focusing on the more basic problematic – the bifurcation of critical cultural studies itself into cultural materialism and poststructuralism.[115] Pitting cultural studies (always in such instances represented as a unity) against political economy not only depicts the 'enemy' as being outside the discourse (where it must remain, according to Grossberg), thereby making the fundamental debate 'us versus them' rather than 'us versus us,' it also renders cultural studies (again, depicted as a unity) hard to pin down and hence to critique – because, for one thing, the ontologies of cultural materialism and poststructuralism are *so* antithetical.

I would like to conclude with a call to integrate, or rather reintegrate, political economy and cultural studies. Reintegrating critical political economy and cultural studies entails, most fundamentally, setting aside poststructuralist cultural studies. In fact, if poststructuralist cultural studies are disregarded, political economy and cultural studies (cultural materialism) are united already. They were never divorced, and hence need no reconciliation.

Why, then, is it of some human benefit to abandon poststructuralist cultural studies, or at least turn from its most extreme instances as represented here particularly by Poster and Grossberg? One set of benefits flows simply from jettisoning a mode of thought that is falsified in self-reference and is plagued by inconsistencies; if clarity of thought is in fact a benefit, casting aside poststructuralism is certainly an advantage.

Stuart Hall, who often seemed to have a toe testing the poststructuralist waters, inadvertently gave another advantage. He declared, 'Postmodernism attempts to close off the past by saying that history is finished, therefore you needn't go back to it. There is only the present, and all you can do is be with it, immersed in it ... What it says is this: this is the end of the world. History stops with us and there is no place to go after this.'[116] Harold Innis termed this kind of thinking *present-minded*, and he argued convincingly that contemporary scholarship, for this very reason, leads to a lack of understanding.

Kevin O'Donnell, echoing Grossberg and Poster, has pointed to another potential benefit of casting aside poststructuralist thought. O'Donnell observed that a chief contention of poststructuralism is that 'there is no way to escape language, no way to stand outside discourse *to get at pure, raw truth.*'[117] O'Donnell's qualification, 'to get at pure, raw truth,' which I have italicized, is of momentous importance, but that qualification is usually ignored in poststructuralist literature: both Jean Baudrillard and his disciple, Mark Poster, for example, proposed that language and discourse are 'all there is,' that there is simply no way to escape language, *tout court*, nevermind getting at 'pure, raw truth.' To agree with Poster and Baudrillard on this, however, is to subvert any and all quests for social justice simply because social justice pertains to lived conditions and our knowledge of lived conditions. Harold Innis, by contrast, while certainly agreeing that 'pure, raw truth' is difficult if not impossible to attain on account of 'biases' in our ways of perceiving, communicating, and understanding, also insisted that we must continually strive through reflexivity to stand outside the biases of media and discourse sufficiently to at least glimpse truth, even if but as through a glass darkly, and that for him is precisely what the task and duty of scholarship is. Poststructuralism's allegation that there is no truth to seek ought be judged by poststructuralism's own standard, namely that all-encompassing statements cannot be true.

Consider as well the environmental implications of the strict poststructuralist insistence that we are forever trapped in language. A poststructuralist would be inclined to say that in principle the environment may impinge upon the life of each individual, community, society, and country. But all that is completely unknowable, for we live within language and cannot escape language. Environmental discourses for poststructuralists, therefore, are simply that – verbal structures concocted and engaged in by groups of people; and one such discourse is no better than any other. 'This group over here speaks about global warming,' a poststructuralist might remark, 'and that group over there about species' extinctions. May they enjoy their dialogues! Only let us be sure there are other groups with *their* discourses to neutralize them. If there are not, then we run the risk of constructing "grand narratives," which means OPPRESSION, and the only way out of that deleterious situation would be to "deconstruct" the discourses – certainly not to weigh their claims and predictions against observations in the material world because, as Baudrillard says, "truth, reference and objective causes have ceased to exist."[118] Everything is simulation nowadays, and everything is interpretation, and one person's interpretation of a simulation is no better or no worse than any other.'

At the turn of the last century, there were two founding fathers of semiotics/semiology. The more influential was Ferdinand de Saussure. According to de Saussure, 'signs,' or words, are *unmotivated*, by which he meant there is nothing but convention or social agreement that gives a word its meaning. The meaning of signs (words), and of sentences ('syntagms'), de Saussure insisted, can be comprehended by studying the structure of language as it exists at present, without referring to either the history of the language (synchronic, as opposed to diachronic linguistics) or to the material world (internal, as opposed to external linguistics). De Saussure is the exact opposite of Raymond Williams, who insisted that one must study not only the history of meanings of words but relate those meanings to changes in the lived conditions. In de Saussure, then, we find the seeds of major contemporary poststructuralist contentions: that we live in language and cannot extricate ourselves from it, that the relation between language and outside reality is broken, and that we can safely disregard history.

The 'road not taken'[119] was the semiology of the field's other founder, C.S. Peirce. Peirce grounded his semiotics in material reality, by insisting on a tripartite relationship among the sign (word), its object or referent in the material world, and the mental image of the person experiencing the sign. Meaning for Peirce, unlike for de Saussure, comes not just from the structure of language but also from one's experiences in the material world. According to Peirce, moreover, language bears an interactive (dialectical) relationship to material reality, as witnessed, for example, by the famous plethora of names Inuit people have for snow and Trobianders for yam.[120] Peirce made a direct connection between sign and referent, which is precisely what de Saussure rejected.

A major difference between Grossberg and Garnham, between Poster

and Innis, between Baudrillard and Williams, between poststructuralists and political economists/cultural materialists, one suspects, is that
the former in each case are at least implicitly descendants of de Saussure, and the latter of Peirce.

Raymond Williams was the pre-eminent inaugurator of cultural
studies. It seems, then, only fitting to conclude by citing him once more.
As his final remarks in *Culture and Society*, Williams wrote, 'The human
crisis is always a crisis of understanding ... There are ideas, and ways
of understanding, with the seeds of life in them, and there are others,
perhaps deep in our minds, with the seeds of a general death. Our
measure of success in recognizing these kinds, and in naming them ...
may be literally the measure of our future.'[121]

NOTES

1 John Hartley, *A Short History of Cultural Studies* (London: Sage, 2003), 1.
2 Wikipedia, 'Cultural Studies' (n.d.), http://en.wikipedia.org/wiki/Cul-
tural_studies.
3 Valda Blundell, John Shepherd, and Ian Taylor, 'Editor's Introduction,' in
Relocating Cultural Studies: Developments in Theory and Research (London:
Routledge, 1993), 4.
4 Richard Johnson, 'What Is Cultural Studies Anyway?' *Social Text* 16 (Winter 1986–7): 38.
5 Blundell, Shepherd, and Taylor, 'Editor's Introduction,' 4.
6 Ziauddin Sardar and Borin Van Loon, *Introducing Cultural Studies* (St Leon-
ards, AUS: Allen and Unwin, 1998), 8.
7 Williams referred to his position as 'cultural materialism,' which he
defined as 'a theory of the specificities of material cultural and literary
production within historical materialism.' Raymond Williams, *Marxism
and Literature* (Oxford: Oxford University Press, 1977), 5.
8 The terms *postmodern* and *poststructural* will be used here almost interchangeably. For a nuanced demarcation, however, see Ben Agger, 'Critical
Theory, Poststructuralism, Postmodernism: Their Sociological Relevance,'
Annual Review of Sociology 17 (1991), http://www.uta.edu/huma/illumi-
nations/agger2.htm.
9 David Macey, *The Penguin Dictionary of Critical Theory* (London: Penguin
Books, 2000), 77.
10 Lawrence Grossberg and Janice Radway, *Cultural Studies* (London:

Routledge, 1992), 111; as quoted in Richard E. Lee, *Life and Times of Cultural Studies: The Politics and Transformation of the Structures of Knowledge* (Durham, NC: Duke University Press, 2003), 2.

11 In this regard, Grossberg is fully in accord with poststructuralism's 'founding texts.' Adam Katz, for example, maintains that Baudrillard, Delueze, Guattari, Derrida, Foucault, Lacan, and Lyotard – poststructuralism's founding fathers – all privileged 'the local and specific' and resisted 'totalizing abstraction.' Adam Katz, 'Postmodern Cultural Studies: A Critique,' *Cultural Logic* 1, no. 1 (Fall 1997): 11.

12 Lawrence Grossberg, 'Aims and Scope,' *Cultural Studies* (2007), http://www.tandf.co.uk/journals/routledge/09502386.html. Emphasis added.

13 Stuart Hall, 'On Postmodernism and Articulation: An Interview with Stuart Hall' (1986); repr. in *Stuart Hall: Critical Dialogues in Cultural Studies*, ed. David Morley and Kuan-Hsing Chen (London: Routledge, 1996), 141. See also, Tim O'Sullivan, John Hartley, Danny Saunders, Martin Montgomery, and John Fiske, *Key Concepts in Communication and Cultural Studies*, 2nd ed. (London: Routledge, 1994), 17–18.

14 Mark Poster, *Critical Theory and Poststructuralism: In Search of a Context* (Ithaca, NY: Cornell University Press, 1989), 126.

15 Mark Poster, *The Mode of Information: Poststructuralism and Social Context* (Chicago: University of Chicago Press, 1990), 130.

16 Poster, *Critical Theory*, 107ff.

17 Lawrence Grossberg, 'Cultural Studies vs. Political Economy: Is Anybody Else Bored with this Debate?' *Critical Studies in Mass Communication* 12, no. 1 (1995): 72–81.

18 The antagonisms between political economy and cultural studies are well known. See, for example, Kevin Robins and Frank Webster, 'The Communications Revolution: New Media, Old Problems,' *Communication* 10, no. 1 (1987): 71–89; and Oscar H. Gandy Jr, assoc. ed., 'Colloquy,' *Critical Studies in Mass Communication* 12, no. 1 (1995): 60–100.

19 Poster, *Mode of Information*, 15.

20 Poster, *Cultural Theory*, 15.

21 Terry Eagleton, *Figures of Dissent* (London: Verso, 2003), 74.

22 Williams, *Marxism and Literature*, 108.

23 Raymond Williams, *Keywords: A Vocabulary of Culture and Society*, rev. ed. (1976; Oxford: Oxford University Press, 1983), x.

24 Graham Murdock, 'Across the Great Divide: Cultural Analysis and the Condition of Democracy,' *Critical Studies in Mass Communication* 12, no. 1 (March 1995): 89.

25 Fred Inglis, *Raymond Williams* (London, UK: Routledge, 1995), 320–2; Alan

O'Connor, *Raymond Williams* (Lanham, MD: Rowman and Littlefield, 2006), 115–19.

26 Raymond Williams, *Culture and Society 1780–1950* (1958; Harmondsworth: Penguin Books, 1984), 11–12.

27 Ibid., 13, 15.

28 Ibid., 16. Emphasis in original.

29 Ibid., 285.

30 Ibid., 16.

31 For example, Allan Bloom, *Closing the American Mind* (New York: Simon and Schuster, 1987).

32 Williams, *Culture and Society*, 298. According to Williams, 'A very large part of English middle-class education is devoted to the training of servants. This is more its characteristic than a training for leadership, as the stress on conformity and respect for authority shows.' Ibid., 315.

33 Ibid., 229.

34 The official start of the grouse-shooting season in the United Kingdom.

35 T.S. Eliot, *Notes towards a Definition of Culture* (New York: Harcourt, Brace, 1949), 31; qtd in Williams, *Culture and Society*, 230.

36 They viewed democratic culture as a moving away from an ideal. Ibid., 226.

37 Ibid., 310.

38 Ibid., 313.

39 Ibid., 297.

40 Ibid.

41 Ibid., 311.

42 Ibid., 312.

43 Ibid., 307.

44 Smith wrote, 'In opulent and commercial societies to think or to reason comes to be, like every other employment, a particular business, which is carried on by a very few people, who furnish the public with all the thought and reason possessed by the vast multitudes that labour.' Adam Smith, draft of *The Wealth of Nations*, qtd in Williams, *Culture and Society*, 52.

45 Williams, *Culture and Society*, 52.

46 Ibid.

47 Ibid., 60. The quote is from Shelley's *A Defence of Poetry*.

48 Williams, *Culture and Society*, 60.

49 Ibid., 307–8.

50 Ibid., 301.

51 Ibid.

52 Ibid., 16.
53 Ibid. Emphases in original.
54 Ibid., 287.
55 Robert E. Babe, *Cultural Studies and Political Economy: Toward a New Integration* (Lanham, MD: Lexington Books, 2009).
56 Compare J.M. Bernstein, introduction to *The Culture Industry* by Theodor W. Adorno, ed. J.M. Bernstein (London, UK: Routledge, 1991), 3.
57 David Held, *Introduction to Critical Theory: Horkheimer to Habermas* (Cambridge, UK: Polity, 1980), 78.
58 Simon Jarvis notes that while Adorno 'illuminated an extraordinary range of subjects' he addressed two key questions: 'What is the relationship between power and rationality? Can there ever be a kind of thinking which does not live off the suffering of others?' Simon Jarvis, *Adorno: A Critical Introduction* (Cambridge, UK: Polity, 1998), 1–2.
59 Max Horkheimer and Theodor W. Adorno, *Dialectic of Enlightenment* (New York: Continuum, 1991), 120; originally published in German in 1944. Statements of this sort have attracted critique. J.M. Bernstein suggests, for example, that Adorno overemphasized the culture industry's goal of homogenization. J.M. Bernstein, 'Introduction,' 23. See also, Douglas Kellner, 'Critical Theory and the Culture Industries: A Reassessment,' *Telos* 62 (1984–5): 196–206.
60 Grant McCracken, *Culture and Consumption: New Approaches to the Symbolic Character of Consumer Goods and Activities* (Bloomington: Indiana University Press, 1988).
61 Stephen Crook, introduction to *The Stars Come Down to Earth* by Theodor Adorno (1994; repr., New York: Routledge, 2007), 35.
62 Horkheimer and Adorno, *Dialectic of Enlightenment*, 126.
63 Theodor Adorno, *The Culture Industry*, ed. and intro. J.M. Bernstein (London: Routledge, 1991), 85.
64 Adorno quoted in Deborah Cook, *The Culture Industry Revisited: Theodor W. Adorno on Mass Culture* (Lanham, MD: Rowman and Littlefield,1996), 27.
65 Robert Hughes, *The Shock of the New: Art and the Century of Change* (London: BBC, 1980), 66–80.
66 Horkheimer and Adorno, *Dialectic of Enlightenment*, 131.
67 Adorno, *The Culture Industry*, 86.
68 Horkheimer and Adorno, *Dialectic of Enlightenment*, 158.
69 Cook, *The Culture Industry Revisited*, 3.
70 Adorno, qtd in ibid.
71 Theodor Adorno, 'On the Fetish Character in Music and the Regression of Listening' (1938); repr. in *Culture Industry*, 26.

72 Ibid., 28–9.
73 Ibid., 27.
74 Adorno, 'Culture Industry Reconsidered' (1975); repr. in *Culture Industry*, 85.
75 Ibid.; see also Adorno, 'Fetish Character in Music,' 31.
76 Adorno, 'Culture Industry Reconsidered,' 90.
77 Adorno, 'Stars Down to Earth.'
78 J.M. Bernstein, 'Introduction,' 12.
79 Ibid., 14.
80 Horkheimer and Adorno, *Dialectic of Enlightenment*, 122.
81 Ibid., 121. Emphasis added.
82 Ibid., 144.
83 Ibid., 126.
84 Adorno, 'Free Time,' in *The Culture Industry*, ed. and intro. J.M. Bernstein (London: Routledge, 1991), 170.
85 Horkheimer and Adorno wrote, 'Amusement under late capitalism is the prolongation of work. It is sought after as an escape from the mechanized work process, and to recruit strength in order to be able to cope with it again. But at the same time, mechanization has such power over a man's leisure and happiness, and so profoundly determines the manufacture of amusement goods, that his experiences are inevitably after-images of the work process itself.' Horkheimer and Adorno, *Dialectic of Enlightenment*, 137.
86 Adorno, 'Free Time,' 168.
87 Theodor W. Adorno, 'The Schema of Mass Culture,' in *Culture Industry*, 77; originally published in German in 1981.
88 Arthur Asa Berger, *Media Analysis Techniques* (Newbury Park, CA: Sage, 1991), 106–17; Michael Mandelbaum, *The Meaning of Sports: Why Americans Watch Baseball, Football and Basketball and What They See When They Do* (New York: Public Affairs, 2004); Michael R. Real, 'The Super-Bowl: Mythic Spectacle,' in *Mass-Mediated Culture* (Englewood Cliffs, NJ: Prentice-Hall, 1977), 92–117.
89 Horkheimer and Adorno, *Dialectic of Enlightenment*, 137.
90 Theodor Adorno, 'How to Look at Television' (1954); repr. in *Culture Industry*, 138.
91 Cook, *The Culture Industry Revisited*, 61.
92 Ibid., 7–8.
93 Adorno, 'How to Look at Television,' 141.
94 Ibid., 142.
95 According to Adorno, since film, for example, accommodates various

levels of response, 'this would imply that the ideology provided by the industry, its officially intended models, may by no means automatically correspond to those that affect the spectators.' Theodor W. Adorno, 'Transparencies on Film' (1981–2; repr. in *Culture Industry*, 157.

96 Ibid., 156.
97 Horkheimer and Adorno, *Dialectic of Enlightenment*, 123.
98 Raymond Williams, *The Year 2000* (New York: Pantheon, 1983), 118.
99 Horkheimer and Adorno, *Dialectic of Enlightenment*, 123.
100 Ben Bagdikian, *The Media Monopoly*, 6th ed. (1983; Boston: Beacon, 2000); Robert McChesney, *Rich Media, Poor Democracy* (New York: New Press, 1999).
101 Adorno, 'Culture Industry Revisited,' 89.
102 Ibid., 91, 90.
103 Ibid., 89.
104 Ibid., 91.
105 Nicholas Garnham, 'Political Economy and Cultural Studies: Reconciliation or Divorce?' *Critical Studies in Mass Communication* 12, no. 1 (1995): 69.
106 Grossberg, 'Cultural Studies,' 79.
107 Ibid., 77.
108 Poster, *Critical Theory and Poststructuralism*, 90.
109 Grossberg, 'Cultural Studies,' 79. Emphasis added.
110 Lawrence Grossberg, *We Gotta Get Out of This Place: Popular Conservativism and the Postmodern Culture* (New York: Routledge, 1992), 54; qtd in Jennifer Daryl Slack, 'The Theory and Method of Articulation in Cultural Studies,' in *Stuart Hall: Critical Dialogues in Cultural Studies*, ed. David Morley and Kuan-Hsing Chen (London: Routledge, 1996), 115.
111 Lawrence Grossberg, 'The Formations of Cultural Studies: An American in Birmingham,' in *Relocating Cultural Studies: Developments in Theory and Research*, ed. Valda Blundell, John Shepherd, and Ian Taylor (London: Routledge, 1993), 59; emphasis added. One is reminded here of Ivy Lee's dictum, 'Truth happens to an idea.' Lee was founder of the U.S. public relations industry, and according to Stuart Ewen's gloss, Lee proposed that 'something asserted might become a fact, regardless of its connection to actual events.' Stuart Ewen, *PR! A Social History of Spin* (New York: Basic Books, 1996), 79.
112 Stuart Hall, 'Encoding/Decoding,' qtd in Slack, 'Theory and Method,' 115.
113 At the very least, combining or disassembling structures requires time, energy, and a range of resources (including monetary).

114 Garnahm, 'Political Economy and Cultural Studies,' 69.
115 Although the terminology differs, a related demarcation was made by
Stuart Hall, who distinguished between 'culturalist' and 'structuralist'
modes. Derived from sociology, anthropology, and social history, the 'cultural mode' regards culture as a whole way of life; it is accessible through
concrete (empirical) descriptions that capture the unities of commonplace cultural forms and material experience. The 'structuralist mode' is
indebted to French linguistics, literary criticism, and semiotic theory, and
conceives cultural forms as being '(semi)autonomous inaugurating "discourses" susceptible to rhetorical and semiological analyses of cognitive
constitutions and ideological effects.' Vincent B. Leitch, 'Birmingham Cultural Studies: Popular Arts, Poststructuralism, Radical Critique,' *Journal of
the Midwest Modern Languages Association* 24, no. 1 (Spring 1991): 74.
116 Stuart Hall, 'On Postmodernism and Articulation,' 137, 134.
117 Kevin O'Donnell, *Postmodernism* (Oxford: Lion, 2003), 6.
118 Jean Baudrillard, *Simulations*, trans. Paul Foss, Paul Patton, and Philip
Beitchman (New York: Semiotext[e], 1983), 6.
119 See Paul Cobley, introduction to *The Communication Theory Reader*, ed.
Paul Cobley (London: Routledge, 1996), 26–32. Cobley suggests that 'the
increased attention given to Peirce's work ... often looks as though it
might upset the whole applecart of post-structuralism ... [It] appears to
offer a new perspective on how communication might be thought to refer
to the real world.'
120 Barrington Nevitt, *The Communication Ecology: Re-presentation versus Replica* (Toronto: Butterworths, 1982), 109–10.
121 Raymond Williams, *Culture and Society: 1780–1950* (1958; repr., Harmondsworth: Penguin, 1963), 323.

18 Political Economy of Economics[1]

It is now nearly fifty years since Milton Friedman famously (and controversially) claimed that economics is and should be a 'positive' social science. Friedman distinguished between 'positive' and 'normative' economics, the former describing how things are, the latter how they should be. He elaborated that positive economics is 'in principle independent of any particular ethical position,'[2] that it is scientific, objective, value-neutral, and predictive. Most neoclassical economists today claim that their marginalist approach to understanding economic phenomena *is* 'positive' and scientific. This is a claim I intend to dispute.

Economics is concerned with prices. Indeed the discipline is sometimes defined as the study of the price system. Prices, in turn, are quantitative indicators of relative value.[3] There are also many non-price indicators of value (the Ten Commandments, the Code of Hammurabi, the U.S. Declaration of Independence, hierarchies in family and schoolyards, the performance of hockey teams, and so on). Neoclassical economics, however, scarcely recognizes non-price systems of valuation and thereby at least implicitly advocates the replacement of non-quantitative modes of valuation with prices (a trend that economic historian and communication theorist Harold Innis referred to derogatively as the 'penetrative powers of the price system').[4] Indeed a thrust of neoclassicism is that prices are a sufficient means of denoting and communicating value.[5] A discipline that authenticates or valorizes the authority of prices as indicators of value, however, cannot in truth be deemed 'positive' or 'value-neutral' if and when that entails trivializing, denigrating, or ignoring other modes of valuation – ones based on custom, kinship, ethical pronouncements, community sentiment, and so on.

Modern economic discourse, then, *is* value-laden. Indeed, it is the study of one mode of relative valuation (the price system) to the exclusion of (thereby implicitly denigrating) other modes of valuation. This normative dimension of mainstream (neoclassical) economics can perhaps be seen even more clearly when the economics discipline is viewed historically. At every stage of its evolution, mainstream economics has been aligned with, and has doctrinally served, a class interest.

Consider first the physiocrats – 'founders of economics as a science.'[6] They held sway, particularly in France, in the last decades of an essentially agricultural, extractive economy (1756–76), meaning that the landed aristocracy was still at the apex of the social-economic hierarchy. The physiocrats affirmed the existing power structure by proffering *a land theory of value*; that is, they maintained that all economic activity depends ultimately on agriculture and on resource extraction. Bountiful harvests, according to these theorists, give rise to surpluses that can be saved and reinvested, and that allow some workers to pursue non-farming activities, such as manufacturing. All non-agricultural pursuits, in contrast, according to the physiocrats, are 'sterile' in the sense that they yield no surplus.

Their argument made, and makes, a lot of sense.[7] As noted by David Suzuki, today developmental efforts in the third world often degrade human health and increase poverty because they undermine local communities and their air, water, and soil – 'the real basis of well-being.'[8] Possibly to our peril, we have lost the physiocrats' understanding that wealth ultimately derives from nature.

On the other hand, returning to our theme of the political economy of knowledge, the physiocrats did not question the enclosure movement and the resulting priva te ownership of land. It is only right, they claimed, that landowners receive rent (albeit subject to taxation) from those who work their land; the surplus, in other words, according to the physiocrats, *should* accrue to land owners ('*rentiers*'). Their insistence on this normative point effectively condoned class differentiation based on land ownership.

With the rise of industrialism, the physiocrats' influence waned quickly. An economics endorsing rents to the aristocracy while denigrating activities of the 'captains of industry,' after all, did not suit the changing economic climes. The classic economics text, bumping physiocracy to the margins and bolstering the claims of the emerging capitalist class, was of course Adam Smith's *The Wealth of Nations*, first published in 1776. Smith's economic system, like that of subsequent major classical political economists (for instance, Malthus, Ricardo,

Bentham, Mill, Marx), is premised on a *labour theory of value*. At first this might seem paradoxical: on the one hand a mainstream economics attributing all value to labour and, on the other, burgeoning capitalist power. The paradox is partially resolved, however, as soon as it is recognized that the classical economists defined *capital* as 'stored-up labour' (owned, of course, by capitalists). Workers possess only 'labour power,' that is their own capacity to do work. Unlike most other classical economists, Marx, of course, went further, sowing the seeds for the demise of classical economics. He claimed that if labour is the source of all value, then workers *should* receive that value; more on this below.

The conservative classical political economists, however, had a response, at least implicit, to Marx's later criticism. They proposed an 'iron law of wages.' They claimed that workers' propensity to reproduce and multiply their numbers whenever their standard of living rose above bare subsistence invariably forces wages back down once more to the subsistence level. They foresaw, then, a permanent immiserization of the working class – a position that 'justified' great income inequality, as the capitalist class (they alleged) knew how to control *their* numbers in the face of wealth.

From a propagandistic perspective, however, classical economics was flawed. The eighteenth and nineteenth centuries were characterized by social upheaval, revolution, and strident demands for increases in human rights and democracy – and classical economics could be seen as inflaming that situation. Consider the following passages respectively from the epic tomes of Smith and Malthus:

> In the progress of the division of labour, the employment of the far greater part of those who live by labour, that is, of the great body of the people, comes to be confined to a few very simple operations, frequently to one or two. But the understandings of the greater part of men are necessarily formed by their ordinary employments. The man whose whole life is spent in performing a few simple operations, of which the effects too are, perhaps, always the same, or very nearly the same, has no occasion to exert his understanding, or to exercise his invention in finding out expedients for removing difficulties which never occur. He naturally loses, therefore, the habit of such exertion, and generally becomes as stupid and ignorant as it is possible for a human creature to become. The torpor of his mind renders him, not only incapable of relishing or bearing a part in any rational conversation, but of conceiving any generous, noble, or ten-

der sentiment, and consequently of forming any just judgment concerning many even of the ordinary duties of private life.[9]

The poor laws of England tend to depress the general condition of the poor in these two ways. Their first obvious tendency is to increase population without increasing the food for its support ... Secondly, the quantity of provisions consumed in workhouses, upon a part of the society that cannot in general be considered as the most valuable part, diminishes the shares that would otherwise belong to more industrious and more worthy members, and thus, in the same manner, forces more to become dependent ... The parish laws of England appear to have contributed to raise the price of provisions, and to lower the real price of labour. They have therefore contributed to impoverish that class of people whose only possession is their labour.[10]

One response to (and cause of) unrest was Marx's revolutionary call to overthrow an inegalitarian and class-based economic order. A second, and much more conservative response, however, was (and remains) neoclassical economics.

As it developed at the turn of the previous century, neoclassical economics is based on yet another theory of value. According to neo-classicism, the value of a commodity depends directly not upon its land content, nor upon its labour content, but ultimately on subjective considerations of 'utility.' True, 'land' and 'labour' are recognized as factors of production, and hence enter the cost equations, but it is fundamentally the aggregation of subjective preferences, ever shifting, that renders these factor inputs (and hence the products they embody) 'valuable.'

This new *psychological* or *utilitarian theory of value* serves the power structure well. First, it makes things *seem* to be democratic and egalitarian: after all, *everyone* has preferences, wants, and desires, and everyone expresses these in the marketplace through dollar 'votes,' contributing thereby to the valuation of things. Second, through the neoclassical doctrine of Pareto optimality, initial conditions are taken as given, thereby leaving unchallenged (and unconsidered) great concentrations of wealth, even though as is widely known, wealth begets wealth and poverty begets poverty. Third, the theory ostensibly absolves any individual or class of responsibility for bad outcomes: if there is poverty, no one is to blame, because ultimately the 'marketplace' is the expression of every individual's 'utility' (indeed, as if the notion of 'utility' were not abstract and metaphysical enough, of their *marginal* utility!). The self-correcting market, according to this thinking, ensures everyone is compensated appropriately, including those with riches and those in dire need.

And so, there we stand. Two revolutions in mainstream economic thought, three theories of value, each aligned with a class interest and thereby affirming a power structure.

Neoclassicism, today, remains the economics mainstream. And, given the history of economic thought and, more generally, the political economy of mainstream knowledge, it is unlikely to be dislodged unless and until a *powerful* class interest becomes ill-served by the existing paradigm. Many theorists indeed argue that we have entered a new era, variously termed post-industrial society, postmodernism, the information society, the information revolution, the Third Wave, and so on. If correct, this would imply the emergence of a new dominant class, namely those controlling modern information and communication technologies – and pari passu, the ascent of *a new theory of value based on knowledge and information*. To this point, however, we see little indication of an emerging theory of value to challenge neoclassicism, Rather, the attempt is made continuously to incorporate information and knowledge within the established paradigm by treating information like a commodity (a procedure, as noted previously, that is rife with contradictions!).

NOTES

1 Reprinted with the permission of Hampton Press.
2 Milton Friedman, 'The Methodology of Positive Economics,' in *Essays in Positive Economics* (Chicago: University of Chicago Press, 1953), 3, 4.
3 F.A. Hayek, 'The Use of Knowledge in Society,' *American Economic Review* 35, no. 4 (September 1945): 525.
4 Harold A. Innis, 'The Penetrative Powers of the Price System' (1938); repr. in *Essays in Canadian Economic History*, ed. Mary Q. Innis (Toronto: University of Toronto Press, 1956), 252–72.
5 Kenneth Arrow, 'The Economics of Information,' in *The Computer Age: A Twenty-Year View*, ed. Michael Dertouzos and Joel Moses (Cambridge, MA: MIT Press, 1979), 313–14.
6 Jacob Oser, *The Evolution of Economic Thought* (New York, NY: Harcourt, Brace & World, 1963), 29. See also Joseph Schumpeter, *History of Economic*

Analysis, ed. Elizabeth Boody Schumpeter (New York: Oxford University Press, 1954), 223–43.

7 See, for example, Clive Ponting, *A Green History of the World* (New York: Penguin Books, 1991), on the necessity of an agricultural surplus for the formation of cities, the division of labour, etc.

8 David Suzuki and Holly Dressel, *From Naked Ape to Superspecies* (Toronto: Stoddart, 1999), 174.

9 Adam Smith, *An Inquiry into the Nature and Causes of the Wealth of Nations,* ed. Edwin Çannan (1776; New York: Modern Library, 1937), 734.

10 T.R. Malthus, *An Essay on the Principle of Population* (1803; repr., selected, intro. Donald Winch, Cambridge: Cambridge University Press 1992), 100–1.

PART FIVE

Concluding Thoughts

19 Political Language: The Political Economy of Knowledge

WARREN J. SAMUELS*

... the invisible hand of some economic god.

— Mario Cuomo (1992)

... Federal Reserve Chairman Alan Greenspan, whose hand is on the control lever of the U.S. economy.

— Editorial, *Lansing State Journal* (1989)

Words are so precise that they always go too far.

— Georges Simenon (1978)

In most of the markets with which I am familiar the invisible hand is all thumbs.

— Ray Marshall (n.d.)

Thus science must begin with myths, and with the criticism of myths.

— Karl Popper (1957)

There is no established economic usage for anything in economics.

— Frank H. Knight (1933)

'Reality.' What a concept.

Robin Williams (1979)

* Michigan State University

Philosophical realism satisfies, for some people, at least two concerns. For those whose mindset requires determinacy and closure, philosophical realism assures them that there really is something 'out there,' given and transcendental. Those with this mindset consider, or at least hope, that philosophical realism will defeat philosophical idealism. These thinkers have several goals: One is to identify the given and transcendental. Another is to establish philosophical realism not as just another mindset but as the actual definition of reality. The third is to preclude or overrun philosophical idealism, in part because they identify with the status quo, however selectively perceived and pursued, and in part because their need for determinacy and closure renders anathema the open-ended opportunity for change in the social construction of reality congenial to the other mindset that is comfortable with open-endedness and ambiguity as part of the process of working things out. In short, realists are not comfortable with choice, idealists are.

These considerations and motivations characterize the jockeying for positions through the deployment of language. In such matters the political nature of language is transparent.

The problem to which the foregoing leads is this: if everyone were a philosophical realist, each likely would differ on the substantive content of what his or her realism considers given and transcendental. This predicament means that the realist, no less than the idealist, has the burden of choice. In short, there is no necessary substantive difference between philosophical realism and philosophical idealism: they both face the ineluctable necessity of choice, to which a good deal of wishful thinking is applied. The result is that all people – philosophical realists and idealists – must choose that definition of reality that suits them. A further result is that it is in the interest of most people, perhaps especially the hierarchic levels, to influence other people's definition of reality. Doing so is one of the functions of language.

Whatever one's philosophical preference, in working things out each necessarily confronts the roles of power and language – power, understood non-pejoratively as participation in decision-making based on rights; and language, understood to be a means of communication and of influencing people's definition of reality and their actions. This points to a society with people whose power and language has to be worked out. Much of the time all that is obfuscated; the rest of the time it is finessed by rendering it oblique and opaque.

More than power and language as pure, abstract categories are involved, however. There are, for example, the media and other institutions (such as government and non-media enterprises) engaged in generating and marshalling information and ignorance.

Robert Babe's work comports with the foregoing. He is concerned with the media, whose pages or viewing screens use language to define the world. Not only that, the media are an important part of the social control forces in society, the therapeutic forces that define problems, policies, and solutions, and hence contribute to the belief, mythic, and symbolic systems of society. The media also contribute, in addition to social control, to psychic balm and the social construction of reality. The media are so ubiquitous, so largely a part of our scheme of things that they are conventionally taken for granted – and thereby reinforce a nation's way of life and one or another version of societal values. Accordingly, Babe's work has also focused on the institutions and theories in which telecommunication business and policy control the culture of a social system and the political economy of knowledge. Babe is very sensitive to the media as an industry seemingly different from every other industry, and from government and religion as well, but similar in that all use the media and language in order to define and control the world in which they operate. Babe's work is truly foundational and, as such, rare and either praiseworthy or suspect.

This paper outlines one view of the foundations – a supporting paradigm – of Babe's work, not of Babe's work itself. It suggests a fundamental chain of reasoning that supports the conclusion that language is political and something of that conclusion's importance. The reasoning is so fundamental that every challenge made to it illustrates the reasoning. Section 1 takes up Adam Smith's system of social science and the argument from his *History of Astronomy* on the role that language plays in setting minds at rest. Section 2 illustrates his argument by summarizing some conclusions from my study of Smith's and others' conceptions of the invisible hand and relates them to my present purpose. Section 3 suggests what results when one considers primitive terms and metaphors in the light of the argument of sections 1 and 2. Section 4 examines what can be said about language as political argument resulting from the foregoing.

1. Smith's System of Social Science and His *History of Astronomy*

Smith's system of society was tripartite. It has been widely understood only within the last fifty years or so, even though he endeavoured to call attention to it. The three parts into which he divided society are the moral sentiments and moral rules, law and government, and the market. The system was a blend of synoptic and synthetic processes. Interdependence and tensions between all parts of the system take up much space in Smith's works. His *Theory of Moral Sentiments*[1] dealt with the formation and evolution of moral rules; the *Wealth of Nations*,[2] markets and market activity; and his *Lectures on Jurisprudence*,[3] which he did not write up but which we have in the form of two sets of student notes. The key point for us is that this system went through stages in an evolutionary way. Competition among moral and among legal rules and between both evolving sets of rules characterized the process of working them out. Smith held that the rules were worked out by humankind, driven, first, by the principles of approbation and disapprobation, which God had planted in humankind and, second, by a desire for recognition and approval both by others and by oneself (status emulation). Power was pervasive in his system but so was language. In particular, the use of language enabled him and others to express the history of social, political, and economic spheres.

The process of working all this out was language. Language was one means deployed to achieve social control and psychic balm as well as the belief, mythic, and symbolic systems of society, including working out the control of morals and government in part through linguistic manoeuvres. Because Smith found that the tripartite synoptic and synthetic system covered all aspects of human nature and of people in society, he had no need to enforce some rigid definition of an economic problem or of an economics insulated from non-economic factors and forces or from factors interfering with economic equilibrium by ruling out all forces that may have interfered with the market process and its putative determinate and unique solutions. Whatever one thinks of those practices, the fictional picture that emerges can, should disciplinary criteria otherwise allow, provide a sense that the analysis is correct as a description, an explanation, or a tool. The satisfaction of disciplinary requirements is all that is required, not establishing the truth of the matter.

In his *History of Astronomy* Smith argues that our imagination is disturbed by sentiments of wonder, surprise, and admiration, due to new phenomena, the unexpected, and the great or beautiful. Such disturbances induce philosophical (that is, scientific) inquiry into 'the invisible chains which bind together all these disjointed objects' in order to introduce order into this chaos of jarring and discordant appearances, to allay this tumult of the imagination, and to restore it ... to that tone of tranquility and composure, which is both most agreeable in itself, and most suitable to its nature.'[4]

For present purposes, the several different interpretations given to the question of proportions need not be examined, but it is clear that some propositions acquire status as a contribution to knowledge, and others as a contribution to the composure of the imagination, and still others to both. Indeed, in the concluding paragraph of the *History*, Smith says, in regard to his treatment of Newton, that even we – while we have been endeavouring to represent all philosophic systems as mere inventions of the imagination, to connect the otherwise disjointed and discordant phenomena of nature – have insensibly been drawn in, to make use of language expressing the connecting principles of this one, as if they were the real chains that Nature uses to bind together her several operations.

Smith goes on to suggest how the foregoing works out. He is obviously concerned with propositions that soothe the imagination, whatever their truth value. Some language is received as describing and/ or explaining phenomena; some, with setting minds at rest, and some accomplishing both. Smith's inquiry was less about their truth than about 'how far each of them was fitted to sooth(e) the imagination, and to render the theatre of nature a more coherent, and therefore a more magnificent spectacle, than otherwise it would have appeared to be.'[5]

It is clear that whatever the respective proportions of uses, for Smith, propositions that set minds at rest are numerous enough to warrant his attention and discussion.

Either an implication from the foregoing or an importation from experience is the proposition with which interested parties attempt to soothe the imagination or to manipulate the thought and action of others. The preceding sentence might apply, say, to two competing political groups, political parties, each of which understands and practises manipulation. An alternative scenario also has two groups, but one of them naively seeks to offer true propositions that people need to study before voting for or against them. The other group offers propositions that soothe the mind, even lull the mind, perhaps even manipulate the mind.

Cognitive behavioural therapy (CBT) holds that the emphasis in traditional psychology upon the patient's need to come to terms with the past in order to satisfactorily exist in the present, may be unnecessary, if not counterproductive. CBT, on the other hand, can lead the patient to correct current cognitive disorders that lead an individual to act dysfunctionally in the present. Whereas reviewing the past could be therapeutically important in helping patients construct narratives of their lives in terms of cause and effect, reviewing the present, or the recent past, can help patients find a rational explanation for their disturbing experience, and that may be all they need. The use of CBT and rational explanation – the rationalization – that emerges can be effective even when the explanation is not correct. As the Harvard psychologist Richard J. McNally concluded, merely asserting a logical sequence (or one that appears logical) of cause and effect lets people feel that they have some control, that they are not victims of unexplained forces.[6]

2. The Invisible Hand

The surviving papers of Adam Smith contain the language of 'invisible hand' three times. One refers to the explanation of irregular events, attributing them to the invisible hand of Jupiter.[7] The other two are unspecified but are clearly economic. In his *Theory of Moral Sentiments* Smith maintains that spending by the rich gives employment to the poor and thereby makes the distribution of consumption more equal than the distribution of wealth.[8] In the *Wealth of Nations* Smith maintains that the pursuit of private interest often contributes to social welfare; his example is how the concern of businessmen about the security of their investment can lead to increased domestic investment and more domestic power. In both types of cases the pursuit of private interest contributes to social welfare.[9] Several points should be made:

- Contrary to much common usage, Smith wrote that the businessman 'is led by an invisible hand,' and not 'as if by an invisible hand.'
- Smith does not write that the pursuit of private interest always and necessarily contributes to social welfare; he qualifies his claims by using such phrases as 'in this, as in many other cases' and 'frequently.'
- The term *invisible hand* is so widely used that Adam Smith himself has become a symbol or metaphor of the capitalist system.
- People have interpreted the operation and function(s) of the invisible hand in terms of order, self-regulation, general harmony and beneficence, harmony among self-interests or Pareto optimality, and harmony of self-interests with the social interest. This is ironic because people, including Smith, nonetheless have observed a great deal of conflict and need for social control.
- Meanings nourished by ideology, emulation of scholarly status, wishful thinking, and so on are often superimposed on the elements of a model.

The sources of conflict in Smith's system are numerous:

- In Smith's tripartite model of society, moral rules, legal rules, and the market operate, interact, and conflict. Economic actors with various interests have conflicting attitudes towards whose interests should be recognized and be given protection in morals, in law, and in the market.
- The market does not have a given transcendental existence; it is a function of morals and law and of the strategic decisions and actions of the managers of firms. Conflicts arise from issues of law versus morals, the scope and rate of change of law and of morals, and so on.
- Three other sources of multiplicity and conflict are (1) the definition of the central problem of economics, (2) the scope of included variables, and (3) the use of assumptions with which to dispose of inhospitable topics.

The basis and consequences of multiplicity are numerous. Every element in every model can be given different identities, interpretations, and explanations. This is because each element of a model can have a different relationship to the total model; that is, people exist differently and interpret differently, and the objects of inquiry can be perceived and interpreted differently. There are no independent tests. Moreover, when an element is given multiple definitions, the result is enormous ambiguity.

There are two characteristics of conflict:

- Solutions to problems have to be worked out; they are not found.
- Each element is over-determined, by which is meant not that they simply interact but that each element is what it is because of actions within each element and the impact of other elements.

There are a few other points with varying degrees of importance:

- Religion (supernaturalism) and naturalism comprise frameworks of analysis that, like schools of academic disciplinary thought, tell distinctive sets of stories, each putatively defining reality. With no independent test available, the result is ambiguity and selective perception.
- Much of human history involves hard-fought conflicts over land, water, and other natural resources; the structure of governance; the direction of the human labour force. Belief, symbolic, and psychic balm systems in society are used to rationalize, legitimize, and change elements of these systems.

- There is no reason why the concept of the invisible hand cannot apply to all institutions, including the market activity of economic organizations.

That Smith addressed language and imagination in such terms underlines Babe's recognition of a central paradox in contemporary political economic relations – that neoclassicists have extracted from Smith a methodological individualism that clouds the complexities of the author's own ruminations. Indeed, the invisible hand now masks and obfuscates the use of language by economic and other agents, now including the media on a massive scale, in pursuit of their respective self-interests. From the history of economic thought, political and cultural agents borrow the concept of the invisible hand in their practice of making things look different from what they actually are and to recruit government on their side. Smith himself indicates how, acting not as a saccharine and harmonious invisible hand, employers can combine and enlist Parliament to lower wages while prohibiting workers from combining and raising wages.[10] The invisible hand may account for unintended and/or unforeseen consequences, but that does not prevent businessmen's quest for control of government and, with its aid, their control of markets, in every phase of which language is brought to bear.

3. Primitive Terms, Other Practices, and Metaphors

This section deals principally with primitive terms, certain practices and metaphors, and their place in the fundamental chain of reasoning leading to the conclusion that language is political.

Every term encountered in economics and in all the social sciences, even the most technical jargon, has multiple identifications. Economics, having benefited from Smith and the Scottish Enlightenment, went on to have numerous such multiple identities. The term *nature*, for example, has been given well over a dozen different definitions. Specifications of the identity of the invisible hand number about four dozen. Identification of the functions performed by the invisible hand number about a dozen categories, each of which has numerous variations. Suggestions of combinations of identity and function are enormous.

Two propositions pertain to the use of the invisible hand and may say the same thing. One is that symbols are important, even when they do not relate to some putative reality, because they introduce and/or connote policy, action, and wishful thinking. The other is that it is what people believe, and not what they know, that is important, because they act on the basis of what they believe, regardless of whether it is true.

At a certain level of abstraction or generalization, the line between fact and fiction, between reality and creative imagination, may well be vague at best. Another line separates truth and tools. As Babe recognizes, myths may be more important than realities, insofar as they define reality as the basis of action. The theory of psychic balm says, inter alia, that through words we impose meaning and order upon the chaos of experience. We choose explanations that minimize discomfort. The manipulation of symbolic concepts through words is a principal mode of governing and a tool for the social construction of reality through the mobilization of psychology.

The assumption is widespread of a putative natural harmony of interests, if only it could be allowed to come to fruition, and be enabled, selectively, to be used as invocation and justification of the legal change that, it is believed, will permit it.

One linguistic practice is the use of primitive terms.[11] A primitive term is one used in a generic sense and has no specified meaning. Such terms are kaleidoscopic, subject to selective perception, and almost invariably given variable specification. Their use facilitates the entry into analysis, discussion, or argument of selective normative premises. Their use allows an author or speaker to escape questions of both substantive content and the mode of its determination. Primitive terms include *private, public, freedom, voluntary, coercion, property*, and *morality*. When a writer or speaker uses one of those terms without providing a definition, even if all auditors nod in seeming agreement, each will attribute to it his or her own definition.

The invisible hand typically is given a so-called free-market connotation. Interdependence between agents and elements, etc., is strongly seen as opportunity-enhancing, although interdependence also connotes opportunity restriction. From an analytical and non-pejorative perspective, the invisible hand serves as a system of social control. Not only has Adam Smith himself become a symbol of the capitalist system, the invisible hand is a metaphor for the dominant Western economic paradigm itself. The invisible hand and its connotations and implications are a key part of what the social belief system, the mythic system, and the psychic balm system have in common. As Babe writes, through its use in mediating social relations, 'analysts need not delve into contradictions and conflictual relations ... because, it is held, each person exercising her power and seeking her own interest contributes automatically, albeit inadvertently, to the "common good."' The same can be said of the divine right of kings, the cunning of history, the Golden Age, and some other mythic system in other societies or other stages, all of which endorse a particular sovereignty of authority, either concentrated or 'democratized.'

Some people have believed that certain topics should not be discussed in public, in part because doing so might have dangerous consequences. An argument deployed in favour of the status quo institutional order held that it was the work of God. Such arguments reinforced the view that only some people should have 'policy consciousness,' a sense that the social system is a product of the social construction of reality – of human policy, and not of God. The special people were the rulers, those who practised statecraft, as in Niccolò Machiavelli's The Prince (1513); the masses were to be kept from such knowledge.

Eventually these practices were entitled manifest and latent function. When a person enters a church, he or she feels a sense of awe, of being in the presence of the sacred. This is the manifest function of entering a church, even if only as a tourist. The latent function is the reinforcement of the social system that is brought about by the experience. The average churchgoer senses only the awe. Performance of the latent function is the duty of the priest, notably the high priest, to create conditions leading to the reinforcement of the status quo. If the latent function and its intricacies were to be widely publicly discussed, that function would not be achieved. Language could be used in favour of ignorance.

Beyond his critique of neoclassicism, Babe's later work extends this very point to the writings of many poststructuralists. Reflecting the symbolic fluidity of a dawning digital age, the postmodernist similarly obfuscates and, like the priest, unwittingly deepens status quo relations.

A classic nineteenth-century trope was to camouflage all this by obliquely and haltingly but sometimes explicitly referring to 'things unseen.' Two of my former students and I have worked out elements of a theory of knowledge, ignorance, and policy. In encapsulating this theory we have identified sources of ignorance (the unseen):

1. Radical indeterminacy: that the future cannot be known until it has been created
2. Simple ignorance, or ignorance of the knowable
3. Knowing what is not so, but thought so nonetheless, what one thinks one knows but does not
4. Selective perception

5. Selective manufacture of belief, including false and/or incomplete knowledge; manipulation of what is seen and not seen; creation of beliefs masquerading as actual definitions of reality
6. Obfuscating definitions

Among the structure of ignorance are the forms that ignorance takes:

1. Limits to knowledge
2. Asymmetrical distribution of ignorance
3. That for which no evidence is provided, only claimed
4. Local and tacit knowledge
5. Exercise of manifest vis-à-vis latent function
6. Manufacture of belief, including false knowledge; pseudo-knowledge intended to mobilize and manipulate political psychology
7. Creations of particular definitions of reality to influence behaviour and policy
8. The unseen as what is obfuscated by special pleaders, including misrepresentation

I also have a long list of the consequences of ignorance.[12]

The detailed evidence comes from case studies of two men who used these techniques to advance their policies. One was George Douglas Campbell, the eighth Duke of Argyll (1823–1900) and Edwin L. Godkin (1831–1902) an Irish-born, American reporter, editor, and publisher. Both men represented and promoted the most conservative, even reactionary, positions in politics. (Earlier, efforts were made to price newspapers and opinion journals out of the reach of workers.) Both were very explicit as to what they were doing and how, using belief, symbolic, and mythic structures as the basis of their writing. It was, incidentally, Godkin who campaigned to have Richard T. Ely fired from Johns Hopkins University for raising certain issues and adopting certain positions in his writings. Babe, from his history of public relations to the contemporary falsities propagated by corporations, identifies more contemporary examples – from Walter Lippmann's pioneering construction of 'pseudoenvironments' to the fatal blindness now threatening our ecological survival.

Moving on to metaphors, consider that 'the market' is given as the answer to the question of what constitutes the invisible hand. Some people believe that Smith's invisible hand is literally an invisible hand. Others believe that both the invisible hand and the market are figures of speech, each standing for something else, such as the forces that govern markets. The informational value of the invisible hand as the market, therefore, is limited and perhaps non-existent. The next question, then, is whether the invisible hand is to be taken as a specification of reality or as a figure of speech. In large part this is because no independent test exists by which to identify the invisible hand either literally or figuratively, or by which one can identify the invisible hand as the market and reject all the other definitions. In this case, the invisible hand is a figure of speech, as is the market; saying, therefore, that the invisible hand is the market is to define one figure of speech by another figure of speech, and the informational value of doing so is again limited and perhaps non-existent. The same is true when the invisible hand is believed to literally exist and be the market (or anything else). But informational value is hardly the whole exercise. Whether treated as a metaphor or something else, the invisible hand has the role(s) that Smith's *History* analysis articulates: to soothe the imagination or to set minds at rest, to provide a definition of reality and the social construction of reality, to provide for social control and psychic balm. Smith taught rhetoric and, as we have seen, identified and stressed language as providing for these roles. Most people seem to believe that the answer that the market is the invisible hand is essentially metaphysical if not imaginary – a figure of speech that has by itself no empirical content. Surely Popper had this type of situation in mind when he claimed, 'Thus science must begin with myths, and with the criticism of myths.'[13]

As for metaphoric status, most people seem to believe that the invisible hand is a figure of speech. But which figure of speech? Most people seem to believe that the invisible hand is a metaphor; a sizeable number seem to consider it to be a simile,[14] with others believing it to be analogy, euphemism, synecdoche, or a trope. It is beyond my present purpose to seriously take up the question of which figure of speech a certain usage may be. The overwhelming majority of people who use the term *invisible hand* seem to consider it a metaphor for the market (or a close substitute such as the price mechanism). The informational content of any answer, however, is asymptotic to zero but, as already remarked, it is hardly the only point of the exercise.

Whether the invisible hand is believed to be the market or something else and whether the invisible hand is believed to be a metaphor or something else, it seems clear that the term *invisible hand* is a primitive term. It has in itself no informational content except what is selectively added through embracing and adding one or more specification of the invisible hand, such as private property, the entrepreneur, competition, and so on. As with any other primitive term, members of an audience hearing the term used by a speaker will automatically, one might say instinctively, think of some specification of the invisible hand and, more than likely, most auditors will choose differently. Though some people may take offence in my saying this, except for what the auditors provide in their own minds, there is no more substantive content inhering in any answer that has professional disciplinary status than to say that the invisible hand is a metaphor for a group of monkeys, in a tree in New York City's Central Park, who control the allocation of resources for the country. There is neither ontological nor epistemological content except for specifications provided by the auditors – or by those people who promote and/or reinforce the invisible hand as a foundational concept in the promotion of capitalism. The meaning of the invisible hand as figure of speech is promoted by its devotees.

In all these cases, whether a primitive term, a metaphor, a simile, or something else, the language situation is not unlike propositions that either have truth value or have little or no truth value but soothe the imagination.

4. Language as Political Argument

Both the breadth and depth of Robert Babe's work and what I have presented in this chapter inexorably lead to the conclusion that language is critically involved in social decision-making. As such, language has political significance. A simple example is this: X can be defined in terms of A or B. If XB is chosen, its use will tend to support the corresponding policy. If XA is chosen, its use will do likewise. Another but not so simple example is that of Ludwig Wittgenstein who first believed that words have meanings that correspond to social and physical reality. Eventually Wittgenstein reversed his explanation. Words and their definitions do not necessarily derive from and correspond with reality but instead are conventional; if anything, reality is defined by words rather than the other way around. This section presents several treatments found in the literature.

Let us first ask two questions: who are the politically active people, and toward what end(s) are they active? The politically active are of two types: One is conservative or liberal in the generic sense of being for continuity and for change, respectively and selectively, driven by a sense of identity and psychological attachments or pressure from others. The other is seeking to control government and thereby his or her financial fortunes through favourably influencing the distributions of wealth, income, and opportunity. A third question will be taken up below.

William Harold Hutt distinguished three different modes of thought. By *rational thought* Hutt meant objective and, especially, disinterested inquiry, inquiry that can result in the accumulation of undisputed knowledge in the social sciences. By *custom thought* Hutt meant inquiry that is infused with implicit premises and ideas directed from traditional and customary ways of doing and looking at things, a tradition sometimes dominated by the interests of upper hierarchic levels and ' at times by the wishful-thinking romanticism of the masses. By *power thought* he meant modes of thinking and expression that are constructed to have intended effects on power, politics, and policy, and whose significance derives principally if not completely from their service in psycho-political mobilization.[15] Hutt seems at first reading to have identified the three modes of thought with particular social groups, but close attention to his text does not rule out the possibility of individuals and groups each having thought-ways of each type. This concern aside, Hutt's modes of thought are in the same tradition as Vilfredo Pareto's distinction between logico-experimental and non-logico-experimental thinking; Thorstein Veblen's distinction between teleological and matter-of-fact preconceptions and also Pareto's notion of derivations; and James Harvey Robinson's concept of rationalization.

Vilfredo Pareto developed a wide-ranging model of society, a large part of which was constructed of theory dealing with the political role of language. This included logico-experimental versus non-logico-experimental knowledge; logical and non-logical conduct; derivations; the social utility of falsity; three dimensions of policy – knowledge, psychology, and power – each one of which is a function of the other two; all within a general model of mutual manipulation, with language (derivations) a means of mobilization and manipulation, driven by power and psychology.[16]

I come next to *The Vocabulary of Politics* first published by T.D. Weldon in 1953. The crux of Weldon's exposition is that the 'whole business' of politics, political institutions, and political philosophy is 'simply a discussion about linguistic usage.'[17] He criticizes 'carelessness over the implications of language [arising] from the primitive and generally unquestioned belief that ... the words which normally occur in discussions about politics such as "State," "Citizen," "Law," and "Liberty," have intrinsic or essential meanings which it is the aim of politi-

cal philosophers to discover and explain.'[18] One must avoid nonsensical
assumptions, especially those that are inconsistent with the view that
there is something 'behind or beyond actual political institutions which
those institutions express, copy, or realize,' assumptions 'reinforced by a
series of confusions between historical, scientific, and linguistic propositions.'[19] On the one hand, there are 'traditional questions in political
philosophy' for which 'we do not know how to set about looking for
answers to them'; on the other hand, 'the real trouble about the pronouncements is that we do not know what kind of evidence we should
need to demonstrate that they are either true or false.'[20] Expanding on
the point about linguistic usage, Weldon says that 'it is not surprising
that no answers to the questions of politics have been discovered, for in
the nature of the case no answers can be discovered ... Unquestionably a
lot of discussion which is called political philosophy is on just this level.
It has no factual content and is simply argument about verbal definitions.' Such discussion has 'practical importance,' but there is 'no method of proving one view to be correct and the other false,' for the rules
of mathematics or of bridge and of politics 'are not the kind of things
which can be proved or disproved.'[21] Again, 'many discussions about
the meanings of political words are purely verbal, that is, they concern
linguistics habits and conventions but tell us nothing about matter of
fact.'[22]

Weldon identifies three objectives in the book: 'to show that the questions put by traditional political philosophy are wrongly posed ... and
cannot be answered'; to show that the theoretical foundations of political theory are all equally worthless; and 'to show that this conclusion
... does not involve cynicism, scepticism, or the rejection of moral or
political evaluations.'[23] Following through with his insistence that many
political terms are not matters of truth or falsity, he writes that any 'sup-
posed foundation of politics is completely useless. It is not false but vac-
uous.'[24] Such a view does not mean that institutional choices and their
performance cannot be evaluated. But it does mean that the evaluation
is based in part on subjective inputs. Using the due process clause of the
U.S. Constitution's Fourteenth Amendment as an example, he argues
that it has no meaning. 'It is a formula which has no application until the
variables which it contains are replaced with actual values.'[25] It must be
said that non-quantitative values are subjective and subject to selective
perception and that 'actual values' do not exist. They are a matter of the
accounting protocol, whose construction is variable, and their application, which is also variable. Subjectivity is ubiquitous. This is evident,

for example, in benefit-cost analysis, where the valuations do not derive from numbers but the numbers derive from valuations.[26]

Weldon proceeds from linguistics to symbolism, still concerned with the vocabulary of politics. 'It has been easy and natural enough ... to assume that "courage," "justice," "freedom," and "authority" ... designated precisely demarcated and permanent entities of some sort, that each of them must have one single, nuclear meaning, and that it was important to discover that meaning ... [thus] to ascertain the true or real meanings of words, or alternatively to become acquainted with the immutable essences for Ideas for which political words stand ... [But] words and sentences are not magical incantations ... words as we have them now are almost entirely conventional symbols ... [that] often inherit something from their more primitive uses.'[27]

Bringing to mind the very invocation popularized in economics by George Stigler and Gary Becker (1977), Weldon somewhat humorously denigrates its condescending position, first saying that if one goes through life with a particular (perhaps intolerable) taste, 'there is nothing to be done about it except to say de gustibus non est disputandum.' The 'same line [can be taken] about political institutions. One can say "Well, some people seem to like slavery or secret ballots or proportional representation. As a matter of fact, I don't; and that is all there is to be said about it"'[28] – a way of protecting the status quo.

Weldon brilliantly shows how one linguistic essentialism can be subtly combined with another: 'Thus it comes to be held not merely that nouns are always the names of identifiable things, but also that the things of which they are the names are unchanging and eternal.'[29] 'The root of the trouble is the mistaken search for absolute standards.'[30]

In a different context, Weldon argues that both the contract theory of the state, including even the theory of absolute monarchy, and statements about those topics 'at best ... [represent] a sweeping psychological hypothesis about human beings, and at worst it is just a fraud.'[31] In connection with the last preceding clause, it should be noted that to Pareto governance is a matter of force and fraud. A few pages later Weldon argues that 'words of appraisal are not descriptive at all. They are [either] just exclamations ... [or] are descriptive but describe not the factual situation but the psychological state of the speaker.'[32]

Weldon incisively considers the concept of the 'rule of law,' which is often 'turned into a kind of slogan or propaganda phrase.' His point is that when used that way it 'is a slippery term because it covertly implies approval of a particular type of legal system while purporting only to approve of the maintenance of law in general.'[33] To the same critical evaluation of the term *laissez-fare*,[34] Weldon thinks that 'the whole of the distinction between positive and negative States and legislation is misleading and has propaganda rather than informative value ... In a trivial sense it is true that all rules restrict freedom ... And in an equally trivial sense, all laws promote freedom.'[35]

Much political language refers 'to the psychological state of the speaker and not to the things he is speaking about';[36] after all, the reason for manipulating what Pareto considered pseudo-knowledge, the derivations, is to influence psychology and through it to influence policy.

Finally, notice should be taken of the organizational frameworks in which political language is used. All of the writers whose foundational work is examined here – most notably Edwin Godkin, the editor and publisher – seem to have been cognizant of the influence exercised by media institutions on language and by language on media institutions. What transpires may be called, pace Thorstein Veblen, the higher learning of political language. Indeed, the work of Robert Babe displays the boldness and the subtleties of that reciprocal process.

. The media have influenced political language in all manner of ways, from the wider dissemination of political language to the form the language takes, such as the sound bite and the spin terminology of political commentators. One historical reason for the media is that the provision of political knowledge – once the press was accepted by the governing class and reinforced by advertising-financed radio and television – came to be in high demand in a mass market. The opportunity to sell newspapers and advertising in all mass media markets meant the need for catchy and seemingly informative language. The law governing concentration in media ownership and the technology engaged in its dissemination have reinforced both the demand and the use of political language. The media have formed the arena in which information of differing levels of superficiality have been formed and used. It is no accident that news departments in radio and television have such basic a role in formulating our civic discourse.

Two further points need attention. First, the use of political language is inescapable. We must communicate, and language, or signs, is the way it is done; and the language is political by virtue of what is being discussed. Second, as disagreeable and repugnant as the media can be, for many, perhaps most people, reading or listening to the media is the way they acquire political information.

My third question, to which I alluded above, is whether the arguments put forth in this essay are self-referential. I would answer (1) in principle, yes; (2) I do not seek either public office or wealth; I do not have much respect for most of those who seek public office and wealth – though perhaps the problems reside in how campaigning for public office and seeking wealth is conducted; and (3) inasmuch as I seek in my work to understand what is actually going on (or the meaning thereof) objectively and without ulterior motives, whether or not I like what is going on is secondary.

When I first met Robert Babe, he was highly defensive about Canadian culture in relation to the aggressive culture of the colossus to the south. Eventually Bob came to understand that cultures do not have independent existence; they are worked out through people living their lives and interacting. Frank Knight used to declare that the chief product of an economy is the people to which it gives rise. For Bob, the chief product of an economy is the culture of its people. But the culture of a people is not something independent and transcendental. If, for present purposes, we combine belief, mythic, and symbolic systems, including language, and have a belief system stand for all such systems, one can say that culture is a product of a belief system and that belief system is a function of culture.

Bob's concentration on the media has been important. For one thing, the media were critical to the creation, restatement, and application of belief systems. The process of working things out is a matter of power and thus of whose interest and whose values are to count, and the media, doing what comes naturally to them, are at the centre of that process. The media are, for the most part, among the higher hierarchic levels of power and their activities typically promote the interests of those at that level of power.

NOTES

1 Adam Smith, *Theory of Moral Sentiments* (New York: Oxford University Press, 1976).
2 Adam Smith, *An Inquiry into the Nature and Causes of the Wealth of Nations*, ed. Edwin Cannan (1776; New York: Modern Library, 1937).
3 Adam Smith, *Lectures on Jurisprudence* (New York: Oxford University Press, 1978).
4 Adam Smith, *Essays on Philosophical Subjects* (Dublin: Messrs Wogan et al., 1795), 27.

5 Ibid., 28.
6 Alex Spiegel, 'More and More, Favored Psychotherapy Lets Bygones Be Bygones,' *New York Times*, 14 February 2006, http://www.nytimes. com/2006/02/14/health/psychology/14psyc.html?ei=5070&en=a10b75. Emphasis added.
7 Smith, *Essays on Philosophical Subjects*, 34.
8 Smith, *Theory of Moral Sentiments*, IV.I.11, 183–4.
9 Smith, *Inquiry*, 456.
10 Ibid., 83–5.
11 Warren J. Samuels, 'Some Problems in the Use of Language in Economics,' *Review of Political Economy*, vol. 13, no. 1 (2001): 91–100. Repr. in *The Legal-Economic Nexus*, 291–397 (New York: Routledge, 2007).
12 Warren J. Samuels, Marianne Johnson, and Kirk Johnson, 'The Duke of Argyll and Edwin L. Godkin as Precursors to Hayek on the Relation of Ignorance to Policy,' *Storia del Pensiero Economico* 1, no. 1 (2004): 5–32; 1, no. 2 (2004): 37–67; 2, no. 1 (2005): 35–71; and 2, no. 2 (2005): 19–38. Repr. in *Legal-Economic Nexus*, 384–8.
13 Karl Popper, *Conjectures and Refutations: The Growth of Scientific Knowledge* (London: Routledge & Kegan Paul, 1963), 66.
14 William D. Grampp, 'What Did Smith Mean by the Invisible Hand?' *Journal of Political Economy* 108, no. 3 (June 2000): 441–65.
15 William Harold Hutt, *Economists and the Public* (1936; New Brunswick, NJ: Transaction, 1990), 3.
16 Vilfredo Pareto, *The Mind and Society: A Treatise on General Sociology* (1916; New York: Dover, 1963); Warren J. Samuels, *Pareto on Policy* (New York: Elsevier, 1974).
17 T.D. Weldon, *The Vocabulary of Politics* (Baltimore: Penguin, 1953), 39.
18 Ibid., 11–12.
19 Ibid., 36.
20 Ibid., 37–8.
21 Ibid., 39.
22 Ibid., 13.
23 Ibid., 14–15.
24 Ibid., 110.
25 Ibid., 98.
26 Indeed, for Babe, questions concerning value – particularly modern culture's marginalization of intrinsic values – are profoundly important.
27 Weldon, *Vocabulary of Politics*, 21–2.
28 Ibid., 13.
29 Ibid., 20.
30 Ibid., 148.

31 Ibid., 40.
32 Ibid., 43.
33 Ibid., 68–9.
34 Ibid., 71.
35 Ibid., 72.
36 Ibid., 181.

20 Robert Babe, Personal Reflections

JAMES WINTER*

Following in the footsteps of Harold Innis, Marshall McLuhan, and Dallas Smythe, Robert Babe has now clearly established himself as Canada's foremost communications scholar. To Bob's credit, he's much easier to understand than was Innis, and not at all glib or uncritical in the way that McLuhan sometimes could be. As for Smythe, commenting on Babe's *Telecommunications in Canada*, he wrote, '[Babe] has done what will be the definitive analysis of [this] subject for a long time to come. And there is nothing of comparable scope and depth for any other country, as far as I am aware.'[1]

As a result of his restless intellect, for more than thirty years Bob has published on topics with an extraordinary range encompassing telecommunications policy, theory, ecology, and the political economy of communication. An authority on Innis, Bob published his seminal work on *Canadian Communication Thought* in 2000. In 2006, he published the *Culture of Ecology*, in which he demonstrates the radical proposition that the price system of neoclassical economics must undergo a fundamental transformation to conform to the principles of ecology. His most recent work argues for the integration of the cultural studies and political economic approaches to communications, and it's in this work that he successfully tackles the postmodernists.

Professor Babe has written of McLuhan's dictum that to understand the world one must stand apart from it. The great thinkers about whom he wrote in *Canadian Communication Thought* 'are outsiders, by birth or disposition.' Babe himself embodies this in several respects, a fact one might gather simply by observing him ride his motorcycle, or fleeing urban life for the simple pleasures of his cottage.

* University of Windsor

First of all, trained as an economist, Bob has stood outside of main-stream economics and used media and communication to critique his former discipline. He applied media and communication to economics, critiquing it from a communications view. Paradoxically, despite most economists' assertions about the emergence of an information econo-my, he discovered that few in the discipline knew much about informa-tion. Bob evidently took delight in deconstructing economics discourse.

Like Innis and Smythe, Babe forsook mainstream economics for political economy and media studies, and like them he placed himself on the outside of both his old and these relatively new disciplines. Over the years, his position on the periphery has migrated to – at least in my view – the centre of a significant body of contemporary research. His work, for example in ecology, resonates with many young scholars today.

I've known Bob Babe for more than twenty years now. We met at an annual meeting of the Council of Canadians in Ottawa in the mid-1980s. We liked each other immediately. I was impressed by his genu-ine warmth and surprisingly unpretentious nature. In addition to our shared nationalism and radicalism, over the years we've discovered a mutual fondness for Indian food, motorcycles, pints of beer, and bil-liards. Our conversations frequently range from American foreign poli-cy to commiserating over the inevitable pitfalls of parenting.

Briefly, I managed to lure Bob from the University of Ottawa, where he taught for over fifteen years, to the University of Windsor. Wind-sor turned out to be a way station for Bob, en route to his alma mater of the University of Western Ontario, and a prestigious research chair appointment. Windsor and Western actually entered into a bidding war over him. (How gratifying this must be for a professor!)

Bob is a valued colleague, whose advice I seek regularly. He is a tire-less thinker and writer, who always has several projects in the works. He has been instrumental in developing graduate communications programs at Windsor and Western.

Perhaps most significant is the impact Bob has had on students, amongst whom he appears to be universally admired and respected. As Jenepher Lennox-Terrion, a former student and eventually colleague at the University of Ottawa told me in a personal communication, 'Bob was a respected and revered professor at the Department of Commu-nication at U of O. I was a student there when he began his career and we were all impressed with his formal and professional ways, not to mention his remarkable beard. As he became more experienced as a professor, he loosened up his attire, going from a suit and tie at first to the suit, no tie, and a pair of white running shoes by the time I graduated a few years later.'[2]

Inspired largely by Bob's critical teachings, students at the University of Ottawa organized an extraordinary multi-day conference with leading critical thinkers in 1994. As but one example, former student Kerry Pither is a human rights advocate and author, who played a pivotal role in Maher Arar's release and the public inquiry into his case. In 1998, based on a flood of petitions and letters of support, Bob received an OCUFA teaching award.

I've listened to Bob lecture, and enjoy the way he employs the Socratic method, drawing answers from the students, rather than talking at them the way some professors do. He frequently uses texts with which he disagrees to provide students with another perspective, or he goes back to the readings that informed his own work and critiques them.

Fortunately for all of us, as he approaches retirement age, Bob seems to have no real plans to do so in a hurry. The explanation partially takes us back to his adolescence. As a teenager, Bob's family cottage was in Bobcaygen, Ontario, where he worked at Belbeck's Garage, pumping gas, and eventually changing tires and doing grease jobs. (In his typical self-deprecating fashion, Bob disavows any mechanical ability.) But the station owner was a master mechanic who could fix anything, a carpenter and very skilled tradesman. When the owner 'retired' and sold his gas station, he opened a little shop at the back of his house and began taking in lawnmowers and other repairs. He still runs this shop, in his late eighties.

When Bob *does* retire, he will be like the retired master mechanic, continuing to write and publish. Indeed, I believe he should do so: he is a master academic.

His next book project is tentatively titled *Meet Harold Innis*. In it, Bob will introduce eminent scholars from the communication field to the ideas of Innis, show how their thought differs, and how Innis could have been incorporated into their work, or, in some cases, how a knowledge of Innis's writings might have modified their perspectives. Figures like Wilbur Schramm come to mind, but perhaps even McLuhan, the wayward disciple, will be included, along with Noam Chomsky and others. I look forward to this with great relish!

Meanwhile, this book will make it possible for current and future students – and faculty – to benefit from an extensive collection of work by Canada's greatest contemporary communications scholar.

NOTES

1 Dallas Smythe, personal correspondence, 6 May 1990.
2 Jenepher Lenox-Terrion, personal correspondence, 14 July 2008.

Influential Writings Selected by Robert E. Babe

The following, for me, have been among the most influential scholarly writings. A few listed here with which I have disagreed that fundamentally animated some of my critical observations; with some others, I have, in part, both agreed and disagreed. The rest, the majority, have inspired.

Arrow, Kenneth. 'The Economics of Information.' *The Computer Age: A Twenty-Year View*, ed. Michael Dertouzos and Joel Moses, 306–17. Cambridge, MA: MIT Press, 1979.

Bell, Daniel. 'The Social Framework of the Information Society.' In *The Computer Age: A Twenty-Year View*, ed. Michael Dertouzos and Joel Moses, 34–65. Cambridge, MA: MIT Press, 1979.

Beniger, James R. *The Control Revolution: Technological and Economic Origins of the Information Society*. Cambridge, MA: Harvard University Press, 1986.

Boorstin, Daniel J. *The Image: A Guide to Pseudo Events in America*. 1961. New York: Atheneum, 1978.

Boulding, Kenneth E. *The Image: Knowledge and Life in Society*. Ann Arbor: University of Michigan Press, 1956.

– *A Primer on Social Dynamics: History as Dialectics and Development*. New York: Free Press, 1970.

– *Ecodynamics: A New Theory of Societal Evolution*. Beverly Hills, CA: Sage, 1978.

Braman, Sandra. 'Defining Information: An Approach for Policymakers.' *Telecommunications Policy* (September 1989): 233–42.

Bronowski, Jacob. *The Origins of Knowledge and Imagination*. New Haven, CT: Yale University Press, 1978.

Carey, James W. 'Harold Adams Innis and Marshall McLuhan.' *Antioch Review* 27, no. 1 (Spring 1967): 5–39.

- 'Technology and Ideology: The Case of the Telegraph.' In *Communication as Culture: Essays on Media and Society*, 201–30. Boston: Unwin Hyman, 1989.
Chaffee, Steven, and John Hochheimer. 'The Beginnings of Political Communication Research in the United States: Origins of the "Limited Effects" Model.' In *Mass Communication Review Yearbook* 5, ed. Michael Gurevitch and Mark R. Levy, 75–104. Beverly Hills, CA: Sage, 1985.
Charland, M. 'Technological Nationalism.' *Canadian Journal of Political and Social Theory* 10, nos. 1 and 2 (1986): 197–220.
Chazen, Leonard. 'The Price of Free TV.' *Atlantic*, March 1969.
Chomsky, Noam. *Necessary Illusions: Thought Control in Democratic Societies*. Toronto: CBC Enterprises, 1989.
- 'Force and Opinion.' In *Chomsky, Deterring Democracy*, 351–406. Cambridge, MA: South End, 1991.
Coase, R.H. 'The Problem of Social Cost.' *Journal of Law and Economics* 3 (1960): 1–44.
Comor, Edward A. 'Harold Innis's Dialectical Triad.' *Journal of Canadian Studies* 29, no. 2 (1994): 111–27.
- *Consumption and the Globalization Project: International Hegemony and the Annihilation of Time*. New York: Palgrave Macmillan, 2008.
Czitrom, Daniel. *Media and the American Mind: From Morse to McLuhan*. Chapel Hill: University of North Carolina Press, 1982.
Daly, Herman E., and John Cobb. *For the Common Good: Redirecting the Economy toward Community, the Environment and a Sustainable Future*. Boston: Beacon, 1989.
Danielian, N.R. *AT&T: The Story of Industrial Conquest*. 1939. New York: Arno, 1974.
Delia, Jesse. 'Communication Research: A History.' In *Handbook of Communication Science*, ed. Charles R. Berger and Steven Chaffee, 20–98. Newbury Park, CA: Sage, 1987.
Ellul, Jacques. 'The Power of Technique and the Ethics of Non-power.' In *The Myths of Information: Technology in Post-Industrial Society*, ed. Kathleen Woodward, 242–7. Madison, WI: Coda, 1980.
Ewan, Stuart. *PR! A Social History of Spin*. New York: Basic Books, 1996.
Galbraith, John Kenneth. *The New Industrial State*. Boston: Houghton Mifflin, 1967.
Galtung, Johan. 'A Structural Theory of Imperialism.' *Journal of Peace Research* 2 (1971): 81–117.
Ginsberg, Benjamin. *The Captive Public: How Mass Opinion Promotes State Power*. New York: Basic Books, 1986.
Grant, George. *Time as History*. Toronto: CBC Learning Systems, 1969.

Hayek, F.A. 'The Use of Knowledge in Society.' *American Economic Review* 35, no. 4 (September 1945): 519–30.

Hubbert, M. King. 'Exponential Growth as a Transient Phenomenon in Human History.' In *Valuing the Earth: Economics, Ecology, Ethics*, ed. Herman E. Daly and Kenneth N. Townsend, 113–26. Cambridge, MA: MIT Press, 1993.

Hughes, Robert. *The Shock of the New: Art and the Century of Change*. London: BBC, 1980.

Hyde, Lewis. *The Gift: Imagination and the Erotic Life of Property*. New York: Vintage Books, 1979.

Innis, Harold A. *The Bias of Communication*. Toronto: University of Toronto Press, 1971.

– *Empire and Communications*. Toronto: University of Toronto Press, 1972.

Kroker, Arthur. *Technology and the Canadian Mind: Innis, McLuhan, Grant*. Montreal: New World Perspectives, 1984.

Kuhn, Thomas. *The Structure of Scientific Revolutions*. Chicago: University of Chicago Press, 1962.

Lazarsfeld, Paul Felix. 'Administrative and Critical Communications Research.' 1941. In *Mass Communication and American Social Thought*, ed. John Durham Peters and Peter Simonson, 166–73. Lanham, MD: Rowman and Littlefield, 2004.

Lippmann, Walter. 1922. *Public Opinion*. New York: Free Press, 1965.

Macpherson, C.B. *The Political Economy of Possessive Individualism: Hobbes to Locke*. Oxford: Oxford University Press, 1962.

– 'Liberal-Democracy and Property.' In *Property: Mainstream and Critical Positions*, ed. C.B. Macpherson. Toronto: University of Toronto Press, 1978.

McLuhan, Marshall, Eric McLuhan, and Kathy Hutchon. *City as Classroom*. Agincourt, ON: Book Society of Canada, 1977.

McLuhan, Marshall, and Wilfred Watson. *From Cliché to Archetype*. New York: Pocket Books, 1971.

Mitchell, Wesley C. *Types of Economic Theory: From Mercantilism to Institutionalism*. 2 vols. New York: Kelley, 1967–9.

Murchie, Guy. *The Seven Mysteries of Life: An Exploration in Science & Philosophy*. Boston: Houghton Mifflin, 1978.

Neill, Robin. *A New Theory of Value: The Canadian Economics of H.A. Innis*. Toronto: University of Toronto Press, 1972.

Nevitt, Barrington. *The Communication Ecology: Re-presentation versus Replica*. Toronto: Butterworths, 1982.

Ong, Walter. *The Presence of the Word*. New Haven, CT: Yale University Press, 1967.

Peers, Frank. *The Politics of Canadian Broadcasting 1920–1951*. Toronto: University of Toronto Press, 1969.

Polanyi, Karl. *The Great Transformation: The Political and Economic Origins of Our Time*. Boston: Beacon, 1957.

Ponting, Clive. *A Green History of the World: The Environment and the Collapse of Great Civilizations*. New York: Penguin Books, 1991.

Pooley, Jefferson. 'The New History of Mass Communication Research.' In *The History of Media and Communication Research: Contested Memories*, ed. David W. Park and Jefferson Pooley, 43–69. New York: Lang, 2008.

Popper, Karl. *Conjectures and Refutations: The Growth of Scientific Knowledge*. New York: Harper & Row, 1963.

Poster, Mark. *The Mode of Information: Poststructuralism and Social Context*. Chicago: University of Chicago Press, 1990.

Preston, William Jr, Edward S. Herman, and Herbert I. Schiller. *Hope and Folly: The United States and UNESCO 1945–1985*. Minneapolis: University of Minnesota Press, 1989.

Robins, Kevin, and Frank Webster. 'The Communications Revolution: New Media, Old Problems.' *Communication* 10 (1987): 71–87.

Roszak, Theodore. *Where The Wasteland Ends*. Garden City, NY: Anchor Books, 1973.

Samuels, Warren J. *The Classical Theory of Economic Policy*. Cleveland, OH: World, 1966.

– 'Interrelations between Legal and Economic Processes.' *Journal of Law and Economics* 14, no. 2 (1971): 435–50.

Schiller, Herbert I. *Mass Communications and American Empire*. New York: Kelley, 1969.

Scitovsky, Tibor. *The Joyless Economy: An Inquiry into Human Satisfaction and Consumer Dissatisfaction*. New York: Oxford University Press, 1976.

Serafini, Shirley, and Michel Andrieu. *The Information Revolution and Its Implications for Canada*. Ottawa: Information Canada, 1980.

Simpson, Christopher. *Science of Coercion: Communication Research & Psychological Warfare 1945–1960*. Oxford: Oxford University Press, 1994.

Smith, Adam. *An Inquiry into the Nature and Causes of the Wealth of Nations*. 1776. Modern Library ed., ed. Edwin Cannan. New York: Modern Library, 1937.

– *The Theory of Moral Sentiments*. 1759. Ed. D.D. Raphael and A.L. Macfie. Indianapolis, IN: Liberty, 1982.

Smythe, Dallas W. *The Relevance of United States Legislative-Regulatory Experience to the Canadian Telecommunications Situation: A Study for the Telecommission, Department of Communications*. Ottawa: Information Canada, 1971.

Sontag, Susan. *On Photography*. New York, NY: Farrar, Straus and Giroux, 1973.

Stigler George J., and Gary Becker. 'De gustibus non est disputandum.' *American Economic Review* 67, no. 2 (1977): 75–90.

Suzuki, David, and Amanda McConnell. *The Sacred Balance: Rediscovering Our Place in Nature*. Vancouver: David Suzuki Foundation and Greystone Books, 1997.

UNESCO, International Commission for the Study of Communication Problems (MacBride Commission). *Many Voices, One World: Communication and Society Today and Tomorrow*. New York: UNESCO, 1980.

von Bertalanffy, Ludwig. *A Systems View of Man*, ed. P.A. LaViolette. Boulder, CO: Westview, 1981.

von Weizsäcker, Carl Friedrich. *The Unity of Nature*. New York: Farrar, Straus and Giroux, 1980.

Watson, Alexander John. *Marginal Man: The Dark Vision of Harold Innis*. Toronto: University of Toronto Press, 2006.

Webster, Frank. *Theories of the Information Society*. New York: Routledge, 1995.

Weizenbaum, Joseph. 'Once More: The Computer Revolution.' In *The Computer Age: A Twenty-Year View*, ed. Michael Dertouzos and Joel Moses, 439–58. Cambridge, MA: MIT Press, 1979.

Williams, Raymond. *Television: Technology and Cultural Form*. Glasgow: Fontana/Collins, 1974.

– *Problems in Materialism and Culture*. London: Verso, 1980.

– *The Year 2000*. New York: Pantheon, 1983.

– *Culture and Society 1780–1950*. Harmondsworth, UK: Penguin Books, 1984.

Winner, Langdon. *Autonomous Technology*. Cambridge, MA: MIT Press, 1977.

Worster, Daniel. *Nature's Economy: A History of Ecological Ideas*. 2nd ed. Cambridge: Cambridge University Press, 1994.

Publications and Conference Papers by Robert E. Babe

1974

'Public and Private Regulation of Cable Television: A Case Study of Technological Change and Relative Power.' *Canadian Public Administration* 17, no. 4
(1974): 187–225.

1975

Cable Television and Telecommunications in Canada. East Lansing: Bureau of Business and Economic Research, Michigan State University, 1975.

1976

'Pay Television.' Canadian Council of Filmmakers Conference on Pay-TV.
Toronto, September 1976.
'Regulation of Broadcasting by the CRTC.' Canadian Broadcasting League
Conference. Halifax, August 1976.
'Regulation of Private Television by the Canadian Radio-Television Commis-
sion: A Critique of Ends and Means.' *Canadian Public Administration* 19, no. 4
(1976): 552–86.

1978

'Vertical Integration and Productivity: Canadian Telecommunications.' American Economics Association. Chicago, August 1978.

1979

Canadian Television Broadcasting Structure, Performance and Regulation. Ottawa: Supply and Services for the Economic Council of Canada, 1979.

1980

'Broadcasting: In Whose Interest?' *In Search / En quête* (Summer 1980): 20–7.

'Concentration of Control in the Canadian Cable Television Industry.' *Regulatory Reporter* (1980).

'Empires in TV Land.' *In Search / En quête* (Winter 1980): 12–19.

'Future Prospects of Canadian Television Programming.' *Conference '80.* Ottawa: Canadian Broadcasting League, 1980.

'The New Technology: Changing or Drifting?' *Closed Circuit* (March 1980): 12–13, 26.

'The New Technologies.' Plenary session, founding conference of the Canadian Communications Association. Montreal, May 1980.

'Public Policy and the Problem of Structural Change in Canadian Broadcasting.' *National Symposium on Law and Policy on Canadian Communications*, Law Society of Upper Canada and Canadian Bar Association, 277–300 (Ottawa: University of Ottawa, January 1980).

'Regulating the Canadian Telephone Industry.' Mid-West Economics Association. Chicago, March 1980.

Review of *The Public Eye* by Frank Peers. *Canadian Public Policy* (Spring 1980): 412.

1981

'Vertical Integration and Productivity: Canadian Telecommunications.' *Journal of Economic Issues* 15, no. 1 (March 1981): 1–31.

1982

'Cable Ownership Patterns and Economic Analysis: Policy Makers Beware.' *Tenth Annual Telecommunications Policy Research Conference.* Annapolis, MD, April 1982.

Review of *Fact and Fancy in Television Regulation* by Harvey Levin. *Canadian Journal of Economics* 15, no. 1 (February 1982): 176–9.

1984

Broadcasting Policy and Copyright Law: An Analysis of a Cable Rediffusion Right.

Ottawa: Government of Canada, Department of Communications, 1984 (co-authored).

'Comment.' In *Cultures in Collision: The Interaction of Canadian and U.S. Television Broadcast Policies*, 178–80. New York: Praeger, 1984.

1985

'Alexander Melville Bell.' *Canadian Encyclopedia*.

'Bell Canada Enterprises (BCE).' *Canadian Encyclopedia*.

'Sir Leonard Brockington.' *Canadian Encyclopedia*.

'Cable Television.' *Canadian Encyclopedia*.

'Francis Dagger.' *Canadian Encyclopedia*.

'Economics of Broadcasting.' Background paper. *Conference on the Future of the Canadian Broadcasting System*, Ottawa, 15–18, 1985.

'Information Industries and Economic Analysis: Policy Makers Beware.' In *Proceedings from the Tenth Annual Telecommunications Policy Research Conference*, ed. Oscar Gandy Jr. et al., 123–35. Norwood, NJ: Ablex, 1983; reprinted in *Mass Communication Review Yearbook* 5, ed. Michael Gurevitch and Mark Levy, 535–46. Beverly Hills, CA: Sage, 1985.

'Media Ownership.' *Canadian Encyclopedia*.

'Sir William Mulock.' *Canadian Encyclopedia*.

'Nathan Louis Nathanson.' *Canadian Encyclopedia*.

'Official Broadcasting Inquiries' (co-authored). Background paper. *Conference on the Future of the Canadian Broadcasting System*, Ottawa, 15–18, 1985.

'Pay Television.' *Canadian Encyclopedia*.

'Alan Plaunt.' *Canadian Encyclopedia*. Edmonton: Hurtig, 1985, 1988; revised, electronic version Toronto: McClelland and Stewart, 1996, 2000.

'Predatory Pricing and Foreclosure in Canadian Telecommunications.' *Telecommunications Policy* (December 1985): 329–33.

'Regulation and Incentives.' Paper presented at the *Conference on Canadian Broadcasting*, University of Alberta, November 1985.

'Graham Spry.' *Canadian Encyclopedia*.

'Telecommunications and Electronic Publishing.' Paper presented at the *Canadian Conference on Electronic Publishing*, University of British Columbia, August 1985.

'Telegraph.' *Canadian Encyclopedia*.

'Telephones.' *Canadian Encyclopedia*.

'TransCanada Telephone System (Stentor).' *Canadian Encyclopedia*.

1986

'Emergence and Development of Canadian Communications.' Paper presented at the Transcom Project Conference, Simon Fraser University / University of British Columbia, Vancouver, August 1986.

'Regulation and Incentives: Two Sides of any Policy.' In *Canadian Broadcasting: The Challenge of Change*, ed. Colin Hoskins and Stuart McFadyen, 23–6. Edmonton: University of Alberta Press, 1986.

'Size of Canada's Copyright Industries.' *Canadian Patent Reporter* 9, no. 4 (August 1986): 449–60.

'Telecommunications and Electronic Publishing.' In *Selected Proceedings of the Canadian Conference on Electronic Publishing*, ed. Dave Godfrey. Vancouver, 1986.

1987

'Let's Make a Deal.' Conference on *Unequal Partners: A Comparison between F.R. of Germany/Austria Canada/U.S.A.*, Carleton University, Ottawa, 25 September 1987.

'Technological Determinism and Technological Nationalism: A Critique of Prevailing Myths.' International Communications Association, Montreal, May 1987.

1988

'Control of Telephones: The Canadian Experience.' *Canadian Journal of Communication* 13, no. 2 (1988): 16–29.

'Copyright and Culture.' In *The Strategy of Canadian Culture in the 21st Century*, ed. Ian Parker, John Hutcheson, and Pat Crawley, 57–65. Toronto, ON: Innis Foundation, 1988.

'Copyright and Culture.' *Canadian Forum*, special supplement (February/March 1988): 26–9.

'Emergence and Development of Canadian Telecommunications: Dispelling the Myths.' In *Communication Canada*, ed. Rowland Lorimer and Donald Wilson, 58–79. Toronto: Kagan and Woo, 1988.

1990

'Guest Editor's Introduction.' *Canadian Journal of Communication* 15, no. 2 (May 1990): vi–vii.

Review of *Missed Opportunities* by Marc Raboy. *Communiqué* 10, no. 4 (December 1990).

Telecommunications in Canada: Technology, Industry and Government. Toronto: University of Toronto Press, 1990.

1991

'Free Trade Agreement, Communications and Telecommunications.' Trilateral Studies Symposium, Michigan State University, East Lansing, 23–4 May 1991.

1993

'Canadian Communication and the Legacy of Graham Spry.' *Queen's Quarterly* (December 1993): 989–1003.

'Communication: Blindspot of Western Economics.' In *Illuminating the Blindspots*, ed. V. Mosco, J. Wasko, and M. Pendakur, 15–39. Norwood, NJ: Ablex, 1993.

'The Place of Information in Economics.' Paper delivered to Twenty-Third Annual Telecommunications Policy Research Conference, Solomons, MD, October 1993; paper also presented to International Communications Association, Ottawa, May 1993.

1994

Information and Communication in Economics. Boston: Kluwer, 1994 (volume editor).

'Information, Economics and Ecosystem.' Paper delivered to Symposium on Critical Communication Studies, University of Ottawa, Ottawa, 24–6 October 1994.

'Information Theory in Economics.' In *The Elgar Companion to Institutional and Evolutionary Economics*, ed. Warren J. Samuels, Marc R. Tool, and Geoffrey M. Hodgson, 360–366. London: Elgar, 1994.

'Neoclassicism and Political Economy.' In *Mediating Culture: The Politics of Representation*, ed. Kosta Gouliamos and William Anselmi, 13–45. Montreal: Guernica Editions, 1994.

'The Place of Information in Economics.' *Information and Communication in Economics*, ed. Robert E. Babe, 41–67. Boston: Kluwer, 1994.

'Real World of the Information Highway.' *Point of View Magazine* (Summer 1994): 16–19.

1995

'Comments on "Economic Internationalization and the Internationalization of Telecommunications Policy" by Mark Brawley and Richard Schultz.' Carleton University Conference on the Internationalization of Canadian Public Policy, Ottawa, 25–6 May 1995.

Communication and the Transformation of Economics. Boulder, CO: Westview, 1995.

'Media Technology and the Great Transformation of Canadian Cultural Policy.' Duke University Symposium on Media Policy, National Identity, and Citizenry in Changing Democratic Societies: The Case of Canada, Durham, NC, 6–7 October 1995.

'Review Essay of Discursive Acts by R.S. Perinbanayagam.' In *Research in the History of Economic Thought and Methodology* 13 (1995): 295–301.

1996

'Bell Canada.' In *Encyclopedia of Television,* ed. Horace Newcombe. Chicago: Fitzroy Dearborn, 1996. http://www.museum.tv/eotvsection .php?entrycode=bellcanada.

'Canada.' In *Media Ownership in an Age of Convergence,* ed. Vicki MacLeod, 23–46. London: International Institute of Communications, 1996.

'Convergence and New Technologies.' In *Cultural Industries in Canada,* ed. Michael Dorland, 283–307. Toronto: Lorimer, 1996.

'Economics and Information: Toward a New (and More Sustainable) Worldview.' *Canadian Journal of Communication* 21, no. 2 (1996): 161–78.

'Guest Editor's Introduction.' *Canadian Journal of Communication* 21, no. 2 (1996): 159–60.

'The Information Highway, Self, and Community, Pitfalls and Possibilities.' Saint Paul University Conference on Information Highway, Ottawa, February 1996.

'Overview of Cultural Ecology.' International Institute of Communications Conference on Cultural Ecology, Sussex, UK, May 1996.

'Paeans to Dallas Smythe.' *Journal of Communication* 46, no. 1 (1996): 179–82.

Review of *ReConvergence* by Dwayne Winseck, and of *The Audience Reflected in the Medium of Law* by Myles Ruggles. *Canadian Journal of Communication* 21, no. 2 (1996): 302–6.

'Symbolic Environment.' University of Ottawa Conference on 'L'hybridation des Cultures à l'heure de la globalisation des marches,' University of Ottawa, 24 October 1996.

1997

'Communication Thought of George Grant.' International Communications Association, Montreal, May 1997.

'Red Toryism: The Communication Philosophy of George Grant.' *Journal of Communication* 47, no. 3 (Summer 1997): 96–101.

Review of *Communication by Design* by Robin Mansell and R. Silverstone. *Journal of Economic Issues* (September 1997), 865–7.
Review of *Whose Brave New World?* by Heather Menzies. *Canadian Journal of Communication* 22, no. 1 (Winter 1997): 128–9.
'Telecommunications: From Old to New Models of Control.' Leicester University MA Program in Mass Communications, Leicester, UK, 1997.
'Understanding the Cultural Ecology Model.' In *Cultural Ecology*, ed. Danielle Cliche, 1–23. London: International Institute of Communications, 1997.

1998

'Convergence and Divergence: Telecommunications, Old and New.' In *Understanding Telecommunications and Public Policy: A Guide for Libraries*, ed. Karen Adams and William F. Birdsall, 15–33. Ottawa: Canadian Library Association and School of Library and Information Studies, Dalhousie University, 1998.
'Media Technology and the Great Transformation of Canadian Cultural Policy.' In *Media Policy, National Identity and Citizenry in Changing Democratic Societies: The Case of Canada*, ed. Joel Smith, 104–22. Durham, NC: Canadian Studies Center, Duke University, 1998.
Review of *An Ecology of Communication: Cultural Formats of Control* by David L. Altheide. *Canadian Journal of Communication* 23, no. 2 (Spring 1998): 267–9.
'Charles Fleetford Sise.' *Dictionary of Canadian Biography, 1911–1920*. Vol. 14. Toronto: University of Toronto Press, 1998: 932–5.

2000

Canadian Communication Thought: Ten Foundational Writers. Toronto: University of Toronto Press, 2000.
'Foundations of Canadian Communication Thought.' *Canadian Journal of Communication* 25, no. 1 (Winter 2000): 19–37.
'McLuhan and Canadian Communication Thought.' McLuhan Symposium, University of Ottawa, May 2000.

2001

Review of *Telecom Nation* by Laurence Mussio. *Scientia Canadensis* 25 (2001): 92–4.
'Twentieth-Century Canadian Communication Theory.' Distance Learning MA Program in Canadian Studies, St Boniface College, University of Manitoba, St Boniface, August 2001.

2002

'The "Information Economy," Economics, and Ecology.' In *Networking Knowledge for Information Societies: Institutions & Interventions*, ed. Robin Mansell, Rohan Samarajiva, and Amy Mahan, 254–9. Delft, Netherlands: Delft University Press, 2002.

'The Political Economy of Information and Communication.' In *An Institutionalist Approach to Public Utilities Regulation*, ed. Warren J. Samuels and Edythe Miller, 99–126. East Lansing: Michigan State University Press, 2002.

'Retrospective on *Canadian Communication Thought*.' Plenary Session, Canadian Communication Annual Meetings, Toronto, ON, 29 May 2002.

2003

'Money and Culture.' *Topia: The Canadian Journal of Cultural Studies* 9 (Spring 2003): 3–13.

2004

'Alexander Graham Bell.' *The Oxford Companion to Canadian History*, ed. Gerald Hallowell, 68. Toronto: Oxford University Press, 2004.

'Bell Canada.' *The Oxford Companion to Canadian History*, 68.

'George Grant.' *The Oxford Companion to Canadian History*, 380–81.

'John Grierson.' *The Oxford Companion to Canadian History*, 271.

'Innis, Environment and New Media.' In *Seeking Convergence in Policy and Practice: Communications in the Public Interest*. Vol. 2, ed. Marita Moll and Leslie Regan Shade, 383–412. Ottawa: Canadian Centre for Policy Alternatives, 2004.

'Innis, Saul, Suzuki.' *Topia: The Canadian Journal of Cultural Studies* 11 (Spring 2004): 11–20.

'Marshall McLuhan.' *The Oxford Companion to Canadian History*, 378–79.

'McLuhan and Canadian Communication Thought.' In *At the Speed of Light There Is Only Illumination: A Reappraisal of Marshall McLuhan*, ed. John Moss and Linda Morra, 37–62. Ottawa: University of Ottawa Press, 2004.

'C.B. Macpherson.' *The Oxford Companion to Canadian History*, 380–81.

'Guglielmo Marconi.' *The Oxford Companion to Canadian History*, 389.

Review of *Harold Innis* by Paul Heyer. *Canadian Journal of Communication* (2004).

'Graham Spry.' *The Oxford Companion to Canadian History*, 595.

'Telecommunications.' *The Oxford Companion to Canadian History*, 610.

'Transatlantic cable.' *The Oxford Companion to Canadian History*, 620–21.

2005

'Culture of Ecology.' Joint Session of Canadian Communication Association and Environmental Association of Canada, University of Western Ontario, London, June 2005.

'The Dialectic of Information.' *Topia: Canadian Journal of Cultural Studies* 13 (Spring 2005): 5–17.

'Innis and McLuhan: Environmentalists,' Probe 2004: The McLuhan Festival of the Future, Drake Hotel, Toronto, 17 October 2004.

'Preface.' In *Automating Interaction*, by Myles Ruggles, vii–xiv. Cresskill, NJ: Hampton, 2005.

Review of *No Time: Stress and the Crisis of Modern Life* by Heather Menzies. *Canadian Journal of Communication* 30, no. 4 (2005): 699–701.

2006

'Canadian Critical Communication.' In *Radical Media Criticism: A Cultural Genealogy*, ed. John Theobold and David Berry, 140–60. Montreal: Black Rose Books, 2006 (co-author).

Culture of Ecology: Reconciling Economics and Environment. Toronto: University of Toronto Press, 2006.

'Harold Innis and the Press.' *Fifth-Estate-Online* (August 2006). http://www.fifth-estate-online.co.uk/comment/haroldinnisandthepress.html.

'Newspaper Discourses on Environment.' In *Filtering the News*, ed. Jeffery Klaehn, 187–222. Montreal: Black Rose Books, 2006.

'The Political Economy of Knowledge: Neglecting Political Economy in the Age of Fast Capitalism (as Before).' *Fast Capitalism* 2, no. 1 (2006). http://www.uta.edu/huma/agger/fastcapitalism/2_1/babe.html.

'Political Economy, Cultural Studies and Postmodernism.' *Topia: Canadian Journal of Cultural Studies* 15 (Spring 2006): 91–102.

'Poster Meets Innis: Poststructuralism and the Possibility of Political Economy.' *Topia: Canadian Journal of Cultural Studies* 16 (Fall 2006): 5–21 (co-author).

2007

'Harold Innis and the Paradox of Press Freedom.' The Association for Canadian Studies in the United States, 19th Biennial Conference, Toronto, November 2007.

'Harold Innis and the Paradox of Press Freedom.' *Fifth-Estate-Online*, May 2007. http://www.fifth-estate-online.co.uk/criticsm/haroldinnisandthepar-adox.html.

'McLuhan and the Electronic Archives. *Old Messengers New Media: The Legacy of Innis and McLuhan*. Ottawa: Archives and Library Canada, 2007. http://www.collectionscanada.gc.ca/innis-mcluhan/index-e.html.

'Valuing Ecosystem Services and Resources.' Workshop on Valuing Ecological Goods and Services: An Ontario Perspective. Peterborough Naval Association, Peterborough. 1 March 2007.

2008

'Innis and the Emergence of Canadian Communication/Media Studies.' *Global Media Journal: Canadian Edition*, 2008. http://www.gmj.uottawa.ca/inaugural_e.html.

Review, *Lies the Media Tell Us* by James Winter. *Topia: Canadian Journal of Cultural Studies* 19 (Spring); repr., Fifth-Estate-Online, 2008. http://www.fifth-estate-online.co.uk/reviews/lies.html.

2009

Cultural Studies and Political Economy: Toward a New Integration. Lanham, MD: Lexington Books, 2009.

'Poststructuralism and the Political Economy of Scholarship.' *Fifth-Estate-Online*, 2009. http://www.fifth-estate-online.co.uk/comment/Babe_comment_june09.pdf.

Forthcoming

'Comment on "The Pathologies of Persuasion." In *Kenneth E. Boulding's Engagement in Sciences*, ed. Wilfred Dolfsma and Stefan Kesting. London: Routledge.

'Culture Industry / Consciousness Industry: Adorno, Smythe and the Political Economy of Media and Communication.' In *Frankfurt School Revisted*, ed. David Berry. London: Ashgate.

'Political Economy, and the Double Dialectic of Information.' In *Messages and Messengers: Angeletics as an Approach to the Phenomenology of Communication*, ed. Rafael Capurro and John Holgate. Munich: Verlag.